ROYAL HISTORICAL SOCIETY

STUDIES IN HISTORY 69

THE OLDEST ALLY

IN MEMORY OF
MY PARENTS

THE OLDEST ALLY

BRITAIN AND THE PORTUGUESE CONNECTION
1936–1941

Glyn Stone

THE ROYAL HISTORICAL SOCIETY

THE BOYDELL PRESS

First published 1994

A Royal Historical Society publication
Published by The Boydell Press
an imprint of Boydell & Brewer Ltd
PO Box 9 Woodbridge Suffolk IP12 3DF UK
and of Boydell & Brewer Inc.
PO Box 41026 Rochester NY 14604–4126 USA

ISBN 0 86193 227 7

ISSN 0269–2244

British Library Cataloguing-in-Publication Data
Stone, Glyn
   Oldest Ally:Britain and the Portuguese Connection, 1936–41. –
(Royal Historical Society Studies in History, ISSN 0269–2244;No.69)
I. Title II. Series
327.410469
ISBN 0–86193–227–7

Library of Congress Cataloging-in-Publication Data
Stone, Glyn.
   The oldest ally : Britain and the Portuguese connection, 1936–1941
/ Glyn Stone.
       p.   cm. – (Royal Historical Society studies in history, ISSN
0269–2244 ; 69)
   Includes bibliographical references and index.
   ISBN 0–86193–227–7 (alk. paper)
   1. Great Britain – Foreign relations – Portugal. 2. Great Britain –
Foreign relations – 1936–1945. 3. Portugal – Foreign relations –
Great Britain. 4. Portugal – Foreign relations – 1933–1974.
I. Title. II. Series: Royal Historical Society studies in history ;
no. 69.
DA47.9.P8S76 1994
327.469073'09'043–dc20   94–7840

The paper used in this publication meets the minimum requirements
of American National Standard for Information Sciences –
Permanence of Paper for Printed Library Materials, ANSI Z39.48–1984

Printed in Great Britain by
St Edmundsbury Press Ltd, Bury St Edmunds, Suffolk

Contents

The Society records its gratitude to the following whose generosity made possible the initiation of this series: The British Academy; The Pilgrim Trust; The Twenty-Seven Foundation; The United States Embassy's Bicentennial funds; The Wolfson Trust; several private donors. Publication of this volume was supported by a further grant from the Scouloudi Foundation

Acknowledgements

This book would not have been completed without the active assistance and co-operation of a large number of people. The PhD thesis upon which it is based was accepted by the University of London in 1986. The subject of the Portuguese connection in British foreign policy was first suggested by my supervisor, the late Esmonde Robertson, who provided advice, guidance and encouragement over many years. My debt to him is enormous and gratefully acknowledged. Thanks are also due to the Humanities Faculty Research Committee of the University of the West of England, the Scouloudi Foundation of the Institute of Historical Research and to the Calouste Gulbenkian Foundation for their financial assistance. I am grateful to the library staffs of many institutions and archives for their expertise. In particular, I should wish to thank the following and, where appropriate, acknowledge permission to quote from collections in their care: the Archive Centre of Churchill College, Cambridge, for the Cadogan, Halifax, Hankey, Phipps and Vansittart papers; the British Library for the Cecil of Chelwood and Harvey of Tasburgh papers; the British Library of Political and Economic Science for the Dalton and Webster papers; the Library of the University of Birmingham for the Neville Chamberlain and Avon (Eden) papers; the Bodleian Library, Oxford, for the Attlee, Dawson, Hemming and Simon papers; Cambridge University Library for the Templewood papers; the Library of the National Maritime Museum, Greenwich, for the Chatfield papers; Trinity College Library, Cambridge, for the Butler papers; and the Franklin D. Roosevelt Library, New York.

Thanks are due to the staff of the Public Record Office, London, for their courteous assistance; copyright material located there appears by kind permission of Her Majesty's Stationery Office. The staff of the University of Bristol Library and the University of the West of England Library have provided much assistance with unfailing courtesy and generosity of their time; in particular, I should wish to thank Glen Kilbey and the late Joyce Davies.

For their helpful criticism and advice I wish to thank Professor Ian Nish, Professor Paul Preston, Professor Denis Smyth and the anonymous referee who reviewed the manuscript on behalf of the Royal Historical Society. This study has also gained much from the assistance of friends and colleagues including Felix Bihlmeier, Professor Geoffrey Channon, Professor Charles Harvey, Dr Andrew Lambert, Christian Leitz, Dr Bob Moore, Dr Steven Morewood, Dr Philip Ollerenshaw, Christopher Parker and Dr Rafael Pepiol. I am indebted to Christine Linehan of the Royal Historical Society for her expert editorial guidance and assistance. For their spendid hospitality I am grateful to Nial and Anne Maynard, Terry and Jane Murden, Dr Michael Tadman and Dr Ian Taylor. I should wish to record my appreciation of Mrs Janet Major and Mrs Margaret Thompson for their assistance in producing earlier drafts of the manuscript and of Cathryn Gallacher for her professional compilation of the index. Finally, I must record my gratitude to my wife Jane for her tolerance and forbearance. The true cost of this study has been borne by my family.

Glyn Stone
June 1994

Abbreviations

DAPE   *Dez anos de política externa, 1936–1947: a nação portuguesa e a se-*
        gunda guerra mundial, i, Lisboa 1961; ii, Lisboa 1962; iii, Lisboa
        1962; iv, Lisboa 1965; v, Lisboa 1967; vi, Lisboa 1971; vii, Lisboa
        1972; viii, Lisboa 1973; ix, Lisboa 1974; x, Lisboa 1974

DBFP   *Documents on British foreign policy, 1919–1939,* 2nd ser. xii, Lon-
        don 1972; xv, London 1976; xvi, London 1977; xvii, London
        1979; xviii, London 1980; xix, London 1982; xx, London 1984
        Documents on British foreign policy 1919-1939, 3rd ser. iii, London
        1951; v, London 1952

DGFP   *Documents on German foreign policy, 1918–1945,* ser. D, i, London
        1949; ii, London 1950; iii, London 1951; vii, London 1956; xi,
        London 1961; Xii, London 1962; xiii, London 1964

DDF   *Documents diplomatiques français, 1932–1939,* 2nd ser. iii, Paris
        1966; iv, Paris 1967; v, Paris 1968; vi, Paris 1970; vii, Paris 1972;
        ix, Paris 1974; xii, Paris 1978; xv, Paris 1981

FRUS   *Foreign relations of the United States,* 1936, ii, Washington 1954;
        1937, i, Washington 1954; 1938, iv, Washington 1955; 1940, ii,
        Washington 1957; 1941, i, Washington 1958; 1941, ii, Washing-
        ton 1959

RIIA   Royal Institute of International Affairs

Introduction

The position of continuing importance which Portugal occupied in Britain's external policy during the period 1936–41 cannot be explained simply in terms of a common economic and political identity. The economic position of Britain and Portugal during the inter-war years was not one of equals. Despite her pressing economic problems Britain was a mature and advanced industrial power while Portugal remained a backward, agriculturally orientated country with a population only a sixth of that of its ally. Between 1929 and 1939 government revenues in the United Kingdom were, on average, more than fifty times greater than those of Portugal while expenditure was almost fifty times as high.[1] Politically, there was a considerable divide in the experience of the two countries. The *Estado Novo* (New State) of António de Oliveira Salazar had been created during the years following the overthrow, in 1926, of the Portuguese parliamentary republic which had itself succeeded the monarchy in 1910[2], both of which had been to some degree modelled on foreign, and in particular British constitutional experience.[3] The *Estado Novo*, on the other hand, was antipathetic to liberal parliamentarism (monarchist or republican); it was authoritarian, apparently corporatist and, in an age of ideological division between the political left and right, possibly fascist too. While it is true that many British academics and politicians on the centre and right rejected the fascist label they could not deny the authoritarian and religious character of the *Estado Novo*, nor that its constitution differed markedly from that of the United Kingdom.[4] Historians have generally confirmed the view that the Salazarist regime was not fascist by emphasising the absence of an established fascist party or movement, Salazar's rejection of the cults of force and personality and of totalitarian state structures, and the partial and limited character of the so

---

[1] The statistical evidence presented here is derived from B. R. Mitchell, *European historical statistics 1750–1950*, London 1975, 723, 726.
[2] For the transition period between the establishment of a military dictatorship in 1926 and the formal creation of the *Estado Novo* in April 1933 see T. Gallagher, 'The mystery train: Portugal's military dictatorship 1926–1932', *European Studies Review* xi (1981), 325–53.
[3] H. J. Wiarda, *Corporatism and development: the Portuguese experience*, Amerst, Mass. 1977, 43.
[4] For contemporary opinion of the *Estado Novo* and its leader see: Lord Harlech, 'Salazar: Portugal's prime minister', *The Listener*, 6 June 1940; E. A. C. Ballard, 'Salazar of Portugal', *Contemporary Review*, Sept. 1940; M. Derrick, 'Portugal and Dr Salazar', *The Dublin Review*, Oct. 1937; E. Wakenham, 'Portugal to-day', *Nineteenth Century and After*, Sept. 1938; T. J. O'Donnell, 'Salazar and the new state of Portugal', *Studies*, Mar. 1936; W. C. Atkinson, 'The political structure of the Portuguese "New State" ', *Nineteenth Century and After*, Sept. 1937 and 'The polity of Portugal', *Fortnightly Review*, Mar. 1938; S. G. West, 'The present situation in Portugal', *International Affairs* xvii (1938).

called corporatist revolution in Portugal.[5] All are agreed, however, as to the authoritarian nature of the Portuguese 'New State'.[6]

The absence of a common economic or political identity between Britain and Portugal was irrelevant to the Portuguese connection which was based firmly on strategic grounds. Both before and after 1936 it was subjected to scrutiny and reassessment by the foreign office, the cabinet and the service departments in terms of the United Kingdom's own perceived strategic and commercial interests. Before this period, as previous research has shown, the alliance between the two countries had endured precisely because it continued to secure those interests; in return British governments had upheld their promise to guarantee, albeit reservedly, the integrity of Portugal and her empire. However, it would be incorrect to assume that discussion amongst British policy makers on the subject of the alliance had always produced complete agreement. Before 1936 a number of divergent views were expressed and the possibility of terminating the alliance was discussed, notably in 1912–13 and again in 1927, and occasionally received at least some government support.[7]

In examining the Portuguese connection in British foreign policy between 1936 and 1941 a whole series of important events and developments of long- and short-term duration have been identified. Pre-eminent was the Spanish Civil War. Portugal's intervention on the nationalist side conflicted with Britain's commitment to non-intervention which made for a period of difficult, not to say delicate, diplomacy on London's part, not least because of the prospect of a deterioration in relations, to the advantage of Italy and Germany. Indeed, the growing German and Italian influence in Portugal, largely as a result of their support for General Francisco Franco's forces in Spain, meant that the British government had to give priority to countering Axis propaganda, to improving economic relations and above all, at a time of scarce provision at home, to meeting the escalating Portuguese demands for supplies of British military equipment including artillery and aircraft. The response of the

5   See Wiarda, *Corporatism and development*; S. G. Payne, A *history of Spain and Portugal*, ii, Madison, Wisc. 1973, and 'Fascism in western Europe', in W. Laqueur (ed.), *Fascism: a reader's guide – analyses, interpretations, bibliography*, Berkeley, Ca. 1976; C. F. Delzell (ed.), *Mediterranean fascism 1919–1945*, New York 1970; H. Kay, *Salazar and modern Portugal*, London 1970; E. Nolte, *Les mouvements fascistes: l'Europe de 1919 à 1939*, Paris 1969; P. C. Schmitter, 'The social origins, economic bases and political imperatives of authoritarian rule in Portugal', in S. V. Larsen, B. Hadtvet and J. P. Myklebust (eds), *Who were the fascists?: social roots of European fascism*, Oslo 1980; T Gallagher, 'Conservatism, dictatorship and fascism in Portugal, 1914–1945', in M. Blinkhorn (ed.), *Fascists and conservatives: the radical right and the establishment in twentieth century Europe*, London 1990.
6   For details on authoritarianism and repression in Portugal see M. Soares, *Portugal's struggle for liberty*, London 1975, 46–7; T. Gallagher, 'Controlled repression in Salazar's Portugal', *Journal of Contemporary History* xiv (1979), 387, 400; D. L. Wheeler, 'In the service of order: the Portuguese political police and the British, German and Spanish intelligence, 1932–1945', *Journal of Contemporary History* xviii (1983), 9–15; Wiarda, *Corporatism and development*, 158–61; Delzell, *Mediterranean fascism*, 346; Payne, *History of Spain and Portugal*, ii, 669–70; H. Martins, 'Portugal', in S. J. Woolf (ed.), *European fascism*, New York 1969, 322–7.
7   G. A. Stone, 'The official British attitude to the Anglo-Portuguese alliance, 1910–1945', *Journal of Contemporary History* x (1975), 729–31, 732–4.

government in sending an official military mission to Lisbon in February 1938 made a crucial contribution to countering the Axis in Portugal.

In their efforts to maintain the Portuguese connection prior to the second world war Britain's policy makers also had to take cognisance of the fears of the Salazar regime that the Portuguese empire in Africa, notably Angola and Mozambique, might, as before August 1914, provide the basis for an Anglo-German settlement at Portugal's expense. For their part, in the pursuit of colonial appeasement between 1935 and 1938, the governments of Stanley Baldwin and Neville Chamberlain had to consider the extent to which the Portuguese should contribute towards a colonial settlement in Africa and whether this was compatible with the need to consolidate Portugal's position within their political orbit.

In the aftermath of the Spanish Civil War, which ended in March 1939, Britain sought, through co-operation with Portugal and in the knowledge of Franco's debt to the Axis powers for their constant support throughout the conflict, to achieve an improvement in relations between London, Paris and Madrid by closely observing the withdrawal of all German and Italian forces from Spain and resolving the tension and ill-feeling which permeated relations between Franco's regime and the French government. At the same time, the negotiations for alliance with Soviet Russia from April 1939 onwards, no matter how reluctantly entered into by Britain and France, had important implications for London's relations with the Iberian powers in view of the declared and unremitting anti-communism of the Salazar and Franco regimes.

The outbreak of war in September 1939 did not automatically exclude Axis influence from Portugal for despite the alliance, and with the approval of London, Lisbon adopted an official policy of neutrality. Britain was thus forced to continue the policy of countering German influence in Portugal through a variety of means including greater emphasis upon propaganda, the continuation of armaments supplies to the Portuguese military forces, the concession of military conversations during 1941 and economic warfare. In the latter case Britain, with reluctant American support, sought to co-operate with Salazar to ensure the continuation of Portuguese benevolent neutrality and Spanish non-belligerency. On a quite different level, British strategic planning after the fall of France in June 1940 had to consider seriously the possibility of a German occupation of the Iberian Peninsula with the possible loss of Gibraltar. The alternative to an operational strategy based on Britain's Spanish colony was to take possession of the Spanish and Portuguese Atlantic islands, that is, the Canaries, the Azores and the Cape Verde islands. Between June 1940 and December 1941 (and beyond) British military planners devoted much attention to contingency and operational planning for the seizure of the Azores and, though a lesser option, the Cape Verde islands. Eventually, the administration of Franklin Delano Roosevelt in the United States and the governments of Southern Rhodesia and of the Union of South Africa – as well as Salazar's regime – became involved.

The early years of the second world war also witnessed increased attempts by the Japanese at economic penetration of Portugal's far eastern possessions – Macao and Timor. This was a serious and growing problem for British (and Australian) policy makers. Japan's intentions concerning Portugal's tiny far eastern empire, and specifically Macao, were discussed in official circles as early as 1935; thereafter it was Timor which attracted greater attention because of its location at the southern end of the Netherlands East Indies which were vital elements in Japan's projected Greater East Asia Co-Prosperity Sphere. Before December 1941 Britain sought to counteract Japanese economic penetration by encouraging and supporting Australian demands for concessions in Timor while discouraging Salazar from granting similar concessions to the Japanese for oil exploration and commercial airway and steamship communications. However, strategic considerations involving the defence of northern Australia – Port Darwin was a mere 300 miles from Portuguese Timor – were obviously paramount since the actual economic prospects of the colony for either Japanese or Anglo-Australian interests were negligible. The Timor question came to involve Britain's relations not only with Portugal and Japan but also with the governments of Australia and the Netherlands East Indies. The concern of the Australian and Dutch governments for the defence of their interests in the south east Asian archipelago and northern Australia was accentuated by the German victories in western Europe in the Spring and early Summer of 1940. The Japanese attack on Pearl Harbour on 7 December 1941, followed by the loss of the *Prince of Wales* and *Repulse*, provided the incentive for joint Australian-Dutch action in Portuguese Timor. Taking advantage of its inadequate garrison, a combined Australian-Dutch force, with the belated approval of London, occupied the Portuguese colony on 17 December. There followed the most serious crisis in Anglo-Portuguese relations since 1890. It divided the British government and did not abate until February 1942 when Japanese forces in turn occupied Portuguese Timor.

While the British foreign policy making process in the period 1936–41 had to take into account relations with many and varied countries, particularly the great European powers, Japan and the United States, the Portuguese connection was of sufficient importance occasionally to merit consideration at the highest levels; in peacetime the cabinet, the cabinet foreign policy committee and the committee of imperial defence, and during the second world war the war cabinet, the defence committee and the chiefs of staff committee. At foreign office level the department most concerned was the league of nations and western department and after 3 September 1939, the central department. Inter-departmental consultation on Portugal within the foreign office and between foreign office departments and other institutions of government such as the colonial office, the dominions office and the service ministries was a frequent occurrence. On these occasions the foreign office usually acted as co-ordinator either through the medium of inter-departmental correspondence or in convening *ad hoc* meetings. However, on a number of occasions Portuguese issues were discussed within formally constituted committees. For example, the question of Portuguese armaments requirements before 1939 was discussed at length within a number of committees of the committee of imperial defence – the chiefs of staff sub-committee, the committee for armaments orders from foreign countries and its successor the allied demands committee.

In the conduct of relations with Portugal, British foreign policy formulation was necessarily dependent upon clear and precise information and advice from the embassy in Lisbon which by the mid-1930s was established with ambassa-dorial and counsellor representation. It lacked, however, other permanent and important personnel such as military, air, naval and press attachés. It is perhaps a measure of the growing importance of the Portuguese connection in British foreign policy that by the end of 1939 British representation in Portugal in-cluded permanent attachés for all of these previously neglected areas. Consulta-tion with British representatives abroad on matters affecting Portugal were also commonplace and included the embassies in Paris, Berlin, Madrid, Washington and Tokyo; the consulates at Beira (Mozambique), Lobito (Angola) and Batavia (Netherlands East Indies); and government house in Pretoria, Salisbury, Canberra and Wellington. Contact was also maintained with the high commissions of Australia, New Zealand and the Union of South Africa in London.

In Portugal the foreign policy making process operated differently. Within the *Estado Novo* the executive was independent of the national assembly and increasingly functioned on a bureaucratic rather than political basis.[8] The administrative establishment was dominated by a small civilian and bureau-cratic élite located in the ministry of the president of the council of ministers, the council of ministers and in central ministerial organisations such as finance, interior, army, foreign and colonial affairs. Salazar stood at the apex of this hierarchical structure and his immediate subordinates – ministers, secretaries and under secretaries – were all, as events were to show, expendable. During this period the Portuguese dictator occupied a number of key positions within the *Estado Novo*: president of the council and prime minister (from 1932); finance minister (from 1928); and as foreign minister in succession to Dr Armindo Monteiro (from 1936) and as minister of war (from 1936). However, he did recognise the significance of the support of the armed forces for his regime and therefore accepted that the president of the republic should be a senior military figure.[9]

In the sphere of foreign policy formulation too the process was bureaucratic and personalised. Even before he became foreign minister Salazar presented himself as the key decision-maker receiving advice from Monteiro and the officials of the foreign ministry.[10] Its permanent head, Luís Teixeira de

---

[8] Templewood Papers, XIII:11. See also L. S. Graham, *Portugal: the decline and collapse of an authoritarian order*, London 1975, 14.

[9] The first president of the authoritarian republic was General Oscar Fragoso Carmona who remained in office until 1951. According to Douglas Wheeler, after 1936 the highly privileged status of the military was diminished, for example, officers were less immune to police arrest: 'The military and the Portuguese dictatorship 1926–1974: "the honor of the army" ', in L. S. Graham and H. M. Makler (eds), *Contemporary Portugal: the revolution and its antecedents*, Austin, Texas 1979, 198–9, 205. See also Gallagher, 'Conservatism, dictatorship and fascism', 163–4.

[10] The ministry of foreign affairs was reformed in 1938 in an attempt to improve its efficiency in dealing with the representations of foreign countries. For details of how the ministry worked see F. Nogueira, 'Portugal: the ministry of foreign affairs', in Z. Steiner (ed.), *The Times survey of the foreign ministries of the world*, London 1982. The foreign service of the *Estado Novo* was small. In 1944 there were 92 members of the diplomatic corps of whom only 5 were ambassadors; there were just 58 in the consular service of whom 8 were consul-generals. See D. L. Wheeler, 'And

Sampaio,[11] reported directly to Salazar and action on main lines of policy affecting Portugal's relations with other states, including Britain, had to await his approval. The same was true in matters of colonial and military policy. The net effect of this concentration of power was to slow down the machinery of government, although, as will be shown, Salazar was sometimes prepared to expedite matters concerning Portugal's long standing ally. Moreover, delays in the deliberation and communication of decisions were as frequent on the British side as on the Portuguese.

During the period 1936–41 the foreign policy making processes of Britain and Portugal worked to preserve the Anglo-Portuguese relationship while, at least on the British side, maintaining other more vital interests at a time of increasing crisis in the established international order. At the same time, Britain could not afford to remain complacent about the alliance. 1936 was a significant year for the Anglo-Portuguese relationship. The outbreak of civil war in Spain in July, which created an active Italian and German interest in Portugal, the proposed rearmament of the Portuguese armed forces, and the revival of official German claims to colonial territory, altered the diplomatic climate and accordingly brought relations with Portugal closer to the forefront of Britain's foreign policy priorities. Certainly, from 1936 onwards Britain could no longer afford to take for granted Portuguese acquiesence in the British view of the alliance.

who is my neighbor? a World War II hero or conscience for Portugal', *Luso-Brazilian Review* xxvi (1989), 125.
[11] Sampaio started his career in Portugal's foreign service in 1896. He was and remained a monarchist at heart: ibid. 125, 131.

1

The Origins of Non-Intervention in Spain

The outbreak of civil war in Spain in July 1936, the most momentous event in the Iberian Peninsula since the war of resistance to Napoleon during the early nineteenth century, was bound to cause shock waves which would reverberate throughout Portugal, particularly in view of Lisbon's persistent apprehensions concerning developments within the second Spanish Republic from its inception in 1931. The effects of the war were not confined to the Iberian countries: until its conclusion in March 1939 it continued to exercise an influence, occasionally profound, upon relations between the European powers, greater and lesser, and this included the Anglo-Portuguese relationship. While the fascist dictatorships of Germany and Italy supported the rebel nationalist forces of General Francisco Franco, Soviet Russia provided increasing aid to the Spanish republicans and France gave limited support, Britain from the outset adopted a strictly neutral political-military position, enshrined in the official policy of non-intervention.[1] Portugal, on the other hand was throughout a

[1] For Germany's role in the Spanish Civil War see H.-Henning Abendroth, *Hitler in der spanischen Arena: die deutsch-spanischen Beziehungen in Spannungsfeld der europäischen Interessenpolitik vom Ausbruch des Bürgerkrieges bis zum Ausbruch des Weltkrieges 1936–1939*, Paderborn 1973; M. Merkes, *Die deutsche Politik gegenüber dem spanischen Bürgerkrieg 1936–1939*, Bonn 1969; R. H. Whealey, *Hitler and Spain: the Nazi role in the Spanish civil war*, Lexington, Kentucky 1989; G. L. Weinberg, *The foreign policy of Hitler's Germany*, I: *diplomatic revolution in Europe 1933–1936*, Chicago 1970, and *The foreign policy of Hitler's Germany*, II: *starting World War Two, 1937–1939*, Chicago 1980; H.-Henning Abendroth, 'Die deutsche Intervention im spanischen Bürgerkrieg: ein Diskussionsbeitrag', *Vierteljahrshefte für Zeitgeschichte* xxx (1982); D. Smyth, 'Reflex reaction: Germany and the onset of the Spanish civil war', in P. Preston (ed.), *Revolution and war in Spain 1931–1939*, London 1984; P. Monteath, 'German historiography and the Spanish civil war: a critical survey', *European History Quarterly* xx (1990). The most comprehensive study of Italian policy is J. F. Coverdale, *Italian intervention in the Spanish civil war*, Princeton, NJ 1975. For Soviet policy see D. T. Cattell, *Communism and the Spanish civil war*, Berkeley, Ca. 1955, and *Soviet diplomacy and the Spanish civil war*, Berkeley, Ca. 1957; J. Haslam, *The Soviet Union and the struggle for collective security in Europe 1933–1939*, London 1984; E. H. Carr, *Comintern and the Spanish civil war*, London 1984; and J. Hartley, 'Recent Soviet publications on the Spanish civil war', *European History Quarterly* xviii (1988). France's role in the Spanish conflagration awaits detailed treatment. Meanwhile, R. J. Young, *In command of France: French foreign policy and military planning 1933–1940*, Cambridge, Mass. 1978; J. E. Dreifort, *Yvon Delbos and the Quai d'Orsay: French foreign policy during the Popular Front 1936–1938*, Lawrence, Ka. 1973; J. B. Duroselle, *La décadence (1932–1939)*, Paris 1979; and G. Warner, 'France and non-intervention in Spain, July–August 1936', *International Affairs* xxviii (1962), provide relevant and interesting material. D. W. Pike, *Les français et la Guerre d'Espagne 1936–1939*, Paris 1975, is a comprehensive and useful study of French opinion in relation to the civil war, based upon a wide range of French newspaper sources. There are two detailed studies of Portugal's role in the Spanish civil war: Iva Delgado, *Portugal e a Guerra Civil de Espanha*, Lisboa 1980, and César Oliveira, *Salazar e a Guerra Civil de Espanha*, Lisboa 1987. Oliveira's is by far the best treatment. Finally, for Britain's pursuit of non-intervention in Spain see J.

wholehearted supporter of the nationalist cause. Naturally, this imposed a severe strain upon Anglo-Portuguese relations, especially during the early months of the civil war when Britain sought to persuade an extremely reluctant Portugal to adhere to the Non-Intervention Agreement and subsequently to serve on the Non-Intervention Committee in London. Indeed, during August and September 1936, for the first time since at least the years immediately preceding the Great War, Portugal found herself occupying the centre stage of European diplomacy, and her determination to resist any diplomatic moves that might threaten to undermine the early successes of the rebel forces in Spain severely taxed Britain's diplomatic resources. Before examining, however, this particular aspect of Spanish civil war diplomacy it is necessary to establish clearly and in some detail the respective positions adopted by Portugal and Britain in the Spanish conflict.

Contrary to the opinion of certain writers, Portugal could not manufacture even small scale weapons for her own armed forces, let alone supply Franco, though it is possible that the Portuguese authorities denuded their own imported stocks.[2] Franco obtained virtually all his armaments requirements from Nazi Germany and fascist Italy and from those parts of Spanish industry which fell increasingly under his control.[3] However, according to César Oliveira, Portuguese companies regularly supplied Franco's forces with war material such as gunpowder, dynamite, cartridges, fuses and grenades.[4]

From the beginning of the war Salazar's government provided moral and political support through its representatives in the London Non-Intervention Committee, the League of Nations in Geneva and the International Control Committee at Tangier.[5] In addition, between July 1936 and the end of the civil war, and particularly during the early months, Portuguese radio and press propaganda was incessant and forthright in espousing the rebel cause.[6] Even before

Edwards, *The British government and the Spanish civil war, 1936–1939*, London 1979; D. Carlton, 'Eden, Blum and the origins of non-intervention', *Journal of Contemporary History* vi (1971); E. Moradiellos, 'British political strategy in the face of the military rising of 1936 in Spain', *Contemporary European History* i (1992), and 'Appeasement and non-intervention: British policy during the Spanish civil war', in P. Catterall and C. J. Morris (eds), *Britain and the threat to stability in Europe 1918–45*, London 1993; G. A. Stone, 'Britain, non-intervention and the Spanish civil war, *European Studies Review* ix (1979), and 'Britain, France and the Spanish problem 1936–1939', in R. C. Richardson and G. A. Stone, *Decisions and diplomacy: essays in twentieth century international history*, London 1994.

2   For the erroneous claims that Portugal manufactured weapons for Franco see R. G. Colodny, *Spain: the glory and the tragedy*, New York 1970, 78, and V. Alba, *Transition in Spain: from Franco to democracy*, New Brunswick, NJ 1978, 180. For evidence that the Portuguese denuded their stocks see FO 371/24508 C7778/40/41.

3   For details relating to the provision of war material to the nationalist forces by Germany and Italy see H. Thomas, *The Spanish civil war*, 3rd edn, London 1977, 977–9. With reference to nationalist self-help see C. E. Harvey, *The Rio Tinto company: an economic history of a leading international mining concern 1873–1954*, Penzance 1981, 283–4, and R. H. Whealey, 'How Franco financed his war – reconsidered', *Journal of Contemporary History* xii (1979), 142.

4   Oliveira, *Salazar e a Guerra Civil*, 149.

5   C. R. Halstead, 'Spanish foreign policy, 1936–1978', in J. W. Cortada (ed.), *Spain in the twentieth century world: essays in Spanish diplomacy 1898–1978*, London 1980, 46.

6   FRUS, 1936, ii. 456. For details see Oliveira, *Salazar e a Guerra Civil*, 202–12.

the war Salazar provided General José Sanjurjo, the ill-fated leader of the July military *coup*, with a place of exile and Portuguese territory, notably Lisbon and Estoril, became the focal point of military conspiracy against the Spanish Republic. After the outbreak of hostilities the rebels were permitted to establish a 'black embassy' in the Aviz hotel in Lisbon where José Maria Gil Robles, leader of the Spanish Catholic party, *Confederación Española de Derechas Autónomas* (CEDA), and Franco's brother Nicolás, organised supplies, propaganda and financial assistance. The Lisbon headquarters also provided a central telephone exchange through which the military authorities in the two nationalist controlled zones (separated by republican held territory) communicated with each other until unification made this unnecessary.[7] Significantly, the Portuguese not only allowed but apparently sanctioned certain of Franco's police and intelligence agents to operate independently within Portugal.[8]

During July and August 1936, before the Portuguese – Spanish frontier area ceased to be a battlefield, the Portuguese government demonstrated its solidarity with the nationalist cause through its discriminatory treatment of captured republican troops. While officers of the nationalist army had free entry into Portugal at all times, members of the Spanish government militia who had fled across the Portuguese frontier were incarcerated[9] and in many cases handed over to the authorities in rebel-held Spain.[10] Moreover, during the early crucial weeks, the Portuguese authorities allowed German war material to be moved through their territory and did what they could to ease financial-military transactions. As early as 26 July 1936 the German legation in Lisbon informed the *Wilhelmstrasse* of a request from the rebel generals for Junker transport aircraft and German bombers adding that negotiations had taken place at the private residence of the adjutant to the Portuguese president.[11] These negotiations had been conducted in the strictest secrecy but Portuguese involvement in the movement of foreign-supplied war material to the rebel forces could not for long remain concealed. The arrival of the steamships *Kamerun* and *Wigbert* in Lisbon during the second half of August 1936 did not pass unnoticed. *The Times*, for example, reported that both ships unloaded military supplies, 800 tons of them from the *Kamerun*. The cargoes were alleged to have included light tanks, aeroplanes, bombs and hand grenades, all consigned to the Spanish insurgents.[12] The British ambassador in Lisbon, Sir Charles Wingfield, was

[7] See FO 371/20533 W9085/62/41; 371/20573 W9964/9549/41. See also Thomas, *Spanish civil war*, 360; Delgado, *Portugal e a Guerra Civil*, 34–5; Oliveira, *Salazar e a Guerra Civil*, 182–4; P. Fryer and P. McGowan Pinheiro, *Oldest ally: a portrait of Salazar's Portugal*, London 1961, 120; P. A. M. van der Esch, *Prelude to war: the international repercussions of the Spanish civil war 1936–1939*, The Hague 1951, 39–40; Alba, *Transition in Spain*, 140.

[8] Wheeler, 'In the service of order', 15–16. The Portuguese also supplied Franco with intelligence on republican activity, for example, the shipment of arms from Mexico to the Spanish republic during 1937: Oliveira, *Salazar e a Guerra Civil*, 152–3.

[9] Most of the captured Spanish militiamen were incarcerated in three locations: the fortress at Caxias, the Graça fortress at Elves and the concentration camp of Herdada da Coitadinha in Alentejo: Oliveira, *Salazar e a Guerra Civil*, 158.

[10] *New Statesman and Nation*, 29 Aug. 1936. See also DGFP, D, iii, no. 53, p. 55; Julio Álvarez del Vayo, *Freedom's battle*, London 1940.

[11] DGFP, D, iii, no. 12, p. 14.

[12] *The Times*, 26 Aug. 1936; *New Statesman and Nation*, 29 Aug. 1936. See also Delgado,

informed by the French minister, Amé Leroy, that the war material had been disembarked on 21 August and hastily forwarded by rail.[13] German war material was moved through Portuguese territory via the German trade association *Compañía Hispano-Marroquí de Transportes* (HISMA), headed by a Nazi party official, Johannes Bernhardt.[14]

After August 1936 Portugal's role as a conduit for arms supplies to Franco was somewhat modified in the face of increasing public awareness abroad, Anglo-French pressure upon Lisbon to participate in the Non-Intervention Committee, and the increasing ability of the nationalists to receive arms supplies directly through their own ports. British intelligence sources confirmed that during October 1936 there was no evidence of any appreciable transit traffic in arms through Portugal; this was also the view of the Lisbon embassy.[15] In addition, the foreign office noted in December 1936 that there was no evidence of any Portuguese breach of the Non-Intervention Agreement.[16] However, the same intelligence sources did report, at monthly intervals from December 1936 onwards, an appreciable small-arms traffic from Germany via Antwerp into Portugal for the rebel forces in Spain.[17] According to these sources Portugal imported 200 cases of machine guns, 120 cases of rifles and 300 cases of revolvers during December 1936.[18] Moreover, from January 1937 until August 1938 when the small arms traffic ceased, approximately 320,000 rifles and 555,000 revolvers were sent from Germany via Portugal to the nationalist forces.[19] The finances for this operation were probably provided by the German trade cartel, the *Ausfuhrgemeinschaft für Kriegsgerät* (AGK), which was part of the *Reichsgruppe Industrie*.[20] In 1937 the AGK, in co-operation with HISMA, concluded an arrangement with Portugal for the supply of war material to the value of 4.1 million reichmarks; this material was processed and forwarded to the nationalist forces in Spain by the materials procurement office established

---

Portugal e a Guerra Civil, 88–93; Oliveira, *Salazar e a Guerra Civil*, 146; W. C. Frank Jr, 'Politico-military deception at sea in the Spanish civil war, 1936–1939', *Intelligence and National Security* v (1990), 90–1.

13 FO 371/20574 W10214/9549/41.

14 For details of HISMA's activity in Spain see Harvey, *Rio Tinto company*, 271–2.

15 FO 371/20584 W15431/9549/41.

16 FO 371/20588 W18100/9549/41.

17 These monthly intelligence reports were sent to the foreign office by the war office in the form of 'Arms Traffic Summaries' which detailed all illicit arms supplies to the republican and nationalist forces in Spain. Although it is not possible to confirm the reliability or otherwise of these intelligence sources it is pertinent to note that the foreign office viewed them as reliable. See *Dalton Diaries*, i. 18, diary entry 24 June 1937.

18 FO 371/21321 W1698/7/41.

19 These statistics are derived from a series of monthly figures which appear in various files in the FO 371 series. See G. A. Stone, 'The oldest ally: Britain and the Portuguese connection 1936–1941', unpublished PhD diss. London, 1986, app. i.

20 For details of the AGK and its role in Spain see M. Einhorn, 'Die ersten Massnahmen des deutschen Imperialismus zur wirtschaftlichen Ausplünderung Spaniens (Juli bis August)', in W. Scheider and C. Dipper (eds), *Der spanische Bürgerkrieg in der Internationalen Politik 1936–1939*, München 1976, 155.

previously in Lisbon by the Spanish military. The office was organised under the name of Fernández Aguilar, an alias for Nicolás Franco.[21]

The least observed yet most positive form of intervention by Portugal concerned the number of Portuguese volunteers fighting on Franco's side.[22] Writing in the early 1950's Sir Robert Hodgson, Britain's semi-official representative with the nationalist authorities at Burgos after September 1937, estimated that some 20,000 Portuguese took part in the civil war and incurred losses totalling some 8,000.[23] While a number of historians have accepted Hodgson's assessment others have remained somewhat sceptical, arguing that probably no more than a few thousand actually participated in the war.[24] During the hostilities both official circles in Lisbon and the Portuguese press – much of the latter was government controlled – were extremely vague when referring to Portuguese nationals fighting for Franco.[25]

The United Kingdom showed little interest in the involvement of Portuguese volunteers in Franco's forces. A foreign office appraisal at the beginning of 1937 referred to French, German, Italian, Russian and British volunteers (numbered in hundreds fighting on the side of the Spanish Republic), but excluded the Portuguese.[26] Similarly, in March 1937 *The Times* estimated that roughly 60,000 foreign combatants were actually fighting on Franco's side but did not mention Portuguese volunteers.[27] Indeed, it was not until the spring of 1938 that official concern in the matter was shown in London.[28] Even the parliamentary left appeared unconcerned. While on many occasions labour MPs questioned ministers in the house of commons on the subject of German and Italian volunteers it was only in December 1938 that the issue of the Portuguese was actually broached.[29]

The end of the civil war brought with it a loosening of Portuguese inhibitions. On 8 June 1939 some seventy Portuguese officers who had fought in Spain returned to Lisbon and were greeted enthusiastically at a demonstration attended by the minister of commerce, João da Costa Leite, and General Sousa

---

[21] Ibid. 161, n. 60. See also *DGFP*, D, iii, no. 80, p. 85 and Oliveira, *Salazar e a Guerra Civil*, 151–2.

[22] The Portuguese volunteers were known as *Viriatos* (named after Viriatus who had led the Lusitanian resistance to Rome in the second century BC) and the majority of them were enlisted in the Spanish foreign legion. See *The Times*, 14–15 Mar. 1939. A small number of Portuguese volunteers fought on the side of the Spanish Republic during the earliest days of the civil war: Pike, *Les français*, 156. César Oliveira estimates that between 500 and 2000 Portuguese combatants fought for the Republic: *Salazar e a Guerra Civil*, 271–2.

[23] R. Hodgson, *Spain resurgent*, London 1953, 70.

[24] For example, the Spanish historian Ricardo de la Cierva argues that using all the Portuguese volunteers scattered throughout the whole nationalist army it was impossible to form even a brigade of 3,000 men, though there was apparently a plan to do so: 'The nationalist army in the Spanish civil war', in R. Carr (ed.), *The Republic and the civil war in Spain*, London 1971, 206. In the first edition of his mammoth work on the civil war Hugh Thomas readily accepted Hodgson's figures. The latest edition notes only that 'several thousand' Portuguese volunteers fought for Franco: *Spanish civil war*, 360. See also Oliveira, *Salazar e a Guerra Civil*, 244–7.

[25] For example, FO 371/22644 W5816/83/41.

[26] *DBFP*, 2, xviii, no. 34, p. 53.

[27] 9 Mar. 1937.

[28] FO 371/22644 W6403/83/41.

[29] *Hansard parliamentary debates*, HC, 5th ser. cccxlii, col. 841.

Teles, respectively the civilian and military heads of the *Legião Portuguesa*. At the same time, the Portuguese press claimed that some 10,000 Portuguese had enlisted in Franco's army, fighting not as Portuguese units but as individuals enlisted in the foreign legion and units of the *Falange Española* and *Requetés*. Of these 10,000 it was claimed some 6,000 were killed or wounded.[30] During the previous month Salazar admitted in his address to the Portuguese national assembly that 'several thousands of Portuguese' had gone to fight and die for Spain.[31] However, his denial of any official connection contradicted his declared intention of 1 August 1936 to help the rebels 'with all available means' including the intervention of the Portuguese army should that be necessary.[32] What is not in dispute is the fact that many thousands of Portuguese fought and died on the side of Franco and that in terms of actual foreign combat commitment to the nationalist cause Portugal ranked second only to Italy.[33]

In supporting Franco the Portuguese authorities were strongly motivated by ideological fears and prejudices. From the outset they viewed their support for the nationalist cause as a crusade against anarchy and communism which, they believed, threatened the whole fabric of western civilisation.[34] The strong antipathy of the Portuguese authorities for atheistic communism was a natural ideological corollary of the Catholic corporatism of the *Estado Novo*. Even before the civil war the major focus of Portuguese hostility in international affairs was the Soviet Union with whom Portugal had no formal diplomatic relations.[35] Soviet support for the republican forces simply confirmed the widespread nature of the communist conspiracy. A victory for the republicans in Spain would mean the end of the *Estado Novo* since it was clearly believed, with some cause in view of their statements, that a republican success would soon be followed by the invasion of Portugal and the establishment of a Portuguese communist republic.[36] In addition, Salazar was extremely concerned at the possible effect of events in Spain upon the Portuguese working class which, he believed, might easily succumb to the influence of the Spanish and Portuguese left. According to Amé Leroy, even before the outbreak of hostilities in Spain the Portuguese were very apprehensive about the possibility of a communist *coup de main*, sustained financially by Spanish extremists and supported by

30 FO 371/24121 W9629/5/41. Captain Jorge Botelho Moniz, chief of the 'attendance section for Portuguese combatants in Spain', claimed, in the *Diário de Lisboa* of 7 June 1939, that between 10,000 and 12000 Portuguese enlisted to fight for the nationalist cause: Oliveira, *Salazar e a Guerra Civil*, 244–7.

31 Kay, *Salazar*, 126–7.

32 Thomas, *Spanish civil war*, 360; DGFP, D, iii, no. 25, p.25.

33 German casualties, with about 300 dead, were extremely light in comparison with Portuguese casualties. The Italian forces at their maximum numbered between 40,000 and 50,000 troops while losses amounted to around 4,000 dead and 11,000–12,000 wounded: Thomas, *Spanish civil war*, 977–9; Coverdale, *Italian intervention*, 418–19.

34 FO 371/20530 W8431/62/41; A. O. Salazar, *Doctrine and action: internal and foreign policy of the new Portugal 1928–1939*, London, 1939; DAPE, i: no. 37, p. 86.

35 Russian citizens were prohibited from entering Portugal or the Portuguese colonies. In 1934 the Portuguese had opposed vigorously Russia's entry into the League of Nations: West, 'The present situation'.

36 FO 371/20527 W7918/62/41; DAPE, iii, no. 111, pp. 90–1; DGFP, D, iii, nos 53 and 76, pp. 54, 77–8.

certain Portuguese political exiles. The authorities were also uncertain as to the loyalty of the navy and feared, in the event of a *coup*, defections within the Lisbon garrison.[37] The emergence of a left-orientated government in Spain following the general election of February 1936 had added considerably to these fears.[38] Indeed, the contrast between the excellent relations enjoyed by the Salazar regime with the rightist Spanish government of Niceto Alcalá Zamora and Alejandro Lerroux and the serious deterioration in relations with the Spanish Popular Front government after the elections of February 1936 could not have been more marked.[39]

The conflagration in Spain increased official concern in Lisbon for the internal stability and security of Portugal. The mutiny on board two Portuguese warships, the cruiser *Afonso d'Albuquerque* and the destroyer *Dão*, on 8 September 1936 seemed to provide clear proof of the extremely dangerous effects of the civil war in Spain. According to the official explanation in Lisbon some members of the crew of the *Afonso d'Albuquerque*, which had recently visited the Spanish republican port of Alicante, became infected with bolshevik ideas and committed acts of indiscipline on the return journey. Similarly, members of the crew of the *Dão* had been in contact with communist ideas while visiting Spanish ports.[40] Salazar's response was immediate. On 10 September a decree was published which made it obligatory for all public servants to sign a document accepting the social order established by the constitution of 1933 and repudiating 'communism and subversive ideas'. A week later the Portuguese legion was founded to combat communism and anarchy.[41] During the next year or so the state's repressive apparatus was enlarged and strengthened.[42]

Although the naval mutiny was easily suppressed and remained an isolated incident, and while no proof of an international communist conspiracy was forthcoming at the subsequent trial of the mutineers, the episode reinforced official Portuguese determination to support Franco.[43] Indeed, for the Portuguese government the restoration of 'law and order' in Spain by the Spanish military – no matter how brutally carried out – could only benefit Portugal's own social and political order. Salazar was personally very critical of the failure of the Spanish Republic to maintain order and control both before and after the outbreak of the civil war.[44]

The authorities in Portugal were also firmly convinced that if the Spanish

[37] Pike, *Les français*, 74 n. 23. Leroy also reported the rapid organisation of communist cells amongst the Portuguese tramway employees, the dockworkers and even amongst certain sections of the military, in particular, the Republican Guard. According to César Oliveira the Portuguese secret police, the *Polícia de Vigilancia e Defesa do Estado* (PVDE), were extremely active at this time in gathering intelligence on the Portuguese oppositionist forces in Portugal and abroad: *Salazar e a Guerra Civil*, 119–21.

[38] See FO 371/20511 W2540/W2976/W3674/478/36. See also Delgado, *Portugal e a Guerra Civil*, 27; D. Little, *Malevolent neutrality: the United States, Great Britain and the origins of the Spanish civil war*, Ithaca NY 1985, 196–7.

[39] Oliveira, *Salazar e a Guerra Civil*, 100–4.

[40] FO 371/20511 W11421/403/36.

[41] Ibid.; Kay, *Salazar*, 95.

[42] See introduction.

[43] FO 371/20511 W14272/403/36. See also FO 371/20511 W11421/403/36.

[44] See FO 371/21277 W20511/923/36.

republican forces triumphed in Spain not only would Portugal go communist but it would cease to be a truly independent state because the ambitions of the Spanish left were not confined to the defence of the Spanish Republic but included the establishment of a federation of Iberian soviet republics with Portugal, possibly associated with Galicia, merely one amongst many. In such an eventuality the Portuguese colonial empire would cease to exist.[45] According to the American journalist Edward Knoblaugh, the republican prime minister, Largo Caballero, was committed to Portugal's absorption into a Spanish soviet republic.[46] Even in defeat many republicans continued to believe in the idea of a federation of Iberian states which might include Portugal.[47]

Although they wanted Franco to win, the Portuguese authorities were conscious that a regenerated national and imperial Spain might seek, like Castile in the sixteenth century, to incorporate their country into one national Iberian state. Indeed, during the civil war reports reached Lisbon of maps seen pinned to the wall of the military headquarters at Burgos and Salamanca in which Portugal appeared as a province of Spain. Moreover, during 1938 a great stir was created in Lisbon with the circulation of a pamphlet entitled The Spanish Empire believed to be a copy of a publication by the Spanish fascist movement the Falange Española, which portrayed a double headed eagle bearing the arms of Spain and Portugal, and those of Philip II of Spain, the monarch who in 1580 annexed Portugal – a state of affairs which lasted until 1640 when Portugal regained her independence. For the Portuguese the implications were all too obvious.[48] Salazar too was uneasy but remained convinced that an enduring relationship could be established between himself and Franco and thus between their two countries. The appointment of Nicolás Franco as Spanish ambassador at Lisbon in April 1938 seemed to herald a more harmonious future for relations between the two Iberian states.[49] The signing of the Pacto del Bloque Iberico, a treaty of Hispano-Portuguese Friendship and Non-Aggression, in March 1939, confirmed Salazar's faith in Franco and the wisdom of the original decision to support his cause by all available means.[50]

---

[45] A. J. Toynbee, Survey of international affairs 1937, II: The international repercussions of the war in Spain (1936–1937), London 1938, 205; M. Chaves Nogales, 'Franco's Spain', Fortnightly Review, Oct. 1937, 414–15; West, 'The present situation', 215. Portuguese association with Galicia is usually based upon linguistic similarities.

[46] M. Derrick, The Portugal of Salazar, London 1938, 20.

[47] See memorandum by Catalan and Basque separatisits to the Royal Institute of International Affairs, Mar. 1940: Attlee Papers, MS Attlee dep 1.

[48] Derrick, Portugal of Salazar, 19–20; Wakenham, 'Portugal to-day', 266. See also D. Puzzo, Spain and the great powers 1936–1941, New York 1962, 70–1; Fernando Rosas, O Salazarismo e a aliança Luso-Britânica: estudos sobre a política externa do Estado Novo nos anos 30 e 40, Lisboa 1988, 45. The Falange Española was founded in October 1933. In the spring of 1934 it amalgamated with the fascist group the Juntas de Ofensiva Nacional Sindicalista (JONS), founded in 1931, to form Spain's only significant fascist party, the Falange Española de las JONS. In April 1937 Franco forcibly fused it with the Carlists and the rest of the Spanish right to form a new political organisation under his leadership, the Falange Española Tradicionalista y de las JONS. See M. Blinkhorn, 'Conservatism, traditionalism and fascism in Spain, 1898–1937', in his Fascists and conservatives: the radical right and the establishment in twentieth century Europe, 129–34.

[49] Kay, Salazar, 89–90, 116–17.

[50] For details concerning the Iberian Pact of March 1939 see ch. vii.

From the beginning of the civil war in Spain, Britain was determined to avoid direct military and political intervention and to adhere to a policy of strict neutrality regardless of the actions of other European powers including France and Portugal. Thus the British government readily accepted a French proposal for an agreement by which the European powers would refrain from interference in the civil war. Indeed, Britain was more committed to the principle of non-intervention than was France; so much so that when the Non-Intervention Agreement became operative towards the end of August 1936 Britain was the only European power prepared to impose a strict embargo on the supply of war material to the belligerents.[51]

Throughout the Spanish Civil War the government strenuously resisted calls for the abandonment of non-intervention.[52] In this Britain's policy makers, including the foreign secretary, Anthony Eden, and the foreign office, were motivated from the outset by a genuine desire to confine the conflagration to Spain and thereby avert the possibility of a general European war based on ideological divisions.[53] It was felt that any involvement in Spain might irretrievably jeopardise their efforts to reach a general European settlement to replace Locarno through the proposed five power conference.[54] In addition, by pursuing a politically non-partisan policy the British government believed they would receive favourable treatment from whichever side emerged victorious; because Britain alone among the great European powers had not intervened to kill Spaniards.[55] Added to this was the conviction that by means of her superior financial resources Britain could overcome Italo-German influence in Spain should Franco win the civil war.[56] Finally, from August 1936 onwards the chiefs of staff continued to advise that the maintenance of non-intervention was the best means of preserving Britain's considerable strategic interests in the western Mediterranean and eastern Atlantic.[57]

Broad strategic and political considerations apart, many in British governing circles shared Salazar's vehement condemnation of the left-wing Spanish authorities especially during the early stages of the civil war. This was particularly true of the senior naval authorities who continued to condemn unreservedly the killing of Spanish naval officers by republican sailors during the early weeks of the civil war, despite the fact that these officers were in open revolt against

[51] For Britain's pusuit of non-intervention during the crucial early weeks of the civil war in Spain see Edwards, *British government and the Spanish civil war*, 1–37; Carlton, 'Eden, Blum', 40–55; Moradiellos, 'British political strategy', 123–37; Stone, 'Britain, non-intervention', 129–49.

[52] Ibid. 134–5.

[53] FO 371/20534 W9331/62/41.

[54] For details of Britain's attempts to convene a five power conference see W. N. Medlicott, *Britain and Germany: the search for agreement 1930–1937*, London 1969, 25–30.

[55] See Eden's speech of 19 Jan. 1937 in *Hansard parliamentary debates*, HC, 5th ser. cccxix, col. 95. For Neville Chamberlain's views which were virtually identical see CAB 23/90 CM 47(37), 15 Dec. 1937.

[56] See, for example, I. Maisky, *Spanish notebooks*, London 1966, 146.

[57] CAB 24/264 CP 234(36). *DBFP*, 2, xvii, no. 126, pp. 151–8. See also G. A. Stone, 'The European great powers and the Spanish civil war, 1936–1939', in R. Boyce and E. M. Robertson (eds), *Paths to war: new essays on the origins of the Second World War*, London 1989, 215–16.

the elected government of Spain.[58] During the early months of the war senior foreign office officials, including Sir Robert Vansittart, the permanent under-secretary, his deputy, Sir Alexander Cadogan, and Sir George Mounsey, super-intending assistant under-secretary to the league of nations and western department, tended to share the admiralty's distaste for the Spanish Republic. They were horrified by what they considered the breakdown of law and order in republican controlled areas.[59] Despite this, the foreign office was not prepared to advise the abandonment of non-intervention in favour of the nationalist forces even though, on the one hand, the parliamentary opposition persistently claimed that non-intervention implicitly favoured Franco since the republicans were denied their legal right to purchase arms and munitions in Britain and France; and on the other Eden and some of his foreign office advisers, including his private secretary, Oliver Harvey, and Vansittart, reached the conclusion during 1937 that the survival of the republican government in Spain was in Britain's best interests.[60]

British ministers, at the highest level, rarely expressed pro-Franco sentiments whether at meetings of the cabinet or of the foreign policy committee. How-ever, with the notable exceptions of Eden and Leslie Hore-Belisha, secretary of state at war, ministers were generally disposed in the *Caudillo*'s favour. Prime Minister Neville Chamberlain, implied that this was the case when he warned his colleagues during January 1939 that the government 'should avoid showing any satisfaction at the prospect of a Franco victory'.[61] Moreover, in the eco-nomic, if not the political and/or the military sphere, the government actually went out of its way to curry favour with the nationalists in order to counter the growing German economic offensive in rebel territory and thereby safeguard established British economic interests. In November 1937 it went so far as to appoint an agent, Sir Robert Hodgson, to the nationalist government in Burgos and to receive the Anglophile duke of Alba in exchange. Although there was no formal political recognition of Franco's government until the end of the civil war, these agents were effectively accorded full diplomatic status.[62]

---

58 Chatfield Papers, CHT/3/1; L. Pratt, *East of Malta, west of Suez: Britain's mediterranean crisis 1936–1939*, London 1975, 34 n. 35; CAB 27/623 FP(36) 23rd mtg, 5 Feb. 1938; Simon Papers, MS 7 Simon, diary entry 5 Feb. 1938; Thomas, *Spanish civil war*, 258; S. Roskill, *Naval policy between the wars*, II: *the period of reluctant rearmament 1930–1939*, London 1976, 374.

59 Foreign office minutes 20 Aug. and 12 Sept. 1936: FO 371/20573 W9717/9549/41; 371/20575 W10779/9549/41. For further details see Stone, 'Britain, non-intervention', 136–7 and Little, *Malevolent neutrality*, 251–6.

60 In this connection see Stone, 'Britain, non-intervention', 147–8 n. 35. Eden was already reaching the conclusion that the Spanish Republic's survival was in Britain's best interests in November 1936: 'My own feeling is at present *against* the granting of belligerent rights to Franco for international rather than Spanish reasons. I do not want even to appear to follow Hitler and Mussolini at this moment but would prefer to "show a tooth" in the Mediterranean; still less do I want to facilitate an attempt at a blockade that is maybe intended to starve Madrid': Eden Diaries, diary entry 21 Nov. 1936.

61 CAB 27/624 FP(36) 35th mtg, 23 Jan. 1939.

62 For a full discussion on the subject of British and German economic intervention in the Spanish civil war see G. T. Harper, *German economic policy in Spain during the Spanish civil war*, The Hague 1967 passim; Harvey, *Rio Tinto company*, 270–89; Edwards, *British Government and the Spanish civil war*, 64–100; Weinberg, *The foreign policy of Hitler's Germany*, ii, 146–54,

Notwithstanding such pro-Franco tendencies, the official policy of non-intervention was faithfully adhered to despite the many breaches of the agreement by other European powers including Portugal. Moreover, since the government's commitment to non-intervention was patently at odds with Lisbon's support (together with that of Germany and Italy) for General Franco, a deterioration in the Anglo-Portuguese relationship was a distinct possibility, particularly as during August and September 1936 it fell to Britain to persuade an extremely reluctant Portugal to adhere to the Non-Intervention Agreement and to join the London based Non-Intervention Committee. Indeed, the early months of the war in Spain imposed a considerable strain on the Anglo-Portuguese relationship. From the beginning the foreign office expected the question of Britain's commitment to defend Portugal against attack by Spanish forces to be raised: such action by the British would naturally have terminated the policy of neutrality before it had been firmly established.

The foreign office received the French proposal for non-intervention on 2 August 1936. It was initially conceived as a three-power agreement between France, Italy and Britain, other countries to join at a later stage, but the foreign office regarded this as insufficient and wished to include other important powers such as Germany and Soviet Russia, particularly the former. To avoid singling out Germany as a fourth additional party Portugal was to be included as 'Spain's nearest neighbour and the Power most vitally concerned in the course of events in that country'. The French readily agreed and requested immediate British diplomatic assistance at Rome and Lisbon. Wingfield was instructed to support the French *démarche* in whatever way he thought cogent.[63]

The French minister made his approach on 5 August and was immediately supported by Wingfield. The following day the Portuguese foreign minister, Armindo Monteiro, announced that before reaching a decision his government felt bound to make a number of observations concerning the position of the international zone at Tangier,[64] Soviet adhesion to the proposed non-intervention agreement, and the possibility of Portuguese recognition of the belligerency of the Spanish military. Monteiro also stressed that Portugal's national safety depended on the defeat of the Spanish government. Leroy was asked in general terms for Franco-British assurances relating to the security of Portugal while Wingfield received a more specific request which amounted to an appeal to the alliance in certain eventualities:

If [the] Portuguese Government sign away their liberty to render such assistance [to the Spanish military] will His Majesty's Government compensate this renunciation by an understanding to come immediately to the defence of

---

156–60; Whealey, *Hitler and Spain*, 72–94, and 'How Franco financed his war', 133–52; Schieder, 'Spanischen Bürgerkrieg und Vierjahresplan', in Schieder and Dipper, *Spanische Bürgerkrieg*, 162–90.

[63] FO 371/20526 W7504/62/41; 371/20527 W7808/62/41; *DDF*, 2, iii, no. 76, p. 119.

[64] Monteiro charged that Spanish warships, navigated by the crews who had murdered their officers or held them to their post under duress, were using Tangier as a base of supply. For details of the Portuguese position regarding Tangier at this time see Delgado, *Portugal e a Guerra Civil*, 44–5.

Portugal against a Spanish invasion . . . Will British soldiers be on [the] Portuguese frontier and British aeroplanes be above Portugal within 24 hours?

Monteiro also recalled the declaration made at Madrid in 1873 and asked 'whether His Majesty's Government were prepared as a condition of Portugal joining in [the] non-intervention agreement to take some similar action now', and further that 'His Majesty's Government guarantee the integrity of Portugal'? [65]

The French government emphasised that they would assist the Portuguese in the eventuality contemplated by Monteiro only so far as their obligations under the covenant would allow.[66] The foreign office were equally anxious to limit their commitments to Portugal and held strongly to the view that Portuguese adhesion to non-intervention would reduce considerably the likelihood of an attack from Spain. While reassuring the Portuguese on the subjects of Tangier and Soviet adhesion, the foreign office insisted that as far as belligerent rights were concerned it was highly desirable that all the principal powers should act in agreement and that it would be 'entirely premature and strongly to be deprecated for one power closely, such as Portugal, to take such a step at this stage'.[67] The forthright views of the British authorities compelled the Portuguese to make an early decision. On the evening of 13 August Monteiro, after a prolonged conference with Salazar and Sampaio, informed Leroy and Charles Dodd, the British chargé d'affaires, that, in deference to the views of their respective governments, his government adhered in principle to the proposed non-intervention agreement. However, the Portuguese were not prepared to give an absolutely binding commitment, insisting that 'the adhesion given in principle does not diminish the freedom of Portugal to judge of circumstances and take such action as may be dictated by their duty to preserve domestic peace in Portugal, the lives, property and liberties of the people and security, integrity and independence of the country'.[68]

On the same day that Britain and France exchanged diplomatic notes thereby inaugurating the Non-Intervention Agreement, Monteiro told Dodd that in view of the control exercised by the rebel forces along the Spanish-Portuguese frontier his government could not rule out the possibility of recognising the belligerent rights of the Spanish military authorities, though he admitted there would be considerable advantage in such recognition being granted by the interested powers in common accord.[69] While the Portuguese recognised the difficulties of pursuing an independent policy in isolation from other powers, and especially Britain, it was obvious, at least to the foreign

---

65 FO 371/20527 W7918/62/41; DDF, 2, iii, no. 96, p. 147; DAPE, iii, no. 111, pp. 88–93. For the declaration of 1873 see Foundations of British foreign policy 1792–1902, ed. W. Temperley and L. M. Penson, Cambridge 1938, 341–3.

66 FO 371/20528 W7964/62/41; DDF, 2, iii, no. 99, p. 151.

67 FO 371/20527 W7918/62/41. See also DBFP, 2, xvii, no. 76, pp. 80–1; DAPE, iii, no. 141, pp. 119–20.

68 FO 371/20530 W8634/W8645/62/41. See also DBFP, 2, xvii, nos 89, 90, pp. 96–7; DDF, 2, iii, no. 142, pp. 208–9; DAPE, iii, no. 155, pp. 132–6; FRUS, 1936, iii. 486.

69 FO 371/20531 W8781/W8782/62/41.

office, that even if they adhered to the Non-Intervention Agreement they would do so with any number of mental reservations.[70] Indeed, acceptance in principle of non-intervention did not halt Portuguese assistance to Franco. On 17 August the United States minister in Lisbon, Robert Caldwell, reported that substantial quantities of foodstuffs and other supplies were said to be reaching the rebel forces through Portugal.[71]

Although the French had expressed initial satisfaction with Monteiro's response, by 18 August there was growing impatience with Portuguese procrastination. Leroy was conscious of a certain reticence at the Portuguese ministry of foreign affairs. Although the Portuguese had not dared refuse to adhere in principle, the French minister was convinced that they would seek to evade signature by every quibble conceivable in the hope 'that victory of the rebels may render signature superfluous meanwhile continuing to afford the rebels all assistance in their power'. Leroy's concern was shared by the *Quai d'Orsay*. Paul Bargeton, acting permanent head, told Lloyd Thomas, British minister in Paris, that British collaboration would be more necessary at Lisbon than at Berlin or Rome as the Portuguese were being extremely tiresome and had made no effort as yet to reply to the French proposals.[72] Accordingly, on 19 August, the Lisbon embassy was authorised to inform the Portuguese that His Majesty's Government were beginning to share the impatience of the French minister and that they were finding 'it extremely difficult to reconcile their [Portuguese] request for assurances of support in the event of an attack from the Spanish Government with the tendency now becoming apparent on the part of the Portuguese Government to throw in their lot with the rebel factions'.[73]

On the same day, Wingfield told Sampaio that it was vital to European tranquillity that all the powers agree not to intervene in Spain, since 'we should otherwise have different Powers taking an active part on different sides with incalculable results'. Subsequently, Wingfield spoke to Leroy, now apparently convinced that the Portuguese were merely wasting time and had no intention of adhering to the Non-Intervention Agreement since 'they hoped for an early victory of the insurgents in Spain which would spare them the necessity of taking any decision'. The ambassador then wrote to Sampaio urging immediate Portuguese adhesion which was confirmed on 21 August.[74] The Portuguese text, however, differed from the original British and French in insisting that certain acts could not be defined as intervention, for example, Portugal's right to defend herself against 'any regime of social subversion which may be established in Spain', in other words a left-wing regime, and the possibility of recognising the belligerency of Franco's military authorities or of establishing relations with them. The Portuguese also insisted that the enlistment of

---

[70] FO 371/20530 W8645/62/41.

[71] *FRUS*, 1936, ii. 487.

[72] FO 371/20530 W8645/62/41; 371/20533 W9060/62/41; 371/20534 W9339/62/41.

[73] FO 371/20533 W9060/62/41.

[74] FO 371/20573 W9906/9549/41; 371/20535 W9444/62/41. On 19 Aug. the Portuguese minister in Berlin, Veiga Simões, had informed his government that the German government was 'disposed to adhere, definitely and finally, to the multilateral accord concerning Spain': Oliveira, *Salazar e a Guerra Civil*, 305.

volunteers and the opening of subscriptions, activities which favoured the Republic in August 1936, were contrary to the spirit of non-intervention.[75] Following renewed Franco-British pressure the Portuguese published a decree of prohibition on 27 August.[76]

Before that date French concern for their proposal, together with the British government's own conviction that it was the only viable policy in the circumstances, undoubtedly accounted for the cumulative pressure exerted on the Portuguese authorities. At the same time, senior members of the foreign office had some sympathy with Portugal despite her overt support for the rebel forces. Horace Seymour, head of the league of nations and western department, thus wrote on 26 August that:

> In general, is there not perhaps some excuse, or at any rate some explanation, if the Portuguese have not behaved in the last six weeks with entire wisdom? It is one thing to look at these events from London: it is quite another to be in the position of a small country, with a large land frontier to Spain.

Mounsey agreed that this was the right line for them to take. Portugal's difficult position must be taken into account, and only if all the other powers accepted this would there be any hope of bringing her in.[77]

Foreign office sympathy was put to the test on 28 August when the Portuguese decree of prohibition and note of adhesion was published. While its first article acknowledged that arms should not be transported to Spain through Portuguese territory, the second allowed the Portuguese authorities to raise the prohibition if any of the signatories to the Non-Intervention Agreement was discovered to be allowing either the direct or indirect enlistment of volunteers, or the opening of subscriptions for the continuation of the war. The final article confirmed that the decree took effect immediately and would be enforced as long as the prohibition was effectively applied in their respective territories by the German, British, French, Italian and Soviet governments. The same day Monteiro advised Leroy that his government would hold firmly to their reservations and conditions.[78]

The Portuguese attitude aroused considerable anxiety in Paris. It was feared that the reservations stipulated by the Portuguese might justify other governments in maintaining that Portugal's stance negated the condition of unanimity, which had been laid down in the original proposal for non-intervention.[79] The French authorities were particularly critical of the Portuguese statement that their adherence was conditional on their recognition that the provisions were being effectively carried out by the other powers. The French felt this was a matter to be determined by all the governments concerned through the medium of the proposed co-ordinating committee.

---

75 FO 371/20573 W9906/9549/41.
76 DDF, 2, iii, no. 201, p. 281; FO371/20573 W9682/W9781/9549/41; 371/20574 W10214/9549/41.
77 FO 371/20573 W9964/9549/41.
78 FO 371/20574 W10214/W10163/9549/41; DDF, 2, iii, no. 211, p. 317.
79 In this connection see FRUS, 1936, ii. 515.

Following the intervention of Roger Cambon, French *chargé d'affaires* in London, Wingfield was authorised to make representations on the subject.[80]

The Portuguese foreign ministry responded to the ambassador's *démarche* by assuring him that the export and transit of arms had definitely been prohibited, that the prohibition would be strictly enforced and that a new decree would be required to suspend its terms: the Portuguese government would not take such a step without previously notifying their intention and reasons to the other powers. Articles two and three simply indicated what would happen if other powers failed to keep their engagements.[81] These assurances, while confirming Portugal's commitment to non-intervention, did little to allay suspicions and anxieties in Britain, and especially in France, particularly as Lisbon was reluctant to accept membership of the London based Non-Intervention Committee, and there was a growing number of allegations of continuing Portuguese involvement in arms deliveries to the rebel forces. During the ensuing weeks these issues severely taxed the patience of the British and French authorities and threatened the fragile structure of the non-intervention policy.

Before Portugal's decree and note of adhesion were published, reports had begun to appear in British and French newspapers concerning the unloading in Lisbon of war material destined for the rebel forces. The British labour movement was particularly incensed and on 26 August a deputation, led by Sir Walter Citrine, general secretary of the TUC, and Arthur Greenwood, deputy leader of the labour party, raised the issue with Eden and Lord Halifax, lord president of the council. The view was strongly expressed that 'unless Portugal could be got to come into the agreement [for non-intervention] at once and to put it into strict force, the whole object of the non-supply of arms policy would be defeated'. Although Eden emphasised the 'unique and difficult position in which Portugal is placed, both geographically and politically *vis-à-vis* the present troubles in Spain', he also assured the delegation that 'everything is being and has been done to exert pressure from here on the Portuguese Government with a view to bringing them into the proposed agreement'. In the opinion of the foreign secretary this was the only practical way of resolving the difficulties presented by the Portuguese. The matter of the transit of arms would be solved as and when the majority of the other powers adhered to the agreement. Eden stressed that Portugal was not in a position to export any quantity of arms to Spain.[82]

Lisbon's public commitment to non-intervention did not halt further allegations of Portuguese breaches. Indeed, the day after publication Cambon drew Mounsey's attention to the activities of the *City of Manchester*, a British ship which was alleged to be carrying arms from Germany to Lisbon.[83] Shortly afterwards, reports appeared in the British press to the effect that German and British ships were loading cargoes of munitions for Portugal with Spain as the ultimate destination. Consequently, Citrine and Greenwood insisted upon

80 FO 371/20573 W9781/9549/41.
81 FO 371/20574 W10917/W10231/9549/41; *DAPE*, iii, no. 243, pp. 212–13.
82 PREM 1/360. See also *DBFP*, 2, xvii, no. 136, 172–3.
83 FO 371/20574 W10231/9549/41.

21

raising the issue with the foreign office.[84] Eventually, official enquiries confirmed that the *City of Manchester* was owned by a respectable British shipping firm, Ellerman Lines, and was in Australia. Viscount Cranborne, parliamentary under-secretary of state for foreign affairs, accordingly informed the Labour party leader, Clement Attlee, that as far as he was concerned there was no truth in the story at all.[85] While this may well have been the case with the *City of Manchester*, it is established that a German ship, the *Usaramo*, apparently unbeknown to the British embassy, sailed into Lisbon without warning on 31 August 1936. Unloading was refused by the Portuguese authorities and the cargo of war material was subsequently unloaded at Vigo in northern Spain. According to German naval intelligence the Portuguese had acted under British pressure.[86] There is no record in the foreign office archives of any such pressure being applied but Wingfield's enquiries about the *City of Manchester* had probably influenced the Portuguese to act quickly in the case of the *Usaramo*.

Press reports alleging Portugal's continuing involvement on the side of the Spanish insurgents naturally contributed to growing anti-Portuguese feeling amongst the left in Britain and France. A number of left-wing French newspapers postulated a definite relationship between Portugal and Nazi Germany, while British Labour criticisms of Portugal's role in the civil war were clearly expressed at the meetings of Citrine and Greenwood with the foreign office on 26 August and 1 September.[87] Animosity towards Portugal in British and French left-wing circles was exacerbated by the persistent refusal of Salazar's government to join the Non-Intervention Committee in London. On 10 September, for example, during its annual conference in Plymouth, the TUC passed a resolution by an overwhelming majority which included an appeal to the government to use their influence with Portugal to bring her into line.[88] At the same time, both the British and French governments, especially the latter, feared that Portugal's non-participation in the Non-Intervention Committee could wreck the non-intervention policy before it had been properly established. Consequently, and despite the strain which it necessarily imposed on the Anglo-Portuguese relationship, British pressure was maintained throughout September 1936.

The idea of an international committee to supervise non-intervention had first been broached by the French on 24 August.[89] By the beginning of September the International Committee for the Application of the Agreement for Non-Intervention in Spain was established in London under the temporary chairmanship of W. S. Morrison, financial secretary to the treasury. Of the original most closely involved powers – Britain, France, Germany, Italy, Soviet Russia and Portugal – only Germany and Portugal remained unrepresented. By the

---

84 FO 371/20574 W10289/9549/41.
85 FO 371/20574 W10231/W10289/9549/41.
86 DGFP, D, iii, no. 77, p. 77. Merkes, *Deutsche Politik*, 61.
87 For details of French press opinion see Pike, *Les français*, 132.
88 *The Times*, 11 Sept. 1936.
89 DBFP, 2, xvii, no. 128, p. 161.

time of the first meeting of the committee on 9 September only Portugal was not a member.

The Portuguese were first approached on the matter on 26 August.[90] When, on 1 September, they made up their minds they attached a formidable series of conditions to Portugal's membership, including insistence that the competence of the committee should be strictly limited; that it should have the necessary powers to carry out its mission; and that the impartiality of its actions should be guaranteed. They also insisted that the competence and methods of procedure of the committee should be strictly defined and that it should not receive or examine unsubstantiated or unofficial information.[91] The British authorities realised the dangers of the Portuguese response. As a result of the meeting with Citrine and Greenwood on 1 September it was clear that 'if it transpired that Germany and Portugal, or either of these powers, delayed or turned down the summoning of the proposed committee of collation, the extreme elements both in the United Kingdom and France would at once make this a pretext for forcing the French Government and His Majesty's Government to give up the whole idea of non-intervention'.[92] This was not an exaggerated view because the French government was again facing demands from within the broader Popular Front movement to abandon non-intervention since the fascist powers, including Portugal, were continuing to supply arms to the insurgents. Portuguese intransigence towards the Non-Intervention Committee was, moreover, seen by the French left as a delaying tactic in favour of the insurgents. Portuguese counter-accusations of French breaches of non-intervention on the Spanish republican side, when most members of the French left still thought that their government was strictly adhering to non-intervention, confirmed their belief in the futility of that policy.[93] Despite left-wing demands for pro-republican intervention the socialist leadership stood firm and the socialist prime minister, Léon Blum, was able to maintain his party's support for the non-intervention policy in a major speech at Luna Park in Paris on 6 September.[94]

A further attempt was made to persuade the Portuguese to send a representative to the Non-Intervention Committee. On 4 September, Wingfield assured Monteiro that a Portuguese representative would be free to express his government's views on its functions and duration. For his part the foreign minister admitted that his government would have nothing to do with the committee were it not for their desire to co-operate with the British authorities. He did not conceal Portugal's difficulties in participating in a committee which included a representative of the Soviet Union, and where all sorts of questions connected with the Spanish Civil War could be raised in the presence of the representatives of twenty or more states.[95]

[90] FO 371/20573 W9781/9549/41; 371/20574 W10214/9549/41.
[91] FO 371/20574 W10282/9549/41; DBFP, 2, xvii, no. 153, pp. 193–4.
[92] FO 371/20574 W10289/9549/41.
[93] In this connection see FO 371/20574 W10198/9549/41; 371/20575 W10618/W10619/W10772/9549/41.
[94] The Times, 4, 5 and 7 Sept. 1936.
[95] FO 371/20574 W10398/9549/41; DAPE, iii, no. 258, pp. 229–30; FO 371/20576 W10932/9549/41. See also DGFP, D, iii, no. 70, p. 71.

Although all the other interested powers, including Germany and Italy accepted membership of the Non-Intervention Committee, the Portuguese declined on 7 September, two days before the committee's first meeting. The foreign office were dismayed. Cranborne believed it was 'very stupid' because it would 'make a deplorable impression and give rise to every sort of suspicion', while Mounsey thought the Portuguese reply was 'childish' and that the absence of a Portuguese representative would 'have a disastrous influence on the work of the Committee'.[96] Wingfield was accordingly instructed on 8 September to make an urgent and immediate appeal for reconsideration. The Portuguese authorities were to be left with no illusions as to the great importance which the British government attached to the successful operation of the Non-Intervention Committee:

> It was the view of His Majesty's Government that on the successful constitution of the Committee the policy of non-intervention materially depended. If it failed, a dangerous European situation might develop from which Portugal could not, any more than other nations, be immune. It was their earnest hope, therefore, that the Portuguese Government would not by any decision they might make imperil still further an already difficult and delicate international situation.[97]

The Portuguese were unmoved.[98]

The French were particularly displeased at Portugal's intransigence. Charles Corbin, French ambassador in London, specifically referred to the absence of a Portuguese representative at the first meeting of the Non-Intervention Committee on 9 September and expressed the hope that the difficulties would soon be overcome so as to allow Portugal to take part, since it was clear that the participation of a country adjacent to Spain was of the utmost importance.[99] Following the meeting Corbin spoke to Cranborne, Vansittart and Mounsey and reiterated the importance of Portugal's participation in the committee. Vansittart expressed his own incomprehension at the Portuguese attitude despite repeated representations in Lisbon. According to Corbin the foreign office believed that once she realised she was really isolated Portugal would accept membership.[100] Meanwhile the foreign office endorsed a further effort by the French government in Lisbon. On 10 September Leroy saw Monteiro and emphasised that Portugal would suffer no loss of sovereignty; that the Portuguese absence was liable to misinterpretation and would place in doubt the real aims of their policy with regard to Spain; that it was difficult to see what more effective form of control could be achieved than the Non-Intervention Committee; and that it was only through participation that the Portuguese government could expect to judge the scope and method of work of the committee or could satisfy themselves of its qualities of impartiality and

---

96 Neville Chamberlain Papers, NC 7/11/29/14; FO 371/20575 W10771/9549/41.
97 FO 371/20575 W10771/9549/41; 371/20577 W11420/9549/41.
98 FO 371/20576 W10853/9549/41.
99 NIS(36) 1st mtg, FO 849/1. The minutes of the Non-Intervention Committee meetings, thirty in all, are also to be found in the Hemming Papers at the Bodleian Library, Oxford.
100 *DDF*, 2, iii, no. 243, p. 353.

efficiency. Monteiro, however, insisted that his government were quite determined to take no part in the committee until they were satisfied with its workings in practice. It would be intolerable, for instance, were the Soviet representative to demand an investigation in Lisbon of Portugal's relations with the insurgents. Moreover, the very recent naval mutiny which, according to the foreign minister, was caused by the action of Spanish communists showed that Portugal was being forced into the Spanish struggle. Indeed, Monteiro admitted that he did not know how long his government could remain bound by the Non-Intervention Agreement which they had never liked.[101] When, on 11 September, Wingfield sought to reinforce Leroy's démarche Monteiro remained immovable, citing the communist menace as the reason.[102]

Portugal's continued intransigence was greeted with increasing signs of anxiety in the foreign office. For some time it had recognised the threat posed to the whole of the non-intervention policy and in particular to the French government's efforts to hold the political ring against the more extreme elements in the Popular Front coalition. Blum's government remained extremely nervous about the political capital these elements could make out of Portugal's refusal to be represented on the committee. Indeed, in conversations with the French ambassador on 12 and 14 September, Mounsey had great difficulty in convincing him to dissuade his government from taking some drastic line about Portugal pending one further effort to bring her at least into contact with the committee.[103] To this end the embassy was instructed on 14 September to convey to the Portuguese government 'the profound disappointment of His Majesty's Government at their present decision'; to express the hope that 'the decision would be revised at an early date'; and to warn that the continued refusal of the Portuguese to participate in the work of the Non-Intervention Committee 'may affect the activities of that body so adversely as to undermine the whole basis of collaboration on which it must rely for any successful results'.[104] At the second meeting of the Non-Intervention Committee the same day, Morrison informed the representatives of this latest British démarche while Corbin reiterated the 'utmost importance' which his government attached to securing Portuguese collaboration which they considered highly desirable.[105]

By this time Lisbon's attitude was provoking demands that the Spanish arms embargo be extended to Portugal herself.[106] At the first meeting of the chairman's sub-committee on 15 September the question whether to raise the export of war material to Portugal, in view of her special geographical position and her attitude towards the Non-Intervention Committee, was discussed at some length. Both the German and Italian representatives, Prince Bismarck, chargé d'affaires in London, and Count Dino Grandi, Italian ambassador to the Court of St James, rushed to the defence of the Portuguese government while the

---

[101] FO 371/20576 W10853/W11199/9549/41; 371/20578 W12154/9549/41.
[102] FO 371/20576 W11201/9549/41; 371/20578 W12154/9549/41. DAPE, iii, no. 308, pp. 272–3.
[103] FO 371/20511 W10925/403/36.
[104] FO 371/20576 W11201/9549/41.
[105] NIS(36) 2nd mtg, FO 849/1 and Hemming Papers. For the German position on this issue see DGFP, D, iii, no. 82, p. 90.
[106] See the Spectator, 11, 18 Sept. 1936; New Statesman and Nation, 12, 19 Sept. 1936.

French and Swedish representatives, respectively Corbin and Baron Palmstierna, were more critical. In the event, it was decided to discuss the position of Portugal at the sub-committee's next meeting on 18 September.[107] Before then the Portuguese authorities raised the question of a possible arms embargo on their country with the British ambassador. Sampaio, who believed the French government were working towards this, asked what the British attitude would be, given they had not even accused the Portuguese of sending war material to Spain and that Portugal herself was very short of arms of all kinds. Wingfield advised the foreign office that he had no reason to believe that breaches of the Non-Intervention Agreement were taking place in Portugal and added that such an embargo would cause deep resentment whilst encouraging those Portuguese elements who would like to overthrow Salazar's government.[108] On 18 September Morrison expressed to the sub-committee the view that it was not possible to embargo arms exports to Portugal on the grounds that they might then be transferred to the Spanish insurgents. The sub-committee should assume, until they had evidence to the contrary, that Portugal was abiding by her word in the matter. As a foreign power, Portugal had her own arms requirements and it would be inconsistent to hold that she was abiding by the agreement while denying her arms for her own use. Although the French and Soviet representatives criticised Portugal's absence, there was general agreement with Morrison that a decision on the issue should be deferred until a thorough and lengthy discussion could take place. Meanwhile, the sub-committee did not wish to prejudice Portugal's possible membership by making any premature statement.[109]

Before 18 September the efforts of the British and French governments had been to a large degree characterised by remarkable patience, and, on the British side at least, with some understanding of Portugal's difficulties. But the patience of the French government had evaporated. In what appears to have been a concerted action they simultaneously told the British League of Nations delegation to Geneva, the British embassy in Paris and the foreign office in London that France might have to reconsider her position with respect to non-intervention because of the continuing Portuguese intransigence.[110] Blum personally confirmed French apprehensions on 20 September when Eden stopped in Paris on his way to Geneva. The French prime minister emphasised the great difficulty in which his government was being placed by Lisbon's refusal to be represented on the Non-Intervention Committee. There were only two countries with frontiers contiguous to Spain, namely Portugal and France, and if Portugal refused to play her part 'the position of the French Government would become well nigh intolerable'. The French premier knew that the British government had already spoken with Lisbon, but he begged Eden to make some further effort. While Eden appreciated the difficulties of the situation and was anxious that Portugal should take her place in the committee in London, he

---

107 NIS(C) (36) 1st mtg, 15 Sept. 1936, FO 849/27; Hemming Papers. For the origins of the chairman's sub-committee see *DBFP*, 2, xvii, no. 182, pp. 252–3.
108 FO 371/20577 W11616/9549/41.
109 NIS(C) (36) 2nd mtg, 18 Sept. 1936, FO 849/27; Hemming Papers.
110 For further details see Stone, 'Britain, non-intervention', 143.

believed it would be a mistake to exaggerate the effect that Portugal's non-inclusion in the committee could have. Portugal did not have vast supplies of arms which she could furnish to the rebels and was indeed short of arms herself. Moreover, she had accepted the principle of non-intervention and the latest information from Lisbon seemed to show that no flagrant violations of this undertaking were taking place. Eden also made reference to Portugal's very real fear of the consequences of a victory for the extreme left in Spain.[111]

Although the Portuguese could still count on German and Italian support[112] their resistance began to crumble in the face of sustained British pressure. On 21 September Eden saw Monteiro at Geneva and in the course of a long conversation 'did his utmost to dissipate Portuguese reluctance to serve on the committee in London'. On the following day at a further meeting between the two foreign ministers Monteiro, influenced by Eden's written assurance that the committee's role was 'primarily one of conciliation and consultation', agreed that subject to his government's approval a Portuguese representative should participate in its work.[113] Formal approval was given by the Portuguese government on 27 September and a Portuguese representative attended the meeting of the chairman's sub-committee the following day.

After five weeks of British and French diplomatic pressure the Portuguese had given way but with their mental reservations intact. The problems encountered by Britain signified the difficulty of dealing with a small but determinedly obdurate sovereign power and demonstrated that the Anglo-Portuguese alliance provided no guarantee that Portugal would bend easily to the British will. Others, notably the British left, took a different view, believing that Portuguese intransigence was merely the result of a lack of governmental determination and effort.[114] At the same time, the German foreign ministry held to the view that in the last resort Portugal 'could do nothing against the desire of England'.[115] Certainly, Portuguese adhesion to the Non-Intervention Agreement was largely a consequence of their desire to co-operate with their British ally and, despite the numerous *démarches* of August and September 1936, the Portuguese government still retained a strong attachment to their alliance partner. Salazar, in a published note of 22 September 1936, referred to the British connection in somewhat friendly and flattering terms and expressed his conviction that despite their differences with regard to the civil war in Spain Britain treated Portugal's opinion with respect even when it differed from her own, so that better mutual understanding and co-operation for common interests could only result.[116] Despite foreign office pressure, maintained often at French insistence, there remained in London a strong residue of sympathy and understanding for Portugal's position in relation to the Spanish

[111] FO 371/20577 W11797/9549/41.
[112] See *DGFP*, D, iii, nos 84, 86, pp. 91–3.
[113] FO 371/20577 W11872/9549/41. See also *DBFP*, 2, xvii, no. 216, pp. 296–7; *DAPE*, iii, no. 365, pp. 318–19; FO 371/20577 W11957/9549/41.
[114] *New Statesman and Nation*, 29 Aug. 1936, 12 Sept. 1936.
[115] *DGFP*, D, iii, no. 50, p. 51; Abendroth, *Hitler in der spanischen Arena*, 51–2.
[116] *DAPE*, iii, no. 363, pp. 316–17.

conflict. However, from October 1936 onwards as chairman of the Non-Intervention Committee the British government necessarily had to pursue an impartial role when confronted with powers whose sympathies lay clearly with either the Spanish republicans or the nationalist forces, and Portugal most certainly belonged in the latter category. The difficulties and dilemmas of Britain's position *vis-à-vis* Portugal were realised fully in the ensuing months.

2

Britain, Portugal and the Non-Intervention Committee, 1936–1939

In the course of the discussions surrounding Portugal's membership of the Non-Intervention Committee it became abundantly clear that Salazar's government was very anxious to avoid providing a target for Soviet and republican accusations. Unfortunately for Anglo-Portuguese relations, the British government was placed in a very difficult position because, as chairman of the Non-Intervention Committee, Lord Plymouth would be required at some point to receive Soviet and republican allegations and place them on the agenda for discussion. Twice during September, Julio Álvarez del Vayo, the Spanish foreign minister, accused the governments of Italy, Germany and Portugal of breaking the Non-Intervention Agreement.[1] At the beginning of October, Álvarez del Vayo saw Eden in Geneva and referred to Portugal's constant breaches. The British foreign secretary refuted this; according to the ambassador in Lisbon the Portuguese were in fact carrying out the policy of non-intervention.[2] A secret report received from the foreign office's own sources confirmed that there was insufficient evidence to convict Portugal of a breach of the Agreement.[3]

The lack of firm evidence did not deter either the left in Britain or the Soviet government from returning to the matter. On 3 October 1936, an unofficial left-wing 'Committee of Inquiry into the Alleged Breaches of the Non-Intervention Agreement in Spain' published a report based upon newspaper sources which contained many examples of Italian, German and Portuguese breaches of non-intervention.[4] These were reinforced on 6 October when Samuel Cahan, the Soviet *chargé d'affaires* in London, drew the attention of Francis Hemming, the British secretary of the Non-Intervention Committee, to Portuguese infractions. Cahan insisted that these were of such importance as to warrant priority over all other matters discussed by the committee and should be urgently investigated. In order to make the investigation as exhaustive as possible he proposed that an impartial commission should be sent to the Spanish-Portuguese border to make on the spot investigations, and that this commission should leave some of its members there 'to control the fulfilment of the Non-Intervention Agreement on that border in the future'.[5]

---

[1] FO 371/20578 W12363/9549/41; 371/20579 W12722/9549/41. See also Álvarez del Vayo, *Freedom's battle*, 74.
[2] FO 371/20581 W14106/9549/41.
[3] *DBFP*, 2, xvii, no. 265, p. 363.
[4] FO 371/20579 W13158/9549/41. See also *The Times*, 5 Oct. 1936; the *Spectator*, 9 Oct. 1936. For details of the committee see Thomas, *Spanish civil war*, 397–8.
[5] FO 371/20579 W13061/9549/41; *DAPE*, iii, no. 481, annex 2, pp. 413–17.

Vansittart was convinced that if the Soviets pressed the proposal for such a commission the Non-Intervention Committee would break up with dangerous consequences.[6] His conviction was reinforced when the following day Cahan addressed a further communication which, while mentioning specific German and Italian infringements, concentrated its attack upon Portugal. Cahan threatened that if such violations were not stopped immediately his government would consider itself absolved of its obligations arising out of the Non-Intervention Agreement.[7] By targetting Portugal the Soviets no doubt hoped to eliminate the smallest of those countries supporting Franco within the Non-Intervention Committee and thereby establish a successful precedent for further assaults on Italy and Germany. Moreover, Moscow remained genuinely convinced that Portugal was the main channel of rebel supplies, particularly from Nazi Germany.[8]

Britain's policy makers nevertheless continued to give Portugal the benefit of the doubt. It was Corbin's considered opinion that whenever Portugal became a target for accusations and suspicions the British government manifested a desire to take her side. On 8 October Plymouth told the ambassador that he believed that since adhering to the Non-Intervention Agreement Portugal had ceased to allow the transit of war material. Furthermore, when Corbin raised with Mounsey the Soviet proposal for an investigative commission he received little encouragement.[9] The foreign office line of thinking was confirmed the following day by the Non-Intervention Committee itself.[10] Naturally, the Portuguese found the Soviet proposal extremely distasteful. Lisbon's representative on the Non-Intervention Committee, Francisco Calheiros, Portuguese *chargé d'affaires* in London, actually withdrew from the discussion of the Soviet proposal which he considered insulting. On 10 October Monteiro told Wingfield that the Soviet accusations against Portugal and other states were quite unfounded and that it was most distasteful for the Portuguese government to have to respond to such people.[11] However, that the Portuguese should reply early was underlined on 12 October when the Soviets demanded the immediate establishment of control over Portuguese ports and suggested that this control should be entrusted to the British and French navies. Plymouth, with Eden's approval, refused to summon an early meeting of the committee on the grounds that the Portuguese reply had not yet been received and that the latest note contained no additional evidence whatsoever of violations of the Non-Intervention Agreement.[12] With Franco apparently on the verge of capturing Madrid, the

6 FO 371/20579 W13061/9549/41.
7 FO 371/20579 W13242/9549/41. See also *DBFP*, 2, xvii, no. 270, pp. 368–9; *DDF*, 2, iii, no. 321, pp. 479–80.
8 Cattell, *Soviet diplomacy*, 43.
9 *DDF*, 2, iii, no. 322, p. 482.
10 For details of the discussion see the minutes of the 5th and 6th meetings on 9 Oct. 1936: NIS (36) 5th mtg; NIS (36) 6th mtg, FO 849/1; Hemming Papers. See also *DBFP*, 2, xvii, no. 278, pp. 377–96; Thomas, *Spanish civil war*, 444; Abendroth, *Hitler in der spanischen Arena*, 137.
11 FO 371/20581 W14264/9549/41.
12 FO 371/20580 W13672/9549/41; *DAPE*, iii, no. 496, annexes 2, 3, pp. 442–6. See also Abendroth, *Hitler in der spanischen Arena*, 137; Cattell, *Soviet diplomacy*, 51; Maisky, *Spanish notebooks*, 48.

Soviets interpreted the chairman's reply as 'an obvious playing for time'. On 18 October a *Pravda* editorial repeated the charge that after the agreement was signed the supply of German and Italian material through Portugal not only did not cease but on the contrary increased formidably.[13] The British authorities remained unconvinced. They readily agreed that Franco's success in uniting his northern and southern armies had made the transit of war material via Portugal somewhat superfluous and Wingfield continued to insist that he still had no evidence that Portugal was committing breaches of the agreement.[14]

The charges against Portugal were finally examined at the eighth meeting of the Non-Intervention Committee on 28 October in the light of Lisbon's extremely detailed reply to both of her accusers.[15] Since the Spanish republicans were not represented, Plymouth presented both their accusations to the meeting and the Portuguese counter arguments. Thus the republican charges were examined quickly and systematically. In conclusion, Plymouth recommended that the committee should record that no proof had been found of breaches of the Non-Intervention Agreement by the Portuguese. This was accepted by all members of the committee with the exception of Ivan Maisky, the Soviet ambassador. After a long statement from Maisky the committee adopted an identical approach in relation to the Soviet charges with Plymouth again dominating the proceedings despite some spirited interjections from the Soviet representative. A number of Soviet charges were dismissed as irrelevant, either because they concerned incidents which occurred before Portugal's adhesion to the agreement or because they did not come under the purview of the committee, like the establishment of a Spanish military committee in Lisbon which could at most be argued to constitute indirect intervention. Moreover, where certain charges did constitute a definite breach of the Non-Intervention Agreement the evidence was declared inconclusive. At the conclusion of the examination the committee, with the exception of Maisky, endorsed Plymouth's view that Portuguese breaches of the agreement were not proven. During the meeting Calheiros took the opportunity to declare that his government could not tolerate any discussion of the proposal for the supervision of the Portuguese ports.[16] Plymouth's conduct of the meeting went a long way towards allaying Portuguese resentment at what they considered to be a violation of the committee's rules of procedure by Britain in sponsoring the republican complaints without prior verification.[17] Eden's defence of Portugal in the commons on 29 October removed any residue of resentment or suspicion in Lisbon. In his speech the foreign secretary expressed considerable sympathy for Portugal's position in the Spanish crisis and described the Soviet accusations as

---

[13] Ibid. 48; Cattell, *Soviet diplomacy*, 147–8.

[14] FO 371/20581 W14119/9549/41. See also *The Times*'s editorials 16, 20, 23 Oct. 1936.

[15] The Portuguese replies, translated into English, are reproduced in full in *DAPE*, iii, no. 520, annexes 1, 2, pp. 473–84, 494–504. See also FO 371/20583 W14545/9549/41; Kay, *Salazar*, 98–101.

[16] NIS (36) 8th mtg, FO 849/1; Hemming Papers.

[17] The introduction to the Portuguese reply to the charges of the Spanish republicans consisted of a sharp attack upon Britain for her failure to follow procedure: *DAPE*, iii, no. 520, annex 1, pp. 473–4.

completely unfounded.[18] In Lisbon the leading article of the *Diário de Notícias* of 30 October asserted that Eden's declaration constituted 'the most notable, most significant of the series of important incidents which have marked the activities of European diplomacy during these last weeks'. For many years past the alliance between the two Atlantic nations 'had not been recalled to the attention of Europe with so much firmness and with such renewed vitality'.[19]

While the British government could be satisfied that the outcome of the Non-Intervention Committee's examination had prevented a deterioration in their relations with Portugal, they were still confronted with the difficulties arising out of Lisbon's recent decision to break off formal diplomatic relations with Madrid and by the reluctance of the parliamentary opposition to accept the verdict that Portugal was not deeply involved in the exportation of war material to the Spanish insurgents. Thus Eleanor Rathbone MP, a leading member of the unofficial 'Committee of Inquiry', wrote to Eden on 2 November to complain about his statement in the Commons that there was 'no first hand evidence available that the Portuguese Government are breaking the agreement'. This statement was simply not compatible with the presence of an unofficial rebel Spanish embassy at the Hotel Aviz in Lisbon, with the exclusive reservation of telephonic communications between Lisbon and Seville for the use of the Spanish generals and with the granting of favourable exchange rates for the *peseta*. Three weeks elapsed before Eden replied and when he did he reminded Rathbone that whether these allegations were true or not, the only thing which the Portuguese government undertook to do, when acceding to the Non-Intervention Agreement, was to prohibit the supply of war material to Spain through their territory. The forms of assistance alluded to by Rathbone, did not, therefore, constitute a breach of the Agreement.[20]

The foreign secretary's reply did nothing to allay opposition suspicions and on 30 November he faced some vigorous questioning in the commons from Rathbone and from Labour MPs including Hugh Dalton. When the latter expressed the view that it was notorious that 'Portugal had become simply a conduit pipe through which munitions of war poured in', Eden replied with his by now familiar theme that his information did not show this to be the case and that purely for military reasons it was extremely unlikely.[21] This line of argument carried little conviction and drew instead continued expressions of incredulity from Labour MPs including Philip Noel Baker, Clement Attlee and Stafford Cripps.[22] Confronted with Labour's hostility Eden, while not denying her obvious sympathies for the nationalist forces, continued to make a positive defence on behalf of Portugal. He failed, however, to remove Labour's suspicions of Portuguese policy with regard to the Spanish crisis.[23]

[18] *Hansard parliamentary debates*, HC, 5th ser. cccxvi, cols 46–7.
[19] FO 371/20512 W15081/762/36.
[20] FO 371/20584 W15121/9549/41. Eleanor Rathbone was the Independent MP for the Combined Universities.
[21] *Hansard parliamentary debates*, HC, 5th ser. cccxviii, cols 821–2.
[22] Ibid. cc. 1063–4, 1109–10, 1141.
[23] Ibid. cc. 1101–2. See also *The Times*, 2 Dec. 1936.

The labour party's anti-Portuguese stance, adopted from the earliest days of the civil war, was strengthened by Lisbon's decision to break off formal diplomatic relations with the Spanish government in October 1936, a decision which also embarrassed the British government and further complicated Anglo-Portuguese relations. The unremitting hostility of the *Estado Novo* towards international communism and its activities in Spain was at the root of its action,[24] but a number of specific incidents were used to justify the decision: violation of Portuguese diplomatic correspondence and property by the Madrid authorities; humiliation of Portuguese diplomatic officials; alleged outrages committed by a band of red militiamen on Portuguese territory; and the threatened attack against a Portuguese warship at Tarragona which was in process of repatriating a number of Spanish reds who had, at various times, taken refuge in Portugal. The Portuguese had also been greatly irritated by what they regarded as the persistent and fraudulent claims that the Spanish ambassador was deprived of his liberty in Lisbon.[25]

The foreign office was totally unprepared for the news that Portugal intended to break off relations with Madrid. When Eden and Vansittart saw Calheiros on 23 October they urged him to contact his government immediately to ask them to refrain from taking any such action until there had been an opportunity for further consultation with His Majesty's Government.[26] The intervention of the foreign office came too late, however, and relations were declared 'suspended' that very day. The one saving grace appeared to be the use of the term 'suspended' which Mounsey together with Eden and Vansittart interpreted as meaning that the Portuguese did not intend 'a full rupture'.[27]

Be that as it may, for the immediate future at least, communication between the Portuguese and Spanish governments had ceased and the British authorities found themselves in an acutely embarrassing position as both the Portuguese and the Spanish asked them to represent their respective interests in Portugal and Spain. Pablo Azcárate, the Spanish ambassador in London, made the request unofficially to Eden on 26 October.[28] Vansittart insisted that the British government should avoid such a role, not least because of the disastrous effect it would have on Britain's relations with Portugal. The Spanish ambassador was therefore told that although the British government would not actually refuse the request, in view of its active yet impartial position within the Non-Intervention Committee it would prefer the Spanish government to look elsewhere, at least in the first instance. Eden wished to avoid outright refusal.[29]

Discouragement of an official approach from the Spanish government in this matter made it difficult to accede to Wingfield's request on 2 November, that if

---

[24] This was the theme of Salazar's speech before an assembled crowd outside the ministry of finance on 31 Oct. 1936. See Salazar, *Doctrine and action*, 317–20; DAPE, iii, no. 566, pp. 536–8.
[25] FO 371/20544 W14309/62/41; FRUS, 1936, ii. 541; Secretariado Nacional de Informação, *Portugal: the new state in theory and practice*, Lisbon 1937; Delgado, *Portugal e a Guerra Civil*, 74–5.
[26] FO 371/20544 W14309/62/41.
[27] FO 371/20545 W14575/62/41.
[28] DBFP, 2, xvii, no. 335, p. 477 n. 2.
[29] FO 371/20591 W14625/9729/41. See above ch.1, n. 53.

possible the Portuguese request should not be refused.[30] Mounsey and Vansittart believed the embassy should be told that on the general question of taking charge of foreign interests 'His Majesty's Government had decided that they could not, in their position on the Non-Intervention Committee, undertake to look after the interests in Spain of any of the Powers represented on that Committee'. Eden hesitated to go as far as his officials. That morning cabinet had expressed fears that the foreign office was alienating Portugal and the foreign secretary thought there might something in their concern. It was therefore essential to treat the Portuguese gently for a while. Vansittart, however, convinced Eden that it was hardly possible 'to say less than we said to the Spaniards in explaining why we think it better not to take charge of anyone's interests. We can do it as mildly as we did to Azcárate'.[31] Accordingly, Wingfield was informed of the previous decision to discourage the Spanish government and advised that the same consideration would apply to any similar request on the part of the Portuguese government.[32]

One obvious solution to the problems of the representation of Portuguese interests in Spain was official Portuguese recognition of the Spanish nationalists. Early in November 1936, with Madrid apparently about to fall to the insurgent forces and the withdrawal of the Spanish government to Valencia, this had seemed a distinct possibility. Indeed, on 7 November Salazar told Wingfield that after Madrid had fallen to the insurgents it would be difficult to withhold recognition for much longer particularly as Portugal's whole frontier ran along territory occupied by them. The ambassador understood that the insurgents would be given *de jure* recognition.[33] In view of the events in Spain the British government could hardly deny the validity of Portuguese intentions especially as the question of granting recognition of Franco's belligerency was under discussion at the highest levels in London.[34]

Despite French opposition to any form of *rapprochement* with the nationalists the British cabinet, on 11 November, agreed to recognize Franco's belligerency on the fall of Madrid but not to grant *de jure* recognition to his regime.[35] This decision was relayed to Wingfield for communication to Salazar the following day.[36] In discussing their response to the Portuguese intention to grant *de jure* recognition, and in view of cabinet's decision, the foreign office had considered – but then rejected – the possibility of attempting to persuade the Portuguese to act in concert with them in limiting the degree of recognition which they would at first accord to the Franco regime that of *de facto* relations.[37] In the event, Italy and Germany recognised the Franco government on 17 November but Portugal did not, and the successful defence of Madrid by the republican forces cancelled the prospects of *de facto* recognition by either Lisbon or

---

30 FO 371/20591 W14343/W14492/9729/41.
31 FO 371/20591 W14343/9729/41.
32 FO 371/20591 W14492/9729/41.
33 *DBFP*, 2, xvii, no. 360, p. 524.
34 For details see Edwards, *British Government and the Spanish civil war*, 184–6.
35 CAB 23/86 CM 64(36).
36 *DBFP*, 2, xvii, no. 371, p. 541.
37 Ibid. p. 541, n. 3.

London. An impartial observer, the United States minister in Portugal, surmised that if Portugal had followed the German and Italian example it would have been interpreted as an unfriendly gesture to France and especially to Britain, and would have marked too close an identification with the Rome-Berlin Axis. It was Caldwell's belief that Portugal intended to recognise the Burgos government in the near future, if possible together with certain South American countries, such as Brazil, Argentina and Chile.[38]

In late December 1936, following vain attempts by London and Paris to establish a system of supervision in Spanish territory to enable the Non-Intervention Committee to obtain reliable evidence of breaches of the Non-Intervention Agreement, and to initiate a proposal for mediation in the civil war, a revised scheme for the 'supervision of the land and maritime frontiers of Spain and the Spanish Dependencies to control the entry of arms and munitions of war' was sanctioned.[39] During the early months of 1937 the scheme was the main subject for discussion within the Non-Intervention Committee and while some reluctance was displayed by the Italian, German and Soviet authorities it was Portuguese intransigence which provided the greatest obstacle to progress. Portugal's attitude was a source of considerable irritation both to the French and Soviet governments, and Britain's relations with the former and with the Portuguese government were subjected to the same sort of strain as when Portugal had refused to join the Non-Intervention Committee.

The proposed scheme required international supervision on the land frontiers of both France and Portugal as well as control of shipping entering Spanish ports. This was obviously going to be an extremely sensitive issue for the Portuguese. At the chairman's sub-committee on 12 January Monteiro, now ambassador at London, had indicated his fear that his government would not be able to accept a scheme which required the establishment of agents of the committee on the Portuguese side of the frontier.[40] The ambassador was correct. According to Wingfield, the Portuguese believed that their prestige would be seriously damaged by the establishment of international control on their territory and they were unimpressed by the fact that France was willing to allow an identical supervision on the Franco-Spanish frontier; the prestige of a great power like France would suffer little from foreign supervision.[41] The foreign office dismissed German or Italian influence as the reason for Portugal's

---

[38] FRUS, 1936, ii. 570. In the event, the Portuguese approached the Brazilian and Argentinian governments but failed to acquire their support for a simultaneous recognition of the Franco regime: F. Nogueira, *Salazar*, III: *As grandes crises (1936–1945)*, Porto 1983, 61–2.

[39] NIS (36) 14th mtg, FO 849/1; Hemming Papers.

[40] Monteiro was dismissed as foreign minister partly on the grounds of his 'precarious state of health', but also because Salazar's confidence in him had been shaken by his 'indecision and timidity' at Geneva. Initially, Salazar intended to replace him by Fezas Vital but he declined to accept the invitation. Consequently, Salazar assumed the portfolio for foreign affairs in addition to those of prime minister, finance and war. Vital, along with Salazar, was one of four professors who were suspended and then reinstated at the time of the parliamentary republic. The other two professors were João de Magalhaes Colaço and António Carneiro Pacheco: Nogueira, *Salazar*, iii. 55.

[41] DBFP, 2, xviii, no. 62, pp. 84–6.

rejection. It was decided that until definite proposals were ready 'it would be best to leave them alone and then put the alternatives to them'. Plymouth agreed and suggested that pressure should not be brought to bear until the control scheme had been agreed by all other countries.[42]

The detailed scheme for international supervision prepared by a technical advisory sub-committee of military and naval experts from certain countries, including the United Kingdom, was submitted to the chairman's sub-committee on 28 January. It included supervision by agents of the committee of both the land frontiers of countries bordering on Spain and of vessels proceeding to the ports of Spain and Spanish dependencies.[43] It was soon clear that the main obstacle to agreement was the attitude of the Portuguese representative who declared repeatedly that his government would not accept foreign control on Portuguese soil. The British government therefore decided to make an unequivocal approach to Lisbon and to enlist the support of the French, German and Italian governments.[44]

When Wingfield saw Salazar on 2 February he urged him to agree to Portugal's active participation in the scheme. Salazar, however, held out little hope: the whole nation intensely disliked any suggestion of foreign influence in their internal affairs. This he reiterated to the French minister, received immediately after Wingfield, with further emphasis on Portugal's dislike and most unwilling acceptance of non-intervention. On the same day Sampaio told the German and Italian ministers that national susceptibilities made a favourable reply most unlikely.[45] Salazar reaffirmed his attitude shortly afterwards in a long personal letter to Wingfield:

> We cannot believe that, in the face of the Communist menace in Spain, or at least of the danger to the peace of other people arising from its establishment in the peninsula, British policy can be merely to go on supporting in any way possible the non-intervention agreement which has already failed . . . it cannot be expected that we should with closed eyes participate in the English policy in questions which we consider to be ones of life and death for us, whatever may be the confidence we repose in the nobility, clearsightedness and energy with which the English Government would defend Portugal, should occasion arise.[46]

It was hardly surprising therefore that the British government should learn on 5 February that the Portuguese were unable to consent to international supervision on their territory. As a concession, however, they would be prepared to accept British agents, attached to the embassy, who would certify that neither arms nor volunteers were passing through Portugal into Spain in order 'to show their desire to be helpful and their confidence in their allies'.[47]

---

42 Ibid. nos 79, 80, pp. 105–6; *DAPE*, iv, no. 736, pp. 13–14.
43 FO 371/21320 W1171/7/41; *DBFP*, 2, xviii, no. 80, p. 106 n. 2.
44 FO 371/21321 W2109/7/41.
45 *DBFP*, 2, xviii, no. 138, pp. 176–7; FO 371/21323 W2865/7/41; *DDF*, 2, iv, no. 385, pp. 666–7; *DGFP*, D, iii, no. 217, pp. 238–40; *FRUS*, 1937, ii. 238–9.
46 *DAPE*, iv, no. 763, pp. 43–4. See also Nogueira, *Salazar*, iii. 76.
47 *DBFP*, 2, xviii, no. 151, pp. 198–9; *DDF*, 2, iv, no. 406, p. 707.

Portugal's refusal was predictably ill-received in London and especially in Paris. On 7 February Corbin told Mounsey that it had placed his government in a most difficult position as it now seemed impossible for them to accept the scheme for land control to which they had previously agreed in principle; the French were convinced that Portugal's attitude was dictated by the nationalists at Salamanca. In Eden's absence Plymouth authorised a further *démarche* at Lisbon: it was to be made perfectly clear that Portugal's attitude placed the French government in a very difficult position and threatened to destroy a scheme whose object was to relieve the dangerous tension in international relations arising from the Spanish troubles.[48]

Wingfield left an *aide mémoire* to this effect with the Portuguese foreign ministry on 8 February.[49] By 10 February there had been no reply, thus confirming, as Plymouth told the cabinet, that the Portuguese were not changing their position on the presence of foreign officials on their land frontier. In order to provide the assurances which some powers (France and Russia) would now require, it would therefore be necessary to extend naval supervision to Portuguese ports, an addition of 400 miles of naval patrol. Plymouth had discussed the matter with Monteiro who believed that it might be easier for his government to accept, under duress, an international scheme which they could not prevent than to agree to the proposals affecting the land frontiers. Although cabinet expressed doubts on the feasibility of operating an extended system of naval patrol in the face of a hostile and unwilling Portugal, Plymouth was authorised to take part in a technical evaluation of the proposal.[50] When, later the same day, at a meeting of the chairman's sub-committee, Monteiro duly confirmed that his government could not accept the scheme for the supervision of the Portuguese-Spanish frontier, extension to Portugal of the system of maritime supervision seemed the most practicable alternative.[51]

The foreign office, however, wished to explore other alternatives and the most likely appeared to be that involving the attachment of British agents to the embassy, made by the Portuguese themselves. In his *aide mémoire* of 8 February to the Portuguese foreign ministry, Wingfield had asked what facilities the Portuguese would be willing to afford to British agents to enable them to fulfil their duties.[52] There was no reply, but on 11 February Mounsey showed Monteiro a draft memorandum containing British proposals relating to the use of British agents in Portugal. The assistant under-secretary explained that it was not an official communication and the proposals were not officially approved. Nevertheless, Monteiro telegraphed Salazar the same day with an account of the British proposals.[53]

The ambassador's apparently favourable reaction raised hopes in the foreign office that the proposals might have a chance of acceptance by his government;

48 FO 371/21322 W2586/7/41.
49 DAPE, iv, no. 772, pp. 56–7; FO 371/21324 W3998/7/41.
50 CAB 23/87 CM 7(37); FO 371/21323 W2983/7/41.
51 NIS (C) (36) 25th mtg, FO 849/27; Hemming Papers. FO 371/21322 W2586/7/41; DDF, 2, iv, no. 417, p. 730.
52 DAPE, iv, no. 772, p. 57.
53 FO 371/21323 W3386/7/41; DAPE, iv, no. 782, pp. 73–4.

in which case there would probably be no need to extend naval supervision to Portugal.[54] None the less, on 12 February Wingfield was informed of the chairman's sub-committee's decision of 10 February to refer the question of extending the naval patrol scheme to Portugal to a special sub-committee and was authorised to seek an immediate interview with Salazar in order to induce him to give the necessary instructions to Monteiro to attend and report its proceedings.[55] The ambassador embodied his instructions in a memorandum which he gave to Sampaio on 13 February and later the same day he was received by Salazar. The Portuguese dictator was in 'a mood of suppressed irritation' because, according to Sampaio, he regarded the embassy's note as 'an implied ultimatum'. Eventually, he was persuaded by his secretary general that the British communication was 'entirely friendly' but he remained adamant that his government could not be represented or collaborate in the work of the special sub-committee.[56] Salazar's government was also receiving increasing criticism from Italy and Germany. On 13 February Ribbentrop told Monteiro that in holding up a settlement Portugal was helping the republican forces more than Franco since the French frontier remained open. As proof of his assertion, the German ambassador pointed to the restrained response of the French and Soviet representatives in the Non-Intervention Committee to the Portuguese stand. For their part, the Italians made a number of representations in Lisbon explaining to the Portuguese that Germany and Italy had agreed to what had been proposed in the committee and that really there was no need for Portugal to be 'more royalist than the King'.[57]

Clearly, by 16 February, the only scheme which the Portuguese government would contemplate concerned the use of British observers on Portuguese soil. Indeed, they had anticipated that the memorandum shown unofficially to Monteiro on 11 February would be followed by an official British communication and were obviously disappointed when this failed to appear. For their part the British government, constrained by their chairmanship of the Non-Intervention Committee, hoped that the suggestion would be officially communicated by Portugal to that committee. The dilemma was acutely summed up by Ray Atherton, the United States *chargé d'affaires* in London:

Foreign Office informs me British Government are in an embarrassing position since the Portuguese Ambassador has informed them that his Government is willing to accept British observers attached to the British Embassy in Lisbon, but that the British Foreign Office is not free formally to advise the Non-Intervention Committee [of] this.[58]

It was becoming extremely urgent, however, to resolve the dilemma in view of growing French anxieties at the delay in reaching a solution to the Portuguese problem. As Plymouth explained to the cabinet, on 17 February, the French

54 *DBFP*, 2, xviii, no. 173, pp. 229–30.
55 FO 371/21322 W2586/7/41.
56 FO 371/21323 W3065/7/41; 371/21324 W3997/7/41; *DAPE*, iv, nos 786, 800, pp. 81–2, 96–9.
57 *DAPE*, iv, no. 792, pp. 88–9; FO 371/21324 W3696/7/41.
58 *FRUS*, 1937, i. 243.

gesture in accepting land supervision had as yet resulted in no assurances whatsoever that Portugal would co-operate. Unless the situation was cleared up immediately, it would be very difficult for the French government to continue with the Franco-Spanish frontier scheme and in that event the whole control scheme might be delayed since all acceptances had been made on the condition that every country represented on the committee would agree to carry it out. Plymouth reminded cabinet that the ban on foreign volunteers to Spain was made dependent on supervision being applied within a reasonable time.[59] Fortunately for the government, and for that matter the control scheme, the Portuguese government agreed the following day to the appointment of a certain number of British observers attached to the embassy in Lisbon.[60]

The British authorities now needed to produce a scheme which would work effectively while not alienating the Salazar regime. Initial disagreement on the actual number of British observers was eventually resolved on 26 February when the two governments agreed that 129 observers would be sent to Portugal.[61] On 3 March the Portuguese gave official approval to the revised observation scheme for the Hispano-Portuguese frontier which took the form of a separate Anglo-Portuguese agreement linked with the Non-Intervention Committee's overall control scheme. At the same time, Monteiro made it perfectly clear to Eden that his government agreed to the presence of British officers on their frontiers only so long as there was supervision in the Pyrenees too.[62]

The complete scheme for supervision by sea and land was finally adopted on 8 March by a resolution of the Non-Intervention Committee which recognised the efficacy of the separate Anglo-Portuguese agreement.[63] Portugal was to play no part in the naval patrols, in accordance with her wishes, even though during the planning stages she had been allotted responsibilities on the northern coast of Spain. The Lisbon authorities, as Monteiro informed the chairman's sub-committee on 26 February, were content to accept a four-power naval patrol consisting of Britain, France, Germany and Italy, and thus excluding, of course, Soviet Russia.[64]

The adoption of the scheme, despite Portuguese obstinacy, was a rare success for Anglo-French diplomacy. Unfortunately, it was short-lived. Despite the painstaking efforts of the Non-Intervention Committee the scheme remained fully operative for a mere three months until the withdrawal of Germany and Italy from the naval patrol following attacks, one substantiated the other not, on the German patrol ships *Deutschland* and *Leipzig*, and Portugal's suspension of land observation on the Portuguese-Spanish frontier. For the last time during

[59] CAB 23/87 CM 8(37). For French anxieties see FO 371/21323 W3305/7/41; *DDF*, 2, iv, nos. 427, 434, 446, pp. 742–3, 755–6, 772; *FRUS, 1937*, i. 241.
[60] FO 371/21324 W3418/7/41; *DAPE*, iv, no. 803, pp. 101–2. See also *DBFP*, 2, xviii, no. 192, pp. 269–70; *DDF*, 2, v, no. 3, p. 4.
[61] *DAPE*, iv, no. 820, annex i, pp. 129–30; *DBFP*, 2, xviii, no. 227, pp. 322–4.
[62] FO 371/21325 W4457/7/41; *DAPE*, iv, no. 832, pp. 161–2.
[63] For details of the Non-Intervention Committee land and sea control scheme see *Parliamentary papers 1936–1937*, xxviii, cmd. 5399.
[64] NIS (C) (36) 35th mtg, FO 849/27; Hemming Papers.

the civil war Portugal's action aroused critical responses in both London and Paris though eventually in the British case the criticism became somewhat muted.

The suspension of the observation scheme on the Portuguese frontier arose directly from German and Italian withdrawal from the naval patrol on 23 June. This enabled republican ships and ports to escape supervision while those of Franco remained under the effective control of the British and French naval forces. In the absence of equality of treatment the Portuguese informed both Wingfield and the foreign office on 25 June of their decision to suspend the facilities granted to the British observers in Portugal.[65] Even though the British authorities knew that the observation scheme in Portugal was ineffective[66] Eden was particularly angry at the lack of prior consultation on Portugal's part, especially in view of the special relationship which existed between the two governments by virtue of the alliance. On 26 June the foreign secretary insisted via Monteiro that the Portuguese government should continue to allow and facilitate British observation on the Portuguese frontier.[67] In reply Salazar reiterated the disadvantageous position in which Franco was placed as a consequence of the German and Italian withdrawal. He added that the suggested extension of the Franco-British naval patrol, to fill the gap left by Germany and Italy, did not commend itself: there was little confidence in French supervision of the coasts of Barcelona and Valencia.[68]

On 28 June Eden warned Monteiro that the French government might now take similar action over the Pyrenees frontier, which would be calamitous for the control scheme and for the policy of non-intervention as a whole. He urged that while a joint Franco-British plan to close the gap was being examined by the Non-Intervention Committee British observers should continue their work.[69] Salazar, however, refused to reverse his decision since he did not see any prospect of finding a scheme for restoring maritime observation which would be acceptable to Germany and Italy. He criticised the fact that the new proposals were being developed by Britain and France alone without consultation with other powers. There was no real confidence in French or British impartiality. Germany, Italy and all Europe believed the British government supported the republicans and Britain's close collaboration with France, whose sympathies with the 'Reds' of Valencia and Barcelona were not concealed, simply confirmed this view.[70] Unsurprisingly, the French were extremely exercised by the Portuguese decision to suspend the observers. Blum's government, supported by most of the French press, considered that international control on the Pyrenees frontier could not continue if it came to an end on the Portuguese frontier.[71] Delbos stressed the importance of this issue to the British ambassador, Sir Eric

---

65 FO 371/21338 W12344/W12345/W12406/7/41; *DAPE*, iv, no. 1124, pp. 453–4; *DDF*, 2, vi, no. 136, p. 213. See also Nogueira, *Salazar*, iii, 106.

66 FO 371/21336 W11628/7/41.

67 *DBFP*, 2, xviii, no. 659, pp. 943–4.

68 FO 371/21341 W13262/7/41; *DAPE*, iv, nos 1134, 1140, pp. 460–2, 469–72.

69 *DBFP*, 2, xviii, no. 662, pp. 946–7.

70 FO 371/21341 W13250/7/41

71 FO 371/21339 W12645/W12652/W12735/7/41; 371/21340 W12787/7/41.

Phipps, on 7 and 10 July. Soon after, the French authorities suspended observation on the Franco-Spanish frontier: it was to remain open until the Nyon Conference in September.[72]

Britain reacted less stridently to Portugal's suspension of land observation. This was partly because of a shift in the government's Spanish policy in mid-July 1937 – from co-operation with the French towards a point 'midway between France on the one hand and Germany and Italy on the other'. This was intended to break the deadlock within the Non-Intervention Committee and to achieve a compromise on the three major issues confronting member powers, namely closing the gap in the control scheme left by Germany and Italy, the withdrawal of foreign volunteers from Spain and the recognition of belligerent rights.[73] Despite reservations later on the part of Eden and Vansittart this modified policy continued until the end of the Spanish civil war and was reinforced in particular by Britain's search for a *rapprochement* with Italy during 1938 and 1939 and by the decision, in November 1937, to exchange agents with Franco's administration.[74] While this decision was based on economic, political and strategic considerations as they affected British interests, the confident expectation that the proposed exchange of agents would be well received by Franco owed something to Portugal's intervention with the *Caudillo* during June 1937.

The first indication that Franco might not be irrevocably wedded to the Axis powers and that he was seeking to distance his government from its erstwhile partners occurred on 14 June when Nicolás Franco, through an intermediary sent from Lisbon, informed the British ambassador, Sir Henry Chilton, that the Salamanca government was anxious for closer relations with Great Britain.[75] Shortly afterwards, the duke of Alba, acting on Franco's personal instructions, assured Cranborne that 'there was nothing that the General desired so much as good relations with England'. Further confirmation came on 28 June during an interview between Eden and Monteiro. The latter told Eden that his government had recently determined to ask for some clarification of Franco's views on foreign policy. Accordingly, the former Portuguese consul general at Madrid, Vasco da Cunha, had been instructed to go to Salamanca to explain 'the Portuguese Government's great preoccupation lest General Franco should have committed himself beyond a certain point to Germany and Italy' and to emphasise that 'the Portuguese Government attached great importance to knowing whether General Franco's policy would be "within the orbit" of British policy'. In his response Franco had made it clear that his indebtedness to Germany and Italy would be repaid only in the commercial sphere; that no territorial concession was contemplated or would be granted; and that as to the future it was his desire that the nations of the Iberian Peninsula should work together within the orbit of British foreign policy. Further, he had entered into no

---

[72] FO 371/21341 W13324/7/41.
[73] FO 371/21342 W13561/7/41. See also *FRUS*, 1937, ii. 360–1.
[74] For details of the decision to appoint a special agent see Edwards, *British Government and the Spanish civil war*, 188–92; C. E. Harvey, 'Politics and pyrites during the Spanish civil war', *Economic History Review*, 2nd ser. xxxi (1978), 98–100.
[75] FO 371/21295 W11819/1/41.

engagements with third countries and did not contemplate any payment on a political basis.[76]

In view of their constant complaints concerning Britain's apparent lack of sympathy for Franco's cause and their encouragement of improved Anglo-Nationalist relations during June and July 1937, it was to be expected that the Portuguese should welcome the British initiative in exchanging agents. Indeed, the Portuguese ambassador told Eden that the exchange of agents had been very well timed and that it had already removed most of the sense of hostility on the part of Franco's supporters towards the United Kingdom.[77] Later, in December 1937, the Portuguese appointed their own special agent, the minister of commerce, Dr Pedro Theotonio Pereira, to the Salamanca government. Emulating the British position, the Portuguese government made it clear that their action did not constitute *de jure* recognition but was being taken for practical reasons because of the difficulty of establishing direct contact with Franco's administration.[78]

Despite Portugal's obvious collaboration with Germany and Italy within the Non-Intervention Committee during the last six months of 1937, there was no danger of a rupture in Anglo-Portuguese relations because of their policies *vis-à-vis* the civil war in Spain. This was illustrated clearly in September 1937 by the mild reaction of the British authorities to the negative vote of the Portuguese delegate who, with the Albanian, ensured the defeat of a League of Nations resolution which was, in the words of one historian, 'nothing more than a referendum for Britain's policy outside the League'.[79] Later, Chamberlain's efforts to get on better terms with Italy, which culminated in the Anglo-Italian Agreement of April 1938 and Britain's ready acceptance of Portugal's reasons for granting *de jure* recognition to Franco's regime, in the same month, served to reconcile further the different positions of the two countries.[80]

The extent of Anglo-Portuguese reconciliation – which also owed something to the presence of a British military mission in Portugal during most of 1938 – was demonstrated during the summer months by the government's refusal to comply with French, and British labour and liberal party requests to pressurise Portugal into restoring observation on the Portuguese-Spanish frontier. The French government were particularly critical of the lack of supervision on the Portuguese frontier since thay had decided in mid-June to close their own

[76] DBFP, 2, xviii, no. 664, pp. 948–9. See also CAB 27/622 FP(36) 15th mtg, 28 June 1937; DAPE, iv, no. 1145, pp. 475–8; FRUS, 1937, i. 354. See also Rosas, O Salazarismo, 46; Nogueira, Salazar, iii, 103, 107.
[77] DAPE, i, no. 74, pp. 142–3; FO 371/21270 W21787/25/36.
[78] FO 371/21384 W21943/W22151/100/41. See also Kay, Salazar, 115. In June 1937 Vasco da Cunha had been installed at Salamanca as 'Consul General of Portugal', accredited to the nationalist secretariat for external relations: Oliveira, Salazar e a Guerra Civil, 328.
[79] W. Kleine Ahlbrandt, The policy of simmering: a study of British foreign policy during the Spanish civil war 1936–1939, The Hague 1962, 76–7. See also Rosas, O Salazarismo, 96–7; R. Veatch, 'The League of Nations and the Spanish Civil War 1936–1939', European History Quarterly xx (1990), 197–8. Although the resolution was not adopted because the requirement for unanimity had not been fulfilled, Veatch claims the vote constituted a victory for the Spanish Republic because 'Britain, France and sixteen other states which were parties to the non-intervention policy had voted in favour of a threat to end it'.
[80] For British reactions to Portugal's recognition of Franco see FO 371/22641 W4211/83/41.

frontier with Spain; which had been reopened in March 1938 by the short-lived second ministry of Léon Blum. Contrary to the views of certain historians, the decision to close the French frontier was not taken in response to strong British pressure.[81] As Georges Bonnet later told Phipps, the French government were convinced that if they did not close the frontier the risk of war would have been increased by 100 per cent; they had heard that a number of ships heavily laden with Russian war material intended for the republicans had set out, or were about to set out, for Havre and Bordeaux for onward transportation into Spain. The French foreign minister deplored Russia's 'renewed and unhealthy wish to fish in troubled Spanish waters far removed from her own territory, which would therefore be immune from the disturbances and damage she wished to cause others'.[82]

However, by the end of June, Edouard Daladier was beginning to have second thoughts on the decision to close the Franco-Spanish frontier while the Portuguese-Spanish frontier and the Franco-held Spanish ports remained open. The French premier told Phipps, on 30 June, that this was a one-sided arrangement which he considered intolerable and which he could not impose on the French people much longer. He warned that if the latest Non-Intervention Committee plan – a modified version of the British proposals of July 1937 to achieve the withdrawal of volunteers and the restoration of observation on all land frontiers – was not soon put into operation the Pyrenees frontier would have to be thrown open again.[83] Feeling on the subject was running higher and higher among the French working classes and workmen told him they would readily work overtime if it was to provide the Spanish government with the means to defend themselves against the two dictators. Daladier, however, hinted that if he were able to say that in order to localise the war all frontiers must be closed he would be able to convince them, but he could not continue indefinitely with the existing discrimination against the Spanish government whilst Mussolini openly boasted that he would not allow Franco to be beaten. Phipps assured him that according to Sir Robert Hodgson, who had stopped off at the Paris embassy that very morning while on his way to London to report to Halifax, nothing appreciable in the way of war material was going across the Portuguese-Spanish frontier even though it might be said to be open. The ambassador impressed upon Daladier 'the absolutely vital importance that His Majesty's Government attached to the continued closure of the Pyrenees frontier in order to give a reasonable time for the British Non-Intervention plan to come into operation', and asked that an assurance to this effect be given through him to Halifax and Chamberlain. Daladier agreed but without enthusiasm.[84]

Criticism of the closing of the French frontier while the Portuguese remained

---

[81] See Edwards, *British Government and the Spanish civil war*, 174; Thomas, *Spanish civil war*, 825; D. Smyth, *Diplomacy and strategy of survival: British policy and Franco's Spain 1940–1941*, Cambridge 1986, 12–13.
[82] Phipps Papers, PHPP 1/20. See also Cecil of Chelwood Papers, MS 51804.
[83] For details of the original British proposals see NIS (36) 24th–27th mtgs inclusive, FO 849/1; Hemming Papers.
[84] FO 371/22427 R5954/240/22. See also Phipps Papers, PHPP 1/20.

open was not confined to the French government; the parliamentary opposition in the United Kingdom was equally hostile. As early as 21 June, David Lloyd George raised the matter and demanded to know whether Portugal had been asked to close her frontier. On this occasion R. A. Butler, parliamentary under-secretary of state for foreign affairs, was not forthcoming.[85] Labour MPs, including Ellen Wilkinson, refused to be put off and on 27 June, and again on 29 June 1938, a number of questions were asked about the Portuguese-Spanish frontier.[86] It was not, however, until 4 July that a question from Eleanor Rathbone elicited a categorical reply from the government. Butler told the commons that since the suspension of observation on 25 June 1937 the government had received no evidence to show that effective control was not being maintained and had not therefore felt called upon to make any communication on the subject to the Portuguese government. Rathbone, supported by Lloyd George, was not in the least satisfied with this reply and demanded to know why strong representations had been made to the French government to keep their frontier closed while corresponding representations had not been made to the Portuguese government. Butler replied that the government had every reason to believe that the Portuguese exercised effective control on their land frontier. He denied that any formal representation or request had been made by His Majesty's Government to the French in relation to the closure of their frontier.[87] A final attempt on the subject was made on 13 July when the government was asked to consider suggesting to the French government that the Franco-Spanish frontier should be reopened until such time as the Portuguese frontier of Spain and the sea inspection scheme were both in operation in order to secure equality of treatment to both sides in the Spanish struggle. Butler rejected the suggestion and asserted that the land frontier between Spain and Portugal, like that between Spain and France, was closed to the transit of those goods whose export was forbidden by the Non-Intervention Agreement.[88]

Butler's statements to the commons, both in terms of British representations to the French and the claim that effective control was maintained on the Spanish-Portuguese frontier, were, of course, misleading. Even if formal representations had not been made to the French government the foreign office was certainly aware that Phipps had personally applied pressure on Daladier on 30 June. Moreover, although the ambassador in Portugal, Sir Walford Selby, informed them that Captain Malcolm MacDonald R.N., head of the British Observation Corps in Portugal, did not consider that the Portuguese government had connived at or facilitated the passage of arms across the frontier it was admitted that large supplies of dynamite, tractors, lorries, petrol, wine and telephone cables, which might be for military use but which were not on the contraband list, had at all times passed freely across the frontier.[89] The foreign office was also aware from the monthly arms traffic (to Spain) summaries supplied by the war office that small arms consignments intended for nationalist

85 *Hansard parliamentary debates*, HC, 5th ser. cccxxxvii, cols 1014, 1032–3.
86 Ibid. cc. 1502, 1877–8.
87 Ibid. cccxxxviii, cc. 7–9.
88 Ibid. cc. 1291–2.
89 FO 371/22649 W8962/83/41.

Spain had been regularly reaching Portugal since the suspension of observation in 1937. Disturbed by the opposition questions Vansittart instituted an enquiry which resulted in a report from Walter Roberts, of the league of nations and western department, on 22 July. it was stated that according to recent war office reports consignments had been made to Portugal but that while the material might be for Spain it might equally be for the Portuguese government or conceivably for plotters against Salazar's regime. Although Roberts advised that an enquiry should be made in Lisbon his suggestion was quickly rejected as 'likely to be highly dangerous',[90] presumably because of its potential effect upon the progress of the Non-Intervention Committee plans for the restoration of full supervision of all frontiers and the withdrawal of volunteers, and upon the military conversations then continuing in Portugal between the Portuguese and the British military mission.

The government's determination to avoid alienating Portugal was further demonstrated towards the end of 1938 when they chose to say and do nothing about reports which indicated that the recruitment of volunteers in Portugal was continuing despite their efforts to achieve the withdrawal of volunteers from Spain.[91] By this time, however, such infringements of non-intervention were unlikely to cause problems for Britain since it was virtually certain that Franco would achieve a complete victory in the civil war. Thus the foreign office was very receptive to the fears expressed by Monteiro during January 1939 that the longer republican resistance continued the more foreign political and economic influence (German and Italian) would gain ground in Spain to the probable detriment of Portugal's independent position in the Iberian Peninsula. He urged British recognition of the nationalists.[92] On 27 February, ten months after Portugal, the British government granted *de jure* recognition to Franco.

At certain specific points during the civil war – September 1936 and February 1937 – Portuguese intentions threatened to destroy the carefully constructed policy of non-intervention. From August 1936 until the summer of 1938 Portugal's ambivalence – as an interested member of the Non-Intervention Committee while intensely disliking its *raison d'être* – presented the British government with a dual problem; how to maintain Portugal's fidelity to the alliance while retaining French goodwill. The civil war failed to disrupt the Franco-British entente because although the two countries sometimes differed on non-intervention, not least over Portugal's attitude, especially on land observation, or on practical matters such as the British plan of July 1937, their essential interests increasingly demanded closer co-operation. The end of the civil war in Spain coincided with the establishment of regular military staff contacts at the highest level and with Britain's commitment, in the event of war, to send an expeditionary force of thirty-two divisions to fight in France. As the Spanish conflagration ended, Anglo-Portuguese relations were also on firm

[90] FO 371/22649 W8962/83/41; 371/22650 W9343/83/41.
[91] FO 371/22657 W15667/83/41.
[92] FO 371/24150 W1076/W3379/1076/41; DAPE, v, no. 1883 and annex, pp. 577–8.

foundations. After a difficult beginning, Lisbon's consistent support for Franco had been accommodated by their British allies. Indeed, at certain points during the civil war Britain saw Portugal as a possible source of communication with the Franco authorities. In February 1937, for example, shortly before Portugal's acceptance of the British observation scheme Lord Cranborne did not fail to appreciate that 'close relations with her may also be of advantage to us should Franco win', and during July 1937 Eden, having spoken previously to Monteiro, suggested to Chamberlain that an approach to Portugal might be useful as a means of discovering the exact position of Franco's guns near Gibraltar – rumoured to be manned by German officers.[93]

Towards the end of the Spanish conflict the Portuguese began to appreciate the dangers as well as the benefits of Italian and German intervention on the nationalist side. Hence, there was an ambivalence: on the one hand, natural anxiety that the Axis powers might continue to exercise undue influence in the Iberian Peninsula after the war; on the other, common support for Franco, and the common ideological bond of virulent anti-communism, might draw Portugal into the Axis orbit. However, despite the fact that Britain's unrelenting pursuit of non-intervention had on occasions threatened to alienate the Portuguese government as in February 1937, and despite the complications created by the Spanish conflict, Britain retained and strengthened the Portuguese connection by means of other positive measures including military co-operation which, significantly, involved the despatch of a military mission to Lisbon.

93 FO 371/21323 W2865/7/41; 371/21269 W14227/25/36. Eden to Chamberlain, 20 July 1937, PREM 1/360 and Avon Papers AP 13/1/42A. A meeting to discuss this issue involving Eden, Sir Thomas Inskip (minister for co-ordination of defence), Duff Cooper (first lord of the admiralty) and Leslie Hore-Belisha (secretary of state at war) actually took place, according to Chamberlain's marginal comment on the letter, the same evening. Further confirmation is provided in the Avon Papers which have become available only very recently. In a letter to Hore-Belisha of 24 July 1937 Eden thought it a 'good thing if the same little committee as discussed the matter [the guns above Gibraltar] the other day in the PM's room should do so again should the need arise': AP 13/1/42C. Unfortunately, information as to what transpired at this meeting cannot be traced in the Public Record Office archives or in the available private papers of Chamberlain, Eden, Inskip or Hore-Belisha. Gibraltar is a sensitive issue and probably the subject of close scrutiny on the part of Her Majesty's Government.

3

Countering the Axis in Portugal

There can be no doubt that the Spanish Civil War gave Germany and Italy the opportunity to advance their political, economic, military and strategic interests. The common struggle against the forces of socialism and communism in Spain contributed to the strengthening of the Rome – Berlin Axis in contrast to the divisions created within French, British and American societies by the Spanish war and the continuing diplomatic estrangement thereby of the western democracies from Soviet Russia. For Germany in particular collaboration with Franco provided real economic and military benefits in the form of enhanced access to key raw materials such as copper, iron ore and pyrites and battle experience for German personnel and equipment, notably the *Luftwaffe*.[1] In view of their considerable assistance, and despite Franco's reservations concerning the *Falangist* movement in nationalist Spain, both Germany and Italy could reasonably expect an end to the previously friendly relations of Spain with Britain and France and, consequently, a general weakening of their strategic position in the eastern Atlantic and western Mediterranean. The end of the civil war and Franco's adhesion to the Anti-Comintern Pact in April 1939 could be taken as confirmation of this and to indicate a strengthening of the strategic position of Germany and Italy.[2]

In their Iberian ambitions the fascist powers were not unmindful of Portugal. During the civil war, both looked forward to the break-up of the Anglo-Portuguese alliance and the inclusion of Lisbon in the Berlin–Rome–Madrid axis. In the course of a lecture, delivered at Leipzig in the summer of 1938 before an audience of national socialist leaders, General Walter von Reichenau, commander of the fourth army group, revealed an acute awareness of the significance of the Portuguese connection for Britain:

> The most important of sea and latterly also air routes lead along Portuguese coasts and can be either defended or attacked from it. Portugal's bridge-like position towards Africa is obvious. So is its close connexion with the Mediterranean basin. Madeira is ideal as an observation post on the entrance to the Mediterranean. The Azores, protruding as they do westwards, are bound to play a big part in international aerial intercourse over the Atlantic. The right to make use of them would free England from many a care

---

[1] For economic benefits see ch. i, n. 62. For the military advantages of German intervention in Spain see Merkes, *Deutsches Politik*, 128–43; E. L. Homze, *Arming the Luftwaffe: the Reich air ministry and the German aircraft industry 1919–1939*, London 1976, 170–4.

[2] For strategic issues see D. C. Watt, 'German strategic planning and Spain 1938–1939', *Army Quarterly* (1960), 220–7; Smyth, 'Reflex reaction'. For the significance of Spain in German war plans see Whealey, *Hitler and Spain*, 95–134.

regarding supplies of food and raw materials in war time. Together with the Cape Verde Islands, the Azores are strung out along the first half of the seaway to South Africa; the southern half of that route leads past Portuguese Guinea, São Tomé, Príncipe and the long coast of Angola. The mere thought that these positions might some day fall into the hands of an enemy is irreconcilable with the existence of the British Empire. This clearly shows why, in view of the altered conditions in the Mediterranean, Britain needs Portugal's friendship more than ever.

Reichenau also made specific reference to the potential significance of southern Portugal for the air defence of Gibraltar. The interests of Germany and of nationalist Spain demanded, the general believed, that Portugal 'cease being consciously or unconsciously a pawn on the Anglo-French chessboard'. Reichenau was certain that Portugal could be won for the Axis either through a successful courtship of Salazar's government or by means of Spanish military intervention.[3]

Reichenau's observations on Portugal, although officially denied,[4] were not isolated; they reflected official thinking in Berlin. Since the outset of the civil war in Spain the German government, and its Italian counterpart, had sought to exploit Anglo-Portuguese differences over Spanish policy. German and Italian official propaganda lost no opportunity in this respect. For example, Italian propaganda sought to exploit Portugal's exclusion from the Nyon Conference in September 1937.[5] Equally, the Italian press was not above fomenting rumours and inventing stories injurious to Britain's standing in Portugal. Towards the end of 1937, for instance, a statement appeared in all government controlled newspapers which claimed that the British government intended to annex the Azores. On another occasion, a report was published which claimed that the attempt on Salazar's life in July 1937 had been arranged by the British secret service.[6] By virtue of their support for Franco the Italians were able to work quite closely with the Portuguese propaganda department and articles appeared in Portuguese newspapers expressing common Latin sympathies and extolling common corporative structures and objectives. Indeed, according to the British embassy 'the parallelism of the tasks of the two authoritarian States in restoring and maintaining order' have been the subject of much lecturing, press articles and mutual felicitation'.[7] The extent of Italy's success

---

[3] CAB 24/277 CP 163(38). See also the *News Chronicle*, 12 July 1938.

[4] The German minister at Lisbon, Baron Hoyningen-Huene, issued an immediate denial which Salazar accepted. According to Franco Nogueira, the Portuguese leader had read the text of the lecture very carefully before concluding that it was a forgery. However, he was impressed by the knowledge it revealed and the detailed argument: *Salazar*, iii. 165.

[5] For German and Italian exploitation of Portugal's exclusion from the Nyon Conference see FO 371/21405 W16941/16618/41. Salazar had expressed regret and surprise at Portugal's exclusion from the conference. His country could not have been excluded on the grounds that the conference was confined to Mediterranean powers because Germany, Russia and Roumania were not and yet they had been invited. At the same time, invitations had not been limited to the powers directly interested in the civil war in Spain, that is, Britain, France, Germany, Italy and Russia because Turkey and Egypt were included: Nogueira, *Salazar*, iii. 129.

[6] FO 371/21341 W13167/W13272/7/41; FO 425/414 W20510/923/36.

[7] FO 371/22601 W3407/3407/36.

could be measured by her complete rehabilitation in Portugal after the nadir of 1935 when the *Estado Novo* imposed sanctions and supported Britain and the League of Nations. The British embassy appreciated that the decline in the influence and authority of the League after the close of the Abyssinian war was a measure of Italy's return to favour.[8] According to the British *chargé d'affaires*, Charles Bateman, the Portuguese increasingly regarded Geneva as Stalin's second capital.[9]

While Italian propaganda was extremely irksome to the British authorities, German propaganda was more dangerous. By the end of 1938 the Germans had virtually ousted Reuters and *Havas* and obtained control of the news agencies in Portugal through the *Deutsches Nachrichten-Büro* (DNB). By supplying international news at a very low price, the DNB had gained access to small local newspapers throughout Portugal which included German propaganda in their news services.[10] At the cultural level too the Germans worked hard to ingratiate themselves. Active centres of Portuguese culture were set up during 1937 in Berlin, Hamburg and Cologne while Portuguese was put on a level with French as an optional romance language in the German *gymnasia*. German vied with English in Portuguese secondary schools while in the universities German was taught jointly with English. German centres of culture were well established in Lisbon and Coimbra.[11] German teachers visited Portuguese lyceums and a German-Portuguese club in Lisbon co-ordinated and fostered Luso-German cultural and social relations while German and Italian influence with the youth movement, the *Mocidade Portuguesa*, and with the *Legião Portuguesa* increased steadily.[12] Contacts between the *Mocidade* and the Hitler Youth had been established since August 1936 when contingents of the former visited Berlin for the Olympic Games.[13] The Germans also strengthened their connections with other movements akin to their own, such as the Portuguese 'National Foundation for Delight in Work' which was established in 1935.[14]

The Germans also lost no opportunity to establish closer relations with the Portuguese military and police authorities. This included their contribution to the training of the Portuguese secret police, the PVDE, and an invitation to the Portuguese police to attend an international police conference held in Berlin under Heinrich Himmler's direction during August 1937.[15] In the same year a number of German warships visited Lisbon – the battleship *Admiral von Scheer* in September and the light cruiser *Köln* in October. German submarines also visited at various times. Early in February 1938 the German flagship *Deutsch-*

---

8 Ibid.

9 FO 425/414 W20510/923/36.

10 FO 371/22597 W14363/153/36.

11 Italian centres of culture existed in Lisbon, Coimbra and Oporto but their activities were somewhat neutralised by their lack of continuity and by the fact that Italian was not a class-based subject in Portuguese lyceums.

12 FO 371/22601 W3407/3407/36; West, 'The present situation', 217–18.

13 FO 425/414 W20510/923/36; DGFP, D, iii, no. 70, pp. 71–2.

14 For a reference to the visit of the 'Strength through Joy' movement to Portugal in April 1938 see undated memorandum, Dawson Papers, MS Dawson 79.

15 Gallagher, 'Controlled repression', 387; Wheeler, 'In the service of order', 9–15; H. A. Jacobson, *Nationalsozialistische Aussenpolitik 1933–1938*, Frankfurt-am-Main–Berlin 1968, 462.

land visited Lisbon accompanied by two submarines.[16] During 1937 the Germans also succeeded, with the help of the Portuguese minister of marine, in installing a wireless air station at Sintra and secured accommodation for *Lufthansa* airlines next door to the Portuguese naval air station in Lisbon, in spite of the strong opposition of several members of the Portuguese air council.[17] The German army played its part in cultivating relations with the Portuguese military. In October 1937 Field Marshal Werner von Blomberg, German minister of war, visited Madeira and the Azores and his visit was followed on 5 November by the presentation to Salazar 'as a symbol of the cordial spirit of cameraderie which now exists between our two armies' of the standard of the 10th Portuguese infantry battalion which was captured at Ferre du Bois during the Battle of Lys on 9 April 1918.[18] Above all, from mid-1936 onwards the Germans declared a keen interest in supplying the Portuguese armed forces with their material requirements and presented formidable competition to British armaments manufacturers.

The British clearly needed to make an extra effort if they were to maintain their leading position in Portuguese affections and foreign policy. Yet, as late as seven months after the outbreak of the Spanish war, in February 1937, Salazar privately complained of Britain's tendency to neglect her oldest ally in that she did not keep her informed of current British policy, particularly in relation to events in Spain.[19] Salazar's complaint was not dissimilar to that made by Armindo Monteiro, while foreign minister, to Eden at Geneva in January 1936.[20] At the beginning of March 1937 Monteiro, now ambassador in London, repeated these complaints. He told Eden that while Britain could contribute more to Portugal than vice versa his country could none the less play a part in helping their ally in the future. The ambassador was very anxious to enlist Eden's support in responding positively to Salazar's complaints, particularly in view of German and Italian propaganda which was extremely active in Portugal.[21] Eden expressed a willingness to see Anglo-Portuguese relations placed on a more intimate footing and on 16 March he gave Monteiro a message for Salazar which clarified his government's reasons for upholding the policy of non-intervention in Spain.[22]

At that same meeting, while dismissive about Italian influence in the peninsula, Monteiro expressed fears about the effect of German propaganda in Portugal which, he reminded Eden, was on a very large scale; almost every sphere, cultural, journalistic and sport was affected. Eden explained that although their resources were more limited than those of Germany, which spent so profusely, they were determined to improve upon previous efforts in the field

16 FO 371/22601 W3407/3407/36; *The Times*, 28, 31 Jan. 1938.
17 FO 425/414 W20510/923/36.
18 FO 371/21278 W21055/923/36; *The Times*, 6 Nov. 1937.
19 *DAPE*, iv, no. 763, p. 43.
20 See Stone, 'Official British attitude', 745, n. 25.
21 FO 371/21325 W4457/7/41.
22 FO 371/21327 W5350/7/41. See also *DBFP*, 2, xviii, no. 298, p. 438; *DAPE*, iv, no. 879, pp. 201–2.

of cultural propaganda.[23] Accordingly, Reginald (Rex) Leeper, head of the foreign office news department, was instructed to improve news communication with Portugal and to expand British cultural propaganda. To facilitate the presentation of British news in Portugal, arrangements were made for Reuters to replace *Havas* as the appropriate news service agency. Reuters' service was made available at cheap rates in Portugal to enable it to compete, to some degree at least, with the free news supplied by the DNB.[24] The news department also persuaded *The Times* to publish articles and editorials which were favourable to the Salazar regime. Between September 1937 and August 1939, having previously paid little attention to Portugal, *The Times* published nine editorials and seven leading articles on Portuguese affairs and on 2 August a thirty-six page special on Mozambique. It was probably no accident that a number of important journals published articles on Portugal during 1938 and 1939 usually praising Salazar's achievements, notably in financial affairs.[25] The British Council was also active in improving Anglo-Portuguese cultural relations during 1937 and 1938. In 1937, for example, the English Institute at Coimbra was provided with increased funds while the director, Professor Downes, organised a series of lectures: the number of students taking English at Coimbra University trebled during 1937–8. A number of scholarships were also provided for Portuguese students to study at the universities of Nottingham, Southampton and Cambridge. Representatives of British universities attended the Historical Congress of the Portuguese Empire, held in Lisbon in July 1937, and the celebrations held at Coimbra from 6–10 December 1937 to commemorate its fourth centenary. Eminent British academics such as Professor Lionel Robbins and Sir Charles Webster delivered lectures at Lisbon and Coimbra between 1937 and 1939.[26] In November 1938 a British Institute was inaugurated in Lisbon by Lord Lloyd who represented the British Council. Earlier in the year, in May 1938, an Anglo-Portuguese Society had been founded in London 'under auspices that provide the friendly promotion of a good understanding between two countries which have been allies for centuries but have still to know each other better'.[27] In February 1939 a Portuguese fortnight was held in London which included lectures, receptions and a Queen's Hall concert. Later, in June 1939, the BBC news service to Portugal began broadcasting in the Portuguese language and included a broadcast of short talks by prominent British figures organised in conjunction with the Portuguese broadcasting corporation, the *Emissora Nacional*. The broadcasts included talks by Lord Baldwin, Lord Hailsham, Lord Stamp and the bishop of London which in general praised Salazar's achievements in Portugal.[28]

The improvements which took place in cultural diplomacy after 1936

23 FO 371/21327 W5350/7/41.
24 FO 371/21280 W21476/21104/36.
25 See, for example, W. F. Deedes, 'Portugal', *Quarterly Review* cclxxii (1939); Wakenham, 'Portugal to-day'; West, 'The present situation'; W. C. Atkinson, 'Portugal and her empire', *Fortnightly Review*, July 1939; W. A. Hirst, 'Greater Portugal', *Contemporary Review*, Sept. 1939.
26 For details of Webster's visit to Portugal see the Webster Papers, 7/9.
27 *The Times*, 20 May 1938.
28 FO 371/22601 W3407/3407/36; *The Times*, 20 May, 23 Nov. 1938, 6 June 1939; FO 371/24008 W7845/398/36.

undoubtedly helped to remove any sense of complacency in Britain's attitude towards her oldest ally. The excellent impression created in Lisbon by articles and editorials in *The Times* – Salazar expressed his personal pleasure at the first of these, published on 14 September 1937 – provided a clear indication of the benefits of carefully considered press contributions.[29] Unfortunately, many of the beneficial effects were undermined by certain sections of the British press who indulged in what the foreign office regarded as ill-considered rumour-mongering and attacks on the Salazar regime. During 1937 a number of articles appeared which created a furore in British governing circles, and in the embassy in Lisbon, as well as causing resentment within the ranks of the Portuguese government. Particularly vexatious were those articles which sought to include Portugal in some deal or other involving the cession of her colonial territory to Germany. One such article, which appeared in the *Sunday Express* on 31 October 1937, emphasised the pre-war Anglo-German negotiations on the Portuguese colonies and included extracts from the recently published Lichnowsky memoirs.[30] On 9 November the government controlled *Diário de Notícias*[31] devoted two pages to an editorial criticising the anti-Portuguese tendency of the British popular press and quoting at length from the *Sunday Express* article. The British embassy was equally critical and while Bateman made a spirited effort to repair the damage with a vigorous speech to an audience of influential Portuguese servicemen and ex-servicemen in Lisbon – which Salazar was apparently pleased with – he was none too sanguine that such efforts would continue to succeed.[32] The foreign office shared his exasperation: Lord Cranborne was particularly incensed by the article in the *Sunday Express*.[33] At the beginning of December 1937 press speculation and leaks concerning the recent visit of Lord Halifax to Germany, in particular references to colonial transfers involving Portuguese and Belgian territory, further fuelled resentment in Portugal and created yet greater irritation in British official circles.[34]

Another unfortunate impression was created during 1937 by the publication of the latest volume of the British *Official History of the Great War* which dealt with the events of 1918 and gave a rather lamentable description of the part played in the Battle of Lys by Portuguese forces. This was compounded by the claims of a retired British officer, Brigadier Frank P. Crozier, in his latest book, *The Men I Killed*, that he had killed Portuguese soldiers to stop the rot on 9 April 1918. These claims provoked a bitter response in the Portuguese press. Although foreign office support for the embassy's expression of official regret

---

[29] FO 371/21269 W17905/25/36.

[30] Prince Karl von Lichnowsky was German ambassador in London before the first world war. He participated in the pre-war Anglo-German negotiations which considered the partition of the Portuguese empire.

[31] According to David Shillan, a member of the directorate of the British Institute during the second world war, the *Diário de Notícias* played a role in Portugal comparable to *The Times*: 'Portugal today', *International Affairs* xx (1944), 219.

[32] FO 425/414 W21064/25/36.

[33] Ibid.

[34] Halifax Papers A4 410 3.1; FO 800/268. For details of Portugal's response to press reports of the Halifax visit see ch. 6.

and disgust at Crozier's claims was officially acknowledged by the Portuguese, the whole episode could not but be compared unfavourably to the return by the German army of the Portuguese standard, captured at the Battle of Lys.[35]

Continuing friction was provided by persistent left-wing criticism in Britain of the Salazar regime and its support for General Franco. Clearly, the Portuguese were annoyed to the extent that sections of the Portuguese press – notably *A Voz*, a Catholic monarchist newspaper, and *O Século* – responded with an anti-British campaign of their own which was of such intensity as to create considerable consternation amongst the French legation at Lisbon.[36] Further irritation was created in official circles in Portugal by the persistence of the British parliamentary opposition in forcing the government to make statements on the validity of the treaties under the alliance and their application in relation to the Portuguese colonies.[37] While, in a major speech before the national assembly on 28 April 1938, Salazar reaffirmed his country's commitment to the alliance and made positive and appreciative references to the British military mission which was visiting Portugal, he could not resist making some acid remarks on the activities of the British opposition which had obviously struck a sensitive nerve.[38]

Fortunately, any long term ill effects of such anti-Portuguese comment were mitigated by events in Europe during March and April 1938. The British ambassador reported on 2 April that since the opening of conversations between London and Rome there had been a marked decline in anti-British propaganda. According to Selby, who had been ambassador to Vienna prior to his recent posting to Lisbon, the Anglo-Italian conversations were being followed with the deepest interest in Portugal, and if they were successful he was convinced that Britain's position in Portugal would be materially assisted. While commentary on the German annexation of Austria was restrained in the Portuguese press, opinion in Portugal had hardened against Germany. Selby confirmed that a weakening of the Rome–Berlin Axis – a likely result of an Anglo-Italian understanding – would not be unwelcome to most Portuguese. The ambassador understood that the German minister's communication to the foreign ministry concerning the annexation of Austria was coldly received.[39] This was perhaps not surprising in view of the close similarities between Portugal and Austria – two small agriculturally-based countries possessing

---

[35] FO 371/22601 W3407/3407/36; 371/21269 W16242/W16893/25/36. A sympathetic article written by Major G. R. Johnson, previously assistant military attaché in Lisbon, to counter the impressions of the Official History's record of the Portuguese role in the Great War, and drawing upon Portuguese sources, appeared in the *Army Quarterly* of October 1937.

[36] *DDF*, 2, viii, no. 187, p. 381. According to Iva Delgado, *A Voz* was an ultra conservative and 'hysterically Germanophile' journal before the Nazi–Soviet Non-Aggression Pact of August 1939 : *Portugal e a Guerra Civil*, 28.

[37] The opposition had raised the question of the validity of the Anglo-Portuguese treaties on five occasions between February 1937 and April 1938, the last two during April 1938: *Hansard parliamentary debates*, HC, 5th ser. cccxx, cols 377–8; cccxxi, cols 341–2; cccxxxvi, col. 1066; and cccxxxiv, cols 742, 1094–5.

[38] Salazar, *Doctrine and action*, 352.

[39] FO 371/22592 W4620/146/36.

Catholic corporatist structures, each overshadowed by a larger powerful neighbour.[40] Certainly, the Portuguese Catholic Church, which still retained great influence in Portugal, disapproved of Germany's absorption of Austria. Indeed, the cardinal patriarch, Monsignor Manual Goncalves Cerejeira, a close friend of Salazar, was a strong Anglophile who consistently advised the prime minister of the dangers of any drift away from Britain since the very independence of Portugal and the preservation of the Portuguese colonial empire depended on the alliance.[41] In addition, a number of articles appeared in the *Diário de Notícias* during April 1938 which argued that opinion in the United Kingdom was hardening against Germany and that the annexation of Austria by the Third Reich had weakened the Rome–Berlin Axis. Selby was informed privately that these articles had been well received by Salazar.[42]

Anschluss and the Anglo-Italian conversations, however, proved only temporary setbacks for German propaganda in Portugal. In October 1938, with the steady monopolisation of Portuguese news services by the DNB in mind, Monteiro expressed his anxieties as to the cumulative effect of German activity in his country. He told Lord Elibank that while there was a certain revulsion of feeling in Portugal against intense German propaganda it 'must leave its mark and make it more difficult in the future for those who wished to maintain the British friendship and connexion'.[43] The British government continued to watch anxiously the development of DNB control in Portugal and during the early summer of 1939 they were disturbed to learn that for reasons of economy the *Diário de Notícias* had found it necessary to terminate its contract with Reuters. On 15 June Selby, reporting on German press activity, warned Halifax that to all intents and purposes 'the daily foreign news fed to Portuguese opinion by the Portuguese press conforms to the political requirements of the propaganda ministry in Berlin with its special section of fifteen officials whose sole duty seems to be to study the Portuguese and Spanish press'.[44] To counteract German ascendancy the government proposed to establish a British news service in Portugal, and in August Selby was instructed to request the provision of all necessary facilities for the circulation of British news in Portugal and to stress the intention of the news department of the foreign office to do everything possible 'to foster interest in Great Britain and the Dominions in everything that pertained to the welfare of Portugal and the furtherance of the friendship which existed between the two countries'.[45] This step coincided with the outbreak of the second world war and together with the appointment of a press attaché to the Lisbon embassy helped serve British interests in Portugal during the critical early war years.

[40] See T. Gallagher, 'The theory and practice of Portuguese authoritarianism: Salazar, the right and the Portuguese military 1920–1968', unpublished PhD diss. Manchester 1978, 163–6.
[41] For example, FO 371/22592 W1757/146/26. The extent of Cerejeira's influence with Salazar is debatable. Tom Gallagher claims that the cardinal's relationship with Salazar was not as close after 1932 as it had been previously: *Portugal: a twentieth century interpretation*, Manchester 1983, 126.
[42] FO 371/22593 W5449/146/36.
[43] FO 371/22597 W14363/153/36.
[44] FO 371/24064 W9627/160/36.
[45] FO 371/24064 W10614/W12374/160/36. See also FO 425/416.

Despite the improvements, however, it cannot be claimed that Britain won the propaganda war with Germany (and Italy) in Portugal before September 1939. If cultural propaganda represented the fifth arm (with the three armed services and financial solvency) of British defence during the 1930s it was certainly inadequate. Research has clearly demonstrated the relative inferiority of British cultural diplomacy in the period.[46] The British Council, for example, began in 1935 with a budget of only £5,000. This increased to £60,000 for 1937–8 and £200,000 for 1938–9, but was still only a fraction of the German and Italian budgets. According to one treasury estimate the Germans were spending £5 million and the Italians £2 million on propaganda during 1938.[47] British tardiness in responding to the propaganda race with Germany and Italy was largely a consequence of treasury resistance to increased allocations, as witness their hostile reaction to the report of the Vansittart Committee of May 1938 which recommended substantial increases for institutions such as the British Council and the Travel and Industrial Development Association, and a considerable expansion of the press attaché service. Treasury resistance was based on political as well as financial grounds in that they believed such proposals ran counter to the main thrust of government foreign policy since in the long run it would not be possible 'to combine the policy of appeasement with a forward policy in propaganda'. As Philip Taylor suggests, Vansittart countered the treasury's optimistic assessment of appeasement with proposals motivated by the need to repair serious deficiencies in the area of cultural diplomacy in the face of a possible future Anglo-German confrontation.[48]

An increase of £150,000 in the propaganda budget was eventually agreed by the treasury. It consisted of £50,000 for the remainder of 1938 and £100,000 for work in 1939. This was well short of Vansittart's original recommendation for an increase of half a million pounds.[49] When, after Munich and even more so after Prague, increased attention was paid to propaganda – exemplified by the appointment of fifteen additional press attachés to embassies such as Lisbon, Athens, Warsaw and Santiago – it proved extremely difficult to make up for lost time in countries such as Portugal before the outbreak of war, though once war was declared Britain possessed an increasingly formidable propaganda machine under the control of the recently established ministry of information.[50]

Britain's failure to counter German activity in Portugal in the cultural sphere

[46] See P. M. Taylor, *The projection of Britain: British overseas publicity and propaganda 1919–1939*, Cambridge 1981; C. Cruickshank, *The fourth arm: psychological warfare 1938–1945*, London 1977; P. M. Taylor, 'British official attitudes towards propaganda abroad, 1918–1939', and D. W. Ellwood, 'Showing the world what it owed to Britain: foreign policy and cultural propaganda 1935–1945', in N. Pronay and D. W. Spring (eds), *Propaganda, politics and film 1918–1945*, London 1982.

[47] Ellwood, 'Showing the world', 54, 56–7; Taylor, *The projection of Britain*, 240–1.

[48] PREM 1/272. Taylor, *The projection of Britain*, 234–44. According to R. B. Cockett, the news department of the foreign office, headed by Rex Leeper 'the most vitriolic anti-appeaser in the Foreign Office after Sir Robert Vansittart . . . his closest personal and political colleague', became a focus of opposition to the government's appeasement of Nazi Germany: 'The foreign office news department and the struggle against appeasement', *Historical Research* lxiii (1990), pp. 75.

[49] Taylor, *The projection of Britain*, 243–4.

[50] For British propaganda activity in Portugal during the early war years see ch. 8.

was not however fatal to the alliance's prospects. No matter how many resources the Germans expended in Portugal the British had tradition on their side and their entrenched position could not easily be breached unless they failed to take appropriate consolidatory measures in the economic and military spheres as well as in counter-propaganda. As long as there was some success there propaganda deficiencies could be overcome, and, indeed, in neither the economic nor military spheres were the British neglectful of their opportunities though the problems associated with both often appeared intractable.

At the economic level Britain had for many years past been Portugal's single most important trading partner. This fact, coupled with relatively large British investments in Portugal and the Portuguese empire, had contributed to Portugal's commitment to the British connection. A successful penetration of the Portuguese economy by Germany would naturally threaten Britain's political standing in Portugal. By 1938 it seemed that German traders, including armaments manufacturers, were making increasingly determined efforts to gain a larger share of the Portuguese market. German activity was sufficient to worry the embassy and Arthur King, the commercial secretary, accordingly warned the department of overseas trade in August 1938. In September Selby added his own warning during an interdepartmental meeting at the foreign office and urged 'the necessity of steps being taken without delay to counter the subsidised efforts of other countries, Germany in particular'.[51] Little or no progress had been made in this direction, however, by November 1938 when four related articles appeared in The Economist which focused upon Germany's trade offensive, notably in south-eastern Europe but also in western Europe and south America. It was asserted in the second of these articles that while German progress in the majority of countries of western Europe was slight, Portugal was an exception: there was a definite decline in the British share of the Portuguese market and although Germany's share was no higher in 1937 than in 1929 there had been a considerable increase during 1938.[52]

King thus prepared a memorandum dealing with Britain's trade position as seen from Lisbon. It was admitted that there had been a drop in the United Kingdom export percentage from 20.96 per cent in 1936 to 18.13 per cent in 1937 and to 16.5 per cent for the first nine months of 1938, while the German share had increased from 14.11 per cent in 1936 to 15.05 in 1937 dropping slightly to 14.83 for the first nine months of 1938. The reduction of the British percentage was largely accounted for by the import of German coal into Portugal. There had also been a steady decline in Britain's share of the tin plate market, falling from about four-fifths in 1930 to less than a third in 1937; the main beneficiaries were the United States and Germany. Finally, the import of sulphate of ammonia from the United Kingdom had been affected by cartel arrangements and there had been a marked deterioration in the share of the motor vehicle market in Portugal to the advantage of France and Germany in particular.

In analysing the German economic challenge King advised that German

51 FO 425/415 W15733/152/36; FO 371/22594 W12933/146/36.
52 The Economist, 5 Nov. 1938.

methods of trade, as practised in south-eastern Europe, could not be applied to Portugal where the essential factor, exchange control, was absent. Indeed, the visible trade balance with Germany was adverse to Portugal which was exactly what the Bank of Portugal wanted so as to avoid the possibility of frozen credits in Berlin. Moreover, while Germany used the weapon of export subsidy in her trade with Portugal, King did not believe that this had resulted in any striking success if coal, motor cars and tin plates were excluded. The commercial secretary was therefore taking a reasonably optimistic view although admitting there was room for improvement in certain areas. He was not prepared, however, to accept Salazar's criticism that British enterprise did not compete for 'undertakings of great value'.[53]

The Portuguese nevertheless remained convinced that Britain, unlike Germany, was neglecting opportunities to be involved in important developments in the Portuguese economy. The head of the economics section of the foreign ministry, the condé de Tovar, was particularly critical. He considered British business methods and enterprises in Portugal to be completely out of date and felt that Britain had failed entirely to keep pace with new developments in Portugal or to understand its possibilities and requirements. Since 1918 Britain had done nothing to improve her commercial opportunities or to take advantage, as other powers had done, of the economic requirements of the 'new' Portugal. In particular there had been no British involvement in the electrical development of Portugal, which was completely in the hands of the Germans. Portugal was on the point of developing a great electrical grid system – which incidentally would affect coal importation – and Tovar wondered whether British enterprise would present itself for competition. Portugal had also much to offer Britain in the way of exports: the afforestation programme, for example, meant that she could provide the sleepers for all British railways.[54]

In passing on Tovar's views Selby was forced to admit that electricity in Portugal was completely in the hands of a German company, *Siemens Schuckert*, which had a large and efficient organisation at their disposal. As regards the new grid system, the ambassador explained that a large scheme involving the development of hydraulic power was under consideration by the Portuguese authorities and it seemed that *Siemens Schuckert* might have the advantage over British firms because of their existing organisation in Portugal. The ambassador also expressed certain anxieties regarding Tovar's low opinion of British commercial effort and capacity. Given his important position in the foreign ministry and the possibility that his views might be widely held by other officials, Selby considered it was 'the most serious warning of what we have to contend with on the economic side, not to speak of the political'.[55]

Tovar's criticisms, communicated to the department of overseas trade during February 1939, were rejected outright. To demonstrate that British firms had not neglected opportunities in Portugal, the department referred to the success of the Anglo-Portuguese Telephone Company of Portugal in securing an

---

[53] FO 425/415 W15733/152/36.
[54] FO 371/24068 W1380/594/36.
[55] Ibid. Tovar was later appointed Portuguese ambassador at Berlin where he served from 1941 to 1945.

important five-year contract, with the possibility of renewal for two further periods of five years, for the supply of telephone equipment to the Portuguese posts, telegraphs and telephone service. Marconi Ltd and Standard Telephones and Cables Ltd were presently tendering for the supply of wireless equipment to Angola while Leyland Motors Ltd were tendering for the supply of motor lorries to the Mozambican authorities. No mention was made, however, of any intention on the part of British companies to tender for future electricity contracts.[56] Despite the rather complacent views of the department of overseas trade some members of the British business community in Portugal were anxious to improve Anglo-Portuguese economic relations, notably Sir Alexander Roger, chairman of the Anglo-Portuguese Telephone Company. Indeed, during April 1939 Roger submitted a number of proposals to the Portuguese government which focused upon the type of goods which might be exported to the United Kingdom in increased quantities – port, fish, cork, timber, resin, fruit, garden produce and mineral products – and upon the development of the economic wealth of Portugal and her colonies in such areas as tourism. Salazar's immediate response was to emphasise that the difficulty standing in the way of the development of Anglo-Portuguese trade, and specifically in armaments contracts, was the question of prices, extended credits and the particular methods by which the totalitarian states entered competition. He did, however, promise to have Roger's memorandum examined carefully by the competent authorities.[57]

Roger was clearly anxious to keep conversations on economic relations away from diplomatic channels to avoid giving the Portuguese government the impression that he was trying to exert pressure via the embassy.[58] His attitude was shared by the board of trade which had previously been approached by the foreign office with a request for early assistance in defining government policy. The foreign office believed it was essential for the government to define their policy without delay for upon it depended not only the future of Britain's export trade but also of her political relations with Portugal.[59]

The foreign office request was eventually answered by the department of commercial relations and treaties at the board of trade in May 1939. The department was strongly of the opinion that discussion on Anglo-Portuguese commercial relations should be avoided because the conditions which offered the greatest probability of successful commercial negotiations with any foreign country – the existence of a balance of merchandise trade or of payments substantially adverse to the United Kingdom and/or the existence of tariff or similar concessions which could be offered the other party – did not apply. The board of trade refused to accept that the balance of trade with Portugal was favourable to the United Kingdom and referred to the considerable discrepancy between British and Portuguese trade statistics. According to United Kingdom trade returns there had been a balance of visible trade favourable, since 1935, to

56 FO 371/24068 W3133/594/36.
57 FO 371/24068 W2152/594/36; 371/24069 W7723/594/36.
58 FO 371/24069 W7367/594/36.
59 FO 371/24065 W4193/257/36.

Portugal where trade figures were notoriously defective.[60] The overall balance of payments between the two countries was, on the other hand, to all intents and purposes, in equilibrium. Despite this, the board could see no possibility of obtaining concessions for British exports to Portugal unless and until steps had been taken to increase British purchases of Portuguese products. There were no tariff or other concessions the government could offer which the Portuguese would regard as being of any practical value. The board of trade concluded that private initiative on both sides was the best way forward.[61]

Having examined Roger's proposals the Portuguese authorities came to the same conclusion, Tovar insisting that discussions between the representatives of the various interests concerned should proceed without official intervention.[62] These, however, had made little or no progress by the outbreak of war in September 1939. An entirely new set of circumstances now demanded a radically different approach to Anglo-Portuguese economic relations.[63]

[60] Board of trade figures for United Kingdom trade with Portugal, excluding the colonies, showed balances in favour of Portugal of £726,000, £847,000 and £440,000 in the years 1936, 1937 and 1938, while the Portuguese returns showed balances favourable to the United Kingdom of £1,343,000, £1,524,000 and £1,380,000 respectively: FO 371/24069 W7224/594/36.
[61] FO 371/24069 W8102/594/36.
[62] FO 371/24069 W10215/594/36.
[63] See ch. 8.

4

The Military Dimension

Despite Portuguese criticism of Britain's apparent lack of interest in their country's economic development there was little danger before September 1939 that this would lead to political difficulties between the two allies. In one area, however, a considerable problem had arisen, causing great anxiety in British governing circles. Intense German competition for Portuguese armaments orders threatened the alliance no less than differences over policy towards Spain. Indeed, Anglo-Portuguese military relations between 1936 and 1939 were the touchstone for the alliance as a whole. Failure to co-operate successfully at this level would have been disastrous, not least because the *Estado Novo* owed its existence to the military *coup* of 1926 and likewise its continued support after 1932, as the Lisbon embassy constantly reminded the foreign office. The German and Italian objective of winning Portugal to the Axis side would almost certainly have materialised if Anglo-Portuguese military relations had not been maintained. As early as August 1936, after the outbreak of civil war in Spain, the German legation advised that advantage ought to be taken of increasing pro-German sentiment in Portugal by 'prompt and generous action with regard to participating in the rearmament programme of the Portuguese armed forces'.[1] The foreign office was under no illusions as to the significance of the Portuguese rearmament programme. As Vansittart told Hugh Dalton in June 1937, Germany and Italy were trying to take Britain's place in Portugal. As well as political influence, the supply of arms generally carried with it a supply of manpower, such as trained instructors. If Britain ceased to supply Portugal, her political influence, already much diminished, would vanish altogether.[2] The problem was how to convince the service departments, confronted as they were by Britain's own escalating defence requirements, to release scarce equipment to Portugal.

The rearming of their armed forces was a major priority for the Portuguese during the middle and late 1930s. Budget surpluses had accumulated over a number of years and it was intended that a considerable proportion of these should be used for armaments. In 1938, for example, the budget allocation of £1,818,000 for the ministry of war and £182,000 for the ministry of marine out of a total of £4,373,000 was exceeded only by expenditure on public works. The budget for 1939 projected extraordinary expenditure to the value of £7,213,000 of which the army accounted for no less than £3,636,000 and the navy £318,000; the ministry of works in comparison received an allocation of

1 *DGFP*, D, iii, no. 53, p. 55.
2 Dalton Diaries, Dalton 1.18, diary entry 24 June 1937.

£2,764,000.[3] In addition, there had been a fairly sizeable expenditure on the reconstruction of the Portuguese navy during the middle of the decade. In 1935 alone £1,040,000 was spent in British shipyards, notably Vickers Armstrong and Hawthorn Leslie. By 1937 the reconstructed navy consisted of six flotilla leaders, five destroyers and three submarines with an aggregate tonnage of 20,000 tons.[4]

Having participated in the reconstruction of the Portuguese navy it was to be expected that Britain would also play a leading part in supplying the requirements of the Portuguese army, including military aircraft. However, as events were to demonstrate only too clearly, Britain's ability to supply Portugal's arms requirements was dependent upon the progress of her own rearmament programme. When, at the beginning of September 1936, the Portuguese made a definite enquiry concerning the immediate provision of the latest British artillery for four divisions, the war office returned a discouraging reply which pleaded Britain's own armaments requirements. The only consolation the war office could offer Portugal was a friendly and well-armed British ally.[5] The foreign office recognised that the Portuguese army might as a result turn to Germany for all its material, and that German officers might train Portuguese troops in its use, but they failed to move the war office who remained singularly discouraging. In Lisbon the war office's response cast doubt on Britain's sincerity and this was reinforced when, during January and February 1937, the Birmingham Small Arms Company failed to offer realistic delivery dates for the supply of 80,000 rifles. In the event, the contract went to a German company.[6]

Portuguese scepticism was confirmed at the beginning of April 1937 when Monteiro contrasted the warm welcome which a recent Portuguese military mission had received in France and Germany with the disinterested reception given to it by the United Kingdom. As a demonstration of British interest the ambassador suggested the despatch of a military mission to Portugal to study present conditions and offer advice to the Portuguese military authorities.[7] In view of the evident anxiety of the Portuguese government, and the increased importance which Portugal might be expected to acquire as a result of the Spanish conflict, the foreign office determined to learn the views of the committee of imperial defence as to whether there was any foreseeable strategic advantage in the acceptance of Monteiro's proposal for positive military co-operation between the two countries.[8]

---

[3] T. W. Fernandes, *Portugal's financial reconstruction: Professor Oliveira Salazar's record*, Lisbon 1939.
[4] Derrick, *The Portugal of Salazar*, 144; Secretariado Nacional da Informação, *Portugal*, 58–9. A. Telo, *Portugal na Segunda Guerra*, Lisboa 1987, 96–7. Salazar had authorised the reconstruction of the navy in face of hostile reactions from the army. The decision to favour the navy was taken in 1932 in grateful acknowledgement of the success of a naval expedition, commanded by the navy minister himself, which during 1931 crushed an oppositionist insurgency in the Madeira islands: Wheeler, 'The military and the Portuguese dictatorship', 202–3.
[5] FO 371/20513 W10615/W10870/W10890/933/36; 371/20514 W12632/W13069/W15175/ 933/36; DAPE, i, no. 3, pp. 21–2.
[6] FO 371/20414 W16768/933/36; 371/21272 W2566/W3524/31/36.
[7] FO 371/21269 W4669/25/36.
[8] CAB 24/270 CP 189(37) CID Paper 1336–B (also COS 602).

Initially, the committee of imperial defence adopted a reserved position at its meeting on 15 April. During discussion on the value of Portugal as an ally it was pointed out that she stood only fifth in priority for delivery of war material, behind Egypt, Iraq, Afghanistan and Belgium. The meeting concluded that the foreign office should temporise with Portugal over the question of sending a military mission, while the chiefs of staff produced a detailed report on the strategic value of the alliance.[9] In fact, more than two months elapsed before the chiefs of staff issued their report but its contents were to prove very influential. It stated that the military facilities, existing and potential, which Portugal's territory both at home and abroad would offer to the armed forces of Britain or any other belligerent would prove of considerable value in time of war. The strategic value of the alliance, therefore, lay in the fact that it enabled Britain to make use of those facilities while denying their use to a hostile power. Since the previous reaffirmation in 1927,[10] certain developments in Europe, such as Germany's rearmament, the civil war in Spain and Italy's new attitude had tended to increase the importance of the alliance in relation to naval strategy. If the Spanish Civil War produced a strongly nationalist government similar to that of fascist Italy, it was possible that Gibraltar might be denied to Britain and the passage of her shipping through the straits might be made extremely hazardous. In such circumstances the alternative facilities possessed by Portugal might well prove of great value to the Royal Navy. In addition, it was felt that the use of air facilities on the islands of Madeira, the Azores and Cape Verde would be of considerable value to Britain in trade protection, given that they formed a triangle through which a large percentage of her normal seaborne trade usually passed. While the chiefs of staff believed that Angola and Mozambique were very vulnerable to 'peaceful penetration' by overseas Nazi organisations and that the existence of a strong hostile element in those territories in time of war might prove a considerable embarrassment to Britain and the Union of South Africa, it would hardly constitute a threat to the security of the Union or to Rhodesia. While the alliance lasted, however, the potential danger from German influences in Angola and Mozambique could more easily be counteracted. The chiefs concluded by reiterating the importance of the Portuguese connection to British air and naval strategy and by confirming the view that its maintenance was of great importance.[11]

The report was discussed at length by the committee of imperial defence on 15 July 1937. It was clear that certain members such as Sir John Simon, the chancellor of the exchequer, and General Sir Cyril Deverell had some reservations about sending a military mission. The chief of the imperial general staff, for example, stressed that if a military mission were to be sent it could only act in an advisory capacity and would not be in a position to offer any equipment to Portugal. The majority, however, including Sir Thomas Inskip, minister for co-ordination of defence, Sir Samuel Hoare, home secretary, Lord Swinton, secretary of state for air, Lord Halifax, lord president of the council, and the prime minister, Neville Chamberlain, were clearly impressed by the report and

9 CAB 2/7 292nd mtg.
10 For details see Stone, 'Official British attitude', 733–4.
11 CAB 24/270 CP 189(37).

its conclusions. The committee accordingly advised that in view of the report and the importance of counteracting the growing influence of Germany and Italy on Portugal the despatch of a British military mission was essential. With the strong support of the foreign office and of senior ministers this was approved by cabinet on 21 July.[12]

Early in August, the foreign office received unofficial approval from the Portuguese government for the visit of a British military mission and thereupon urged the appropriate authorities to prepare a plan of the mission's scope, composition and programme.[13] The chiefs of staff advised that the scope of the mission be confined to the establishment of personal contacts with the Portuguese authorities and consideration of how these might best be continued subsequently, for example, by the appointment of service attachés in Lisbon and London and by visits or attachments of Portuguese officers to the United Kingdom. It was also agreed that the mission should study Portuguese defence problems and offer or arrange to provide advice on any question concerning defence and rearmament submitted to them by the authorities in Lisbon. With the urgings of Monteiro in mind, it was considered appropriate for the mission to study the measures which Portugal could take to improve the facilities available for Britain in the joint defence of the two countries for a war in which they were engaged as allies and to obtain any useful information which the Portuguese might be ready to provide.[14] The chiefs of staff were adamant that British defence plans for specific wars should not be discussed and advised that the mission be guided by the principle that 'anything which they say or write to the Portuguese authorities is liable to reach other countries'. It was envisaged that the duration of the mission should be for three months in the first instance.[15] In order to satisfy the anxieties of Eden and Vansittart that there should be no further delays in formally announcing the despatch of the mission the committee of imperial defence was bypassed and the subject remitted straight to cabinet who, on 6 October, approved the recommendations of the chiefs of staff as the basis for instructions to be issued to the mission.[16] Shortly afterwards, Monteiro was provided with a formal communication of the government's intention to send a military mission to Portugal and informed of the British view concerning its scope and duration.[17]

Unfortunately, Salazar was not entirely satisfied. He also wished the mission to study 'the conditions in which the armed forces of the two countries would be employed in the event of their being called upon to co-operate', and in order 'to avoid a one-sided impression' to include some corresponding examination of the existing organisation and equipment of the British army. Moreover, a postponement of the mission's visit until the spring of 1938 was requested because new military laws had recently been adopted in Portugal under which reorganisation was proceeding and a delay of a few months would allow the mission to

12 CAB 2/7 297th mtg; CAB 23/88 CM 31(37).
13 FO 371/21269 W14944/25/36.
14 DAPE, i, no. 37, pp. 82–7.
15 CAB 24/271 CP 233(37) DCOS 48 and COS 625.
16 FO 371/21270 W18366/25/36; CAB 23/89 CM 36(37).
17 DAPE, i, no. 91, pp. 154–6.

study problems in the light of the new conditions. The request for a delay was also influenced by premature leaks in the British press during October 1937, notably in the London *Evening News*, the *News of the World* and the *Daily Telegraph*. Bateman reported that Salazar needed and expected more time to prepare the ground in Lisbon. He was naturally annoyed and embarrassed by the leaks which he was inclined to regard as an attempt to force the pace. His embarrassment had been increased by vehement Italian protests.[18]

After further consultation with the chiefs of staff the foreign office accepted the Portuguese additions and proposed that the mission should reach Portugal in February 1938. Monteiro was informed accordingly on 29 November and Portugal's formal acceptance was received at the end of December.[19] The proposed despatch of the mission represented a significant success for British efforts to counteract Axis influence in Portugal as could be assessed by the latter's unconcealed chagrin. Monteiro told Eden, on 2 December, that Ribbentrop rang him up on the subject six times a day while Grandi had displayed a notable coolness towards him since the mission had been announced. Indeed, Ribbentrop had questioned Eden about the mission on the previous day and received a courteous but firm reply. In similar vein the Portuguese minister in Berlin had been approached by Hermann Göring who reminded Veiga Simões that it was Germany and Italy which had preserved his country against the dangers of the Spanish contagion. Simões replied that while Portugal was sensible of the friendship of Germany and Italy she could not forget that her friendship with Britain dated from 1347. Finally, even Japan revealed irritation at the proposed visit, with Japanese newspapers claiming that its object was to secure Portuguese agreement for Britain's plan to establish air and naval bases in Macao.[20]

Although the announcement of the military mission signalled a success for Britain there was, of course, no guarantee that it would be successful. There were formidable problems, not least Britain's inability to fulfil the requirements of the Portuguese armed forces owing to the heavy demands of national defence, highlighted during 1937 by the unwillingness of the war office to provide unconditionally export licences for Anglo-Portuguese arms contracts.[21] While the war office made some concessions they remained resolutely determined to oppose any requests for armaments which might affect their own defence programme.[22] This vexed the foreign office in view of the Portuguese decision, early in December, to place a substantial order for artillery equipment before the British government. The Portuguese were specifically interested in modern field and anti-aircraft artillery identical to that being manufactured for the British army so that complete standardisation of material between the two

[18] FO 371/21270 W19702/W19839/W20304/25/36; DAPE, i, nos 114, 117, pp. 178–80, 181.
[19] CAB 53/8 222nd mtg., 15 Nov. 1937; DAPE, i, nos 149, 189, pp. 205–6, 246.
[20] FO 371/21350 W22040/W21756/7/41; DDF, 2, vii, no. 314, p. 604; FO 371/21270 W21905/25/36.
[21] FO 371/21273 W10854/31/36; 371/21274 W17221/W18136/W18998/31/36; DAPE, i, no. 66, pp. 125–6. See also Nogueira, *Salazar*, iii. 91–2.
[22] CAB 16/187 conclusions 1st mtg, sub-committee on armaments orders from foreign countries, 15 Oct. 1937; CAB 16/187 FAO 4, 6, 8; FO 371/21274 W19336/W19530/31/36.

countries might be achieved. In communicating the order, Bateman warned Eden that the Portuguese authorities must not be given the impression that the British government was indifferent to the rearmament of the Portuguese army.[23]

While it was clear to the foreign office that a double opportunity had been provided for achieving closer relations with the Portuguese military authorities – the military mission and the willingness of Lisbon to consider the purchase of a large amount of war material common to both the Portuguese and British armies – the beginning of 1938 was hardly the most propitious time, given the increased urgency of strengthening Britain's own defence capabilities. During November and December 1937 a major re-examination of Britain's defence priorities had been undertaken by cabinet and the committee of imperial defence which culminated in cabinet endorsement for a reappraisal of defence priorities. The two most important priorities were the protection of the United Kingdom against attack and the preservation of the trade routes on which the country depended for essential imports of food and raw materials. The third was the maintenance of forces for the defence of British territories overseas against attack. The fourth, and lowest, priority was co-operation in defence of the territories of any allies Britain might have in war. In the light of chiefs of staff observations it was also recognised that it was essential 'to reduce the number of our potential enemies and to gain the support of potential allies'. However, placing the continental commitment in the lowest priority would naturally make it more difficult for the foreign office to achieve the support of potential allies. Thus Eden had stressed the need 'to draw into closer relationship with us those smaller states whose assistance in time of war would not be negligible, but whose support to the other side might be disastrous'. The foreign secretary had in mind Portugal, Greece, Turkey, Yugoslavia, Roumania and Poland.[24] For the Portuguese the continuation of limited liability meant that there could be no guarantee of armed British assistance on land should the civil war in Spain escalate into an Iberian-wide conflict, a possibility which was never discounted in Lisbon. Britain's inability to offer such assistance, while at the same time revealing a disinclination to denude the existing and potential stock of weaponry in the short term, presented the military mission with an extremely difficult task.

The mission arrived in Portugal towards the end of February 1938 and was preceded by the visit of fourteen units of the British home fleet, the largest number of warships to visit Lisbon since 1931.[25] The naval demonstration was intended to counteract the smaller German naval visit headed by the battleship *Deutschland* and to prepare the way for the arrival of the mission. On 17 February, shortly before its departure, the head of the mission, Rear Admiral

[23] FO 371/21275 W22294/31/36.
[24] For details of this re-examination see CAB 23/90 CM 46(37) and CM 49(37), 8, 22 Dec. 1937; CAB 24/273 CP 316(37); and CAB 2/7 303rd mtg, 1 Dec. 1937. For the chiefs of staff views and those of Eden and the foreign office see *DBFP*, 2, xix, nos 316, 348, pp. 501–13, 578. See also B. Bond, *British military policy between the two world wars*, Oxford 1980, 257–9; N. H. Gibbs, *Grand Strategy*, I: *Rearmament policy*, London 1976, 466–72.
[25] *The Times*, 28 Jan., 2 Feb. 1938. For details of the visit see also W. Selby, *Diplomatic twilight*, London 1953, 91–3.

Norman Atherton Wodehouse, was received by King George VI; according to the foreign office library there was only one precedent, the visit of Sir Maurice de Bunsen and his special mission to South America in 1918.[26] Assistance was also forthcoming from the United States naval attaché in Lisbon and from the French government: Leroy provided regular reports for it on the activities of the mission in Portugal, and it was in fact discussed by the French army staff during April 1938.[27]

The mission nevertheless arrived in Portugal under a very heavy political cloud. Shortly before its arrival considerable apprehension was expressed in Portuguese circles concerning developments in central Europe with *Anschluss* increasingly inevitable. Even the *Diário de Notícias* argued, in a leader of 18 February, that to all intents and purposes Germany had won military hegemony in Europe and all the newspapers agreed that it would be well for Portugal 'to recognise facts'. The director of the Portuguese propaganda department advised the Reuters' correspondent, on 17 February, that it was useless 'to go on backing the lost cause of Great Britain'. Portuguese anxieties were increased further by the British cabinet crisis which resulted in Eden's resignation on 19 February, by Hitler's speech the following day which heralded a further step towards the *Anschluss* and by German recognition of Manchukuo.[28] Finally, during early February the embassy had warned of the intensification of German efforts in Lisbon to obtain the entire artillery order.[29]

As anticipated by Sir Maurice Hankey, secretary to the cabinet and chairman of the deputy chiefs of staff committee, it soon became apparent to the mission that the Portuguese authorities were alarmed at the prospect of their extreme vulnerability to a land attack during the long period which they feared might elapse between the placing of orders in Britain and the actual deliveries. Admiral Wodehouse understood from his Portuguese opposite number, General Tasso de Miranda Cabral, that a statement by the British government assuring Portugal that the whole weight of their influence and other available resources would be brought to bear in the event of an attack, or real threat of attack, during such a period would remove the present hesitation to rely solely on British armaments.[30] The suggestion of a specific British guarantee was given added credence and significance on 15 March when Wodehouse received a message from Fernando Santos Costa, Portuguese under secretary for war, to the effect that if an exchange of notes could be arranged all his difficulties would be removed and all contracts for armaments and ammunition of calibres larger than rifles and light machine guns would be placed in Britain. The significance

26 FO 371/22592 W2144/146/36.
27 AIR 40/1828; *DDF*, 2, viii, no. 519, pp. 949–50; ix, nos 100, 137, 153, 173, 219, pp. 191–4, 280–1, 315–17, 354–5, 459–61; x, nos 3, 203, pp. 4, 371–2.
28 FO 371/22592 W2389/W2461/146/36; Selby, *Diplomatic twilight*, 96–7. For the context of Hitler's speech see Weinberg, *The foreign policy of Hitler's Germany*, ii. 292–3; J. P. Fox, *Germany and the far eastern crisis 1931–1938: a study in diplomacy and ideology*, Oxford 1982, 298–304.
29 FO 371/22589 W1896/W1944/W2585/75/36.
30 FO 371/22589 W3319/W3332/75/36. For Hankey's views see Avon Papers, AP 13/1/63A.

of this communication was not lost on either the admiral or Selby; not least because of Costa's known pro-Axis views.[31]

The foreign office recognised the significance of recent communications from the Lisbon embassy. It was felt that if the artillery order was placed in the United Kingdom it would ensure not only that the Portuguese army would be armed with material similar to their own but that similar contracts would follow; the political importance of preventing the order from going to Germany was self-evident. These points had been fully appreciated by the committee of imperial defence sub-committee on armaments orders for foreign countries when they discussed the question in January, and agreed to authorise Vickers to continue negotiations with the Portuguese with a view to the eventual conclusion of the contract.[32] The foreign office believed that the proposed assurance would allay Portuguese anxieties concerning their future relations with Spain whatever the outcome of the civil war. Moreover, there was good reason to suppose that British interests in Spain might suffer very seriously and, in view of future possibilities, there was every advantage in making it clear – to the world in general and to the victorious Spanish administration in particular – that Britain was strengthening in every way the ties of her alliance with Spain's co-partner in the Iberian Peninsula.

From the legal point of view the foreign office was convinced that Britain had gained no real advantage from the qualifications given in the house of commons with regard to the Anglo-Portuguese treaties through the use of statements such as 'His Majesty's Government reserve to themselves the right to determine the circumstances in which help might be given or withheld'. It was natural for the Portuguese and others to interpret this as meaning that although Britain was in fact bound to go to Portugal's assistance by treaty the government should reserve their right when the time came to decide whether they should fulfil their obligations. Apart from the obvious cynicism about treaty obligations, which was not in accordance with the government's usual attitude, it could be seriously suggested that to make statements of this kind was emphatically to get the worst of every possible world. In effect, the government could provide the necessary assurances without increasing legal obligations by simply reaffirming its existing obligation to provide armed assistance, arising out of the ancient alliance and devoid of the previous ambiguous additions, and by openly placing their obligations to Portugal under the alliance on the same footing as those to Egypt and Iraq.[33]

The urgent need for a breakthrough in the growing impasse in Anglo-Portuguese military relations by means of a positive revision of the treaty obligations was demonstrated the very same day the foreign office presented their arguments to the committee of imperial defence. The sub-committee on armaments orders from foreign countries, having previously been instructed by cabinet to discuss the question, regretfully concluded that commencement of delivery to the Portuguese could not be approved before 1940 without the certainty of very grave damage to the defence programme, in particular to

[31] FO 371/22589 W3418/75/36. For Costa's career see Gallagher, *Portugal*, 105–7.
[32] For details of this meeting see CAB 16/187 FAO 2nd mtg, 19 Jan. 1938.
[33] CAB 16/143 DPR 259 (CID); CAB 24/276 CP 78(38); FO 371/22589 W3332/75/36.

admiralty gun requirements and field artillery.[34] In view of the urgency, and following the advice of the committee of imperial defence, Chamberlain, on 29 March, authorised the foreign office to propose an exchange of notes, along the lines suggested by General Cabral, to the Portuguese authorities.[35]

Salazar, however, rejected the proposal for an exchange of notes on the grounds that it would do nothing to protect his country against a sudden land attack. Given the archaic condition of the Portuguese army it was essential, at least in the short term, to acquire modern equipment for instructional purposes and for arming his covering troops; and the delay inherent in the British arrangements was incompatible with the present situation in the Iberian Peninsula. Although he admitted that British material was desirable for the sake of uniformity and because the United Kingdom would be the only safe source of supply in war, Salazar warned Selby that he had been offered modern artillery by a third power (presumably Germany) on attractive terms, although so far he had refused.[36]

The new foreign secretary, Lord Halifax, refused to accept the inevitability of Germany securing the entire artillery contract, but the position was far from promising. At the beginning of May Selby failed to convince Salazar of the benefits of Britain's own rearmament programme and the deterrent effect of the Royal Navy in the event of any future Spanish action. At the same time, the chiefs of staff doubted whether Salazar could be kept out of Germany's orbit by merely supplying token equipment which would be inadequate for his needs, and which, in any case, could not be provided before 1939 at the earliest – and then only if a slower rate of delivery could be accepted for Britain's own forces and also for those of India, Egypt and the Dominions. Despite these reservations, which were shared by the treasury, Halifax and Inskip were agreed in principle on the need to provide token equipment and their view in the matter was endorsed on 11 May by cabinet after a lengthy discussion, and with the proviso that nothing could be supplied before 1939. The Portuguese were informed of cabinet's decision on 27 May.[37]

In view of Portuguese anxieties concerning future Spanish policy and the urgent need to advance their rearmament programme the concession of token deliveries was hardly likely to affect German efforts to secure the entire artillery order. In a very real sense, as Wodehouse recognised, the government had reached an impasse. While they could not provide arms of the latest type quickly enough to satisfy Salazar's urgent requirements at a low enough price they were also unable to persuade him that his requirements were not as urgent as he thought; and the problem was compounded by the reluctance of the British authorities to press Salazar or put their case frankly to him.

34 CAB 16/143 DPR 260; CAB 24/276 CP 78(38); CAB23/93 CM 14(38), 11 Mar. 1938.
35 CAB 2/7 314th mtg, 24 Mar. 1938; CAB 24/276 CP 78(38); CAB 23/93 CM 17(38), 30 Mar. 1938; FO 371/22590 W4148/W4203/75/36. See also The private papers of Hore-Belisha, ed. R. J. Minney, London 1960, 155; Nogueira, Salazar, iii. 153.
36 FO 371/22590 W4203/W4522/W4782/75/36; DAPE, i, nos 259, 260, pp. 334–7.
37 CAB 16/143 DPR 267 (COS 717); CAB 24/276 CP 113(38); CAB 23/93 CM 23 (38); FO 371/22590 W4524/W4782/W5681/W75/36 and W6167/W6225/W7075/75/36; T 161/989/S41910/1; DAPE, i, nos 274, 283, 301, pp. 354–5, 360–2, 374.

Wodehouse was convinced that while Salazar was quite capable of playing Britain, Germany and Italy off against each other to achieve increasingly favourable terms for the artillery contract his position in Portugal would be shaken if it were thought that such a policy might lead to the abandonment or even the weakening of the alliance. Pressure should therefore be exerted to persuade him to agree to the British proposals. To sugar the pill Wodehouse recommended that air support be offered in the event of Portugal becoming a theatre of operations in war. This would go some way towards reassuring Lisbon, would provide the government with some reason for insisting on the construction of such air bases as they might require, and would possibly help persuade the Portuguese to buy the same type of aircraft as were in use in the Royal Air Force.[38]

Selby, however, did not believe coercion would work and he remained convinced that the present strategy of careful and considered persuasion was appreciated by the Portuguese dictator. At a meeting of the committee of imperial defence on 30 June, Halifax made it clear that the foreign office was in general agreement with the ambassador's view. The committee agreed that nothing should be said which might tend to alienate Salazar. They also supported Hankey's suggestion, that if Portugal could not wait for British armaments she should be encouraged, from the international point of view, to place her orders with Italy rather than with Germany. Halifax was also invited to satisfy himself that every possible argument had been used to convince the Portuguese prime minister of the improbability of any attack upon Portugal; of the overwhelming support, particularly in sea power, which he would receive by virtue of the alliance; and to explain the unenviable position which would confront his government if, having rearmed with German weapons, their country were to be attacked by Spain supported by Germany. No specific recommendation was made on the question of British air support although the service chiefs revealed deep reservations.[39]

The recommendations of the committee of imperial defence were considered by cabinet on 6 July. A decision was, however, postponed to allow circulation of the report of General von Reichenau's lecture at Leipzig, which had seriously disturbed the service departments.[40] At the same time, cabinet amended the committee's preference by broadening their recommendation to include countries other than Italy, notably Sweden.[41] Inskip convened an urgent meeting of the chiefs of staff committee before the next meeting of cabinet. It was generally agreed that nothing had happened since its positive valuation of the Portuguese alliance in July 1937 to alter its conclusions. In fact, the naval staff representatives reinforced them by emphasising that if the Mediterranean were closed to the British in time of war and their trade to India and the far east had to be routed via the Cape, Portugal and her possessions would assume an added

[38] FO 371/22593 W7662/146/36. See also CAB 4/27 CID paper 1440–B.
[39] CAB 2/7 328th mtg.
[40] According to Minney, Hore-Belisha made a note of the lecture and in the margins of his copy marked passages with a red line and a cross thereby confirming how seriously he viewed it: Hore-Belisha, 157–8.
[41] CAB 23/94 CM 31(38).

strategic importance. The chiefs insisted that it was not possible to help Portugal with land forces but, provided circumstances at home permitted, they should be prepared to assist Portugal with air forces in time of war. In reporting to cabinet Inskip emphasised that such an offer would not only benefit Portugal but might also fit in with their own requirements since the air forces based in Portugal could operate as a counter to the activities of air forces (Spanish, German and Italian) operating from bases in Spanish territory against Gibraltar or British shipping. In view of the great importance attached by the chiefs of staff to the maintenance of the alliance, Inskip recommended the concession of deferred payments.[42]

On 13 July cabinet endorsed the proposed air support for Portugal, Britain's own defensive situation permitting, and authorised Selby, in the event of a favourable reaction by Salazar, to raise the subject, and the provision of air facilities in Portugal for Britain's own air forces, with the Portuguese military authorities.[43] The ambassador, however, advised postponement. He felt the offer of air assistance would have little value for the Portuguese who already thought it was implicit in the treaty of alliance. The military mission agreed on the grounds that their work had taken a definite turn for the better, as indicated by a promise from the Portuguese military authorities to construct an air base in southern Portugal as soon as the British government had selected a site. The impression given was that this base was to be primarily for use by British air forces if required in war.[44] As a further sign of improvement Salazar expressed a readiness at the beginning of August 1938 to consider a reaffirmation of the alliance because the treaties were 'rather antiquated and there would be every advantage in a discussion of their terms with a view to ascertaining whether they met existing conditions'. At the same time he intimated that before such a discussion could take place it was essential that the two governments should have before them the reports of the military missions. He understood that the British mission would suspend its work in Portugal from 12 August onwards to enable the senior members to consult in London.[45]

The report of the British military mssion was completed during September 1938 and raised a number of salient issues with regard to Anglo-Portuguese military relations. The authors were particularly anxious to emphasise the real danger which could arise if the United Kingdom should appear to treat Portugal's fear of aggression too lightly. For the Portuguese the fear was very real and pressing. Their country had been forced by its proximity to the civil war to take note of the forces which Spain could put into the field and of the quantity of armaments the Spaniards had acquired, and to realise their own inadequate defence. British offers of naval support had not proved convincing and the Portuguese were only too aware of the benefits which Britain would derive from having the use of Lisbon and the Atlantic islands in the event of war, with Spain hostile and the probability that Gibraltar would become untenable as a naval base; and in this last eventuality the credibility of Britain as a sea power

42 CAB 24/277 CP 164(38).
43 CAB 23/94 CM 32(38).
44 CAB 4/28 CID paper 1474–B (COS 778); FO 371/22594 W10237/146/36.
45 FO 371/22594 W10873/146/36.

would itself be seriously weakened. As far as the Portuguese rearmament pro-gramme was concerned they had stressed that Portugal could not afford to pay the full market price for all the war material she required, and they considered that assistance in this respect was one of the means by which Britain could and should repay Portugal for the strategic advantages and facilities which the alliance afforded. The mission was advised that the sooner the question of armaments was handled at a governmental level the better, since the agents of Vickers were at a disadvantage: German and Italian armaments representatives negotiated with the full backing of their respective governments. Finally, it was clear that the Portuguese expected the British mission to resume its work in Portugal in October in the expectation of something more tangible than dis-cussions.

The mission therefore concluded that in order to ensure the maintenance of the alliance it would be necessary to provide political, financial and military assistance to Portugal (though not armed assistance on land), at least in the earliest phase of a possible war. Moreover, while accepting that the degree to which such help should be given formed no part of the mission's brief they offered a number of recommendations. In view of Salazar's readiness to consider changes in the alliance, it was suggested that negotiations should be entered into in order to define clearly the application of the existing treaties in specific cases, or alternatively to arrange for a revision of the treaties to make them conform to modern conditions. Meanwhile an assurance should be given that timely diplomatic action would be taken by Britain in the event of any threat from Spain. The mission advised that a decision should be reached as to the forms of assistance which could be offered to Portugal, and that in view of the low standard of training which existed in all branches of the Portuguese defence forces, and the possibility that these forces would need to co-operate and collaborate with British forces in war, the Portuguese government should be encouraged to send missions to study in the United Kingdom. It was felt that serious consideration should be given to the question of affording financial assistance to Portugal and it was recommended that the mission, as constituted, should resume its work in Portugal at an early date.[46]

In evaluating the report early in October the chiefs of staff re-emphasised the strategic importance which they attached to the maintenance of the Anglo-Portuguese alliance, which events in central Europe in September 1938 served only to reinforce. For the most part they endorsed the mission's recommenda-tions. They favoured a revision of the treaties and accepted that an assurance of diplomatic support was the natural corollary to the considerable strategic im-portance Britain attached to the alliance. The chiefs also emphasised that Britain's naval dispositions would secure Portugal and her overseas possessions from seaborne attack. At the same time, they appreciated that the Portuguese authorities had been disillusioned as to any expectation of assistance by British land forces in the opening phases of a war against Germany. Air support, however, was recommended and the chiefs of staff made reference to the instructions given to Selby following cabinet's decision of 13 July. They

[46] CAB 4/28 CID paper 1474–B (COS 778).

71

welcomed the mission's success in persuading a very reluctant Portuguese government to reject a strategy for the total defence of Portugal and to concentrate instead upon the defence of Lisbon from sea, land and air attack and the defence of the Atlantic islands from sea and air raids. In their view the defence of Lisbon was all important and should have absolute priority, and in any further negotiations they felt no opportunity should be lost of impressing this policy on the Portuguese authorities. The chiefs of staff agreed that Portuguese missions should be encouraged to visit Britain. Although they knew cabinet had ruled against departing from the ordinary rules of finance in dealing with the Portuguese, the chiefs of staff considered that 'in view of the strategic importance to us of a friendly and independent, if not actively allied, Portugal in time of war' the question of assisting Portugal in some way merited re-examination. From this point of view they ranked the importance of Portugal 'certainly as high as that of Turkey, for whom we have recently floated a loan on favourable terms'.[47]

The Lisbon embassy strenuously urged acceptance of these recommendations in order to arrest the decline in pro-British sentiment and to rally the many elements in Portugal who still remained faithful to the alliance. It was particularly important to recognise the tremendous pressure which was being exerted on Salazar himself. Selby reported that he faced strong criticism that his policy during the Czech crisis had not been sufficiently clear; powerful influences which favoured an orientation towards Germany and away from Britain were at work on the Portuguese leader. He was also criticised for leaving Portugal unarmed. It was widely believed during the Czech crisis that in the event of war Italian divisions as well as German war planes would have been over the Hispano-Portuguese frontier. The army admitted that it could not have put up any sort of resistance and blamed Salazar for the delay in rearmament, while others blamed Britain for not having been more helpful.[48]

The need for urgency was recognised in London. Accordingly, on 20 October, the committee of imperial defence approved the return of the mission to Portugal for a period of four to five weeks provided this was agreeable to the Portuguese. Meanwhile the foreign office proceeded to examine the advisability of revising the existing treaties and to offer the assurance that Britain would take the appropriate diplomatic action if Portugal was threatened by Spain or another power. Despite the reservations of Sir John Simon, the chancellor of the exchequer, the committee of imperial defence also agreed that the service departments, in consultation with the treasury, should examine the possibility of influencing British armaments firms to supply Portuguese requirements on the same financial terms as they gave to government orders. Largely at the insistence of the treasury it was also agreed that, in view of the difficulty of reaching a decision on applications for assistance from particular countries including Portugal, the chiefs of staff should review the relative strategic importance of all the countries which had already asked for, or were likely in the future to seek to obtain, arms or financial assistance in regard to arms from the

47 Ibid.
48 FO 371/22594 W14020/W13847/146/36.

United Kingdom.[49] The committee also acknowledged the observation of the chiefs of staff concerning the relative viability of British land and sea assistance to Portugal.[50] On 28 October Selby informed the Portuguese authorities of foreign office actions with regard to treaty revision and the offer of British diplomatic support, and of the government's readiness to support the recommendations of the chiefs of staff: that while they could offer no support by land forces in the opening phases of a war against Germany they would be prepared, unless the circumstances of their defensive situation should preclude such action, to assist Portugal with air forces in addition to naval forces in fulfilment of their treaty obligations. In addition, the government was prepared to consider the question of financial assistance for the purchase of armaments in the United Kingdom.[51]

Several months were to elapse before the foreign office completed its deliberations and, likewise, little progress was made before February 1939 in armaments negotiations between London and Lisbon. During this time, however, the government completed a serious appraisal of its capacity to fulfil arms orders to foreign countries. As well as from Portugal, Egypt, Iraq, India and the Dominions, the British authorities had received requests to purchase arms from Turkey, Greece, Belgium, Holland, Yugoslavia, Roumania, Hungary, Bulgaria, Saudi Arabia, Afghanistan and China. Most of these countries had also asked for financial assistance. At the same time, there was a clear recognition of Germany's willingness and ability to supply armaments as a means of gaining political and diplomatic advantage. In a memorandum prepared in February 1938, which at the behest of the foreign office was placed before the committee of imperial defence in April, the industrial intelligence committee of the department of overseas trade had emphasised the tremendous benefits the Germans derived from the mass production of armaments, in terms of relatively low prices and the capacity to supply, and had pointed to the important role of the Reich government in providing special facilities and encouragement to manufacturers and dealers.[52]

It was subsequently confirmed at the highest levels that it was not possible to imitate the German system of production in its entirety. Discussion therefore concentrated on the feasibility of adopting or adapting some of the methods of German industry to achieve a greater measure of war preparedness in the United Kingdom and to improve the position of the export trade. As a result, towards the end of July, Inskip was required to consult with the relevant departments.[53] However, when discussion on the general question of armaments exports was resumed within the committee of imperial defence at the beginning of December 1938 it was clear that a full examination of the problem

[49] For treasury views see T 161/989/S41910/2.
[50] CAB 2/8 334th mtg.
[51] DAPE, ii, no. 439, pp. 45–6.
[52] CAB 4/27 CID 1426–B; CAB 24/276 CP 117(38). See also W. K. Wark, 'British intelligence on the German air force and aircraft industry, 1933–1939', Historical Journal xxv (1982), 644.
[53] CAB 2/7 322nd and 330th mtgs, 12 May and 21 July 1938; CAB 23/93 CM 24(38), 18 May 1938.

had still not been undertaken. On the other hand, in line with the decision of 20 October, the chiefs of staff had produced a review of the relative strategic position of those countries which had applied for armaments from the United Kingdom. This placed Belgium and Holland as the joint first priority, Egypt second, Portugal and Turkey equal third, followed in order of importance by Iraq, Greece, Saudi Arabia, Afghanistan, Yugoslavia, Roumania, Bulgaria and Hungary.[54] The committee of imperial defence approved the review and invited Inskip, in consultation with the three service ministers and their advisers, to examine 'the practicability of increasing manufacturing capacity for certain armaments with a view to building up a greater war potential while placing the Government in a position to supply foreign countries'.[55] Subsequent investigation revealed the principal items involved were aircraft, anti-aircraft guns and artillery equipment and armour. While the position in the short term for aircraft was reasonably optimistic, that for anti-aircraft guns and artillery was not since these could only be supplied from new capacity as yet at the development stage.[56] Although for the time being there was little that could be done to meet the demand for arms from foreign countries the government was prepared to help a number of countries under the new Export Credits Act. After consultation between the treasury, foreign office and board of trade China was allocated £3 million, Greece £2 million, Portugal, Egypt and Roumania £1 million, Iraq £500,000, Afghanistan £250,000 and Iran and Saudi Arabia £250,000 with £1 million in reserve.[57]

By the beginning of 1939 prospects for Anglo-Portuguese military relations appeared more favourable than twelve months previously. Shortly before the military mission had taken its final leave of Portugal in mid-December the reclusive Dr Salazar had made a number of 'most cordial' references to its work and expressed the hope that the visit should be regarded as a 'beginning of intimacy between the two armies'.[58] Furthermore, the government had confirmed the importance they attached to improved military relations by sanctioning the appointment of permanent service attachés to the Lisbon embassy,[59] and Group Captain Field, the air attaché, had succeeded in persuading the air staff to sanction the release of thirty Gladiators for the following April.[60] These hopeful signs were apparently reinforced on 6 February 1939 when the foreign office received official Portuguese acknowledgement of the great importance which was attached to the declaration that the British government was now ready to assist the defence of Portugal by naval, land and air forces. The Portuguese authorities were determined to pursue as far as they could the policy of military defence recommended by the British military mission, concentrating

---

54 CAB 16/187 FAO 16 CID paper 1488–8 (COS 800).
55 CAB2/8 340th mtg, 1 Dec. 1938.
56 CAB 24/281 CP 289(38).
57 CAB 24/282 CP 1(39); CAB 23/94 CM 1(39), 18 Jan. 1939.
58 FO 37122595 W16797/146/36. See also *DDF*, 2, xiii, no. 164, pp. 318–19.
59 The foreign office, urged by the Lisbon embassy, had been pressing for the appointment of permanent service attachés since 1936 partly to provide expert advice on the spot in relation to the various armaments contracts. See FO 371/21269 W9033/W12160/W12233/25/36.
60 See FO 371/22591 W13714/W14478/W14550/75/36; W15717/W15764/W16017/75/36.

on the defence of Lisbon. The Portuguese also registered their appreciation of the British offer of financial facilities for the purchase of arms in the United Kingdom.[61] It was therefore a fearful shock to learn on the very same day that the Portuguese military intended, for technical reasons, to award the contracts for 80mm anti-aircraft guns to Germany, for 40mm anti-aircraft guns to Sweden and for light field artillery to Germany and Italy: the latter to provide 75mm guns while the former supplied 105mm guns. Moreover, it was anticipated that the contract for mountain artillery would go to Italy as the British army pattern was too heavy and the Vickers gun too expensive.[62]

The significance of the Portuguese decision, taken on the advice of technical experts, was all too obvious. While continuing to affirm their allegiance to the alliance the Portuguese intended to purchase the bulk of their military equipment from their ally's greatest potential enemies thereby imperilling effective military co-operation in certain foreseeable contingencies.[63] Halifax immediately recognised the danger. He was adamant that Germany must be prevented from acquiring any of the artillery contracts even if it meant some other country such as Italy or Sweden, or possibly the United States taking them over.[64] The service departments were also prepared to exhort British firms to supply the Portuguese at the same sort of prices charged to Britain's armed forces. There was a glimmer of hope that Portugal might change her mind: on 18 February Salazar announced his intention to purchase fifteen Gladiators and fifteen Spitfires, and on 3 March he told Selby that the artillery order had not been finalised.[65] However, the relatively weak bargaining position of British armaments firms remained a serious obstacle. The embassy was firmly reminded of this by the condé de Tovar on 3 March when he emphasised both Salazar's desire to keep expenditure to a minimum and Germany's willingness to consider the sale of armaments partly on a cash basis and partly in Portuguese exports to the benefit of Portugal's producers and the country's standard of living. Selby therefore advised that if Britain still hoped to secure a large share of the armaments order there was no alternative to subsidising British firms.[66]

The position was further complicated by a division of opinion on the order in which the Portuguese order should be supplied. In addition to the artillery contract Vickers were tendering to supply three submarines to the Portuguese navy. On 21 March at a meeting of the committee on special guarantees, chaired by Sir Frederick Leith Ross, the admiralty asked that the submarines be included within the tender covered by the £1 million export guarantee allocated to Portugal, while the war office were anxious that the anti-aircraft guns be included as they considered them essential to keeping the Portuguese ports open. The foreign office wished to give high priority to the field artillery order in view of German competition. In the event, the war office and admiralty

[61] FO 371/24063 W2115/160/36; DAPE, ii, no. 536, pp. 147–8.
[62] FO 371/24065 W2116/W2118/257/36; Nogueira, Salazar, iii. 206.
[63] FO 371/24065 W2140/257/36.
[64] FO 371/24065 W2192/257/36.
[65] CAB 2/8 347th mtg, 16 Feb. 1939; CAB 4/29 CID paper 1525–B; FO 371/24065 W2996/W3112/W3268/W4113/257/36.
[66] FO 371/24065 W3268/W4079/257/36; 371/24068 W4828/594/36.

accepted the foreign office view and placed the anti-aircraft guns first, then the field artillery and then submarines.[67] It was clear, however, that the war office had only reluctantly placed the field artillery order in second place for on 23 March the foreign office was informed of their anxieties that it would absorb Vickers' capacity for foreign orders for a considerable period of time whereas the submarine order would affect neither the anti-aircraft nor field gun capacity in any way. As a result the war office suggested placing the field artillery contract on a par with the submarines in the order of preference. To complicate matters further, Vickers expressed a clear preference for the submarines contract on 29 March, only to be told by the foreign office that they must maintain the order of preference previously agreed.[68] Vickers were most reluctant to do this, informing the foreign office on 5 April that the Portuguese government could hardly be expected to interest itself in the British offer for artillery since the actual delivery date would be delayed for a period of at least two years. Vickers were strongly supported by the admiralty who considered the submarine contract to be more viable than the one for artillery.[69]

Meanwhile, the government was receiving ever increasing requests for armaments from a growing number of European countries, principally France, Poland, Greece and Roumania, while Turkey continued to make heavy demands. In all cases, including Portugal, the conclusion was the same: the material demanded could be released only at the expense of Britain's own requirements. Although the committee of imperial defence invited the service departments on 20 April 'to continue to make every effort to meet demands for armaments from foreign countries who are allies or potential allies of this country', it was obvious that a firm order of priority amongst potential customers would have to be established.[70] In view of the changed European situation following the 'January crisis', the German entry into Prague and the British guarantee to Poland during March 1939, the foreign office questioned whether Portugal's demands for military equipment still retained some priority in the calculations of the British military authorities. It transpired that the war office was unable to guarantee even token deliveries during the remainder of 1939.[71] This was particularly frustrating for the foreign office given Salazar's reaffirmation of Portugal's loyalty to the alliance in a major speech to the Portuguese national assembly on 22 May, sentiments which evoked a personal and appreciative response from Neville Chamberlain.[72] Despite further attempts the foreign office failed to move the war office during June 1939. Indeed, Major General Sir Henry Pownall told Mounsey on 16 June that no offer could be made at all for field artillery since there was not a single new 25 pounder equipment in existence, while the position in relation to anti-aircraft guns was so bad that the war office was unable to meet the increased

---

67 FO 371/24065 W4901/257/36.
68 FO 371/24065 W5292/W5387/257/36.
69 FO 371/24065 W5949/W5950/257/36.
70 CAB 2/8 353rd mtg; CAB 4/29 CID paper 1547–B.
71 FO 371/24066 W7206/257/36.
72 For details od Salazar's speech see his *Doctrine and action*, 379–93. For Chamberlain's response see *The Times*, 27 May 1939.

requirements for British-held ports in the Mediterranean before August 1940. The director of military operations and intelligence also admitted that although several months had elapsed since the committee of imperial defence had made its recommendations, the question of Portugal being permitted to purchase equipment through the war office at British army prices was still under consideration.[73]

By mid-June the escalating demands of several foreign countries for British armaments compelled a reconsideration of the list of countries in order of strategic importance approved by the committee of imperial defence on 1 December 1938, and a further list of April 1939 which included both political and strategic considerations. In the second list Egypt had been assigned first place with Iraq second, followed in order of preference by Belgium, Portugal, Turkey, Greece, Netherlands, Roumania, Poland, Yugoslavia and Afghanistan. In the light of subsequent developments in Europe and purely on political grounds extensive amendments were made by the foreign office during June 1939 with Poland promoted to first place, Egypt second, Turkey third and Roumania fourth. Iraq was demoted to fifth place and Portugal to sixth followed in order of preference by Greece, Belgium, Yugoslavia, Bulgaria and the Netherlands.[74] Strictly in terms of financial assistance Halifax advised cabinet, on 21 June, to consider a slightly modified version:

> These four countries – Poland, Turkey, Greece and Roumania – he would place in the first category. The second category would consist of Portugal, Egypt and Iraq – countries allied to us but less immediately threatened. The third category would consist of countries such as Yugoslavia and Bulgaria and perhaps Spain, which were wavering between the Rome–Berlin axis and the democratic countries, but which might turn in the right direction if given suitable help. The fourth category would include Afghanistan and Saudi Arabia – countries which were unlikely to join the enemy, but which, for various reasons, we would wish to support.[75]

In addition to political evaluations strategic considerations were also fully explored during the first part of July by the deputy chiefs of staff who, having established a 'rough general order of priority', for the first time included a priority order for the three separate categories of land (including anti-aircraft), sea and air armaments. In arriving at their final order the deputy chiefs took into account the purely strategic factors of the broad strategy of the conduct of the war, the fighting value of the forces of the particular countries and the value of a country to Great Britain in so far as it could deny facilities to the enemy. Within this comprehensive appraisal Portugal figured as fourth in priority for naval armaments, sixth for land armaments, eighth for air armaments and seventh overall. The deputy chiefs recognised that the attitude of Franco's Spain might have far reaching effects on the course of a European war: if Gibraltar were denied to Britain by hostile action from Spain the use of

[73] FO 371/24066 W9501/257/36.
[74] CAB 16/219 AD 4.
[75] CAB 23/100 CM 33(39).

Portuguese bases might be required. The use of these bases, of those in the Portuguese Atlantic islands and their denial to a potential enemy was at all times important. They concluded, therefore, that it was of high strategic importance to Britain that Portugal should be in a position to defend herself from invasion by Spain and from seaborne and air attack. Portugal was not placed higher in the list because of the known 'low military value of her forces'.[76]

The defence of Portugal was not only a pressing matter for the Portuguese military authorities it was also a British obligation under the treaties of alliance which had been the object of further foreign office scrutiny. Discussion in the foreign office, and in the committee of imperial defence, centred upon the nature of the assistance which should be given once it was recognised that the *casus foederis* had arisen. In this respect it was felt that any new treaty of alliance with Portugal should include a clause to the effect that should either party become engaged in war the other would come to its aid in the capacity of an ally. Without such a clause the alliance could not be invoked in the event, for instance, of His Majesty's Government going to the assistance of a third power which had been attacked by a fourth. At the same time, it was recognised that Portugal's agreement to the insertion of such a clause would entail fresh commitments which Salazar would be unwilling to accept in the current circumstances. Selby was accordingly instructed, on 31 March, to obtain clarification of the likely Portuguese response but it was not until June that the ambassador reported Salazar's view, which he shared, that an attempt to replace the old treaties by a new instrument, 'free admittedly from their anomalies but devoid of its psychological strength in circumstances which would give rise to close bargaining and perhaps friction', would not be in the best interests of the alliance.[77] The foreign office readily accepted that the existing treaties should be left intact and that they should be amended only when the need arose. The advice of the legal expert, Sir William Malkin, was compelling:

> The case for leaving them [treaties of alliance] as they are has been considerably strengthened since March, for we may now be involved in war as a result of aggression against not only France or Belgium but also a considerable number of other countries, and an attempt to produce a new treaty which would cover all the cases in which we might desire Portuguese assistance might well present insuperable difficulties.[78]

The decision not to proceed with treaty revision served to focus attention more sharply upon the need to make progress on the outstanding Portuguese armaments contracts. At the end of July, Halifax presented Lord Chatfield, as

---

76 CAB 16/219 AD 28 (DCOS 110).

77 In view of developments since March Salazar was clearly aware that there was an enhanced possibility of war in Europe and, in view of his determination to keep Portugal neutral in any European conflagration, the existing treaties provided sufficient flexibility to avoid overt involvement. Any modification might bind Portugal more tightly to Britain than was desirable and make the avoidance of involvement less likely. For details of Salazar's intentions in this connection see ch. 7.

78 CAB 2/8 345th mtg, 26 Jan. 1939; FO 425/416 W4114/160/36; FO 371/24064 W9623/160/36; DAPE, ii, no. 745, pp. 597–9.

minister for co-ordination of defence, with a cogently argued case for giving Portugal preferential treatment. The objectives of British policy were to obtain the full co-operation of Portugal in time of war; to ensure that she would be a useful ally; and to see that the Portuguese government encouraged Franco's Spain to withhold help from the Axis powers. The first objective was retarded by a doubt in Salazar's mind as to how much importance his British partner attached to the alliance. The second could be only partially fulfilled so long as Portugal remained more or less disarmed while Salazar's authority in Spain was weakened not only by Portuguese disarmament, but by the lack of sufficient evidence of the British government's intention, in case of need, to place all their resources behind his country. While the foreign secretary welcomed the recent inclusion of Portugal among those countries which would be allowed to place their orders for arms through the service departments and the financial facilities provided by the export credit guarantee department, he expressed his conviction that these concessions would be insufficient to consolidate the position unless an early and substantial contribution could be made towards equipping Portuguese land forces. Halifax was adamant that 'the political and strategic importance of securing the three policy objectives must be allowed equal weight with the claim of the military advisers', while with specific reference to Portugal's anti-aircraft requirements, he insisted that from the political point of view Portugal had first claim over all other foreign and dominion countries.[79]

Halifax's strong appeal barely moved the military authorities. While the committee of imperial defence agreed to the immediate delivery of four 3.7 inch anti-aircraft guns, as a token, to be followed by further deliveries at the rate of one per month from October onwards, they were not prepared to consider the supply of 25-pounder guns or converted 18-pounders. The British army alone required 4,200 25-pounder guns and it would be July 1942 before current production could meet this requirement. As an alternative, General Lord Gort, the chief of the imperial general staff, was invited to ascertain whether the French military authorities would be prepared to supply any modern 75mm guns to the Portuguese.[80]

The Portuguese government was informed on 16 and 17 August of the British government's view – which accorded with Salazar's – that it was not necessary to review the clauses of the existing treaties which, coupled with the recent declarations of loyalty to the alliance on both sides, were sufficiently explicit in themselves. At the same time, the British offer of assistance to Portugal by sea, air and land – the latter only after an unavoidable time-lag – first communicated to the Portuguese on 28 October 1938, was reaffirmed and attention was drawn to the recent decision to proceed with compulsory military conscription in the United Kingdom which would undoubtedly strengthen the ability of Britain to render assistance to Portugal in time of war. The offer of immediate token delivery of four anti-aircraft equipments was also communicated to the Portuguese authorities but no specific mention was made of the

[79] CAB 16/219 2nd mtg, allied demands committee, 18 July 1939, and AD 22; FO 371/24064 W11368/160/36.
[80] CAB 16/219 AD 35 (DCOS 151); CAB 2/9 372nd mtg, 2 Aug. 1939.

position in relation to field artillery: the imminent visit of a Portuguese military mission to London providing the reason for the lack of a firm decision.[81] In the event, the outbreak of the second world war transformed the whole question of the supply of armaments to all foreign countries; the priorities of home defence and support for France naturally assumed even greater significance than previously. Since the French government was unable to meet the demands of other countries the suggestion that Portugal should obtain some field artillery from France was quite clearly a non-starter.

Despite the great strategic importance of the alliance and the efforts of the foreign office and the service departments, the British government between September 1936 and September 1939 manifestly failed to provide anything substantial in the way of armaments for their Portuguese ally, undoubtedly because of Britain's own rearmament needs. Whether as a consequence of stringent treasury controls on official expenditure, the shortage of skilled labour in key sectors of the armaments industry, the restrictive attitudes of trade unions or the need to retain financial solvency abroad as the fourth arm of defence, the government was in no position to satisfy the demands of the growing number of foreign countries for British armaments.[82] It was also true that the Portuguese authorities demanded only the most modern equipment which was naturally earmarked, in the first instance, for British forces and were quick to recognise the value of setting German and Italian bids in direct competition with British firms in order to reduce overall costs. None the less, despite the advantages which the Axis powers possessed in terms of their ability to supply Portuguese needs, Salazar did not sign any substantial contracts for artillery, aircraft or naval vessels other than that with Italy for mountain artillery. The embassy in Lisbon, the foreign office and the service departments succeeded in countering intense competition from Germany and Italy and in blocking their ambitions in Portugal. The contribution of the British military mission during 1938 was extremely valuable, not least in persuading the Portuguese to give the highest priority to the defence of Lisbon and the Atlantic islands.

In the light of Britain's inability to supply the urgent requirements of the Portuguese armed forces within a reasonable time the Germans missed a favourable opportunity to undermine the Anglo-Portuguese alliance. The authorities in Berlin, however, suffered from Portugal's fear that German demands for colonies were likely to include her African possessions. The Portuguese were aware of their dependence on Britain's goodwill and that the continuation of the alliance would be the only means available of deterring any potential predator or of preventing a repeat of the Anglo-German negotiations preceding

---

81 FO 371/24064 W10614/W12374/160/36; *DAPE*, ii, no. 814, pp. 454–7.
82 For a discussion of these issues see Gibbs, *Grand Strategy*, i, passim; G. Peden, *British rearmament and the treasury 1932–1939*, Edinburgh 1979, passim; R. P. Shay Jr, *British rearmament in the thirties: politics and profit*, Princeton, NJ 1977, passim; R. A. C. Parker, 'British rearmament 1936–1939: treasury, trade unions and skilled labour', *English Historical Review* xcvi (1981), 306–43; F. Coghlan, 'Armaments, economic policy and appeasement: background to British foreign policy 1931–1937', *History* lvii (1972), 205–16.

the first world war. For their part the British government recognised that German colonial demands provided a useful antidote to German ambitions in Portugal and strengthened their efforts to counter those ambitions.[83] However, British efforts to achieve a reconciliation with Nazi Germany by means of a colonial settlement inevitably carried the risk of a rupture with Portugal. The danger for the government was that they might fail to appease Germany yet alienate their ancient ally.

[83] For example, FO 371/21279 W20511/923/36.

5

Origins of Colonial Appeasement

Despite their many differences, Portuguese statesmen of the monarchy, the parliamentary republic and the *Estado Novo* would have agreed on one common objective – the maintenance of the Portuguese empire. Neither the monarchy nor the parliamentary republic would have taken exception to President Oscar Carmona's declaration in 1939 that Portugal was not merely a European but a world power.[1] The noted historian of the Portuguese empire, Richard Hammond, suggests that the Portuguese felt that their overseas possessions were 'a symbol of their place in the world, even a warranty of their independence as a nation'.[2] Notwithstanding the economic burden of the colonies, which claimed the scarce resources of the mother country, Portuguese governments enshrined the view that their very survival as a nation depended upon the continuation of their African empire against all comers, including their oldest ally. No less an authority on imperial affairs than the 3rd marquess of Salisbury admitted that he thought it logical for the Portuguese to argue that the loss of their colonial empire would probably result in their absorption by Spain.[3]

The Portuguese consequently displayed great tenacity in defence of their colonial possessions.[4] Sovereign control did not, however, prevent foreign economic penetration of the most important territories – Angola and Mozambique – and before the advent of the Salazar regime other powers, notably the British, but also the French and Belgians, tended to dominate economic proceedings through a number of companies. These were, in Portuguese East Africa, the *Companhia de Moçambique* and the *Companhia do Niassa* which were both chartered, the Zambezia Company and the Senna Sugar Estates, and in Portuguese West Africa, the *Companhia de Diamantes de Angola* (DIAMANG) and the Benguela Railway Company. The underdeveloped state of the Portuguese colonies, so disparaged by the radical movement in Britain before 1914, was at least partly the responsibility of these companies, and this was particularly true of the two chartered companies in Mozambique. Throughout the forty years of its charter the *Companhia de Moçambique* failed to establish within its territory in the south and west of the country a basic infrastructure of roads and ports, schools and hospitals, sanitary facilities and water supplies. The

[1] R. A. H. Robinson, *Contemporary Portugal: a history*, London 1979, 83.
[2] R. J. Hammond, 'Economic imperialism: sidelights on a stereotype', *Journal of Economic History* xxi (1961), 589.
[3] P. R. Warhurst, *Anglo-Portuguese relations in south central Africa 1890–1900*, London 1962, 68.
[4] For details of Portuguese resolution in the era of the 'New Imperialism' and its aftermath see R. J. Hammond, 'Uneconomic imperialism: Portuguese Africa before 1910', in L. H. Gann and P. Duignan (eds), *Colonialism in Africa 1870–1960*, I: *the history and politics of colonialism, 1870–1914*, Cambridge 1969, 352–79.

energies of the company were devoted instead to the transit trade to the British and Belgian hinterland and to foreign-owned plantation agriculture.[5] The record of the *Companhia do Niassa* in northern Mozambique was even worse. From his extensive research on the company's performance before 1919 Leroy Vail concludes that these years were characterised by 'oppression and exploitation, rebellion and mass emigration'.[6] In 1917 the Portuguese attempted to cancel the company's charter on the grounds of neglect of its charter obligations but their heavy indebtedness to Britain forced them to retreat. The pervasive presence of South Africa around Delagoa Bay reinforced Britain's dominance of the Mozambican economy. Indeed, according to one historian of Portuguese colonialism, the principal commercial centres of Mozambique – Lourenço Marques and Beira – often appeared to visitors more British than Portuguese.[7] The position in Angola was scarcely different. Until the mid-1920s the colony had practically no roads or railways so that settlers had to transport their agricultural produce from the interior by expensive Boer carts or African porters. The renowned Benguela Railway was not completed until 1931. It had taken more than a quarter of a century, at a cost of $40 million (80 per cent from British sources). The railway, with its terminal point at the Katanga copper mines of the Congo, served British and Belgian interests far more than Portuguese. The most important company in Angola was the DIAMANG: diamonds were the most important export.[8]

During the 1920s, despite foreign office protests, successive Portuguese governments, both before and after the overthrow of the parliamentary republic, succeeeded in changing Britain's relationship with Portugal's colonies. For example, laws were enacted requiring the use of Portuguese in mission schools and Portuguese nationals as editors of Mozambique's newspapers which were to be published in Portuguese and not English; and British-backed firms, such as the Delagoa Bay Development Corporation and the Incomati Sugar Estates, were hard hit by currency regulations imposed by the Portuguese.[9] Most significant of all was the cancellation of the charter of the *Companhia do Niassa* in 1929. The process of Portuguese consolidation was carried further during the early 1930s with the colonial reforms of the *Estado Novo* which tranformed the economic, political and administrative relationship between Portugal and the colonies. The essential goal of the reforms was financial stringency and economic stability. To this end the colonies were required to balance their budgets

---

[5] L. Vail, 'Mozambique's chartered companies: the rule of the feeble', *Journal of African History* xvii (1976), 394–7, 416. See also L. Vail, 'Discussion: the Mozambique company: reply to B. Neil Tomlinson', *Journal of African History* xviii (1977), 285.

[6] Vail, 'Mozambique's chartered companies', 397–402.

[7] Ibid., 410–11; A. K. Smith, 'Antonio Salazar and the reversal of Portuguese colonial policy', *Journal of African History* xv (1974), 656.

[8] G. Clarence-Smith, *The third Portuguese empire 1825–1975: a study in economic imperialism*, Manchester 1985, 129–31; G. J. Bender, *Angola under the Portuguese: the myth and the reality*, London 1978, 101–2; W. Minter, *Imperial network and external dependency: the case of Angola*, Beverley Hills, Ca. 1972, 26–9; R. J. Hammond, 'Some economic aspects of Portuguese Africa in the nineteenth and twentieth centuries', in L. H. Gann and P. Duignan (eds), *Colonialism in Africa 1870–1960*, IV: *the economics of colonialism*, Cambridge 1975, 267, 269–70.

[9] Vail, 'Mozambique's chartered companies', 410–12. For further details see L. Vail and L. White, *Capitalism and colonialism in Mozambique*, London 1980, 200–37.

whatever the effect might be on public services and other developments. Salazar's government also refused to stimulate colonial economic growth through the provision of financial support while the hostile attitude of officials served to dissuade foreign capital from investment in the colonies. To achieve financial solvency and economic stability the colonial ministry was reorganised and strengthened and the more independent high commissioners of the territories were replaced by governors-general who were to be subservient to Lisbon. The restrictions placed on economic growth ensured that the colonies would remain underdeveloped and would consequently continue to depend on the primitive exploitation of African labour.[10] The labour laws, which had created the greatest outcry against Portuguese colonialism, were modified by Salazar in the colonial acts of 1928 and 1930 to read like a freedom charter. The act of 1930 stated that 'the system of native contract labour rests on individual liberty and the natives right to a just wage and assistance, public authority intervening only for purposes of inspection'.[11] In practice the labour laws were consistently and flagrantly flouted by the authorities in Mozambique and Angola. As late as 1942 the Portuguese labour system in Angola guaranteed Africans payment of less than $1.50 a month.[12]

Despite the considerable gap between theory and practice in the labour system of the Portuguese empire and the restrictions on foreign investment, Portugal's colonial endeavours received a good foreign press during the 1930s, in particular the self-congratulatory speeches and lectures of Portuguese statesmen such as Carmona and Monteiro. The British press, notably The Times, was particularly impressed by the financial solvency of the African colonies and the slow if unspectacular growth in their trade.[13] A less laudatory and more realistic assessment was made by The Economist during September 1936 which interpreted the steady appreciation in the value of the empire during the previous half century as the result of the opening up of the hinterland of Portugal's colonies by the enterprise of other powers. The hinterland of Angola and Mozambique had been transformed into the Transvaal, Northern and Southern Rhodesia, Nyasaland and the Belgian Congo:

> These derelict Portuguese settlements on the African coast have become the maritime termini of railways that run into the heart of Africa and tap copper mines, cattle-ranges and agricultural regions producing crop exports. Lourenço Marques, Beira and Lobito Bay [in Angola] have become busy and flourish-

---

10 M. Newitt, Portugal in Africa: the last hundred years, London 1983; Smith, 'Antonio Salazar', 663–7. See also J Duffy, 'Portuguese Africa 1930 to 1960', in L. H. Gann and P. Duignan (eds), Colonialism in Africa 1870–1917, II: the history and politics of colonialism 1914–1960, Cambridge 1970, 174–6.
11 Duffy, 'Portuguese Africa 1930 to 1960', 184.
12 Vail and White, Capitalism and colonialism, 245–53; Bender, Angola under the Portuguese, 142.
13 The Times, 11 July 1938, 17 June 1939. See also Atkinson, 'Portugal and her empire'. For a more critical contemporary view of the Portuguese empire see R. G. Woolbert, 'The future of Portugal's colonies', Foreign Affairs xv (1937). For Monteiro's views see his speech at the opening of the 22nd meeting of the International Colonial Institute in Lisbon on 18 April 1933 and his lecture to the Royal African Society in London, 1 February 1939: The Portuguese in modern colonialism, Lisbon 1934, and 'Portugal in Africa', Journal of the Royal African Society, April 1939.

ing *entrepôt* centres. In fact the value of the Portuguese colonies has appreciated all round. And the precariousness of Portugal's tenure has been accentuated in the same ratio.

In the circumstances, the reorganisation of the empire and a more favourable foreign press provided few guarantees for the survival of Portugal's colonial heritage particularly in a world increasingly witnessing the resurgence of militant imperialism on the pre-1914 model, exemplified by the Japanese takeover of Manchuria in 1931–3 and the Italian conquest of Abyssinia in 1936. While the integrity of Portuguese East Africa was threatened by the more obscure, though no less vaulting, ambitions of Southern Rhodesia and the Union of South Africa, which centred on Beira and Lourenço Marques,[14] the single greatest threat to the Portuguese empire during the 1930s came from the revival of German colonial ambitions which had surfaced during the Weimar period.

Although colonial revision was not an immediate priority in German foreign policy it was raised publicly on a number of occasions by the statesmen of Weimar Germany: in the course of negotiations for the 1925 Locarno Agreement; on the occasion of Germany's entry into the League of Nations in 1926; and during the Young Plan negotiations of 1929. While there was no public announcement of German interest in Portugal's African colonies on these occasions, discussions, both within and between official and unofficial circles, took place which revealed that pre-war ambitions to acquire at least part of these territories were far from moribund.[15] Various initiatives were contemplated which ranged from an unofficial plan by German financial interests to acquire control of the *Companhia do Niassa* in Mozambique to a scheme, originating in the *Wilhelmstrasse*, which envisaged a modified version of pre-war Anglo-German agreements by which Portugal might be induced to hand over her colonies to the League of Nations as security for a loan and Germany might be given Angola under mandate. Indeed, during the Young Plan negotiations the former head of the *Wilhelmstrasse*, Richard von Kühlmann, actually raised with Sir William Tyrrell, British ambassador in Paris, the question of reviving the pre-war accords in relation to Angola and Mozambique. As a result the British ambassador in Berlin, Sir William Rumbold, was instructed to inform the German foreign minister, Gustav Stresemann, that Britain was absolutely unable to reconsider 'the former conventions concerning the Portuguese colonies'.[16]

---

[14] For these ambitions see Stone, 'The oldest ally', 160–3.

[15] In 1924 following consultations with interested groups, including business circles and politicians, the colonial department of the *Wilhelmstrasse* submitted 'Colonial Policy Guidelines' which were subsequently endorsed by the foreign minister, Gustav Stresemann. According to Adolf Rüger, the central idea was to achieve equal status with third parties in all colonies. The main emphasis from the economic viewpoint was on the former German colonies and on Portugal's possessions in Africa, with south-west Africa, Angola and Tanganyika singled out for 'germanisation': 'The colonial aims of the Weimar Republic', in H. Stoecker (ed.), *German imperialism in Africa: from the beginnings until the Second World War*, London 1986, 314–15.

[16] For a discussion of Weimar Germany's colonial aspirations as they related to the Portuguese colonies see FO 371/18820 C2595/21/18; 371/18821 C5142/21/18. See also F. W. Pick, *Search-*

Nazi statesmen were no less interested in the Portuguese colonies than were their Weimar predecessors. As early as April 1933 at a meeting of the economic policy committee, prior to the World Economic Conference and under Hitler's personal direction, Hjalmar Schacht, soon to be promoted to the post of Reich economics minister, argued that the Anglo-German Agreement of 1898 on the Portuguese colonies ought to be revived. He felt that this proposal would not be unacceptable to the United Kingdom and suggested compensating Italy with Lourenço Marques should Angola become a German possession.[17] Klaus Hildebrand stresses the fact that neither Hitler nor any foreign ministry official argued against Schacht's line of thinking.[18] Nor was German interest in Portugal's African possessions confined to mere discussion during the early years of Nazi rule. In August 1934 Francis O'Meara, British consul general at Luanda, was informed that the Portuguese authorities had discovered German military-type maps showing southern Angola and the British frontier. The Portuguese were also perturbed by the alleged smuggling of firearms by Germans in northern Angola and by German wireless activities. In December O'Meara revealed that German propaganda in Angola had been much intensified and was partly directed against Britain. Moreover, in late January 1935, at a time when the return of colonies to Germany was becoming a major issue, he reported that there was 'much talk of a possible German rising, either in Angola or with the help of Angola-German settlers in the adjoining mandated territory of South-West Africa'. According to O'Meara these rumours were limked to reports of the intended secession of the whole of the territory from Portugal.[19]

While the likelihood of a German takeover of Angola by force was extremely remote in 1935, officials in Berlin, such as Dr Kurt Weigelt, head of the economics branch of the new colonial policy department of the German foreign ministry and a confidant of Schacht, made no secret of their ambitions.[20] In February, Pierre Flandin, prime minister of France, told a British MP, Captain John McEwen, that 'the Germans had been once again suggesting that their colonial aspirations could be met if they were given the Portuguese colonies in East Africa and then at a later date, no doubt, they might also have Angola'.[21]

light on German Africa: the diaries and papers of Dr W Ch Regendanz: a study in colonial ambitions, London 1939, 137–42, 144–51, 158–70; K. Hildebrand, Vom Reich zum Weltreich: Hitler, NSDAP und Koloniale Frage 1919–1945, München 1969, 131–2, n. 28; H. Pogge von Strandmann, 'Imperialism and revisionism in interwar Germany', in W. J. Mommsen (ed.), Imperialism and after: continuities and discontinuities, London 1986, 98–9; A. J. Crozier, 'Imperial decline and the colonial question in Anglo-German relations 1919–1939', European Studies Review xi (1981), 210–19.

17 Hildebrand, Vom Reich zum Weltreich, 303. For indications of Italian and Japanese interest in Angola at this time see R. F. Holland, Britain and the Commonwealth Alliance 1918–1939, London 1981, 179; E. M. Robertson, 'Mussolini and Ethiopia: the prehistory of the Rome Agreements of January 1935', in R. M. Hatton and M. S. Anderson (eds), Studies in diplomatic history, London 1970, 374. According to Ritchie Ovendale, in late 1934 General Jan Smuts was greatly concerned about Japanese ambitions in Mozambique: 'Why the British Dominions went to war', in Boyce and Robertson, Paths to War, 271.

18 Hildebrand, Vom Reich zum Weltreich, 303.

19 FO 371/18821 C5142/21/18.

20 FO 371/18819 C1822/21/18.

21 FO 371/18828 C1724/55/18.

During the same month support for the idea of transferring Angola to Germany was provided by the South African minister in Berlin, who told his British counterpart that his government did not intend to return south-west Africa and were equally opposed to the return of German east Africa and the Cameroons. However, if it were possible for Germany to be given possession of the Portuguese colonies, that 'would be ideal'.[22]

The foreign office was vehemently opposed to any deal with Germany which involved the Portuguese colonies, even if the South Africa government was inclined to take a different line. As Vansittart minuted during March 1935:

> It is probable that Mr Pirow [South African minister of defence] and possibly some other members of his Government are playing with the idea of keeping for themselves the former colonies of Germany and satisfying her with Portugal's colonies. It is probable too that this idea is not dead in Germany. But it is quite certain that we can have nothing to do with this ancient and dirty game. It was a grave mistake at the time, and the time for it is long past. There is now a League of Nations, and a few of its members have League principles.[23]

Vansittart's view was reiterated in the foreign office brief for the foreign secretary, Sir John Simon, and Anthony Eden, lord president of the council, prior to their departure for Berlin in March 1935. It was thought that Hitler might raise the question of colonial revision and that part of his strategy might be to obtain British assistance – or at least an assurance of non-interference – in securing one of the Portuguese colonies in Africa by means of cession, purchase or the establishment of a chartered company. In the event of such a proposal it was clear that Britain was bound under treaty obligations to defend and protect the Portuguese empire against 'all enemies, as well future as present'.[24]

Hitler's confirmation to Simon and Eden of his determination to seek colonial revision[25] encouraged the foreign office to examine the German colonial claim during the summer months of 1935. As a preliminary step the central department commissioned one of its officials, J. V. Perowne, to produce two memoranda: one to survey the whole course of Anglo-German colonial relations since the late nineteenth century and the other to detail German aspirations regarding the Portuguese colonies during the same period. The two papers, printed at the end of June, provided the basis for subsequent discussion within the foreign office. Indeed, those discussions which took place between November 1935 and February 1936 represented the first occasion upon which the German colonial claim, examined in the context of a general appraisal of British appeasement policy, received the sustained attention of senior foreign

---

[22] FO 371/18819 C1273/21/18.
[23] FO 371/18819 C1738/21/18.
[24] DBFP, 2, xii, no. 564, pp. 632–42.
[25] For details of the Simon-Eden talks with Hitler see DBFP, 2, xii, no. 651, pp. 703–46. See also Lord Avon, The Eden memoirs: facing the dictators, London 1962, 133–8; A. R. Peters, Anthony Eden at the foreign office 1931–1938, Aldershot 1986, 88–91; D. Dutton, 'Eden and Simon at the foreign office, 1931–1935', Review of International Studies xx (1994), 50–1.

office staff – Orme Sargent, Ralph Wigram, Frank Ashton-Gwatkin and above all Robert Vansittart.[26] Critically, this development coincided with a major change in emphasis in Berlin on the colonial question.

During 1933 and 1934, a difference of opinion on Anglo-German relations had arisen between Hitler and the conservative group, which was connected both to German business circles and the *Wilhelmstrasse* and headed by Schacht and Baron Constantin von Neurath, the foreign minister. The conservatives wished to reach an understanding with Britain through the pursuit of colonial interests while refraining from action within Europe. The *Führer*, as was consistent with the ideas he had expressed in *Mein Kampf* and *Zweites Buch*, and in pursuit of European hegemony, whether as an end in itself or merely as a staging post in a phased programme for world dominion, wanted to secure an entente with Britain by renouncing colonial interests. Thus he would secure British disinterestedness in Europe.[27] However, according to Klaus Hildebrand, by the time of the visit of Simon and Eden to Berlin, Hitler had begun to shift the whole emphasis of his colonial policy: 'From now on it would no longer be the renouncing of revisionist plans overseas which was to bring Britain on to Germany's side. It would be the raising of colonial demands in an increasingly threatening way which was intended to make Britain amenable.'[28] It is in the context of this change that the reorganisation of the colonial movement in Germany should be viewed. In other words, from its inception the *Reichskolonialbund* was assigned the function of 'pretending to make overseas demands in order to render the stubborn British more amenable'. By officially adopting the colonial movement Hitler also succeeded in winning over to his foreign policy programme an important class of German society and integrating their demands into it.[29] Despite the benefits of such a *volte face* there was clearly a danger of genuine misunderstanding. According to Wolfgang Michalka, Hitler had apparently allowed himself to be influenced by economic interests and by Ribbentrop's theories on colonial policy and had thereby fallen into line with traditional revisionist colonial demands.[30] Certainly, this was how the foreign

---

[26] For the Perowne papers see FO 371/18820 C2595/21/18; 371/18821 C5142/21/18. For full details of the foreign office debate see *DBFP*, 2, xv, apps i, iv, pp. 713–36, 762–91.

[27] See W. Michalka, 'Conflicts within the German leadership on the objectives and tactics of German foreign policy, 1933–1939', in W. J. Mommsen and L. Kettenacker (eds), *The fascist challenge and the policy of appeasement*, London 1983, 53. For the debate on Hitler's ultimate objectives, including discussion of the so-called *Stufenplan*, see K. Hildebrand, *The foreign policy of the Third Reich*, London 1973, 12–23; M. Michaelis, 'World power status or world dominion? A survey of the literature on Hitler's "plan of world dominion" (1937–1970)', *Historical Journal* xv (1972) 331–60; A. Hillgruber, 'England's place in Hitler's plans for world dominion', *Journal of Contemporary History* ix (1974), 5–22; M. Hauner, 'Did Hitler want a world dominion?', *Journal of Contemporary History* xiii (1978), 15–31.

[28] Hildebrand, *Foreign policy of the Third Reich*, 36–7. See also Hillgruber, 'England's place', 13, and J. Henke, *England in Hitler's politischen Kalkül 1935–1939*, Boppard-am-Rhein 1973, 72–4.

[29] Hildebrand, *Foreign policy of the Third Reich*, 36–7. See also Michalka, 'Conflicts within the German leadership', 54; Crozier, 'Imperial decline', 226–7.

[30] Michalka, 'Conflicts within the German leadership', 54. For the evolution of Ribbentrop's views on the colonial question between 1935 and 1937 see W. Michalka, *Ribbentrop und die deutsche Weltpolitik 1933–1940: Aussenpolitische Konzeptionen und Entscheidungsprozesse im Dritten Reich*, München 1980, 138–9.

office regarded German demands for colonies from early 1935 onwards though it did not make the mistake of believing that colonies were the only obstacle to the successful appeasement of Germany.

Discussions at the foreign office during late 1935 and early 1936 revealed few illusions about German ambitions in central and eastern Europe. It was recognised that a willingness to concede colonial revision did not guarantee that Germany 'would refrain from warlike adventures and would work for change only by methods of peace and agreement'. Yet, for Vansittart at least, the cession of territory in Africa was to be preferred to the cession of territory in Europe.[31] Cabinet, on the other hand – or more accurately the newly constituted cabinet committee on Germany – and the new foreign secretary, Anthony Eden, were still to be convinced. Until 7 March 1936 the most appropriate concession was considered to be a revision of the Treaty of Locarno to allow the gradual remilitarisation of the Rhineland,[32] but the situation was transformed when Hitler remilitarised the region unilaterally. The 'useful bargaining counter' of the Rhineland had been lost but the *Führer*'s demand, in a speech the same day, for colonial revision as part of a proposed German 'peace plan' nevertheless evoked a positive response in Whitehall. On 9 March, at Eden's behest, a committee of imperial defence sub-committee was set up to study the whole colonial question under the chairmanship of the parliamentary under secretary for the colonies, Lord Plymouth.

In carrying out their brief the Plymouth Committee discounted any possibility of using Portuguese or Belgian colonies as an alternative means of satisfying Germany's colonial appetite. Indeed, after three months deliberation the committee concluded that the least objectionable way of transferring territory to Germany would be for France to join with the United Kingdom in surrendering the whole or part of Togoland, or the Cameroons, or both; south-west Africa and Tanganyika were not to be considered. The committee did not in any case believe that such a step would achieve much in the way of appeasing Germany, for no matter how generously she was treated in the colonial sphere 'she would not necessarily be diverted from pursuing her aspirations in Europe'. It was further recognised that even if all of Germany's former colonies were returned to her, her ambitions would not in the long run be satisfied.[33] The foreign office had foreseen this major objection in their submission to the Plymouth Committee of 26 March 1936:

> Judging, however, by her past history it would be well not to overlook the alternative possibility that, having once regained her former colonial empire, she might before long cast covetous eyes on the possessions of others, and particularly on those of small countries like Portugal which, not being Great Powers, had little real justification, in German eyes, for possessing such extensive territories, of a size out of all proportion to the importance and military strength of the mother country.[34]

---

[31] CAB 24/260 CP 42(36). See also *DBFP*, 2, xv, app. iv(b), p. 786; Vansittart Papers, VNST 1/12. For a discussion of the issues involved see Medlicott, *Britain and Germany*, 21, 27–9.
[32] CAB 27/599 G1(36).
[33] *DBFP*, 2, xvi, app. iii, pp. 758–96.
[34] CAB 16/145 CMG 11.

The Plymouth Committee's lack of enthusiasm for colonial revision was mirrored in cabinet, the cabinet foreign policy committee and the committee of imperial defence with the result that Eden, on 27 July, publicly disclaimed any solution of the colonial question.[35] The policy of colonial appeasement, never the first priority during 1935 and 1936, was therefore temporarily shelved while the British authorities sought a general settlement with Germany and Italy through a renegotiated western or 'Locarno' pact.[36]

From early 1936 onwards the authorities in Lisbon, suspicious of British intentions, adamantly refused to contemplate the loss of Portuguese territory in Africa. Monteiro told Eden at Geneva on 22 January that in no circumstances would Portugal 'yield one inch of her colonial territory', and 'there was no divergence of view whatever, either in Portugal or her colonies about the matter'. Eden assured the foreign minister that 'if occasionally, a section of the British public was not as careful as it should be in its comments about the Portuguese colonies no such suggestion was, of course, entertained by His Majesty's Government'. Unfortunately, Portuguese anxieties were not allayed for long owing to a speech in the house of commons on 5 February by David Lloyd George, in which he alluded to the disparity between the non-existent German colonial empire and the considerable territories of the Portuguese, Belgian and Dutch empires. Eden hoped the Portuguese government would draw 'a sharp distinction between Mr Lloyd George, who was a private member of the House of Commons, and not now even the leader of a party, and the attitude of the Government'.[37] The Portuguese, however, could not afford to be so dismissive. Wingfield reminded the foreign secretary that:

> the Portuguese cannot shut their eyes to the fact that the extent of their colonial empire and the underdeveloped state of most of it has formed the subject of criticism in the past and furnished arguments to those who would like to see parts, at all events, of their territories transferred to more vigorous and capable hands.

Moreover, as the Portuguese realised that in the last resort they were dependent upon British support for the retention of their colonies, suggestions such as those 'voiced in the House of Commons by an ex-Prime Minister were all the more disquieting'.[38]

Salazar confirmed this himself towards the end of March 1936. He told Wingfield that he was perturbed by the German government's evident intention to raise the question of colonies. Although it was not clear whether Germany would demand some or all of her former colonies, or whether she would simply ask for economic rights in the colonies of other powers, Portugal

---

[35] CAB 23/85 CM 53(36); CAB 2/6 280th mtg, 10 July 1936; CAB 27/622 FP(36) 3rd and 4th mtgs, 15 and 27 July 1936; *Hansard parliamentary debates*, HC, 5th ser. cccxv, cols 1131–2.

[36] See CAB 27/622 FP(36) 2nd mtg, 15 July 1936; A. J. Crozier, 'Prelude to Munich: British foreign policy and Germany, 1935–1938', *European Studies Review* vi (1976), 364–5.

[37] FO 371/20512 W771/762/36; W1320/895/36; *Hansard parliamentary debates*, HC, 5th ser. cccviii, cols 244–5.

[38] FO 371/20512 W1796/895/36.

and the other small nations with large colonies had 'every right to be anxious and to dislike the new interpretation of "equality", according to which a State had grounds for complaint and could demand compensation because, for instance, another State had more territory, more wealth or more population than her'. The Portuguese leader wished to know the British view of Germany's colonial claims; he hoped they would discuss it together frankly as allies. Finally, he reminded Wingfield that by the Treaty of Windsor of 1899 the British government had undertaken to protect Portugal's colonial possessions and he hoped they would realise that 'there had never been a more Anglophile government in power in Portugal than the present one'. The ambassador avoided making any commitment by recourse to the traditional reply of British representatives in Portugal: that it was a feature of the British national character to dislike taking decisions about hypothetical situations and that accordingly British governments were inclined to deal with each problem as it arose. Eden approved Wingfield's reply and instructed the ambassador to avoid, if possible, discussing the colonial question with the Portuguese but that 'in the event of Salazar returning to the subject in such a manner as to necessitate a reply', he should indicate that 'it would be useless for these problems of raw materials and colonies, affecting as they did so many countries, to be discussed between His Majesty's Government and Portugal'.[39]

In view of the growing international interest in colonial revision the Portuguese recognised that they needed to develop strong arguments to justify the retention of their empire. One such was presented by Salazar, on 8 June 1936, during his inaugural address to the Economic Conference of the Portuguese Colonial Empire. Taking a leaf out of Hitler's book, he justified the empire in terms of Portugal's severely limited economic resources and her consequent demand for living space for her rapidly growing population.[40] Another, often repeated, argument concerned Portugal's political and financial stability. In the pre-war period or even in the 1920s Portugal could have been accused of irresponsible behaviour. That was no longer the case. The Anglo-German negotiations of 1898 and 1912–14, which went so far as to delineate the respective British and German shares of the Portuguese colonies, had been based upon imminent Portuguese bankruptcy whereas under Salazar financial rectitude was the order of the day.[41] However, while Portuguese finances ceased to provide a possible excuse for the redistribution of Portuguese territory in Africa, the Achilles heel of colonial underdevelopment remained. The Portuguese also insisted that their country had not received any of the former German colonies and should therefore be excluded from any discussions on colonial revision.[42] In making such assertions the Portuguese tended to forget that northern Mozambique had been rounded off at the Ruvuma river in 1919 by the acquisition from Germany of the Kionga Triangle. Although only 200 square miles in extent and part of Mozambique until it was seized by the Germans in 1884, the Triangle's future ownership was almost certain to arise in

[39] FO 371/20512 W2977/W3082/895/36.
[40] For details see A. de Figueirido, *Portugal: fifty years of dictatorship*, New York 1976, 74–6.
[41] For example, the *Diário de Notícias*, 28 Mar. 1936.
[42] FO 371/20512 W1796/895/36.

the event of Germany regaining Tanganyika. The central department considered the issue sufficiently important to produce a memorandum for submission to the Plymouth Committee during March 1936. According to the memorandum the Special Commission on Mandates at the Paris Peace Conference, having discussed the cession of the Triangle to Portugal as territory under mandate, had recommended that 'Portugal was the rightful original owner of the territory and its cession might properly be regarded as an act of restitution'. The recommendation was accepted by the Supreme Council and the Portuguese delegation were informed that it had been decided to recognise Portugal as 'le propriétaire original et légitime' of the Triangle.[43]

Early in the summer of 1936 Nazi colonial ambitions were directed towards bigger fish than the Kionga Triangle. In the light of the Plymouth report the central department anticipated that if Germany realised she could not have her old colonies back they could expect that 'she will try for the Portuguese colonies'.[44] Official circles in Berlin had certainly not forgotten them. Hjalmar Schacht in particular continued to press the idea of colonial retrocession in Africa at the expense of Portugal. In Berlin, during May 1936, he told A. L. Kennedy, an editor of *The Times*, that what was really wanted in the colonial sphere was the development by Germany of a territory like Angola, which was very thinly populated and very rich. The Reich economics minister wondered whether Germany could not lease Angola from Portugal. Schacht made these comments even though he acknowledged that under Salazar Portugal was developing its resources much better than they had ever been developed before. Moreover, towards the end of July he told the South African minister in Berlin that the transfer of Angola would be an ideal solution for Germany if this were found practicable,[45] and in September Rudolf Hess emphasised to Lloyd George during his visit to Berlin that 'the present state of affairs was untenable' by which he meant the possession of colonial empires by small powers. The deputy *Führer* insisted that 'a *redistribution* of colonies was necessary'.[46] The Germans were not alone in viewing the Portuguese colonies as important pieces on the colonial chess board. During his visit to London in June 1936 Oswald Pirow assigned Portugal a key role in his scheme for colonial revision. On 9 June he suggested to Eden that Germany might be given the Cameroons and Togoland, with the addition of a small portion of Portuguese territory in Angola; in return Britain might transfer some portion of Tanganyika to Portugal. The previous day the South African minister of defence had expressed similar sentiments to the cabinet secretary, Sir Maurice Hankey. Neither Eden nor Hankey gave any support to Pirow's suggestion and when he took his leave of the foreign secretary on 25 June he did not refer to it again.[47] Early in September 1936 the South African treasurer of the League of Nations, Seymour Jacklin, unlike

---

43 FO 371/19927 C2359/97/18. See also FO 408/66.
44 FO 371/19927 C5027/97/18.
45 FO 408/66; FO 371/19928 C6228/97/18.
46 Simon Papers, MS Simon 85. Emphasis in original.
47 FO 371/19928 C5218/97/18; CAB 24/262 CP 164(36); PREM 1/247, record of a conversation between Eden and Pirow, 25 June 1936.

Pirow, expressed his anxiety to Gladwyn Jebb 'lest Hitler might already be thinking of the Portuguese colonies'. Jacklin was convinced that for South Africa a German occupation of Angola 'would be only one degree less unfortunate than the return to Germany of German South-West Africa'. The only colonial adjustment South Africa could contemplate with equanimity would be the return of the Cameroons.[48]

Despite the continued interest in the colonial question in German and South African circles during the summer months of 1936, the British authorities remained convinced that the most promising way forward in Anglo-German relations lay in a revised Locarno security system. In view of this, and the additional priority of seeking a non-intervention agreement with regard to the Spanish Civil War, there was a natural reluctance to raise other issues, such as the colonial question, which would further complicate relations between London and Berlin. Consequently, the subject might have remained dormant for at least a while longer but for the intervention of the French authorities. The meeting between Schacht and Blum, in Paris during late August 1936, was the first of a series between the German, French and British governments culminating in Sir Nevile Henderson's abortive meeting with Hitler early in March 1938. The prospects of a deal involving the Portuguese colonies, somewhat remote in the summer of 1936, were to increase significantly during 1937 and 1938.

---

[48] FO 371/19928 C6507/97/18. At this time Jebb was a first secretary in the economic relations section of the league of nations and western department.

6

Portugal's African Colonies and Appeasement

The British failure during the summer months of 1936 to secure a five-power conference to discuss European security did not create any enthusiasm for a colonial settlement in government circles. Quite the reverse: Eden and Vansittart were appalled to learn of the conversations held in Paris in late August between Schacht and French ministers, including Blum and Delbos. The Reich economics minister had offered the possibility of a peace treaty 'lasting long enough for its indefinite prolongation to be guaranteed' and an arms limitation agreement, while rejecting Germany's return to the League of Nations as then constituted. The price was to be the return to Germany of her colonies, for reasons of economics and prestige. Blum's response was quite positive: provided the settlement was European-wide and not merely Franco-German, conversations on Germany's colonial demands would not be impossible.[1] When Eden learned the details of the Schacht–Blum conversations from the French premier himself on 20 September he reminded him that Britain's position remained as stated in the house of commons on 27 July. He reiterated his belief that a five-power conference was the most suitable instrument for achieving a European settlement at a meeting with Delbos in Geneva and in writing on 23 September. Significantly, his actions won the approval of the foreign office and of those cabinet members informed.[2] The French government, confronted with British reluctance to disturb the diplomatic process surrounding the five-power initiative, and disturbed by increasing German intervention in the Spanish civil war decided not to pursue discussions on the Schacht proposals; they were not to be renewed until February 1937 when Sir Frederick Leith Ross visited Badenweiler.[3]

Distaste for the Schacht initiative did not preclude further discussion of Germany's colonial aspirations within the foreign office, particularly where Portugal was affected. On 22 October 1936 Phipps told the central department that, according to reliable sources, Germany's present minimum colonial requirements were the Cameroons and Togoland, a small part of the Belgian Congo with a portion of Angola to round it off, former German New Guinea and a Dutch contribution, provided the Japanese gave a guarantee of neutrality in respect of their possessions. Partial confirmation of this was provided by Baron von Stumm who told Vansittart of his conviction that 'a restitution of

---

1 DDF, 2, iii, no. 213, pp. 307–11; Dreifort, Yvon Delbos, 163–4; J. Ballhaus, 'The colonial aims and preparations of the Hitler regime 1933–1939', in Stoecker, German imperialism in Africa, 357; D. J. Dunthorn, 'Britain, France and the colonial appeasement of Germany 1936–1938', unpubl. MA diss. Bristol Polytechnic 1984, 56–7.
2 DBFP, 2, xvii, nos 210, 214, 223, 228, 229, pp. 286–90, 294–5, 306–7, 312–13.
3 For French reactions see Dreifort, Yvon Delbos, 168–9.

94

Kameroun and Togo, perhaps somewhat "rounded off" would be perfectly satisfactory'.[4] Phipps was personally convinced that there was no reason to believe
Hitler would abandon his European aspirations and be satisfied, even for a
measurable period, with colonies; the only result of colonial surrender would be
the acceleration or facilitation of the programme for eastern expansion laid
down in *Mein Kampf*. Moreover,

> the German colonial programme now advocated, viz., a redistribution of the
> Belgian, Portuguese, Dutch and possibly Australian possessions would not be
> mere surrender on our part, it would also be a betrayal . . . of the small States
> concerned. The unscrupulous Dr. Schacht doubtless thinks that His
> Majesty's Government, rather than give up British or Dominions mandated
> territory, would be ready to connive at the blackmailing by Germany of these
> small States, whose possessions, moreover, would be more valuable to her
> than the former German Colonial Empire, the return of which to Germany
> would . . . only constitute an appetising 'hors d'oeuvre' for a really square
> Teutonic meal later.

The ambassador's views were shared by the colonial expert in the central
department, C. W. Baxter, who agreed that 'if Germany were given all her
former colonies, she would covet parts of the Belgian and Portuguese colonies,
she would begin to hope for the realisation of her old dream of a Central
African Empire from coast to coast'.[5]

Towards the end of 1936 the foreign office learnt of rumours that the
Germans were actively engaged in negotiations with the Portuguese for mineral
concessions in Angola; the first indications for them, as for the public, came in
a *Times* report of 10 December 1936. The Berlin correspondent argued that a
speech made by Schacht in Frankfurt on 9 December, in which he vigorously
reiterated the demand for colonies, was intended 'to meet in advance any
criticism likely to be directed abroad against an agreement with Portugal over
the future of Angola'. He continued:

> there is a tendency . . . to believe that negotiations with Portugal, which are
> reported to have been proceeding for some months, may soon bear fruit in an
> agreement giving Germany at least substantial concessions for the exploita-
> tion of the mineral fields of Angola. The reservation should be made, how-
> ever, that no official confirmation is forthcoming.

Shortly afterwards, Phipps reported from Berlin that rumours of the negotiations had been circulating for some days and the counsellor of the Netherlands
legation had informed the British embassy that he had received confirmation
from a usually reliable source. In the absence of reports from the British consul
at Luanda, Wingfield was alerted to *The Times* article on 29 December.[6]

When Wingfield confronted Sampaio on 4 January 1937 the secretary
general denied there was a word of truth in the reports. He could not think

4 FO 371/19929 C7501/C7565/97/36
5 FO 371/19929 C7500/97/18; *DBFP*, 2, xvii, no. 318, pp. 453–4.
6 FO 371/19930 C8934/97/18.

where such rumours had originated and could only suppose that they might be in some way connected with the fact that when the Germans negotiated commercial exchanges they always insisted on taking their quota of Portuguese goods in the form of colonial products.[7] Despite Sampaio's categorical denial rumours persisted and by late January were being given great prominence in the British press. According to the Berlin correspondent of *The Times* arrangements had been made for seven German iron, steel and chemical firms, including *I. G. Farbenindustrie*, to carry out construction work and to exploit mines in Angola. It was presumed that in effect 'Germany had arranged to take as payment for armaments supplied to Portugal raw materials recovered from Angola by German engineers and German capital'.[8] The foreign office had also received several reports from sources other than newspapers which seemed to confirm that negotiations had been taking place. Wingfield was therefore instructed to take the matter up with Salazar who, however, pre-empted any *démarche* by issuing a categorical statement to the Portuguese press on 29 January to the effect that contrary to all rumours 'we are not selling, ceding, leasing, or sharing our colonies. Our constitution does not permit it, neither does our national conscience'. On 2 February Monteiro again emphasised to Eden that 'under no circumstances would Germans be allowed into Angola'.[9]

In the absence of really firm evidence the only option was to accept that negotiations had never taken place. Certainly, Schacht denied the truth of the story: while at Badenweiler he gave Leith Ross, chief economic adviser to the British government, an unqualified assurance that no negotiations of any kind had taken place.[10] This was somewhat disingenuous given his deep interest in Angola. In his mammoth work on German colonial policy, Klaus Hildebrand cites a letter of 5 October 1935 from Dr Jung of the central office of the NSDAP to Hitler's adjutant, Captain Fritz Wiederman, according to which Hans Hoffman, a former plantation owner in Angola, had made a number of suggestions for extending German economic interests in the colony with which Jung basically agreed. The Nazi official, however, expressed the view that direct contact with Salazar was inappropriate owing to Portuguese sensitivity on the question of their colonies. Following consultations with Schacht, Kurt Weigelt, 'the undisputed representative of monopolist big business in the field of colonial planning',[11] and Baron Hoyningen-Huene, German minister in Lisbon, had reached the same conclusion. According to Jung the Reich economics minister and Weigelt had 'a more constructive plan'. Another German historian, Horst Kuhne, writing about German imperial ambitions in the mid-1930s asserts that the first priority of German finance capital was access to raw materials in Africa and that the question of territorial acquisition was of secondary importance. According to Kuhne, German finance capital tried to gain

7 FO 371/20718 C286/37/18; ADM 116/4391.
8 *The Times*, 28, 30 Jan. 1937; *The Economist*, 30 Jan. 1937; *The New York Times* and *The New York Herald Tribune* carried similar stories. See G. E. L. von Glahn, 'The German demand for colonies', unpublished PhD diss. North Western University 1939, 191.
9 FO 371/20719 C1130/37/18; 371/20718 C771/C785/35/18.
10 FO 371/20725 C958/78/18.
11 Ballhaus, 'Colonial aims', 344.

access to raw materials in Liberia and Angola. At the same time, it has to be acknowledged that in this period rumours were prone to exaggeration, for example, that which claimed that Germany intended to take over Angola forcibly. The British consulate at Luanda could find no evidence on the ground that the Germans were indulging locally in political propaganda or in subversive activities, while discreet observation of German colonists by the Portuguese authorities had revealed nothing to substantiate the popular rumours.[12]

At the beginning of 1937 the foreign office was still ambivalent about colonial appeasement. While the Schacht initiative remained dormant, Vansittart, in his end of year appraisal of British foreign policy, had not excluded the possibility of colonial concessions provided they formed part of a political settlement and enabled Britain 'to turn the corner of 1939' without war. It was assumed that the foreign office wanted to provide a breathing space 'to stabilise the position till 1939'. The foreign office did consider publicly refuting Schacht's presentation of the German case for revision in a *Foreign Affairs* article in January 1937,[13] but, in the event, decided to revive his initiative through Leith Ross's visit to Germany in early February. This was partly in response to Germany's rejection of a British invitation to attend a five-power conference: as an alternative Eden wished to pursue the possibility of negotiations for a general settlement based on Schacht's proposals. It was also a means of forestalling a French suggestion for a Franco–British–American initiative, which included colonial restitution, to meet Germany's economic difficulties.[14]

Having conceded conversations with Schacht, the government's approach remained cautious. Leith Ross was to make no proposal other than to remind the Reich economics minister that if his ideas were to form the basis of further discussion Germany would need to consider a number of political undertakings and assurances which should include participation in a new 'Locarno', an end to autarky, the establishment of neighbourly relations with Czechoslovakia, a return to the League and an end to the armaments race.[15] At Badenweiler on 2 February Schacht emphasised economic aid and colonial restitution as a means of modifying the autarky of Germany's four year plan. He assured Leith Ross that Hitler and Neurath shared his views and that in return for economic and colonial concessions he could promise substantial fulfilment of the list of political undertakings and assurances desired by the British government. Hitler was at present 'open to argument' and if he could be shown that 'other means were available to give Germany a chance' he could be persuaded 'to take that chance and give us the guarantees we wanted'.[16]

Although Hitler told Phipps on 3 February 1937 that no real settlement was

---

[12] Ibid. 344–5, 357; Hildebrand, *Vom Reich zum Weltreich*, 891; H. Kuhne, 'Zur Kolonialpolitik des faschistischen deutschen Imperialismus (1937–39)', *Zeitschrift für Geschichtswissenschaft* ix (1961), 519–20; FO 371/20723 C8055/37/18.

[13] *DBFP*, 2, xvii, app. ii, p. 801; 2, xviii, no. 21, pp. 21–3; H. Schacht, 'Germany's colonial demands', *Foreign Affairs* xv (1937), 223–34.

[14] Crozier, 'Prelude to Munich', 366; *DBFP*, 2, xviii, no. 86, pp. 112–14.

[15] Ibid. 2, xviii, no. 92, pp. 120–1.

[16] Ibid. 2, xviii, no. 148, pp. 187–95; C. A. MacDonald, 'Economic appeasement and the German "Moderates" 1937–1939', *Past and Present* lvi (1972), 107–8.

possible until Germany had colonies and that 'it was inadmissible that France, Great Britain, Spain, Italy, Holland, Portugal and Belgium should have colonies and Germany none', the British could not be sure Schacht had any real authority in foreign policy or that the *Führer* shared his views. At the same meeting Hitler told Phipps that he saw little prospect of an agreement on a western pact or disarmament, while on 11 February Ribbentrop's desire for generous treatment in the colonial sphere contrasted sharply with Halifax's view that colonial retrocession depended on a general settlement.[17] Despite uncertainty as to Nazi intentions and motives on the colonial issue, it was agreed at a meeting of the cabinet foreign policy committee on 18 March that exploratory talks with the French should be started with a joint approach to Berlin in mind.[18]

Discussion within the foreign policy committee revealed a willingness to consider colonial revision providing the United Kingdom was not itself required to make any territorial sacrifice. The return of Tanganyika and Ruanda-Urundi (held by Belgium) was ruled out on strategic grounds and it was accepted that, in view of their declared statements, neither the Japanese nor the Dominions would agree to surrender their mandates.[19] The options were therefore narrowed to some deal involving the Portuguese colonies or the cession of the Cameroons and Togoland which were largely French. The question of using Portuguese territory was raised indirectly by Halifax who expressed a preference for gathering together all the powers interested in Africa to see 'whether it might be possible to have some repartition of Africa in which Germany could find a place'. W. G. Ormsby Gore, the secretary of state for colonies, surmised that this would mean satisfying Germany with Portugal's African colonies and the suggestion was therefore dropped.[20] As there was clearly no intention of sacrificing Portuguese territory only the Cameroons and Togoland were left. However, while the French were willing to consider the cession of French mandates to Germany as part of a final general settlement, they would only do so if the British made at least as great a territorial sacrifice.[21]

Eden therefore told the foreign policy committee on 10 May that he was prepared to consider the cession of Gambia to France as compensation for the loss of Cameroons and Togoland. The Gambia option provoked a memorandum by Hankey but was not pressed at the foreign policy committee on 19 May.[22] Taking another line of argument Lord Lothian, who had met Hitler, Göring and Schacht on 4 May, suggested the government should discuss with the United States and with all the colonial powers how a relaxation of the economic pressures on Germany could be met: 'The United States might throw in war debts and tariff adjustments in return for some territorial arrangements by the colonial powers say in Central West Africa.' The problem was, as Vansittart noted, at whose expense should these be made? The government was

17 DBFP, 2, xviii, nos 147, 167, pp. 187, 221–5; Phipps Papers PHPP 1/17.
18 CAB 27/622 FP(36) 7th mtg; DBFP, 2, xviii, no. 307, pp. 449–59.
19 Ibid. 2, xviii, no. 445, pp. 676–82. For Dominion opinion see R. Ovendale, Appeasement and the English speaking world: Britain, the United States, the Dominions and the policy of appeasement 1936–1939, Cardiff 1975, 34–5, 47–8.
20 CAB 27/622 FP(36) 7th mtg, 18 Mar. 1937.
21 DBFP, 2, xviii, nos 462, 477, pp. 701–3, 723–4. FO800/274.
22 CAB 27/622 FP(36) 10th and 11th mtgs; CAB 27/626 FP(36) 32.

'entitled to expect precision on that. I suppose Portugal is intended again'.[23] In fact the government had no intention of using Portugal again, or Belgium or the Dominions, and with France unprepared to move without a reciprocal British sacrifice – which was unacceptable – the prospects for colonial appease-ment on the basis of the Schacht initiative of August 1936 were extinguished.

Despite the impasse in Anglo-German relations during the early summer of 1937 the colonial question was not dead. Certainly, the foreign office did not believe it was. Orme Sargent was concerned that the Dominion prime ministers should not infer from their conversations with British ministers during the recent imperial conference, that the Germans were prepared 'to shelve the colonial question more or less indefinitely', or that it no longer possessed 'very great importance in German eyes'. Vansittart agreed, expressing the view that 'the colonial question is upon us for keeps'.[24] At the same time, there were worrying signs of increasing anti-British feeling in Berlin. Before his departure for the Paris embassy, Phipps had conveyed Göring's regret that 'Germany was beginning to believe that Great Britain must be numbered amongst her enemies'. Soon afterwards, on 4 May, during 'a long and stormy meeting' with Lothian, the Reichsmarschall castigated Britain for not responding positively to his country which had 'nothing but the friendliest feelings for the British people and the British Empire'. He warned Lothian that 'the German man in the street was now beginning to sense that Germany's real enemy was Great Britain'. Göring repeated his warning to Sir Nevile Henderson, the new British ambassador in Berlin, on 24 May 1937.[25] Eden and his advisers were naturally disturbed by the Reichsmarschall's comments and wished to discuss them with Neurath. However, the foreign minister's visit to London was cancelled and Eden therefore asked the Berlin embassy on 15 July to discover the grounds for Göring's allegation of German animosity towards Britain.[26]

More than two months elapsed before Göring provided a written reply and it was scarcely enlightening. However, he was less elusive in his verbal response, claiming German aims to be limited to 'the consolidation of all Germans into one great German State by reason of the right of nations to self-determination' and expressing his government's desire for an Anglo-German understanding based on German recognition of British maritime preponderance and British recognition of German primacy in Europe. When Henderson taxed him on colonial revision Göring replied that Germany was determined to obtain col-onies and must have them, but it was not British colonies she wanted. He hinted that Portugal might be induced to sell some or all of hers to Germany.[27] Following this conversation Halifax received his celebrated invitation to attend an international sporting exhibition in Berlin, held under the auspices of the German Hunting Association. The Halifax visit and its aftermath represented,

[23] Halifax Papers, A4 410 3.1; Vansittart Papers, VNST 2/31; DBFP, 2, xviii, no. 480, pp. 727–31.
[24] Ibid. 2, xviii, no. 592 and n. 6, pp. 867–8; Ovendale, Appeasement, 48.
[25] DBFP, 2, xviii, nos 396, 480, 538, pp. 609–11, 727–31, 803–4.
[26] Ibid. 2, xix, nos 41, 52, pp. 67–72, 93–7.
[27] Ibid. 2, xix, no. 238, pp. 386–8.

in Andrew Crozier's words, the point at which the colonial question reached 'the pinnacle of importance' in Anglo-German relations during the inter-war years.[28]

British interest in colonial revision had revived during September and October in response to the recrudescence of the German colonial campaign. At the Nuremberg party rally during September 1937 Hitler had apparently spoken in 'unrestrained language' on the subject. During the same month Carl Burckhardt, the visiting League commissioner to Danzig, had learned from the *Führer* of his pain over the dismissal of his colonial claim.[29] Both Göring and Hitler confirmed their commitment to colonial retrocession in separate interviews with the Aga Khan. Indeed, the *Führer* indicated that he was 'perfectly prepared to consider giving up Tanganyika if approximately similar territory were given to Germany as a mandate on the West coast'. Chamberlain was particularly impressed by the Aga Khan's report of his conversations, declaring it 'the most valuable I have seen yet'.[30]

German references to the west coast of Africa, coupled with previously declared interest, were bound to imply some rearrangement of territory which would involve Angola. The foreign office certainly considered this was the case, Orme Sargent stating that 'the only commensurate territory in our possession would be Nigeria – or failing that Portuguese Angola'. Vansittart, however, insisted that 'we cannot muck about as we once did with the possible reversion of other people's property'.[31] Eden shared his reluctance to involve the territory of the smaller colonial powers. Noting that it was Halifax's intention to tell the Germans that 'it would almost certainly be found that others were concerned, and that it would be necessary for "African" powers to consider the question in joint conference', the foreign secretary commented: 'This is rather dangerous. The Belgians and Portuguese won't play at helping us to placate Germany.'[32] In this respect Eden was absolutely correct. Bateman had reported on 3 November that the question of Germany's colonial claims had been the subject of much comment and speculation in the Portuguese press which, oblivious of German claims to the Kionga Triangle, was 'united in declaring that Portugal, having gained no colonial territory as a result of the Paris Treaties, should not be called upon to sacrifice any of her possessions in order to help in remedying the injustice caused by those Treaties'.[33] The extreme delicacy of the matter convinced the foreign office that it should not take up the suggestion, made by Sir Peter Hannon MP, that a question be asked in the house of commons with the object of reassuring Portugal and disabusing the Germans of any ideas that they might acquire a Portuguese colony with Britain's connivance. Howard Smith, an assistant under-secretary, was inclined to provide such an assurance if Halifax succeeded in establishing positive contact in Berlin:

28 Crozier, 'Imperial decline', 230.
29 *DBFP*, 2, xix, no. 145, pp. 262–3; Halifax Papers, A4 410 3.2.
30 Chamberlain Papers, NC 7/11/30/1–3; Halifax Papers, A4 410 3.3.
31 FO 371/20723 C7595/37/18.
32 Eden Papers (FO954) GE/37/48.
33 FO 371/20723 C7697/37/18; *The Times*, 2 Nov. 1937; H. Dalton, *The fateful years: memoirs 1931–1945*, London 1957, 106–7. For German interest in the Kionga Triangle see FO 371/20721 C3913/37/18.

But if Lord Halifax visits the Fuhrer at Berchtesgaden, may not Portuguese memories fly back to the visit paid to Berlin [in 1912] by Lord Haldane, especially as the German press, and the English for that matter, is so full of the subject of colonies? I am not sure that it is for consideration that, if Lord Halifax's visit comes off, we should give a clear assurance to the Portuguese Government that there is no intention to repeat what Sir Eyre Crowe called 'the most discreditable episode in our history'.

Vansittart took the view that if the Portuguese asked they should have no option 'but to give the assurance in some form', but he did not think they 'should volunteer it'.[34]

When Halifax visited Hitler on 19 November the *Führer* referred to the colonial question as the only direct issue between their two countries and expressed his confidence that Britain and France together would examine the question and would be able to propose a solution. Halifax was left with the impression that if Hitler could not be accommodated on colonies 'good relations, under which I suppose we might exert a good deal of influence, and without which the present strain continues, would remain impossible'. While Halifax felt that Blomberg regarded the colonial question as secondary to Germany's position in central and eastern Europe, and that Göring would not be 'too difficult about colonies' it was Hjalmar Schacht who had been the most forthcoming on the colonial issue. He had stressed that west Africa, and in particular Angola, was the focal point of the German colonial claim. Halifax concluded that the only way of improving Anglo-German relations was by means of colonial revision, which should be offered to Hitler as an inducement to being a 'good European'.[35] These views were endorsed by the prime minister.

The situation thus seemed clear. The Germans wanted Togoland and the Cameroons but would not insist on Tanganyika provided they could be given some 'reasonably equivalent' territory on the west coast possibly 'to be carved out of [the] Belgian Congo and Angola'. Chamberlain recognised that Portugal would object strongly to parting with any territory, but it was worth discovering 'whether in a Conference of African Powers we could not arrive at such adjustments as would satisfy the Germans compensating the Powers which surrendered territories by money or territory elsewhere'.[36] The foreign office was less sanguine. Orme Sargent recognised that since Halifax's visit had taken place in a glare of publicity, attracting considerable attention and raising many hopes, 'it would be very difficult, not to say dangerous, not to follow it up with some proposals'. Vansittart agreed but feared that the time had passed 'when colonial retrocession would have fetched a price in Europe'. Eden, however, was determined that it should: 'If we do not get; we shall not give.'[37] Chamberlain, in this instance, was of like mind with his foreign secretary. He assured his cabinet colleagues on 24 November, when Halifax presented his report, that 'he would

---

[34] FO 371/21278 W20797/1966/36.
[35] *DBFP*, 2, xix, no. 336, pp. 540–55; *DGFP*, D, i, no. 31, pp. 54–67.
[36] Chamberlain Papers, NC 18/1/1030. See also K. Feiling, *Life of Neville Chamberlain*, London 1946, 332–3.
[37] FO 371/20736 C8161/270/18.

not make any offer in the colonial field except as a factor in a general settlement'.[38] At the Anglo-French conference on 29–30 November, held to co-
ordinate their respective foreign policies in the light of the Halifax visit, the
French prime minister, Camille Chautemps, and his foreign minister, Yvon
Delbos, confirmed the essential link between colonial revision and a general
settlement. During the conference the British prime minister took the opportunity to float a scheme of retrocession:

> The question of the British contribution on the colonial question was a very
> difficult one. What would the French Government think of a British ap-
> proach to Belgium and Portugal with the object of meeting Germany's sug-
> gestion for a mandate in West Africa over Belgian and Portuguese territory in
> compensation for Tanganyika, the basis of such an approach to be territorial
> cession or monetary compensation or both?

The French ministers were non-committal although Delbos thought that such
an approach would be premature. Directly following the conversations it was
announced publicly for the first time that the British and French governments
were prepared to study the colonial question and, as Andrew Crozier notes, the
silence in British political circles was deafening.[39] Encouraged by the lack of
opposition, and aware of the burdens which diplomacy would have to shoulder
in the light of the chiefs of staff's recent evaluation of British defences,
Chamberlain had every incentive to proceed with colonial appeasement.

The study of the colonial question by the British and French governments
required, as Eden told Ribbentrop, a period of relative calm without incessant
German colonial propaganda.[40] While German demands for colonial revision
were less strident during December 1937 there were difficulties as a result of
newspaper reports in western Europe, Britain and the United States which
claimed a colonial deal was being concocted at the expense of the smaller
colonial powers, Portugal and Belgium. On 1 December Ribbentrop expressed
'considerable surprise' at reports in the Belgian press that Germany had suggested some consolidated colony on the west coast of Africa to which Portugal
and Belgium should contribute. The ambassador was convinced that this did
not represent Hitler's view and he asked whether anybody else had spoken to
Halifax in these terms. Eden's answer was a little evasive, indicating that
Schacht might have made such a proposal. Ribbentrop was adamant that
although Angola had always been Schacht's particular interest, his views in this
matter 'did not represent the views of anybody but himself'.[41]

Press reports proved a considerable embarrassment both for Germany and for
Britain's relations with Portugal. On 2 December Ernst von Weisäcker, soon to

[38] CAB 23/90 CM 43(37).
[39] CAB 27/626 FP(36) 40; Crozier, 'Imperial decline', 231–2; W. R. Louis, 'Colonial appeasement, 1936–1938', *Revue Belge de Philologie et d'Histoire* xlix (1971), 1183–4.
[40] *DBFP*, 2, xix, no. 360, pp. 632–4.
[41] Ibid. In his telegram to Berlin of 2 December Ribbentrop claimed that Eden assured him
'that he did not know where this report [German claims on Portuguese and Belgian territory]
came from': *DGFP*, D, i, no. 50, pp. 88–91.

become Ribbentrop's state secretary, informed the German legation in Lisbon that the reports in the British and Belgian press were a deliberate attempt to make trouble. German diplomats in Portugal were accordingly instructed to deny the rumours and refer to Hitler's statement of 30 January 1937 that 'Germany was making no colonial demands on countries that have taken no colonies from her'.[42] Portuguese suspicions had been fuelled not only by press reports but also by information passed on to Monteiro by the Polish ambassador in London, to the effect that while Hitler had not mentioned colonies to Halifax, Göring had proposed the return of all Germany's former colonies in full sovereignty and the establishment of an international company, in which Germany would be the largest shareholder, to administer the Belgian Congo and Angola. The Reichsmarschall assured the Portuguese minister, Simões, that the press reports were completely without foundation and that a satisfactory solution of German colonial claims would be made by England and France exclusively and would not involve third parties, particularly countries such as Portugal with whom Germany was on the best of terms. According to André François-Poncet, the French ambassador in Berlin, Göring had spoken rather severely about Schacht to Simões, claiming that he had no authority to speak for the Reich.[43] These denials were followed on 6 December by a speech by Ritter von Epp, head of the Colonial League, which was given front page prominence in the *Völkischer Beobachter*. Epp claimed the foreign press had invented stories about Angola and the Belgian Congo with the aim of poisoning the atmosphere at a time when the mandatory powers realised the colonial problem was acute and required urgent solution.[44]

When Eden saw Monteiro on 2 December to inform him of the course of Anglo-French conversations the ambassador was very outspoken:

> His Excellency made no attempt to conceal the horror with which he regarded the idea of Germany becoming again an African Power. 'Today', he said, 'Africa is at peace. Nobody wants Germany back. No native anywhere wishes for such an event, nor does any white man. If Germany goes back to Africa you main gain peace in Europe, but you will destroy peace in Africa.'

Monteiro also warned Eden of the great strategic dangers of allowing Germany to control territory on the west coast of Africa: the establishment of submarine bases there would menace British communications in the Atlantic. Eden assured him that Hitler had never suggested the cession of any Portuguese territory and added that British public opinion 'would never consider the cession of colonial territory to Germany except that the cession could be regarded as the final contribution in reaching a settlement which would give Europe better prospects of real peace than the continent enjoyed at present'.[45]

[42] Ibid. D, i, no. 52, p. 92.
[43] *DAPE*, i, nos 154, 159, pp. 211–12, 214–15; *DDF*, 2, vii, no. 313, p. 603. See also A. J. Crozier, 'British foreign policy 1936–1939 and the Portuguese documents relating to the origins of the Second World War', unpubl. MA diss. London 1967, 22.
[44] FO 371/20724 C8425/37/18.
[45] FO 371/20723 C8377/37/18; *DAPE*, i, no. 160, pp. 215–18; Crozier, 'British foreign policy', 22–3; Kay, *Salazar*, 135.

Official German denials were reported prominently in the Portuguese press as were the visits of the Portuguese and Belgian ambassadors to the foreign office. At the same time, special attention was drawn to the remarkable silence emanating from official quarters in London. When Bateman reported this, Eden, unlike Cranborne, was prepared to consider a written reply to a question in the house of commons. The foreign office, however, unanimously denied the need for this.[46] But, on 14 December, the very same day Eden acceded to this view, the Portuguese revived the whole issue: Sampaio contrasted Germany's official and categorical disclaimers, which had cleared her of suspicion in Lisbon, with the silence of Portugal's ally. He told Bateman that the ambiguous language used by Eden in his conversations with Monteiro – specifically his reference to public opinion and the cession of territory – filled his government with misgiving which was increased by growing references in the London press to the negotiations of 1898 and 1913. The secretary general then warned that:

> The time has passed for vague language and consoling phrases. What is urgently necessary is an unequivocal declaration by His Majesty's Government that the pre-war proposals are dead and that His Majesty's Government have no intention of endeavouring to revive them or pursuing any suggestions of a similar nature.

Sampaio refused to be comforted by Bateman's assurances that when Eden spoke to Monteiro he only had British colonial possessions in mind.[47]

When Eden himself saw Monteiro on 16 December he expressed his astonishment that the Portuguese government continued to doubt their ally's attitude. While it was quite true that 'the German Government had issued a *démenti* of their desire for concessions from Portugal' nobody, so far as Eden was aware, had suggested that 'we had ambitions to benefit from Portuguese possessions or colonies'. There had been, therefore, no need for a similar *démenti* from the British government. He did, however, recognise the need to provide some categorical assurance and accordingly he told Monteiro that 'so far as His Majesty's Government were concerned, the pre-war proposals were dead, and we had no intention of endeavouring to revive them or of pursuing any suggestion of a similar nature', and 'our ancient ally was not to be the price paid for the settlement of the German claims'. On 18 December Selby repeated these assurances during his first meeting with Salazar as ambassador to Portugal.[48] A few days later, on 21 December, Eden publicly repudiated the suggestions that the government was 'thinking of reviving certain pre-war negotiations, in regard to Portuguese territories' and emphasised that, 'so far as we are concerned, those pre-war proposals are dead and we have not the least intention of endeavouring to revive them'. On 23 December Monteiro expressed his delight to Eden personally and referred to Anglo-Portuguese relations as being 'in a honeymoon phase once again'. In Lisbon Salazar sent his personal thanks to the

46 FO 371/21278 W21794/1966/36.
47 FO 371/21278 W22304/1966/36; Nogueira, *Salazar*, iii, 135–6.
48 FO 371/21278 W22354/1966/36; 371/21270 W22920/25/36. According to Selby, Salazar was 'really delighted and relieved' to receive Eden's assurances: Avon Papers, AP 13/1/63.

embassy for Eden's clear and unambiguous statement to which the entire press devoted leading articles.[49]

Nevertheless, Monteiro was far from sanguine about the future of the Portuguese colonies. He told Salazar on 30 December that the prevailing temper in Britain was disposed towards reaching a settlement with Germany through the 'just settlement of outstanding claims'. He had no faith in fair words or treaties and suggested a four-point approach: Portugal should oppose any agreement modifying the existing *status quo* in Africa; should demonstrate to the British and French that any alternative arrangements would be detrimental to their interests; should approach Belgium and South Africa for mutual protection; and should build a strong army in Africa.[50] The ambassador's fears were quite justified. Eden's statement had referred to the pre-war proposals, not to any new proposals that might be made, and his public statement did not mention that 'our ancient ally was not to be the price paid for the settlement of the German claims'. Indeed, Orme Sargent had advised the foreign secretary not to go too far in his assurances to Monteiro on 16 December, advising him 'to avoid saying anything which would exclude us at a future date from inviting Portugal with other Colonial Powers to discuss a general reshuffle of African colonies, with a view to satisfying Germany's claims. Such a reshuffle might involve some change in the status quo of Portugal's colonies or part of them'.[51] It was on such a reshuffle that the prime minister was to concentrate his fertile mind during the last days of 1937 and early January 1938.

Following the visit of the French ministers and discussion in cabinet the government intended to study the colonial question over a period of time and in some depth.[52] By the end of December, however, the foreign office, including the foreign secretary, had developed a sense of urgency. In a memorandum for the foreign policy committee of 1 January 1938, Eden stressed that a long delay should be avoided 'to prevent the hopes created by the recent conversations from evaporating'. Yet it was admitted in the same memorandum that there were several difficult questions. The government needed to clarify exactly what it meant by a 'general settlement' and which territories might be considered eligible for transfer. If in the latter case the French were prepared to make colonial sacrifices it was essential to consider what territorial concessions could be made by Britain, the Dominions and also by other colonial powers, specifically Belgium and Portugal.[53]

In view of the urgency, and in the absence of definite proposals from the foreign office, the prime minister developed his own scheme – an African condominium – based on 'a number of valuable and useful suggestions' made by Joseph Avenol, secretary general of the League of Nations.[54] Chamberlain

[49] *Hansard parliamentary debates*, HC, 5th ser., cccxxx, cols 1880–1; FO 425/414; *The Times*, 24 Dec. 1937.
[50] Kay, *Salazar*, 136; Crozier, 'British foreign policy', 23.
[51] FO 371/21278 W22354/1966/36.
[52] FO 371/20737 C8466/270/18; DBFP, 2, xix, no. 395, pp. 682–6.
[53] CAB 27/626 FP(36) 41; DBFP, 2, xix, no. 409, pp. 706–9.
[54] Chamberlain Papers, NC 2/2A; DBFP, 2, xix, app. i, p. 1139.

presented his ideas to his foreign policy committee colleagues on 24 January 1938:

> The new conception would be based on the complete equality of the Powers concerned and of their all being subjected to certain limitations in regard to African territories to be administered by themselves under the scheme. Germany would be brought into the arrangements by becoming one of the African Colonial Powers in question and by being given certain territories to administer. His idea was that two lines should be drawn across Africa, the northern line running roughly to the south of the Sahara, the Anglo-Egyptian Sudan, Abyssinia and Italian Somaliland, and the southern line running roughly to the south of Portuguese West Africa, the Belgian Congo, Tanganyika and Portuguese East Africa.

Although the scheme envisaged the pooling of some British and French territory it was clear that the Dominion mandates were excluded while Belgium and Portugal were required to make a very substantial contribution. As Simon pointed out during the discussion: 'a glance at the map of West Africa would show how very extensive were the possessions of Belgium and Portugal in that part of the world'. Despite the chancellor's reservations and those of his colleagues – only Hoare offered reasoned objections – the committee agreed to proceed with the prime minister's scheme.[55]

The foreign policy committee and cabinet recognised the importance of connecting colonial revision to general appeasement in Europe. In the first instance, it was felt that exploratory talks with the German government should precede concrete proposals. Accordingly, Henderson was instructed to emphasise the importance which not only Britain but other countries attached to German collaboration in appeasement. While Chamberlain's scheme was to be outlined to the German government, Henderson was specifically told not to identify the areas of transfer.[56] Originally, it had been thought the scheme should be communicated to Hitler before his Reichstag speech of 20 February, but the purge in the German high command, Ribbentrop's appointment as foreign minister and Eden's own resignation conspired to delay Henderson's interview with the *Führer* until 3 March.

During the intervening period the foreign office had to consider how to explain its unilateral approach to Berlin to other interested countries. The French were informed as early as 17 February though reference to the colonial question was confined to a general statement to the effect that no definite scheme was being put forward, and no commitments entered into or undertakings given. Paris was also reassured that no proposals would be contemplated which did not involve an equivalent contribution from Britain to any made by

---

[55] CAB 27/623 FP(36) 21st mtg; *DBFP*, 2, xix, no. 465, pp. 777–91; Ovendale, *Appeasement*, 107–8; K. Middlemas, *Diplomacy of illusion: the British government and Germany 1937–1939*, London 1972, 141–3; R. A. C. Parker, *Chamberlain and appeasement: British policy and the coming of the Second World War*, London 1993, 129–30; Louis, 'Colonial appeasement', 1185–9.

[56] CAB 24/275 CP 54(38); *DBFP*, 2, xix, nos 488, 512, pp. 836–50, 890–2; CAB 27/623 FP(36) 22nd mtg, 3 Feb. 1938; CAB 23/92 CM 4(38), 9 Feb. 1938.

France.[57] Draft telegrams for the United States, Italy, Belgium and Portugal were prepared well in advance, but they were to be communicated only after Henderson's interview had taken place. Some countries were to be told more than others:

> We are telling the United States Government rather less than we have told the French, and we are telling the Italian, Belgian and Portuguese Governments rather less than we are telling the Americans. The telegrams . . . to Belgium and Portugal are in identical terms. It is to be anticipated that on receipt of this information, we shall have urgent enquiries from the Belgian and Portuguese Governments as to what we are saying in Berlin about colonies and as to what our ultimate intentions are.

In the event, the foreign office sent off the telegrams to the British embassies in Rome and Washington on 2 March but did not send those to Brussels and Lisbon until 4.30 pm on 3 March, just half an hour before Henderson was due to see Hitler. Officials were only too aware of the problems the communication was likely to cause in their relations with Belgium and Portugal. As Orme Sargent observed:

> We must realise that since we have already forewarned the Americans, and the Germans have probably similarly forewarned the Italians, the news will not come as a surprise to *them*. But to the Portuguese and Belgians it will come as a bolt out of the blue, and the mention of the colonial issue is likely to provoke suspicions and questionings. But I don't see that this can be helped.[58]

The first part of the communication to the Lisbon embassy on 3 March, brief and couched in general terms, merely informed Selby that as a first step in achieving a measure of appeasement in Europe it was considered desirable to take soundings in Berlin 'with the object of finding out on what lines it might be possible to find a solution to the various problems at issue, including the colonial question, Central Europe and disarmament'. In view of the discussions which had taken place during January and February the second part, which contained the ambassador's instructions, was at best misleading:

> You can assure the Portuguese Government that there is no departure in this regard from the assurances contained in my predeccessor's speech of December 21st in the House of Commons, to the effect that there is no intention whatever of trying to reach a settlement with Germany in the colonial field on the basis of a deal at the expense of other Colonial Powers.

Selby carried out his instructions on the evening of 3 March and the following day received a message from Salazar, who was of course unaware of Chamberlain's

---

[57] DBFP, 2, xix, nos 515, 541, pp. 894, 914–5.
[58] FO 371/21655 C1027/C1398/42/18.

scheme, thanking Halifax and expressing his appreciation of the foreign secretary's assurances.[59]

When Henderson saw Hitler, with Ribbentrop, on 3 March, he carried out Eden's precise instructions of 12 February. The *Führer* and his foreign minister, however, were clearly unimpressed by the British attempt to link colonial settlement with appeasement in central Europe. Under close questioning the ambassador then exceeded his instructions, stating that the British colonial scheme did not exclude the possibility of the restoration of former German colonial territory outside the proposed area. Even this did not attract Hitler who explicitly expressed his disinterest in colonial appeasement in the short term. However, in view of the importance of the colonial question he promised Henderson a written reply.[60]

In rejecting Britain's offer to discuss colonies Hitler was acting according to the strategy laid down in *Mein Kampf* and more recently at the Hossbach Conference of 5 November 1937 when he made specific reference to the achievement of German hegemony in Europe by 1943-5 at the latest. Once European power was achieved the *Führer* would seek to establish his *Weltreich*. In this connection, it is significant that, on his instructions, the date for completing the Z-Plan for extensive German naval construction was brought forward during 1938 from 1948 to 1944. In view of Hitler's intentions, the price Britain demanded for colonial retrocession – arms limitation and peaceful collaboration in Europe – was unacceptably high, even for such traditionalists as Weizsäcker and Neurath.[61] Simões, the Portuguese minister in Berlin, recognised this when he assured Salazar on 4 March that as Germany would be required to make large concessions in Europe everything indicated that a colonial agreement would be a non-starter.[62] Certainly, the British authorities had no intention of raising the colonial issue again following Henderson's abortive meeting and the German annexation of Austria. The onus was now upon Germany.[63] In the event, Hitler's promised reply did not materialise and during July Halifax was able to soothe renewed Portuguese fears concerning the possibility of colonial redistribution by assuring Monteiro, this time genuinely, that 'we are not going to negotiate over Portuguese colonies to your cost'.[64] Colonial appeasement was to all intents and purposes a dead letter after March 1938 but the idea lingered in government circles and was temporarily, if weakly, re-kindled after the Munich settlement.

[59] FO 371/21655 C1027/42/18; 371/21656 C1522/42/18; DAPE, i, no. 234, pp. 314–15. See also Crozier, *Appeasement*, 238.

[60] *DBFP*, 2, xix, nos 609, 610, pp. 985–8; CAB 24/275 CP 58(38); *DGFP*, D, i, no. 138, pp. 240–9; W. W. Schmokel, *Dream of empire: German colonialism 1919–1945*, New Haven, Conn. 1964, 117–21; Crozier, *Appeasement*, 239.

[61] See Schmokel, *Dream of empire*, 122–3; Weinberg, *The foreign policy of Hitler's Germany*, ii, 137–8; Crozier, 'Imperial decline', 233; M. E. Townsend, 'Hitler and the revival of German colonialism', in E. M. Earle (ed.), *Nationalism and internationalism: essays inscribed to Carlton J. Hayes*, New York 1950, 425. For the Z-Plan see E. M. Robertson, 'Hitler's planning for war and the response of the great powers (1938 – early 1939)', in H. W. Koch (ed.), *Aspects of the Third Reich*, London 1985, 208–11.

[62] *DAPE*, i, no. 235, pp. 315–16.

[63] FO 800/269.

[64] FO 371/22591 W10020/75/36; Crozier, 'Prelude to Munich', 375.

Although the colonial question was not mentioned during the Munich proceedings both Hitler and Chamberlain had announced, in the Anglo-German declaration of 30 September, their determination 'to continue their efforts to remove all possible sources of difference and thus contribute to assure the peace of Europe'.[65] The foreign office therefore engaged in a post-Munich appraisal of British foreign policy options in which the question of colonies received due consideration to the extent that 'a clear official consensus in favour of a renewed approach to Germany on the colonial question' was achieved.[66] In developing this the foreign office was not unaware of Hitler's recent reiteration, to François-Poncet at Berchtesgaden, that he was prepared to wait three, four or five years for a decision on colonies.[67] They also understood Portuguese anxieties at the revival of the colonial question as an issue of international politics. As early as 6 October Monteiro expressed to Halifax his fear that the idea of a colonial conference had been mooted at Munich. The foreign secretary's assurance that no such suggestion had been made 'brought the Ambassador evident relief'. However, Monteiro had also studied *Mein Kampf* from which he understood it was Hitler's intention to assert colonial demands once European questions had been settled. Salazar shared his ambassador's pessimism and was convinced that Hitler would soon demand the return of Germany's colonies. According to Selby, the Portuguese prime minister entertained 'little confidence as regard Herr Hitler's professions'.[68]

Continuing speculation in the British press concerning the possible redistribution of Belgian and Portuguese colonial territories in Africa did little to allay Portuguese anxieties despite Salazar's declaration in the *Diário de Notícias* of 16 October, of his faith in the Anglo-Portuguese alliance and the disinterest of other powers in the Portuguese colonies.[69] The visit to Portugal, Britain and Germany during late October and November 1938 of Oswald Pirow, the South African defence minster, served only to fuel press speculation: the advanced announcement was greeted with alarm in Lisbon. Although both Monteiro and Ferreira da Fonseca, the Portuguese minister in Pretoria, were told to find out why he was coming they failed to find anything definite,[70] thus exacerbating rumour and press speculation. Before Pirow even arrived in Lisbon, the Marseilles correspondent of *The Times* was telegraphing London with the news that he had told press representatives there that he intended to discuss the question of Portugal's colonies with leading Portuguese statesmen. It was further

---

[65] Feiling, *Life of Neville Chamberlain*, 376, 381.

[66] D Lammers, 'From Whitehall after Munich: the foreign office and the future course of British foreign policy', *Historical Journal* xvi (1973), 855. For a discussion of the post-Munich debate in the foreign office see also S. Newman, *March 1939: the British guarantee to Poland*, London 1976, 63–6.

[67] Phipps Papers, PHPP 1/21; *DBFP*, 3, iii, app. ii, p. 618.

[68] FO 371/22594 W13338/W13847/W14180/146/36.

[69] R. W. Logan, *The African mandates in world politics*, Washington, DC 1948, 152; RIIA, *Germany's claim to colonies*, 2nd edn, London 1939, 71; Townsend, 'Hitler and the revival of German colonialism', 424.

[70] FO 371/22600 W13533/2184/36; D. C. Watt, 'South African attempts to mediate between Britain and Germany 1935–1938', in K. Bourne and D. C. Watt (eds), *Studies in international history*, London 1967, 417.

reported that he might also visit Germany to discuss the colonial issue with Hitler.[71] Pirow's statement provided credence to a report in the *Daily Herald* of 26 October which claimed that political circles in London were discussing colonial retrocession at the expense of Angola and possibly the Belgian Congo. It was not surprising, therefore, that considerable alarm was raised in Lisbon and Brussels, and while Pretoria issued a firm denial Pirow made no public move to deny the reports.[72] The Germans were not slow to exploit the situation and sought to embarrass the British in their relations with Portugal. On 28 October Selby reported that the *Deutsches Nachrichten-Büro* always brought articles, such as the *Daily Herald's*, to the immediate attention of Portuguese opinion while an article in the *Deutsches Allgemeine Zeitung*, which was given great prominence in the Portuguese press, declared its incredulity that the British authorities should demand of friendly countries such as Portugal and Belgium that they cede any part of their territory to the Reich as compensation for the former German colonies held by themselves.[73]

In interviews with Salazar on 27 and 28 October Pirow confined his remarks on the colonial issue to the simple statement that while some of her former colonies should be restored to Germany, South Africa was determined not to relinquish South-West Africa. At the same time, he laid great emphasis upon the importance of Lourenço Marques for the defence of the Union and even offered military assistance in the provision of ammunition and in training Portuguese pilots. Portuguese approval was also secured for the establishment of an air link between Angola, the Belgian Congo and South Africa.[74] During his subsequent visit to London Pirow insisted that his country was prepared only to make 'substantial financial sacrifices', and that for political and military reasons Tanganyika should not be returned to Germany. However, as he told Malcolm MacDonald, the dominions secretary, he was prepared to consider the surrender of Portuguese territory as part of a colonial deal with Germany.[75] Pirow's suggestions were echoed by the Aga Khan, whose followers in Tanganyika numbered about 15,000. In a memorandum forwarded to Halifax from Antibes on 11 November he suggested that as the Kilwo district of Tanganyika was geographically close to Portuguese East Africa it could be safely handed over to Portugal with financial and other concessions in exchange for ceding Angola to Germany. Since Belgium already occupied Ruanda-Urundi she could be asked to cede a substantial part of the western Congo. Tanganyika and South-West Africa would be retained by Britain and South Africa as mandated territory.[76]

Any progress on the colonial question was brought to an abrupt halt by *Kristallnacht* (9–10 November). On 15 November MacDonald warned Pirow

---

71 *The Times*, 26 Oct. 1938; Watt, 'South African attempts to mediate', 417.

72 Ibid. 417–18; DAPE, ii, no. 433, p. 40. The French government was also deeply concerned about these reports: FO 371/21682 C13165/184/18; DDF, 2, xii, no. 217, pp. 379–80.

73 FO 371/22601 W14305/W14458/2184/36.

74 DAPE, ii, nos 429, 434, pp. 37–8, 41; Watt, 'South African attempts to mediate', 418. See also FO 371/22601 W14307/2184/36; Nogueira, *Salazar*, iii, 183.

75 FO 371/21682 C13625/C13874/184/18. See also PREM 1/289; Ovendale, *Appeasement*, 187. Pirow repeated his ideas on a central African federation to the French ambassador on 11 November: DDF, 2, xii, no. 294, 532–3.

76 FO 371/21683 C13967/184/36.

that British public opinion would no longer tolerate any transfer of colonies or mandated territories to the Third Reich. The following day cabinet endorsed Chamberlain's view that in the existing circumstances there could be no question of returning colonies to Germany.[77] Public sentiment against colonial revision was also hardening in France where there was a resurgence of interest in the French empire.[78] As a result of Kristallnacht the United States was also far less inclined towards appeasing Germany either through colonial revision or other means.[79] The British government therefore felt free to reiterate in the house of commons, on 16 November, that the United Kingdom no longer considered herself bound by the secret convention with Germany of 1898 and R. A. Butler was able to reaffirm the nation's commitment to the Anglo-Portuguese treaties, a commitment which included a guarantee of Portugal's colonial possessions against attack. Any lingering doubts, which the Portuguese or other interested powers might have had, were dispelled publicly on 7 December when MacDonald, echoing Hitler's own words to Pirow in Berlin, informed the house of commons that the government was not discussing colonial retrocesion: 'We are not considering it; it is not now an issue in practical politics'.[80]

The Führer, however, was not inclined to let the matter rest. Early in January 1939 Josef Beck, the Polish foreign minister, following a conversation with Hitler at Berchtesgaden, gained the distinct impression that colonies were high on the agenda of Nazi foreign policy.[81] Indeed, at the beginning of December 1938 Hitler had decided that Germany would demand the unconditional return of her former colonies; on 27 January 1939 the decision was taken to begin construction of a powerful German high seas fleet (Z-Plan); and in February preparations were initiated to create a state colonial office out of the national socialist party's colonial policy office. In addition, on 9 March Epp was instructed by the reich chancellery to push on with plans for the 'occupation of colonial

[77] FO 371/21791 C14096/13564/18; CAB23/96 CM 55(38); The diplomatic diaries of Oliver Harvey 1937–1940, ed. J. Harvey, London 1970, 217–20; C. A. MacDonald, 'Deterrent diplomacy: Roosevelt and the containment of Germany, 1938–1940', in Boyce and Robertson, Paths to war, 306–7.

[78] C. Peyrefitte, 'Les premiers sondages d'opinion', in R. Rémond and J. Bourdin, Edouard Daladier; chef de gouvernement, avril 1938–septembre 1939, Paris 1977, 270–1; C. M. Andrew, 'The French colonialist movement during the Third Republic: the unofficial mind of imperialism', Transactions of the Royal Historical Society, 5th ser. xxvi (1976), 164–5; R. J. Young, 'The aftermath of Munich: the course of French diplomacy, October 1938–March 1939', French Historical Studies viii (1973), 316–17; C. Ageron, 'L'idée d'eurafrique et le débat colonial franco-allemand de l'entre-deux-guerres', Revue d'Histoire Moderne et Contemporaine xxii (1975), 473. For British public opinion on this issue see D. C. Watt, 'British domestic politics and the onset of war', in Centre National de la Recherche Scientifique, Les relations franco-britanniques de 1935 à 1939, Paris 1975, 257.

[79] Ovendale, Appeasement, 194–5; C. A. MacDonald, The United States, Britain and appeasement 1936–1939, London 1981, 113–14; Weinberg, The foreign policy of Hitler's Germany, ii, 520; Diplomatic diaries, 219.

[80] Hansard parliamentary debates, HC, 5th ser. cccxli, cols 849–50; cccxlii, col. 1239; CAB 27/627 FP(36) 71.

[81] Poland and the coming of the Second World War: the diplomatic papers of A. J. Drexel Biddle Jr, United States ambassador to Poland 1937–1939, ed. P. V. Cannistraro, E. D. Wynot and T. P. Kovaleff, Columbus, Ohio 1976, 303, 311.

territory' in Africa.[82] However, official circles in Britain and France were loathe to consider the colonial question; an attitude which reflected public opinion in both countries.[83] Moreover, during February the British chiefs of staff produced a report which was highly critical of colonial revision on strategic grounds.[84] Chamberlain, however, remained somewhat ambivalent: he informed cabinet on 3 May that it was quite impossible to discuss the colonial question with Germany, and while towards the end of the month Butler reiterated, in the house of commons, Eden's statement of 21 December 1937 concerning the Portuguese colonies, the prime minister told Lord Francis Scott in June that he did not believe it was possible to establish a permanent peace between Great Britain and Germany without a settlement of the colonial question. He emphasised his conviction that the colonial question went far beyond Britain and Germany and that any modification of the existing position would have to command the assent of other colonial powers.[85] Those other colonial powers, which undoubtedly included Portugal and Belgium, were spared the problem by the outbreak of the second world war in September 1939.

As Sir Eyre Crowe recognised before the first world war, the essence of the alliance for Portugal was British assistance to preserve not only her own independence and territorial integrity but also that of her empire. Although the pre-war Anglo-German negotiations to partition the Portuguese colonies were not repeated, Chamberlain's government was apparently prepared, in the years before the outbreak of the second world war, to sacrifice virtually the entire Portuguese empire in Africa to achieve a general settlement in Europe. This, despite earlier foreign office reluctance even to contemplate an arrangement involving Portuguese territory and despite the fact that only one-third of Angola and a half of Mozambique fell within the existing Congo Basin zone upon which the Prime Minister's scheme was supposedly based.[86] Only Hitler's refusal to consider colonial retrocession as an immediate practical issue in March 1938 spared the government the considerable embarrassment – especially in view of Eden's statement in the house of commons of 21 December 1937 – of explaining to their oldest ally that whereas most of the British empire would remain firmly under British sovereign control an overwhelming proportion of the Portuguese empire in Africa would be subject to limitations of

[82] Weinberg, *The foreign policy of Hitler's Germany*, ii, 512–13. See also the same author's 'German colonial plans and policies 1938–1942', in *Geschichte und Gegenwartsbewusstein: Festschrift für Hans Rothfels zum 70. Geburtstag*, Göttingen 1963, 464–8; K. Hildebrand, 'Deutschland, die Westmächte und das Kolonialproblem: ein Beitrag über Hitler's Aussenpolitik vom Ende der Münchener Konferenz bis zum "Griff nach Prag" ', in W. Michalka (ed.) *Nationalsozialistische Aussenpolitik*, Darmstadt 1978, 395–412; Robertson, 'Hitler's planning for war', 211–12; K. Hildebrand, *The Third Reich*, London 1984, 34; A. Hillgruber, *Germany and the two world wars*, Cambridge, Mass. 1981, 61–2; Ballhaus, 'Colonial aims', 376–7.
[83] Andrew, 'The French colonialist movement', 165; Peyrefitte, 'Les premiers sondages d'opinion', 271; Watt, 'British domestic politics', 257.
[84] CAB 53/45 COS(39) 840.
[85] CAB 23/99 CM 26(39), 3 May 1939; *Hansard parliamentary debates*, HC, 5th ser. cccxlvii, col. 2682; DAPE, ii, nos 733, 740, pp. 380–1, 390–1; PREM 1/304.
[86] FO 371/21679 C1305/184/18.

sovereignty and part, at least, would be placed under German control. In these circumstances a major *raison d'être* for the alliance, as far as the Portuguese were concerned, would have ceased to exist. It is conceivable that with their confidence in their ancient ally profoundly shaken, and faced with a considerable diminution in their imperial standing, the authorities in Lisbon might have concluded – the British military mission, British cultural propaganda and activity, and British trade notwithstanding – that their only realistic course of action involved closer co-operation with Germany as perhaps the only means of avoiding further humiliation and ultimate absorption into Franco's Spain. In that event, and assuming a German appetite unsatisfied by colonial appeasement, Britain's strategic difficulties in any future war, as the chiefs of staff reminded cabinet during 1937, would have been seriously compounded. Indeed, the early period of the second world war, especially after the fall of France, was to bear solid testimony to the importance of maintaining the Portuguese connection.

7

The Portuguese Connection
and Pre-War Diplomacy

During the late 1930s Portuguese fears were not confined to the fate of their empire. Portugal's own political independence and territorial integrity was also clearly at risk. While the federalist ambitions of the Spanish left had presented the most dangerous challenge to Portugal at the beginning of the civil war in Spain, by early 1938 the successful prosecution of the war by Franco's forces, aided and abetted by Germany and Italy, raised the spectre of Spanish nationalism's traditional ambition for a united Iberian state. The disappearance of Catholic Austria in March 1938 emphasised Portugal's exposed position, particularly in view of the presence of German and Italian forces in Spain. In April 1938, Lisbon demonstrated its cognisance of these circumstance when it granted *de jure* recognition to the Spanish nationalist administration at Burgos.[1]

The *Anschluss* and the situation in Spain accounted both for Salazar's insistence on British military support, and for the acceleration of Portuguese rearmament. At the same time, the Portuguese dictator's alarm over events in central Europe prompted him to criticise, in a speech to the heads of the diplomatic corps in Lisbon during June 1938, the dangerous tendency of 'patriotism becoming daily more exclusive'. According to the papal nuncio, Salazar had gone as far as he had ever gone in suggesting that he did not endorse German extremism: the reason for his change of attitude was the demise of Austria. As Selby reminded Halifax, Salazar was an ardent Catholic. Furthermore, it was undoubtedly the case that the Portuguese as a whole (probably influenced by the papal encyclical *Mit brennende Sorge* of March 1937) had become rather more critical of Nazi Germany because of its anti-religious tendencies, especially since the absorption of Austria.[2]

Nevertheless, during the months following *Anschluss* Salazar remained convinced that Chamberlain's continued appeasement of the Axis powers was in Portugal's best interests in view of German and Italian influence in nationalist controlled Spain and the likelihood of a victory for Franco in the civil war.[3] However, the growing crisis over Czechoslovakia in August and early September 1938 threatened a war in which Italy and Britain would be on opposing sides: in that case Spain would cease to be neutral. Moreover, Salazar realised that if Italy sought to attack France through Spain, Britain might

1 FO 371/22639 W3547/7/41; DAPE, v, no. 1574, pp. 226–8; FO 371/22641 W4211/83/41; Kay, *Salazar*, 115–16; Nogueira, *Salazar*, iii, 155.
2 FO 371/22597 W8995/153/36. For the papal encyclical see Hildebrand, *The Third Reich*, 39.
3 FO 371/22597 W9371/153/36.

attack the Italians in Spain by moving through Portugal.[4] Any illusions which the Portuguese might have had concerning Britain's commitment to France in the event of a war arising out of the French obligations to Czechoslovakia were dispelled on 14 September when Halifax told Monteiro that if France were involved in war and her security menaced 'it was almost inevitable that this country would be forced to range itself by her side'.[5] Salazar was determined to remain neutral in the event of such a conflict and he sought to persuade the nationalist regime in Spain to adopt a similar position.[6]

In the event, Franco's government informed the Portuguese at the height of the Czech crisis on 24 September that it intended to remain neutral should war break out in central Europe, provided no power provoked war on nationalist territory.[7] How far this decision was a direct result of Portuguese influence is difficult to estimate. Franco was particularly worried about French actions in the event of war. He was convinced that France wanted to occupy the entire eastern coast of Spain, including the railway lines leading to it, so as to safeguard her troop transports from north Africa. Moreover, it was to be expected that Spanish possessions overseas would be lost immediately and that France would occupy Minorca. Franco was also forced to admit to his powerlessness in face of Anglo-French military action which could cut his supply lines through Portugal at a time when he had only one and a half months ammunition left; and in such circumstances he did not expect effective help from Germany or Portugal. Indeed, the Spanish ambassador at Berlin, Admiral Antonio Magaz, told under state secretary Ernst Woermann on 26 September that Portugal's friendship with England was closer than her friendship with nationalist Spain.[8]

The importance of the Portuguese connection for Britain was highlighted as the Czech crisis was drawing to a close when Halifax sent a personal message of goodwill to Salazar on 29 September as a demonstration of British faith in the alliance.[9] At the same time, the British authorities were willing, even pleased, to give their blessing to proposals, emanating from Burgos, for a non-aggression pact between the Portuguese and Spanish nationalist governments. The proposed pact was not, according to the second legal adviser at the foreign office, William Beckett, inconsistent with the Anglo-Portuguese treaties of alliance; and the recent Iraqi-Turkish pact of non-aggression was cited as a precedent.[10] Only Monteiro had reservations: he felt the pact would cause considerable complications should war break out in central Europe, given German and Italian influence with Franco.[11] However, the peaceful resolution of the Czech crisis considerably reduced the need for a non-aggression treaty to be concluded

4   DAPE, v, no. 1754, p. 445; Kay, Salazar, 117–18.
5   FO 371/21765 C9797/1941/18; DAPE, i, no. 357, pp. 428–30.
6   Ibid, v, no. 1754, pp. 446–7; Kay, Salazar, 118; Oliveira, Salazar e a Guerra Civil, 350–2.
7   DAPE, i, no. 374, pp. 444–5; FO 371/22699 W13006/13006/41; 371/22698 W13118/12909/41; The diaries of Sir Alexander Cadogan 1938–1945, ed. D. Dilks, London 1971, 105.
8   DGFP, D, ii, nos 622, 638, 641, 659, pp. 950–1, 969–70, 972–3, 991; Merkes, Deutsches Politik, 328; Rosas, O Salazarismo, 109.
9   FO 371/22594 W12807/146/36; DAPE, ii, no. 407, p. 14.
10 FO 371/22699 W13006/13006/41; DAPE, i, no. 371, pp. 444–5; Oliveira, Salazar e a Guerra Civil, 352–3.
11 FO 371/22699 W13055/13006/41; 371/22594 W13338/146/36.

urgently, and the nationalist authorities in Spain made no further reference to the subject in the ensuing months.[12]

Franco's successes in Catalonia and the *de jure* recognition of the nationalists by the British and French governments in late February 1939 prompted a revival of the pact, this time in the form of a treaty of friendship and non-aggression which was signed on 17 March 1939. The treaty, by which the two Iberian countries reciprocally undertook 'absolutely to respect each other's frontiers and territories and not to carry out any act of aggression or of invasion against the other Power', was intended to last for ten years.[13] The British left regarded it as an attempt by the Axis powers to win Portugal away from Britain and to extend German and Italian influence over the whole of the Iberian Peninsula.[14] The foreign office, aware of Portuguese fears of an attack from Spain and the poor condition of Portugal's defences, took a more supportive view; they regarded the treaty as 'welcome evidence of the desire of the Portuguese and Spanish Governments to place their future relations on a sure foundation, thus contributing to the re-establishment of peaceful conditions and stability in the Iberian Peninsula'.[15] From the Portuguese point of view, it was an important step towards the neutralisation of the Iberian Peninsula in case of a future European war; which, they believed, would be favourable to Britain's strategic interests.[16]

However, the conclusion of the Luso-Spanish treaty was followed on 27 March by Spain's adhesion to the Anti-Comintern Pact, an act which Franco, and the *Wilhelmstrasse*, had studiously avoided during the civil war for fear of provoking British and French intervention on the side of the Spanish Republic.[17] While this move fell short of an actual alliance with Italy and Germany it did signify Franco's determination to maintain intimate relations with his civil war partners; in his brother's words it was 'a political confession of faith and a clear statement of future policy'. During April the Spanish authorities sounded Salazar on the possibility of joining the pact, but were met with a blank refusal.[18] Spain's membership of the pact also sharpened fears in Lisbon, Paris and London at the continued presence in Spain of Axis, particularly Italian, troops.

Despite efforts since the summer of 1937 the British and French governments had failed to effect a complete withdrawal of Italian forces from Spain. During the visit made by Chamberlain and Halifax to Rome in January 1939 Mussolini

---

12 FO 371/22699 W14124/13006/41.
13 For the full text of the treaty see FO 371/24150 W4814/1076/41. See also *The Times*, 22 Mar. 1939.
14 For example, *Daily Worker*, 20 Mar. 1939.
15 FO 371/24150 W4671/W4589/1076/41; *DAPE*, v, no. 1990, p. 685.
16 Oliveira, *Salazar e a Guerra Civil*, 356; Rosas, *O Salazarismo*, 113. According to António Telo, the Pact also checked the ambitions of those Spaniards who desired a united Iberia. For Franco it provided an important lever in his relations with the Axis powers and a bridge to a new relationship with Britain and France: *Portugal na Segunda Guerra*, 44.
17 Abendroth, *Hitler in der spanischen Arena*, 231. For Mussolini's attitude concerning Franco's possible adhesion to the Anti-Comintern Pact during the civil war see Coverdale, *Italian Intervention*, 324–5. Spain's adhesion to the pact was made public on 8 April 1939.
18 *DGFP*, D, vi, nos 224, 241, pp. 274, 301.

had shown no signs of even contemplating withdrawal until Franco had achieved a complete victory.[19] But even the total collapse of the Republic in March was not followed by an immediate evacuation of Italian forces. Indeed, at the beginning of April the French authorities received information from official sources that between 24 and 31 March 3,500 Italian troops were landed at Cadiz and were quartered in the neighbourhood of Gibraltar. Despite Mussolini's assurances to London on 9 April, that all Italian volunteers would be withdrawn immediately after the forthcoming victory parade at Madrid, the French continued to fear a *coup* against Gibraltar.[20] Furthermore, the French minister in Lisbon was convinced that the landing of fresh contingents of Italian troops could be for 'no other purpose than action in Portugal in certain easily forseeable contingencies'. Weight was given to this view on 12 April when the commander in chief at Gibraltar advised Selby that between 1 and 10 April approximately 5,000 Italians had disembarked in the region of Cadiz and proceeded northwards to the Pyrenees to a point near the Portuguese frontier where their presence, it was said, was intended to ensure Portugal's benevolent neutrality in the event of a European war. When the ambassador raised the matter with Sampaio on 15 April he was told that there was no confirmation of fresh arrivals of Italian troops in Spain nor of their concentration on the Portuguese frontier. Only two days previously the Italian minister in Lisbon had formally denied that any fresh troops had been landed in Spain. On 17 April the Italian minister provided a written statement to the Portuguese government which denied the presence of Italian troops near the Portuguese frontier. The following day General Francisco Gómez Jordana y Sousa, Franco's foreign minister, assured Pedro Theotonio Pereira, the Portuguese ambassador at Burgos, that all foreign troops would leave Spain immediately after the Madrid parade.[21]

The foreign office had indeed no evidence, other than the report from Gibraltar, that any fresh troops had been sent from Italy to Spain since the fall of Madrid. According to their information, corroborated by the French general staff, all Italian troops in Spain were concentrated in the Albacete and Alicante regions although one regiment might still be stationed north of Madrid.[22] Cabinet was therefore prepared to accept Mussolini's word that all his troops would be withdrawn from Spain after the victory parade in Madrid. Indeed, ministers regarded the Italian government's action over Spain as the ultimate test of whether they intended to abide by the terms of the Anglo-Italian Agreement of November 1938.[23] In the event, Italian and German troops did withdraw in late May 1939, after the victory parade, but they left

[19] P. Stafford, 'The Chamberlain–Halifax visit to Rome: a reappraisal', *English Historical Review* xcviii (1983), 93.
[20] *DBFP*, 3, v, nos 96, 106, 110, 132, pp. 143–4, 151–2, 155, 170–3. In a telegram to French diplomatic representatives in London, Berlin, Rome, Cairo, Tunis and San Sebastian Bonnet referred to the disembarkation of 7,000 men: *DDF*, 2, xv, no. 356, p. 570.
[21] FO 371/24069 W5745/658/36; 371/24118 W6109/W6174/5/41 and W6193/W6396/5/41; Nogueira, *Salazar*, iii, 197–8.
[22] FO 371/24118 W6193/5/41.
[23] CAB 23/98 CM 20(39) and CM 21(39), 13, 19 Apr. 1939; *DDF*, 2, xv, no. 353, p. 567. See also Chamberlain's speech in the house of commons, 13 Apr. 1939; *Hansard parliamentary debates*, HC, 5th ser. cccxlvi, col. 14.

behind a considerable supply of aeroplanes, tanks, artillery and other military equipment for use by the Spanish army. Moreover, Italian and German personnel remained to supervise its use.[24]

Rumours about Italy's intentions in Spain were of course linked to her invasion of Albania on 7 April and to the announcement of Spain's adhesion to the Anti-Comintern Pact the following day. Other rumours abounded including intended Italian *coups* at Tunis, Corfu or even Egypt and the possibility of Greece joining the pact. This latter prompted Winston Churchill, encouraged by 'his friends in the French Government', to advise Chamberlain to sanction British naval action to protect Corfu and Crete. As it happened, Britain provided a definite guarantee of support for Greece on 13 April and initiated negotiations with Turkey which culminated in the Anglo-Turkish declaration of 12 May 1939.[25]

It was against this background, and with their commitments in the eastern Mediterranean very much in mind, that the British government learned officially that Germany intended to send a number of warships into Spanish waters. On 15 April the foreign office heard through Selby that the Portuguese had received preliminary notice from Berlin of a visit to Spanish and Portuguese waters by seven German warships, and perhaps ancillary vessels.[26] This raised fears in Portugal of possible combined action by Italian troops in Spain on the one hand and German warships on the Tagus on the other. Selby therefore informed Sampaio on 17 April that he personally considered the time chosen for the German naval visit to Portugal most inopportune; simultaneously, Monteiro told the foreign office of the impending visit, enquired as to government's attitude and asked whether it felt there was any ulterior object in the German move. The next day Corbin asked the same questions on behalf of the French government.[27] Halifax was prompted to seek the advice of the committee of imperial defence and as a result the naval staff were asked to evaluate the German action and to make suggestions for possible British counter moves.[28]

Meanwhile, the French took rather firmer action. Daladier told Phipps on 19 April that he had ordered one battleship, one cruiser, three destroyers and several submarines, over and above the ships already in the Mediterranean, to 'proceed thither and cruise about roughly within the triangle Gibraltar, Tangier and Oran, calling at these ports from time to time'. According to the French prime minister these vessels were to be escorted as far as Lisbon by the big

[24] A. Randle–Elliott, 'Spain after civil war', *Foreign Policy Reports* xvi (1940), 67; RIIA, *Survey of international affairs 1939–1946: the eve of war*, 1939, London 1958, 292–3, 358.

[25] *DBFP*, 3, v, no. 96, p. 143; PREM 1/323. See also D. C. Watt, *How war came: the immediate origins of the Second World War 1938–1939*, London 1989, 206–14; Pratt, *East of Malta, west of Suez*, 159; *Diplomatic diaries*, 274–7; *Cadogan diaries*, 170–2; S. Aster, *1939 – The making of the Second World War*, London 1973, 131–41; C. A. MacDonald, 'Britain, France and the April crisis of 1939', *European Studies Review* ii (1972), 152–61.

[26] CAB 23/98 CM 20(39), 13 Apr. 1939; FO 371/24161 W6110/6087/41.

[27] FO 371/24161 W6238//W6300/6087/41; DAPE, ii, no. 645, pp. 296–7; Harvey, *Diplomatic diaries*, 281.

[28] FO 371/24161 W6238/6087/41.

battleships *Dunkerque* and *Strasbourg* in order to create 'a good effect in Portugal where the atmosphere does not seem too good just now'.[29] Although British ministers, in particular Halifax and Lord Ernest Chatfield, former first sea lord and recently appointed minister for co-ordination of defence, were quite as apprehensive as the French about the German fleet visit,[30] the admiralty was less so. As the prime minister observed on 15 April: 'Our Admiralty are not alarmed at the Spring visits of the German Fleet. No doubt its mission is propaganda in Spain and Portugal. But it is regarded as an indication that war is not intended as if it were the ships would never venture so far from their own ports.'[31] At a cabinet meeting on 19 April Earl Stanhope, first lord of the admiralty, reported that his advisers still believed that on balance the visit of the German fleet to Spain was not a cause for alarm.[32] Indeed, they concluded their assessment by denying that there was any need for action.[33] The foreign office therefore concurred and the matter was dropped.

Britain could not, however, be as dismissive of Spain's adhesion to the Anti-Comintern Pact, despite Franco's assurance to the Portuguese that it was 'his firm intention to remain outside the policy of the Axis'.[34] The serious strategic implications of a hostile Spain in the event of a European war were not lost on the military authorities in London. In August 1936 the chiefs of staff had emphasised the need to ensure Spain's benevolent neutrality a means of ensuring Britain's imperial communications through the Mediterranean and the sovereignty of Gibraltar as a base. They repeated this advice in July 1938. Further, in a major appreciation of Britain's strategic position during February 1939 the chiefs of staff could not emphasise too strongly 'the strategic need of pursuing a policy which will ensure at least the neutrality of Spain, whatever the outcome of the civil war'.[35] In March, after Franco-British recognition of the nationalist regime the joint planning staff reiterated the importance of Spanish neutrality. It also noted 'the possibility of Nationalist Spain being hostile or at any rate affording facilities to German and Italian Naval and Air forces' and, effects on Gibraltar apart, that Spanish hostility would threaten Portuguese territory and hence involve Britain in further commitments under treaty obligation.[36] The importance of a neutral Spain was also apparent to the French. During the second stage of the Anglo-French military conversations in late April and early May 1939 they acknowledged the vulnerability of south and south western France to air attack from aerodromes in Spanish territory and the grave disadvantage of having a third frontier to defend.[37] At the same

---

[29] *DBFP*, 3, v, no. 218, p. 239; Phipps Papers, PHPP 1/22.
[30] FO 800/323.
[31] Chamberlain Papers, NC 18/1/1070.
[32] CAB 23/98 CM 21(39).
[33] FO 371/24161 W6851/6087/41.
[34] FO 371/24118 W6369/5/41; *DAPE*, ii, no. 651, pp. 304–5.
[35] CAB 24/264 CP 234(36) CID 1259–B (COS 509); CAB 5/9 478–C (also CID 1457–B and COS 750); CAB 53/45 COS 843.
[36] CAB 55/15 AFC(39) 1 JP 379.
[37] P. N. Buckley, E. B. Haslam and W. B. R. Neave–Hill, 'Anglo-French staff conversations 1938–1939', in *Les relations franco–britanniques*, 114.

time, they were conscious of Spain's role as a significant supplier of key minerals for war production, in particular of iron ore, copper, pyrites, mercury, lead and zinc.[38]

During the civil war relations between France and nationalist Spain had been at a very low ebb. Even though the French provided only limited support to the republican forces Paris was clearly identified with the cause of the left in Spain, and French activity within the Non-Intervention Committee tended to support this. Certainly, successive governments refused to follow the British example of appointing an agent accredited to the nationalist administration, and the majority of Frenchmen believed that the Spanish nationalists were firmly in the Axis camp.[39] However, recognising the hopelessness of the republican cause Daladier's government sought to repair relations with the nationalist authorities. The result was the Bérard – Jordana Agreement of 25 February 1939 by which France accorded *de jure* recognition to the Franco regime, and undertook to restore all Spanish property and securities in France, including gold, art treasures, ships and arms.[40] In addition, Daladier appointed Marshal Philippe Pétain, one of France's most eminent soldiers of the first world war, as ambassador to the Spanish military regime. The appointment of a great military figure, one who had previously participated in Franco-Spanish collaboration in Morocco, was clearly calculated to impress General Franco and to establish Franco-Spanish relations on a new and firm footing.[41]

That Franco found French attempts at a *rapprochement* inadequate was demonstrated by his adhesion to the Anti-Comintern Pact, by the fortification of the Spanish side of the Spanish-French frontier in Morocco, and by the refusal of the Spanish authorities to accelerate the return of 400,000 Spanish refugees who had fled over the frontier during the last days of the civil war and its immediate aftermath. Daladier therefore became convinced that only a demonstration of 'strength and decision' on the part of France and Britain would prevent a complete Spanish alignment with the Axis powers. Moreover, he told Phipps, who also believed in the virtue of firm action in Spain, that in the last resort 'an openly hostile Spain, would be preferable in case of war to a Spain hypocritically lending its ports and islands to the Germans and Italians for their submarines'.[42] The French government was not prepared to carry out the terms of the Bérard–Jordana Agreement unless progress was made on the refugee question even though it had not been included in the agreement. In particular, the French authorities refused to hand over the large amounts of war material

---

[38] P. Le Goyet, 'Les relations économiques franco-britanniques à la vielle de la deuxième guerre mondiale', in ibid. 198–9. For British interest in Spanish copper and pyrites see Harvey, 'Politics and pyrites', 94–103.

[39] Peyrefitte, 'Les premiers sondages d'opinion', 273.

[40] For the Bérard–Jordana Agreement see A. Adamthwaite, *France and the coming of the Second World War*, London 1977 261–2; G. A. Stone, 'Britain, France and Franco's Spain in the aftermath of the Spanish civil war', *Diplomacy and Statecraft*, forthcoming 1994. Léon Bérard was a member of the French senate and a friend of Pierre Laval. Later, he became Vichy ambassador to the Vatican.

[41] Sir M. Peterson, *Both sides of the curtain: an autobiography*, London 1950, 174.

[42] *DDF*, 2, xv, nos 37, 38, 83, 172, 472, 492, pp. 51–5, 115–16, 234–6, 772–4, 807–8; FO 371/24158 W6422/3719/41; *DBFP*, 3, v, nos 96, 194, pp. 144, 222–3.

brought from Spain by the fleeing republican forces: there was serious concern that if it was returned to Spain it might later be used against France in the event of a general European conflict.

While the authorities in London sympathised with the French predicament they also feared the effect of French recalcitrance on future relations with Spain. Halifax told Corbin on 26 April that if he were responsible in France he would be disposed to take a chance and return the captured war material having regard to 'the supreme importance of improving French relations with Spain'.[43] Portuguese apprehension was even greater. On 18 April Pereira had expressed concern at the French attitude and impressed upon Sir Maurice Peterson, the British ambassador in Spain, that it was essential to strengthen Franco's position in any way possible 'lest he should be pushed aside and replaced by something worse'. On 3 May Monteiro, on behalf of his government, expressed incredulity at French actions in Spain which served only 'to keep alive the spirit of hatred which unfortunately prevails in Spain against France'. Although Salazar had strongly advised Madrid to liquidate the refugee question as quickly as possible Monteiro warned Mounsey that the Spanish authorities were very bitter at the failure of the French to implement the Bérard–Jordana Agreement and their attempt to link it with the refugee problem.[44]

In response Halifax spoke to Corbin on 4 May and told Phipps to sound out the French government.[45] On 8 May, the very day that Spain's withdrawal from the League of Nations was announced, the ambassador was told by Bonnet – who unlike Daladier and Léger was inclined to favour a more conciliatory policy vis-à-vis Franco and Mussolini – that he agreed that Franco-Spanish relations should be put on to a better footing, but he evidently feared the effect on French public and parliamentary opinion of any prompt implementation of the Bérard–Jordana Agreement without some progress on the vexed question of Spanish refugees.[46] Meanwhile, the visit of the French fleet to Lisbon gave Salazar the opportunity to impress upon the French naval commander the fact that Franco had recently told the Portuguese ambassador at Burgos that Spain was 'perfectly free' and had undertaken no commitments for the future with Germany and Italy: her adhesion to the Anti-Comintern Pact was primarily ideological and of no political significance. The Portuguese prime minister considered a Franco-Spanish *rapprochement* essential. He expressed his incredulity that the French government should risk having a hostile country on their Pyrenean flank in the event of war, one which, despite the devastation of the civil war, had in fact increased its military strength. In London, shortly

[43] FO 371/24158 W6806/3719/41.

[44] FO 371/24118 W6396/5/41; 371/24159 W7221/3719/41; DAPE, v, nos 2036, 2037, 732–3.

[45] FO 371/24159 W7221/3719/41.

[46] FO 371/24159 W7361/3719/41. For the divergence of view between Léger, Daladier and Bonnet regarding Mussolini and Franco see R. Girault, 'La décision gouvernementale en politique extérieure', in Rémond and Bourdin, *Edouard Daladier*, 213–14. For the divergence of view concerning Mussolini only see W. I. Shorrock, *From ally to enemy: the enigma of fascist Italy in French diplomacy 1920–1940*, Kent State 1988, 256–71; D. C. Watt, 'Britain, France and the Italian problem 1937–1939', in *Les relations franco–britanniques*, 288–9; S. Morewood, 'Anglo-Italian rivalry in the mediterranean and middle east, 1935–1940', in Boyce and Robertson, *Paths to war*, 189–90.

afterwards, Monteiro expressed official disquiet at the failure of the French to carry out the terms of the Bérard–Jordana Agreement. At the same time, the duke of Alba, Franco's ambassador in London, intimated that without some progress on either gold or war material there was an increasing possibility that the Spanish ambassador in Paris, José Félix de Lequerica, would be withdrawn and Marshal Pétain would be asked to leave Spain.[47]

When Phipps taxed Bonnet and Léger with the Spanish problem on 19 May, it became clear that although the foreign minister himself wished to execute the Bérard–Jordana Agreement fully, Léger and Daladier were inclined to be 'very intransigent'. Halifax then tried to persuade Daladier to adopt a more conciliatory position when he saw him at the ministry of war in Paris on 20 May. He emphasised his belief that Franco would wish to remain neutral in any war and that it was important 'to get on to as friendly terms as possible with him'. Halifax was particularly impressed by what Monteiro had told him, especially 'that Franco was annoyed with His Majesty's government but still more with the French Government: but he wished if we could play our cards well, to establish friendly relations with both governments'.[48] Some improvement was made following Halifax's visit with the return of some captured war material to Spain but while the French persisted in linking the return of the gold with the refugee question, Franco refused to acknowledge any link and demanded its unconditional return.[49] By this time, Chamberlain, already vexed by French refusals to woo Mussolini, was beginning to express his acute anxiety concerning Franco-Spanish relations. He told cabinet on 7 June that they had a strong interest in ensuring relations between France and Spain did not deteriorate and he proposed that advantage should be taken of Phipps's imminent return to London to discuss the matter with him very frankly with a view to bringing pressure to bear on the French authorities.[50]

If extra incentive was needed it was provided on 9 June when Monteiro, acting on Salazar's instructions, gave a frank and detailed account of the extent to which Madrid felt alienated from Paris. He informed Halifax that the Spanish government were so exasperated at the difficulties placed in their way that they had recently approached Lisbon and raised the possibility of withdrawing their ambassador from Paris and of Portugal taking charge of their affairs in France. According to Monteiro this indicated that Franco intended to maintain a neutral attitude for otherwise he would have entrusted his country's interests to Germany or Italy. The ambassador argued further that as the Bérard–Jordana Agreement had been so successfully negotiated by Jordana, the failure of the Daladier government to carry it out and a break in diplomatic relations between France and Spain would undermine the foreign minister's position. The Portuguese regarded Jordana as a prominent member of the

---

47 FO 371/24159 W7701/W7992/3719/41; Nogueira, *Salazar*, iii, 208.
48 FO 371/24159 W8195/W8087/3719/41.
49 FO 371/24159 W8684/W8721/3719/41; Chamberlain Papers, NC 18/1/1102.
50 CAB 23/99 CM 31(39). The extent of Chamberlain's irritation with the French at this time is clearly revealed in a letter to his sister Hilda on 17 June: 'The French for their part continue to keep up a quarrel with everyone with whom they ought to make friends, Italy, Spain, Turkey. And we inevitably get tarred with their brush': Chamberlain Papers, NC 18/1/1103.

moderate party which was sympathetically inclined towards France. If he ceased to maintain his influence in Spanish politics the clique headed by Ramón Serrano Suñer, minister of the interior, would have 'complete ascendancy in General Franco's Government'. This would inevitably push Spain further towards the Axis powers. It was essential, therefore, to achieve an improvement in Franco-Spanish relations. Halifax assured Monteiro that he was speaking to the converted and he promised to raise Portugal's preoccupations with Phipps on his return to London. Meanwhile, he urged the Portuguese authorities to continue to use their influence in Madrid to discourage the Spanish government from taking 'no hasty step in the direction of breaking off relations between France and Spain'.[51]

Although Sir Alexander Cadogan, the permanent head of the foreign office, saw Corbin on 12 June and warned him that Jordana might be replaced by Serrano Suñer should the Bérard–Jordana Agreement collapse, and although Phipps was subsequently briefed to make yet further efforts in Paris, it was recognised on the British side that there was a limit to the pressure they could exert on their most important ally. The advantages of such pressure seemed obvious to Sir George Mounsey:

> Our policy is being bitterly criticised both by Germany and Italy on the ground that it constitutes encirclement. . . . If we brought sufficient pressure to bear on the French to make them start conversations with Italy in particular the Italian cry of encirclement would fall to the ground forthwith. If she [France] would, even at some sacrifice, improve her relations with Spain there would be infinitely less danger than there is at present of the latter country falling into the arms of the Axis powers; while at the same time the fact of a better atmosphere having been produced between this country and France on the one hand and Spain and Italy on the other might at some future time give the best hopes of renewing a means of approach between the democracies and the German Government.

Halifax, R. A. Butler and Cadogan agreed with Mounsey but recognised that timing was crucial and that the time had not yet arrived.[52] However, within a matter of weeks, during mid-July, Phipps was instructed to urge Daladier 'in the strongest possible terms' to make concessions to Italy and to fulfil the Bérard–Jordana Agreement. The French prime minister refused to appease Mussolini but on the issue of Franco-Spanish relations he proved more accommodating and the decision was finally taken to return the Spanish gold to Madrid.[53]

Phipps had not been alone in urging the French authorities to end the deadlock in their relations with Spain. Salazar and Pétain had added their weight. Although, in the end, the French government were not entirely convinced that Spain was not committed to the Rome–Berlin Axis – the visit to Spain of the Italian foreign minister, Count Galeazzo Ciano, in mid-July

51 FO 371/24159 W9069/3719/41; DAPE, v, no. 2056, pp. 769–71.
52 FO 371/24159 W9153/W9252/3719/41; Phipps Papers, PHPP 1/22.
53 Roosevelt Papers, President's Secretary, File 25, located in the Franklin Delano Roosevelt Library in New York.

naturally fuelled their doubts – they were prepared to concede on the gold issue because they had already redistributed the most modern of the captured Republican war material, particularly Czech anti-aircraft guns and motor equipment, within the French armed forces. Moreover, the French themselves ceased linking the refugee question with that of the gold: they had decided to rehabilitate the remaining Spanish refugees and to absorb them into the steadily expanding French economy. With war seemingly drawing near[54] the Spanish republicans in France were no longer a liability and were rapidly becoming an asset. Thus Paris had everything to gain and nothing to lose, other than financially, by returning the gold to Madrid.[55]

Naturally, the French *volte-face* was welcomed in Portugal and according to Monteiro's information it had produced 'an excellent effect in Spain'.[56] However, the Anglo-Portuguese objectives of seeking to prevent a complete alignment of Spain with the Axis powers and to achieve strict Spanish neutrality in the event of a European conflict, were by no means fulfilled. Indeed, on a visit to Italy in early July Serrano Suñer had told Ciano that he considered it fundamental to Spanish and to Axis policy 'to take Portugal out of the British sphere of influence'. The Spanish minister recognised the difficulties but he intended to exert his efforts in that direction and he invited collaboration.[57] Moreover, while Franco claimed in an interview to the *Diário de Notícias* in July that in the event of war Spain would remain neutral if her territory, honour and independence were not affected, he also told Ciano on 19 July that Spain intended, in the event of a short war, to maintain 'a very favourable – even more than very favourable – neutrality towards Italy' and he intimated that should there be a long war it would not be possible to maintain neutrality for events would lead Spain 'to take up a more definite position'.[58]

Not surprisingly, Salazar's doubts were exacerbated by Ciano's visit to Spain, and during early August 1939 he began to express his fears that Spain might irretrievably commit herself to the Rome–Berlin Axis.[59] Halifax and his senior officials decided to take advantage of the situation and, conscious of the Portuguese dictator's anxieties, try to establish closer contacts with Portugal on the Spanish question. Instructed to request collaboration on Spanish matters Selby accordingly saw Salazar on 17 August. The prime minister welcomed further consultation and declared his intention to keep his British ally informed regarding developments in Spain. Selby was convinced that Salazar could be relied on to exert all his influence with Franco against any attempt by the Axis powers to embroil Spain.[60] In the event, on 31 August, at the height of the

54 On 18 July Daladier told William Bullitt, the American ambassador, that he was personally convinced that Hitler intended to make war that summer and would begin by an attack on Danzig: ibid.
55 Ibid; FO 371/24159 W10453/W10599/W10723/3719/41; Peterson, *Both sides of the curtain*, 212–13.
56 FO 371/24070 W11847/658/36; Nogueira, *Salazar*, iii, 217.
57 *Ciano's diary 1939–1943*, ed. M. Muggeridge, London 1947, diary entry 5 June 1939, 100–1.
58 RIIA, *Survey of international affairs 1939–1946*, 359; *Ciano's diplomatic papers*, ed. M. Muggeridge, London 1948, 291.
59 For example, *DAPE*, v, no. 2088, pp. 804–5.
60 FO 425/416.

Polish crisis, Monteiro informed the foreign office of Franco's intention to adopt a neutral position should war break out, in advance of the official Spanish declaration. The following day Salazar emphasised to Selby that the maintenance of Spanish neutrality was essential for Portugal and assured him that Britain could rely upon her to continue to exercise all her influence in this direction.[61]

It is difficult to estimate how far Spain's decision to remain neutral was in fact influenced by Portuguese intervention. After a long and bloody civil war there was every incentive to stay out of further conflict and Franco continued to fear that in the event of Spanish belligerency France might seize Morocco and the Basque country.[62] Furthermore, the announcement of the Nazi-Soviet Non-Aggression Pact on 23 August had created shock waves throughout the Iberian Peninsula. Nationalist Spain's erstwhile German partner in the civil war and the Anti-Comintern Pact had joined hands with her deadliest enemy, Soviet Russia.

The Nazi-Soviet Pact removed any lingering possibility of a genuine Anglo-French-Soviet *rapprochement* and terminated the negotiations between the three countries which had been proceeding since mid-April 1939 following the British guarantees to Poland, Roumania and Greece. While disappointing, failure had its consolations, not least in sparing Britain any embarrassment in her relations with the smaller European powers including Spain and Portugal. Indeed, during the immediate aftermath of the German entry into Prague on 15 March 1939, one of the key arguments in cabinet and the cabinet foreign policy committee in favour of an alliance with Poland rather than with Soviet Russia was that any close association with the latter would frustrate efforts to build up a front against German aggression. On 27 March Chamberlain told the foreign policy committee that communications recently received from Poland and Roumania intimated that any public association of Soviet Russia with the scheme would greatly weaken and diminish its authority. The same message had come from Finland, Yugoslavia, Italy, Spain and Portugal. During the discussion, and two days later at a cabinet meeting, Halifax reiterated the argument claiming Portugal, Spain and Italy would be influenced against them if they entered into a pact which included the Soviets. Meanwhile, Chamberlain was telling a labour party delegation on 30 March that many countries objected to Britain having any dealings with Russia and he referred specifically to Catholic Poland, Portugal and Spain and to Canada with its large Catholic population in Quebec.[63] For a time at least the foreign office shared cabinet's unease. When Maisky proposed, early in April, that the Soviet foreign minister, Maxim Litvinov, should visit Britain, Orme Sargent was clearly appalled; he saw such a visit having an adverse effect on Britain's relations with other powers, including Portugal, Italy, Finland and Poland.[64] For the

---

[61] FO 371/24160 W13054/W13007/5056/41.
[62] FO 371/24160 W12901/5056/41.
[63] CAB 27/624 FP(36) 38th mtg; CAB 23/98 CM 15(39); Dalton, *Fateful years*, 238.
[64] FO 371/23063 C5430/3350/18.

same reason Cadogan was critical of Stalin's proposal of 17 April for a full blown military pact.[65]

There were strategic dangers as well as political difficulties for the British government in too close an association with Moscow. While Portugal's strategic importance, but unremitting hostility to Soviet communism, was mentioned only infrequently cabinet members, including Chamberlain, Chatfield and Stanhope, repeatedly pointed to the risk of driving Spain still further into the Axis camp.[66] Unfortunately for those in official circles who held such views, the chiefs of staff, while recognising the dangers of Spanish hostility including Portugal's obvious vulnerability to invasion from Spain, concluded that 'the possibility of antagonising Franco Spain should not from the military point of view be allowed to stand in the way of the conclusion of a pact with Soviet Russia'.[67] The home secretary, Sir Samuel Hoare, an inveterate anti-communist and Franco supporter during the civil war, agreed with them, informing Cabinet on 17 May that he did not attach importance to the argument that Spain might become alienated and commit herself fully to the Axis powers as a result of a British alliance with Soviet Russia: Spain was already in the anti-comintern camp. Vansittart, in his honorary post as 'Chief Diplomatic Advisor to His Majesty's Government', was equally forthright. He advised Halifax on 16 May that because the Russian issue was of such great importance only issues of real weight 'should be allowed into the scale when considering it', and that consequently the Portuguese and Spanish arguments should be dismissed.[68] Moreover, on the opposition benches in parliament and among the conservative party dissidents, there was a growing inclination to dismiss arguments which warned of alienating smaller powers such as Portugal and Spain. During a major debate on foreign policy in the house of commons on 19 May Churchill, Eden and Sir Archibald Sinclair, leader of the liberal party, were particularly dismissive of Portuguese and Spanish factors.[69]

By 22 May the foreign office, including Halifax, had conceded ground to the point of presenting a memorandum to cabinet which on balance favoured an alliance with Soviet Russia. They had been especially impressed by a chiefs of staff report of 16 May which warned ministers of the need for a triple alliance in order to forestall a Soviet-German *rapprochement* – a possibility considered by the foreign office since at least 1934[70] – and to pose an effective deterrent to any German plans for aggression. The deterrent argument was particularly

65 FO 371/22969 C5460/15/18.
66 CAB 23/99 CM 26(39) and CM 27(39), 3, 10 May 1939. See also CAB 27/624 FP(36) 45th mtg, 5 May 1939; PREM 1/409; Chamberlain Papers, NC 18/1/1099.
67 CAB 24/286 CP 108(39) 10 May 1939; CAB 27/625 FP(36) 47th mtg.
68 CAB 23/99 CM 28(39); Vansittart Papers, VNST 2/43.
69 *Hansard parliamentary debates*, HC, 5th ser. cccxlvii, cols 1845–6, 1860, 1874. See also S. Aster, 'British policy towards the USSR and the onset of the Second World War March 1938—August 1939', unpubl. PhD diss. London 1969, 325–6. Monteiro communicated the views of Churchill, Eden and Sinclair to Salazar on 20 May 1939: *DAPE*, ii, no. 718, 363–5.
70 See R. Manne, 'The foreign office and the failure of the Anglo-Soviet rapprochement', *Journal of Contemporary History* xvi (1981), 725–55; W. Murray, *The change in the European balance of power, 1938–1939: the path to ruin*, Princeton, NJ 1984, 301–4.

effective, as the foreign office recognised, in countering the expected hostility of the smaller powers:

> If Spain follows in the train of the Axis, we remove danger from that quarter if the Axis can be restrained from war by the fear of overwhelming forces against it. Spain is in no mood and is not in a position to make war on her own and the same applies, of course, to Portugal and Yugoslavia.[71]

When Cabinet met on 24 May Chamberlain finally and most reluctantly conceded the argument, though not before insisting upon linking the prospective alliance with the discredited League principle of collective security. He remained unconvinced of the wisdom of including Soviet Russia in the proposed eastern front and while he acknowledged the possibility of a Soviet–German *rapprochement* if an accommodation was not reached with Moscow, he believed that merely cast further doubt on Soviet reliability. He continued to have 'a deep suspicion of Soviet aims and profound doubts as to her military capacity', and clearly lamented the effect of a tripartite pact on his general appeasement policy: 'the alliance would definitely be a lining up of opposing blocs and an association which would make any negotiations with the totalitarians difficult if not impossible'.[72] Moreover, even mere dialogue with Soviet Russia was a source of 'trouble with our friends'.[73]

But that negotiations with the Soviets were a source of 'trouble with our friends' was by no means obvious. The growing demands from many countries for British military equipment and assistance during the last months of peace testified to the lack of impact of the tripartite discussions. Portugal was not alienated from Britain despite her well known aversion to Soviet communism: when informed generally of the Soviet offer of a tripartite alliance by Halifax on 18 May Monteiro merely expressed concern as to 'the effect which a grouping of the Powers which placed Soviet Russia on one side and Germany on the other might have upon the minds of the populations and more especially of the peasant classes in many continental countries'. While he felt that it was 'a weakness rather than a strength for British policy to be too intimately associated with the Soviet Government' that was because in a choice between Hitler and Stalin 'it was quite possible that some simple minds would prefer the immediate domination of the former'.[74] At the same time, in order to deflect any criticism, the British authorities took great care in presenting their decision to proceed with negotiations for a triple alliance. On 26 May Selby was instructed to show Salazar the text of the draft agreement submitted to Moscow for an Anglo-French-Soviet defensive agreement and to assure him that Britain's association with Soviet Russia did not represent 'any departure from

---

[71] CAB 24/287 CP 124(39); M. R. Wheatley, 'Britain and the Anglo-Franco-Russian negotiations in 1939', in *Les relations Franco-Britanniques*, 206–7; R. Manne, 'Some British light on the Nazi-Soviet pact', *European Studies Review* xi (1981), 89–90.
[72] Chamberlain Papers, NC 18/1/1101–1102. See also P. Stafford, 'Political autobiography and the art of the possible: R. A. Butler at the foreign office 1938–1939', *Historical Journal* xxviii (1985), 916.
[73] Chamberlain Papers, NC 18/1/1107; Aster, *Making of the Second World War*, 282–3.
[74] FO 371/24118 W6369/5/41; DAPE, ii, no. 651, 304–5.

the fundamental policy of His Majesty's Government' which was 'directed to assisting the smaller States of Europe in defending their independence against aggression by their large expansionist neighbours'. Indeed, it was in furtherance of this policy that the British government was entering into 'a purely defensive arrangement under definite conditions, and for a specified period, with the Soviet Government' and Halifax felt that it was axiomatic that 'the conclusion of that arrangement signifies no sort of "ideological" union or alliance'.[75]

It was hardly to be expected that the Portuguese authorities would receive such news with pleasure. Salazar lost no time in clarifying his government's position, as one more of sorrow than anger, thus according very closely with the feelings of the British prime minister:

> Although we are in no way concerned with agreements entered into by Great Britain with other States which do not affect our alliance, nevertheless we are led by the attitude we have taken up in the past to affirm our lack of faith in the aid promised by Soviet Russia to any country, and our fear that the drawbacks may outweigh any possible advantages as regards the position of third Powers not only in the east of Europe but also others which we do not want to see attracted to the other side owing to apprehensions derived from the appearance of Russia in the politics of Europe.[76]

Given the horror with which Soviet communism was regarded in Portuguese governing circles Salazar's response was rather mild: it is clear that British involvement with the Soviets was not considered substantial enough to threaten, as far as Portugal was concerned, the Anglo-Portuguese alliance. It is important to recognise here that the Portuguese government was privy, via its minister in Berlin, Veiga Simões, to information which charged that Hitler was attempting to induce Soviet Russia to preserve complete neutrality in the event of a European war arising out of the Danzig question. According to Simões's informant, a high official of the *Wilhelmstrasse*, Hitler needed to achieve Soviet neutrality in order 'to stifle much of the German army leaders' opposition to a war in which Russia would be on the opposite side'.[77]

The announcement of the Nazi-Soviet Non-Aggression Pact was of course ill-received in Portugal. None the less, Salazar was still not inclined towards a policy of unconditional support for Britain in the event of a general conflict. According to German sources, he told Nicolás Franco on 25 August that he would do everything to ensure that Portugal remained neutral although he did not give a binding declaration. Inclination towards neutrality was probably at least partly influenced by strong German pressure. On the day before the German invasion of Poland the German legation in Lisbon was asked by Ribbentrop to enquire whether Berlin might count on 'impeccable neutrality' from Portugal should war break out between Germany and Great Britain, and to stress, in the event of the Portuguese government raising their treaty

---

75 FO 371/23066 C7661/3356/18.
76 CAB 24/287 CP 131(39).
77 FO 408/69.

obligations under the Anglo-Portuguese alliance, that the German government would be unable to admit such an appeal. In response Salazar told the German minister, Baron Hoyningen-Huene, on 1 September, that his country's alliance with Britain placed her 'under no obligation whatever to render assistance. Not even in the case of a defensive war'. Moreover, he could not see 'the slightest reason which might compel Portugal in the future to render assistance'. In the long term, he thought, 'it must be in Britain's interests to confine the theatres of war to as few as possible, and that the most welcome solution for her would be for the whole of the Iberian Peninsula to constitute a neutral zone'.[78]

In the event, Salazar's British ally required no more of his country than that she should maintain a benevolent neutrality. This was a somewhat surprising decision in view of previous assumptions made by Britain's military authorities. During the Czech crisis of September 1938, for example, the chiefs of staff had produced a military appreciation of Britain's situation in the event of war with Germany based on a number of political assumptions, one of which anticipated that Portugal would not remain neutral. In a further broad-ranging strategic appreciation in February 1939, in which it was anticipated that Britain and France would be ranged against Germany and Italy with possible Japanese hostility, the chiefs of staff clearly assumed that, provided present relations continued, Portugal would fulfil her treaty obligations; in particular that she would permit the use of Lisbon as an alternative base to Gibraltar in the event of Spanish hostility, although it was admitted this would involve British forces in the defence of Portugal against all forms of attack. The following month, in the course of preliminary planning for the Anglo-French military conversations, the joint planning staff continued to assume that in the event of a general conflict Portugal would fulfil her treaty obligations. As late as July 1939 the deputy chiefs of staff included in their instructions to the British military mission to Russia a political appreciation by the foreign office of the probable alignment of the powers in a European war in which Portugal was ranked as an ally of Britain and France along with Soviet Russia, the Dominions, Egypt, Iraq and Poland.[79] By the end of August, however, when approached by the foreign office the chiefs of staff recommended that it would be in Britain's best interests if Portugal were 'to follow the precedent of 1914, and while remaining neutral at the outset, refrain from making any declaration of neutrality'. They believed this would enable Portugal 'to exercise the maximum of benevolence and would leave both Portugal and ourselves free to reconsider the position at a later stage'.[80]

In arriving at their conclusion the chiefs of staff were certainly influenced by their knowledge of the poor condition of Portugal's fighting forces: the resultant need to provide considerable assistance made her a commitment rather than an asset. Moreover, they feared that Portugal's entry into the war might convert Spanish neutrality into Spanish hostility and, paradoxically, it was only in the

[78] DGFP, D, vii, nos 278, 487, 522, pp. 290, 473–4, 500; DAPE, ii, no. 897, pp. 523–4; Nogueira, Salazar, iii, 236.
[79] CAB 24/278 CP 199(38) (COS 765); CAB 53/45 COS 843; CAB 55/15 JP 379 AFC(39); CAB16/183B DP(P)71 also DCOS 154 (Revise).
[80] CAB 53/54 COS 973; FO 371/24064 W12657/160/36.

event of Spanish hostility that Portuguese facilities became attractive.[81] Salazar had reached the same conclusion by a different route. According to a report by Selby on 1 September, the Portuguese were convinced that by remaining neutral they would be best able to influence Spain in a similar direction and by helping to maintain Spanish neutrality they would serve both their own and their ally's interests.[82]

Unlike their democratic republican predecessors in August 1914, the Salazar regime deliberately embarked on a course of neutrality in September 1939. But how strict would that neutrality be? Would it be the 'impeccable neutrality' demanded by Ribbentrop or the benevolent neutrality sought by the British chiefs of staff and foreign office? During the first two years or so of the second world war Portugal's commitment to her British ally was to be put severely to the test, in particular after the fall of France in June 1940. The policy of countering Axis influence in Portugal, pursued with some success by the Chamberlain administration, did not end in September 1939. On the contrary, the circumstances of war made its continuation in the form of political and economic warfare even more vital.

[81] CAB 53/54 COS 973.
[82] FO 371/24064 W12998/160/36.

8

Countering the Axis in War-time Portugal

From the onset of the second world war the British authorities sought to persuade the Portuguese government to adopt a position of benevolent neutrality. Its initial response aroused optimism. As early as 1 September, Salazar, in communicating his decision to remain neutral, emphasised to Selby his anxiety to assist his British allies in any way possible. Later, he praised publicly 'the heroic sacrifice of Poland' and on 9 October, while revealing that Germany had offered to respect the integrity of Portugal and her overseas possessions if she were neutral, he proclaimed his country's 'friendship and complete fidelity to the English Alliance'.[1] Moreover, during September and October the Portuguese authorities were accommodating when Britain requested protection for British interests in Mozambique and assurances that the coasts of Portugal and the Portuguese islands in the Atlantic would be denied to German submarines or aircraft, although they did refuse permission for the movement of some fifty colonial troops through Mozambique on the grounds that it would infringe their country's neutrality.[2] Early in 1940, however, they were less amenable to further British requests for assistance concerning the transit of Germans through the Azores, the suppression of meteorological broadcasts, the interception of German cable messages, the passage of arms through Mozambique, the purchase of trawlers for the admiralty and the conclusion of a war trade agreement.[3]

This response called into question the British decision to approve Salazar's neutrality. Indeed, during January Selby suggested to Halifax that the position ought to be reviewed: misunderstandings with the Portuguese government would ensue if British requests for assistance jeopardised, or seemed to jeopardise their neutrality. The ambassador emphasised that as a neutral Salazar exercised a restraining influence in Madrid, if not in Rome as well, and that if Portugal were required to adopt a belligerent status her present disarmed state would make her a military liability. While he acknowledged that as a neutral Portugal continued to render Germany 'all those services permitted to, if not incumbent upon, a neutral State in virtue of accepted international law', Selby was inclined, unless Portuguese assistance in the fullest sense became a strategic necessity for reasons of the British blockade or on account of the strategic position in the Atlantic, to leave the position as it was, 'making such use of Portuguese goodwill as we may be able'.[4]

[1]   FO 371/23160 C14393/C16611/13620/36; K. Duff, 'Portugal', in RIIA, *Survey of international affairs 1939–1946: the war and the neutrals*, London 1956, 319; Kay, *Salazar*, 153.
[2]   FO 371/24489 C2886/379/36.
[3]   Ibid.
[4]   FO 371/24489 C1599/379/36.

Sir Maurice Peterson, British ambassador in Madrid, adopted a more critical view. He advised that although the Spanish government probably preferred Portugal to remain neutral it was unlikely that Spain's own neutrality would be affected if Portugal were to enter the war on the allied side. He warned that Lisbon's lack of co-operation on the negotiations for a war trade agreement was impeding the efforts of the allies in Spain to the benefit of Germany. Peterson felt there was a case for calling on Portugal, as an ally and ostensibly friendly neutral, to take more active measures to check the use of her territory as an entrepôt for German trade.[5] Halifax was just as critical; in particular, he deplored the refusal of the Portuguese to consider a war trade agreement. Selby was to ask Salazar to reconsider British requests for assistance.[6]

When Selby was making his representations to Salazar on 7 March, at the same time as Halifax was seeing Monteiro in London, it was in the knowledge that the German minister, Hoyningen-Huene, was exercising the strongest pressure on the Portuguese to remain neutral. Nevertheless Salazar's initial reaction was to announce his willingness to consider each request for assistance with 'the maximum of goodwill and with due regard to Portugal's obligations to her Ally, obligations which he considered he had surely sufficiently empha-sised'.[7] He confirmed this in a written reply on 13 March when he reaffirmed that his attitude was unchanged and referred explicitly to Portugal's 'benevolent neutrality'. Although Salazar alone would decide whether, and to what extent, he would meet the wishes of his ally, the foreign office interpreted his reply as an assurance of benevolent neutrality and Halifax instructed Selby to tell him that his communication was much appreciated.[8]

In re-endorsing Portuguese neutrality Halifax was deeply influenced by a chiefs of staff appreciation of the strategic position. So long as the main strategic requirements of a neutral Portugal continued to be fulfilled – denial of harbours and aerodromes on the mainland and in the Atlantic Islands to Britain's enemies, the continued use of cable stations on the islands and Portuguese protection thereof – the chiefs of staff considered that the advant-ages which Britain would gain from the use of Portuguese bases would be outweighed by consequential defence commitments. On strategic grounds the chiefs argued that Portugal's continued neutrality would be in Britain's best interests and, crucially, that no action should be taken 'which might precipitate a situation likely to lead to Spanish intervention or which could be turned to German advantage'. They considered that all possible means of pressure in the diplomatic and economic sphere should be exercised 'in order to persuade Portugal to accede to reasonable demands' and that German pressure should be vigorously countered.[9]

As long as the 'phoney war' continued the authorities in London remained satisfied with Salazar's assurances of benevolent neutrality while recognising, as Selby had concluded, that the United Kingdom could not expect any

5   FO 371/24489 C2255/379/36
6   FO 371/24489 C2886/379/36.
7   FO 371/24489 C3325/C3610/C3613/C4064/379/36; DAPE, vi, no. 435, pp. 381–4.
8   FO 371/24490 C4067/379/36; DAPE, vi, no. 454, pp. 400–5.
9   CAB 80/8 COS(40)256.

appreciable co-operation from Lisbon until the Portuguese could be sure of British protection by land, sea, and especially by air. Germany's invasion of Norway and Denmark during April 1940, however, aroused fears of increased fifth column activity in Portugal: rumours abounded in diplomatic circles of a possible German engineered *coup* in Lisbon or a Spanish attack on Portugal in the German-Italian interest.[10] The foreign office observed that provided Italy was non-belligerent and Franco's government maintained itself in power, the position was secure. However, if there were a change of government in Spain, there was the possibility of an anti-Salazar movement, assisted by Germans in Spain and Portugal and abetted by the Italians. In the light of these observations the war cabinet, on 15 May, instructed the chiefs of staff, and particularly the admiralty, to prepare a contingency plan setting out the action to be taken if it became necessary for Britain to secure strategic points in the Cape Verde islands, the Azores, or on the mainland of Portugal.[11] Detailed plans were then drawn up for an assault on the Atlantic islands and Mozambique.[12] Moreover, cabinet further advised the foreign office to consider setting up an intelligence centre under the auspices of the Lisbon embassy and to examine the possibility of organising the British communities in Portugal both for intelligence purposes and for combined action in the event of civil disturbances.[13]

Britain's commitment to the continued neutrality of the Salazar regime was clearly brought into question by the collapse of France and the entry of Italy into the war during June 1940. With German troops on the Pyrenean frontier threatening possible invasion, anti-British demonstrations in Spain demanding the return of Gibraltar, Spanish troops occupying Tangier and Franco declaring non-belligerency following Italy's entry into the war, there was every prospect that the Iberian Peninsula would become embroiled in the hostilities.[14] To forestall such an occurrence Salazar negotiated an extension to the Treaty of Friendship and Non-Aggression of March 1939 with Franco's government. Aided by Franco's desire not to be drawn too precipitately into the general conflict, a desire influenced by the attack on the French fleet at Oran which signalled Britain's determination to continue the struggle, the Portuguese dictator brought negotiations to a successful conclusion with the signing and publication of a protocol on 29 July 1940.

The Protocol provided the means for collective action by allowing the signatories to 'concert' if they wished to act upon 'events' – such events presumably being international incidents arising from the war. During the negotiations Salazar had strenuously resisted Spanish attempts to draw Portugal away from the Anglo-Portuguese alliance and included in the Protocol was a statement which implied that Portuguese duties under it were subordinated to their

[10] FO 371/24490 C6527/379/36.

[11] FO 371/24490 C6527/379/36; CAB 65/7 WM 123(40).

[12] The chiefs of staff appreciation is in CAB 66/8 WP(40)180. For details see ch. ix.

[13] CAB 65/7 WM 149(40), 31 May 1940.

[14] Towards the end of April 1940, before the Battle of France, the Portuguese ambassador at Madrid, Pedro Theotonio Pereira, had received assurances from Franco personally that even if Italy entered the war, which he doubted, Spain would remain neutral. This assurance had been divulged to the British government on Salazar's instructions: Telo, *Portugal na Segunda Guerra*, 129.

alliance obligations.[15] The immediate significance of the Protocol in the summer of 1940 was that it gave to the belligerents the clear message that the Iberian powers had a common preference to remain at peace and to keep the war from the peninsula. This, at a time when the Franco regime was under tremendous pressure to bring Spain into the war.[16] While the Germans publicly described the Protocol as 'a link in the chain of British diplomatic defeats', claiming that it meant the end of the Anglo-Portuguese alliance, the British chose to interpret it differently and welcomed it with some enthusiasm. Halifax expressed his appreciation personally to Monteiro on 30 July.[17] For Sir Samuel Hoare, recently appointed British ambassador at Madrid, the Protocol was significant because it was 'a very substantial factor on the side of Spanish peace', and the more definitely this view was stated the less likelihood there was of the Germans using the agreement to attempt to estrange Portugal from the British alliance.[18]

The enthusiastic reception of the Protocol in London was hardly surprising in view of the imperative need to confine the struggle to as few military theatres as possible. By the summer of 1940 Britain was confronting the Axis powers alone in the Atlantic, Home Waters, the Mediterranean and north north-east Africa; and an extension of the war into the Iberian Peninsula, especially if Spain became an active belligerent, would be intolerable. While every endeavour would be made to keep Spain non-belligerent and to preserve the peace of the Iberian Peninsula, the need to counter Axis influence in Portugal, and to maintain that country's benevolent neutrality, was recognised as an important priority by Winston Churchill's government, not least in view of Salazar's willingness to play his full part – as witness the Protocol – in helping to prevent Spain's entry into the war. Thus by encouraging and strengthening Portugal and undermining Axis influence there Britain would be contributing towards the preservation of Portugal's independence and benevolent attitude. At the same time, there was no guarantee that Germany would desist from military action in the peninsula even if Spain remained firmly opposed to entering the war; in such circumstances Portugal would probably be drawn into the conflict. Given the range of possibilities the British authorities were compelled, from the early summer of 1940, to pursue a dual strategy in their relations with Portugal. While they intended to strengthen their position in Portugal by countering Axis activity and by insisting on the maintenance of benevolent neutrality, they also set in motion contingency planning which envisaged, in the event of

[15] For full details on the origins and implementation of the Protocol see C. R. Halstead, 'Consistent and total peril from every side: Portugal and its 1940 Protocol with Spain', *Iberian Studies* iii, (1974), 15–29. For the text of the Protocol see *DAPE*, vii, no. 1066, pp. 323–5.

[16] See Telo, *Portugal na Segunda Guerra*, 163–4.

[17] Halstead, 'Consistent and total peril', 20. According to António Telo, the Italians saw the Protocol as Salazar's first strike against the 'English alliance' and confirmation of Lisbon's capacity to resist British pressure. He also argues that Serrano Suñer, Colonel Juan Beigbeder, the foreign minister, and Franco, interpreted the Protocol as facilitating the entry of Spain into the war and not the contrary: *Portugal na Segunda Guerra*, 212–14. See also Nogueira, *Salazar*, iii. 285–6.

[18] FO 371/24526 C8051/6006/41; 371/24503 C8761/40/41; Chamberlain Papers, NC 7/11/33/102; Templewood Papers, XIII:2.

a clearly perceived German military threat to the peninsula, the occupation of the Portuguese Atlantic islands, the strengthening of Portuguese defences on the islands and the establishment there of a Portuguese government-in-exile. In 1940–1, as in the pre-war period, British efforts to counter Axis influence were concentrated in the spheres of propaganda, trade (economic warfare) and Portuguese rearmament.

The pre-war reorganisation of Britain's propaganda service in Portugal – the appointment of a press attaché, the inauguration of a Portuguese news bulletin by the BBC and the utilisation of a regular British news service – provided the embassy in Lisbon after August 1939 with the means to challenge Germany's strident anti-British propaganda. During the period 1939–41 liaison with the ministry of information and the foreign office was quite effective, often through the device of parliamentary questions and answers, in countering German charges that, for example, the British were dissatisfied with Portuguese neutrality and were scheming for the overthrow of the Salazar regime; that, if they won the war, they intended to substitute a democratic regime; that the British blockade was doing untold harm to the Portuguese economy; or that the British authorities had promised the Union of South Africa part of Mozambique and Angola.[19] At the same time, the British Institute in Lisbon was actively engaged in organising cultural propaganda and arranging visits to Portugal. The most successful of these were those of the duke of Kent during June 1940 and a delegation from Oxford University during April 1941. The duke attended the celebrations of the eight hundredth anniversary of the foundation of Portugal and the tercentenary of Portugal's independence from Spain. The delegation awarded Salazar an honorary degree at a ceremony in Coimbra University, a signal success for British cultural diplomacy: Salazar had previously hesitated to accept the honour because of his fear of jeopardising Portuguese neutrality and because he had already refused honorary degrees from several German universities. The event received abundant publicity in the Portuguese press. It was, according to Sir Ronald Campbell, Selby's successor, 'first class propaganda. The Germans are livid'.[20]

Despite these successes a number of critical voices were raised in Lisbon and elsewhere which claimed that the British propaganda effort was insignificant compared to the German. During the summer of 1940 the ministry of information noted the 'currents and cross currents as reported in the Portuguese Mail' and concluded that apart from the visit of the duke of Kent, Britain had produced very little antidote to 'the insidious German propaganda which permeates the Press and private conversation'. Sections of the British community in Lisbon were also very critical. According to Sir Alexander Roger the German legation was well organised, its propaganda was continuous, its Gestapo was all embracing and its minister was strong and persistent. Roger was extremely critical of the embassy staff, in particular of Selby, and demanded

---

[19] DAPE, vi, annex to no. 199, pp. 169–70; FO 371/26818 C369/C5035/214/36; Hansard parliamentary debates, HC, 5th ser. ccclviii, col. 584; ccclxxi, cols 321–2; ccclxxvi, col. 1916.
[20] FO 371/26811 C4619/C4658/149/36. For the duke of Kent's visit see FO 371/24491 C7649/379/36.

that he be his replaced by 'a man of strong and forceful personality backed by a staff of the same calibre'.[21] Halifax regarded Roger's remarks as 'unduly harsh', which they were since the embassy did not have the financial resources of the legation; German subsidy of the Portuguese news service via the *Deutsches Nachrichten-Büro* was particularly significant. Moreover, the activities of the British community in Lisbon could not be compared with those of the German community, though again there were mitigating circumstances which the embassy staff generously recognised.[22]

Although the quantity of German propaganda during the period 1939 to 1941 was greater, it was not always qualitatively superior to the British. The case of Dr Krawczyk is a good illustration. Krawczyk was a German agent posing as a priest who arrived in Portugal at the end of April 1941 and delivered lectures at Coimbra and at Oporto, which he had previously delivered in Spain, on the subject of 'present day German Catholicism'. The discovery that Krawczyk had been unfrocked by the archbishop of Breslau gave the Portuguese Catholic press the opportunity to contradict his assertions that Germany was not persecuting the Church. A *Voz* published an article on 30 May about the real position of the Church in Poland, including information on the imprisonment of the Polish Bishops Fulman and Goral, which was so frank that the British embassy was surprised it had passed the censor.[23]

The lesson of the Krawczyk affair was that care should be taken not to offend Portuguese Catholic susceptibilities. Portuguese political susceptibilities, especially in official circles, also required careful handling as Campbell, for one, recognised. During May 1941 the ambassador advised that in its broadcasts to Portugal the BBC should avoid the word 'democracy' which was interpreted by the Portuguese as 'an incitement to the forces of disorder'. While he appreciated that the democratic theme was essential for British and American consumption Campbell could see no reason why it 'should *ever* be used in talks addressed exclusively to Portugal'.[24]

The danger of arousing Portuguese political susceptibilities was demonstrated towards the end of 1941 by the Cortesão affair. At the beginning of October Monteiro raised the subject of BBC broadcasts with William Strang, superintending assistant under-secretary to the central department, and complained that they sometimes appeared to be tinged with hostility towards the Portuguese government. Despite Strang's reassurances, the Portuguese censor banned British photographs from 9 October onwards and severely cut the British news service. On 14 October the censor told the press attaché, Marcus Cheke, that this action had been taken on direct instructions from Salazar. The censor referred to the noticeable absence of complimentary references to the Salazar regime in recent British broadcasts and intimated that this was because of the activities of Dr Jaime Cortesão, a Portuguese exile in London who was employed as a translator, and who was erroneously thought to have been

21 FO 371/24488 C8609/C7381/111/36. See also *By safe hand: letters of Sybil and David Eccles 1939–1942*, ed. D. Eccles London 1983, 97.
22 FO 371/24492 C6416/2686/36.
23 FO 371/26818 C6241/214/36.
24 FO 371/26818 C5219/214/36.

promoted head of the Portuguese section of the BBC. The embassy felt the BBC would be well advised to dispense with Cortesão's services.[25] In London, Monteiro assured Strang that the prestige of his government was very high and enjoyed widespread support. He warned that the British government would be making a great mistake if they accepted the small group of oppositionists in Portugal as collaborationists.[26]

While the BBC was prepared to dismiss Cortesão the foreign office was told that he would be very difficult to replace because of the scarcity of first class Portuguese translators. To avoid disrupting Portuguese broadcasts the foreign office was prepared to relent.[27] Campbell, however, took a wholly different view and appealed to the foreign secretary (Anthony Eden had succeeded Halifax in December 1940) to consider the issue from the Portuguese point of view:

> it is difficult to exaggerate the importance which the incident assumes in the eyes of the Portuguese Government in their present sensitive and nervous frame of mind. That a Portuguese subject (known personally to Dr Salazar as an able but wrong-headed man) should engage in subversive propaganda from British soil is bad enough. That he should continue in British official employment after this fact has become known is totally incomprehensible to the Portuguese Government.

The ambassador feared the incident would be viewed as a test of British sincerity and he could not urge too strongly that even at the cost of a temporary loss of efficiency, Cortesão be dismissed.[28] Eden concurred and Cortesão's employment was terminated forthwith.[29]

In the event, the Cortesão affair did not seriously damage Britain's prestige in Portugal, at least partly because the Germans were in no position to exploit the situation for in October 1941 the Portuguese vessel, *Corte Real*, was sunk by a German submarine in the belief that it was carrying wolfram ore to the United States.[30] In any case incidents such as these, even the *Corte Real*, had only a minor effect on the overall policy of the Portuguese government. Not surprisingly, Portuguese public opinion tended to follow closely the ebb and flow of British and German military successes: when German or British military and diplomatic fortunes were in the ascendancy this was reflected in the Portuguese press as was clearly revealed, for example, at the time of the Fall of France and the Battle of Britain.

During the first part of June 1940 the Portuguese press remained loyal to the allied cause. However, as the inevitable allied defeat loomed it became more strident in its criticisms, particularly of the democratic systems of Britain and

---

[25] *DAPE*, ix, no. 2370, pp. 353–5; FO 371/26819 C11489/214/36. Before he went into exile Cortesão had previously been employed by the Portuguese government as a high official in the colonial ministry. During the Spanish civil war he was a leader of the Portuguese Popular Front in exile. See Oliveira, *Salazar e a Guerra Civil*, 269–70.
[26] *DAPE*, ix, no. 2414, pp. 379–82.
[27] FO 371/26819 C11489/C11812/C12213/C12235/214/36.
[28] FO 371/26819 C12818/214/36.
[29] Ibid.
[30] See FO 371/26835 C11422/C11542/C11733/900/36.

France which had brought about their ruin. For example, the *Diário de Notícias* of 20 June was scathing in its direct association of the failed defensive strategy of the French with the democratic mentality which had served to enfeeble the nation. On 22 June, the semi-official *Diário da Manha* was even more forthright in condemning democracy for encouraging 'every vice, every disorder and every corruption'. The *Comércio do Porto* referred on 23 June to the inability of the democracies to follow 'the rhythm of modern life' and to the role of individualism in weakening the moral energies of the nation. In view of such statements, which continued into July, it is perhaps not surprising that the Portuguese press expressed unanimous approval of Marshal Pétain's Vichy government. According to the press section of the British embassy, the German victory in France also exerted a noticeable effect on opinion in official circles with the result that the censor was instructed to insist on a more strict 'neutrality' in all newspapers. During August 1940 there were signs that the Portuguese authorities were reconciling themselves to Hitler's new European order: leaders appeared, for example, which gave a far from hostile reception to a speech by Dr Walther Funk, head of the Third Reich's economics ministry, on the future economic structure of Europe.[31]

The embassy in Lisbon recognised that the success or failure of their propaganda depended in the last resort on the course of the war. In August Selby expressed his belief that the tendency in Portugal to believe that a German victory was inevitable would only be countered effectively by 'a demonstration of Britain's ability to withstand attack and to strike at her enemies'. The Battle of Britain during late August and September was, of course, such a demonstration. Leading articles then appeared in the Portuguese press which revealed a growing confidence in Britain's will to resist and showered praise on the Royal Air Force. During the period from 16 to 26 September widespread coverage of Britain's victories coincided with the exclusion of virtually all DNB messages from the front pages of every newspaper, including the *Diário de Notícias*, which was quite unprecedented. Even the *Diário da Manhã* which was quite sympathetic to the Axis powers, and which printed much DNB and *Radio Roma* material, included the Exchange Telegraph at the top of its foreign press columns.[32] According to 'well documented records held in the *Pálacio das Necessidades* of the [Portuguese] Foreign Ministry' a Luso-German press debate began with a heated exchange in the summer of 1940 and lasted well into 1942, souring relations between the two countries. The Germans complained frequently about the pro-allied tone and content of much of the Portuguese press. Between June 1940 and June 1944 Nazi Germany apparently lodged more than a hundred protests about offensive items in the press; Britain lodged nine.[33]

Despite the Luso-German press debate and favourable military developments for Britain during August and September, Portuguese opinion was still not

[31] FO 371/24494 C6574/4597/36.
[32] Ibid; FO 371/24493 C10958/2686/36. According to American intelligence, the *Diário da Manha* was 70 per cent pro-Nazi and it was only after D-Day in June 1944 that it began to modify its stance: Gallagher, 'Conservatism, dictatorship and fascism in Portugal', 170.
[33] D. L. Wheeler, 'Review of António Telo's *Portugal na Segunda Guerra*', *Luso-Brazilian Review* xxvii (1990), 135-6.

prepared to throw its entire support behind her cause. There remained a considerable residue of respect, if not admiration, for Germany's military prowess. The Portuguese, from Salazar downwards, therefore looked for signs of genuine reversals in Britain's fortunes after June 1940. Britain's developing relationship with the United States was therefore of crucial and lasting importance for it strengthened the credibility of those in Portugal, both British and Portuguese, who argued ceaselessly that Britain would emerge from the struggle victorious.[34] Ultimately, even their deep seated hatred of communism did not blind the Portuguese to the significance of the Russian factor in the military balance of the war.[35]

German propaganda notwithstanding, Salazar's government, like the Spanish generals, realised that Britain had allied herself to Soviet Russia for purely military reasons. It was not a step towards communism. Indeed, when the German military attaché in Lisbon asked the Portuguese authorities for help in raising a corps of volunteers from the *Legião Portuguesa* to fight against Soviet Russia, he was declared *persona non grata*.[36] At the same time, following Monteiro's personal intervention, the BBC was instructed to tone down British support for their Russian ally in its broadcasts to Portugal.[37]

Unquestionably, the most difficult challenge the embassy had to face was Portuguese respect for Germany's military prowess. During the summer of 1941 German propaganda in Portugal naturally stressed the series of German victories over Russian forces, and in particular the capture of Smolensk. Salazar was obviously impressed and, according to Campbell, took an unduly exaggerated view of German industrial and military strength.[38] As the ambassador lacked sufficient information to make an effective impression, he was provided, in an unprecedented move, with a joint intelligence chiefs' memorandum which contained detailed information about German losses in Russia and an assessment of the drain on German resources resulting from the Russian campaign. It also covered recent progress in British military reorganisation and rearmament, improvement in Britain's strategic position in the middle east and the eastern Mediterranean, the extent of American military and economic support and the successes of the Royal Navy and Royal Air Force against

---

[34] FO 371/24494 C10958/C13281//4597/36; FO 371/26811 C1006/149/36; FO 371/26795 C8917/41/36.
[35] FO 371/26795 C8917/41/36. Initially, Salazar (and Franco) anticipated a rapid collapse of Soviet resistance to the German invasion of 22 June 1941. According to António Telo, at the end of 1941 the Portuguese dictator remained convinced that Germany had established a dominant position on the European continent; that the British did not have the power to win the war and should reach an accommodation with Hitler before it was too late; and that, in view of Germany's dominance, United States involvement would needlessly prolong the war: *Portugal na Segunda Guerra*, 416–17.
[36] FO 371/26835 C7748/900/36. For Spanish military views on the extension of the war into Soviet Russia see FO 371/26940 C8416/222/41.
[37] FO 371/26819 C12584/214/36. The foreign office was only too aware of Salazar's dread of communism. In April 1942 the British ambassador in Portugal, Sir Ronald Campbell, reported that Salazar was convinced that unless the *Wehrmacht* succeeded in breaking the Soviets that summer 'Europe would be engulfed in a wave of communism such as no other power on earth could stop': Gallagher, 'Conservatism, dictatorship and fascism in Portugal', 165–6.
[38] FO 371/26795 C9773/C10275/C11211/41/36.

German forces.[39] Campbell made good use of this material in his subsequent interviews with Salazar. This, together with America's entry into the war, meant that by the end of the year Portuguese confidence in an ultimate victory for the allies was greater than at any time since May 1940.[40] There was nevertheless no intention in Portuguese official circles of abandoning neutrality. Fear of German retribution should they actively and openly back the allied cause lingered for a considerable time after 1941 as witness, for example, Portugal's willingness to continue supplies of wolfram to Germany against the wishes both of Britain and the United States.

In acknowledging the limitations of propaganda in their relations with Portugal the British also recognised the importance of not antagonising Salazar's regime in the economic and commercial sphere. Yet the needs of economic warfare, so vital to the long term conduct of the war, inevitably imposed a strain on relations with Portugal. The economic blockade, and its corollary, rationing of imports and exports, was a source of much discontent among the Portuguese who were not prepared to submit meekly to the demands of their British ally. While during January 1940 they concluded commercial agreements with Spain and Italy, they persisted in their refusal to conclude a war trade agreement with Britain; this even though negotiations had begun in October 1939. Indeed, discussions had revealed a wide divergence of interest between the two countries. Salazar wanted the trade agreement to include the supply to Portugal of such essential items as coal, copper and tinplate, and the maintenance of Portuguese exports in pitwood, rosin, turpentine, tinned fish, wolfram and wine. If the British stopped Portuguese exports to Germany he expected compensation.[41] The British wanted Portugal to stop supplying either financial assistance or credits to Germany, to refrain from using British tinplate for the export of tinned goods to adjacent neutrals in excess of normal exports and to institute an export licensing system for an agreed list of commodities.[42] Although there was no agreement during 1940 the Portuguese went some way towards meeting Britain's essential requirements in the financial sphere.[43] However, they proved less accommodating with regard to the introduction, in July, of compulsory navicerts for all shipping approaching Europe.[44] The effect of the navicert system was to prevent the re-export and carriage of Portuguese colonial produce to Germany, Italy and enemy-occupied countries, the main recipients of such trade before the war. Initially the Portuguese may have thought the blockade would be a relaxed affair – a reasonable supposition in view of the leniency with which it had been implemented in the first phase of the war. However, British insistence that rationing quotas be fixed, by means of a temporary embargo on further imports into Portugal, rapidly dispelled that

39 JIC(41) 390(Final) in FO 371/26795 C11055/41/36.
40 FO 371/26795 C12151/C14072/41/36. R. G. Caldwell, 'The Anglo-Portuguese alliance today', *Foreign Affairs* xxi (1942) 157.
41 W. N. Medlicott, *The economic blockade*, i, London 1952, 510–13.
42 Ibid. 512.
43 Ibid. 515–16.
44 For details of the navicert system see ibid. 436–42.

illusion.[45] While negotiations for a quota on petroleum imports were concluded successfully in February 1941, with an agreed figure of 78,000 tons per quarter,[46] the Portuguese proved more obdurate concerning other commodities, particularly colonial produce such as sisal, sugar, cocoa, coffee and oilseeds. In December 1940 Salazar warned Selby that too ready an acceptance of the British blockade would not only affect adversely the economy of Portugal and her colonies, but would also threaten his country's neutrality.[47]

To conciliate Portuguese public opinion, the British ministry of economic warfare agreed at the beginning of 1941 to revised quotas but insisted on the prohibition of exports to undesirable destinations and the avoidance of excessive stocks.[48] Following an exchange of notes, Salazar agreed to the revised quota system though 'with the greatest reluctance as regards the colonial territories' and the extension of the navicert system to the Portuguese colonies. He would still not agree, however, to provide a written guarantee concerning the re-export of colonial produce and insisted that Britain trust him in the matter. He further ruled that materials already stored in Portugal were not covered by the guarantee. Despite these reservations the British accepted that the exchange of notes of 14 and 25 January constituted an agreement 'in principle'; an agreement which was subject to wide interpretation and which became a source of difficulties in the future, especially after the entry of the United States into the war.[49]

There could be no doubt that despite Portuguese concessions, the blockade policy infringed and threatened Portugal's neutrality. In March 1941 Salazar complained bitterly about the activities of the British consulates in Portugal. He warned that such activity was bound to be exploited by German propaganda and that it might lead Hitler to take retaliatory action. He was determined to maintain his country's neutrality even if it meant trading with Germany because Portugal's neutrality remained the best guarantee for the neutrality of the peninsula as a whole.[50] The British authorities recognised the problems which economic warfare created for them in Portugal and they suspected that the Germans were exercising strong and continuous pressure in Lisbon to secure some modification in the operation of the blockade. Nevertheless, Eden rejected any modification, insisting that German policy was guided by strategic rather than commercial considerations.[51]

Economic issues were a source of continuing friction for the rest of 1941. The

45 See CAB 68/7 WP 203(R)40; Medlicott, *Economic blockade*, i. 515.
46 For details of the petroleum negotiations see ibid. 517–19.
47 FO 371/24488 C13062/C13595/36/36. For the impact of British economic warfare policy on the Portuguese colonies see G. Clarence-Smith, 'The impact of the Spanish Civil War and the Second World War on Portuguese and Spanish Africa', *Journal of African History* xxvi (1985), 311–14.
48 *DAPE*, viii, annex to no. 1410, pp. 19–20; Medlicott, *Economic blockade*, i. 521.
49 FO 425/418; CAB 68/8 WP 19(R)41. For difficulties after 1941 see W. N. Medlicott, *The economic blockade*, ii, London 1959, 314–42. See also Eden Papers, PORT/42.
50 FO 425/418; *DAPE*, viii, no. 1610, pp. 310–13. The blockade was also a source of irritation to the Anglo-Portuguese Society in London which formed a trade committee during 1941 to argue for a relaxation of controls on Portugal. In this connection, see *Hansard parliamentary debates*, HL, 5th ser. cxix, cols 173–92.
51 FO 425/418.

ministry of economic warfare suspected that the Portuguese were breaking the spirit of the 'agreement in principle'. At the beginning of 1942 they learnt that goods which required export licences were being disguised as indigenous products, for example, palm oil as turpentine, despite a regulation of September 1941 which required that everything except wool and coal be verified at the frontier or place of loading. The ministry was also compelled to recognise the growth of Portuguese trade in commodities such as sugar, sardines and tin with the occupied countries of western Europe, notably France and Belgium, and with French North Africa.[52] These infractions, however, paled almost into insignificance beside the continuation of Portuguese exports of wolfram ore to Germany, which was a source of considerable strain in relations between Portugal and Britain and the United States.[53]

The allies could not ignore the significance of the wolfram exports because as a tungsten ore its application in war was extremely varied. It was used, for example, as a core for armour piercing projectiles, as an alloy in stellite used for engine valve sealing and as a catalyst for synthetic oil production.[54] During the early years of the war most tungsten ore came from China, Burma or Korea but once the Trans-Siberian route to the far east was closed by the German invasion of the Soviet Union the smaller reserves in Portugal and Spain became increasingly significant. Indeed, during 1941 and 1942 Portugal accounted for over 80 per cent of European production.[55] Even before the German invasion of Russia there had been growing competition in Portugal between British and German buyers which resulted in a price explosion during 1940 and 1941. The British then copied the Americans and substituted molybdenum which could be obtained from the United States at a relatively stable cost. The emphasis, therefore, shifted in late 1941 towards pre-emptive purchases of wolfram in the Iberian Peninsula. Deliberate efforts were made by Britain to raise the price of wolfram in both Spain and Portugal in the hope that higher prices would attract supplies already committed to the Germans as well as exhaust their funds. By the end of November 1941 the price of wolfram was nearly £6,000 per ton compared to £300 per ton in August 1940.[56]

Despite the astronomical increase in price and the highest production rates ever reached, the Portuguese economy suffered some dislocation as a result of the wolfram boom. Thousands of Portuguese living in the areas surrounding the

[52] Medlicott, Economic blockade, ii. 317–19; By safe hand, 351–5.
[53] There exists a sizeable body of literature on the subject of Portuguese wolfram during World War II including Medlicott, Economic blockade, i, ch. xv; ii, chs xi, xx; J. W. Cortada, United States-Spanish relations: wolfram and World War II, Barcelona 1971; Sir L. Woodward, British foreign policy in the Second World War, iv, London 1975, 65–71; J. K. Sweeney, 'The Portuguese wolfram embargo: a case study in economic warfare', Military Affairs xxviii (1974); D. L. Wheeler, 'The price of neutrality: Portugal, the wolfram question, and World War II', Luso-Brazilian Review xxiii (1986), pts 1, 2, 107–27, 97–111.
[54] Cortada, United States-Spanish relations, 19; J. K. Sweeney, 'United States policy towards Portugal during the Second World War', unpubl. PhD diss. Kent State 1970, 107.
[55] For statistical details relating to tungsten production during World War II see C. J. Schmitz, World non-ferrous metal production and prices 1700–1976, London 1979, 178–81.
[56] Medlicott, Economic blockade, i. 527–9; ii. 319–20; Sweeney, 'United States policy towards Portugal', 111–12.

wolfram mines abandoned their fields and small trades, which brought scant financial benefits (the daily wage of many agricultural workers was a mere two shillings), to engage in fossicking for wolfram to the detriment of important sectors of the economy. Moreover, with the British and Germans spending about £1 million a week on wolfram and sardines the enhanced purchasing power of a section of the population greatly increased demand for consumer goods, already in short supply, and accentuated inflationary tendencies which the government's attempts at price control seemed powerless to prevent.[57] In order to impose control over the production and purchase of wolfram Salazar instituted a system of government control in February 1942. Henceforth, all wolfram sales would take place in an officially controlled market and there would be specific allocations for each of the belligerents. To the consternation of the allies the Germans would continue to receive a considerable share of the market under the revised system.[58] While German military power remained substantial Salazar was not prepared to risk counter-reprisals. It was only in June 1944 that he was persuaded to impose a complete embargo on all wolfram exports including those to Germany; by that time the Third Reich had stockpiles adequate for another two years.[59]

British irritation at Portuguese infractions of the blockade was tempered by the knowledge that they were not, apart from wolfram, on a large scale, and by their knowledge of the important part Portugal was playing in helping to preserve Spanish non-belligerency.[60] The idea of seeking Portugal's support with Franco's government arose during the negotiations for an Anglo-Portuguese war trade agreement in May 1940. David Eccles, who represented the ministry of economic warfare, concluded from his discussions with the condé de Tovar that the economic problems of Portugal and Spain were inextricably linked. Accordingly, the best approach would be a British government intitiative to assist Spain economically, with Salazar as intermediary, while ensuring that Portuguese economic needs and Britain's special relations with Portugal were kept to the forefront.[61] The foreign office was convinced that the solution to the Spanish situation lay in consolidating Franco's regime, the main threat to which was economic distress, exploited by Axis agents.[62] Following

[57] Medlicott, Economic blockade, ii. 315–16; Wheeler, 'The price of neutrality', pt 1, 113–16.
[58] Germany's share was 2800 tons per annum but, unlike the British who were permitted to purchase wolfram on the basis of credit, the Germans were required to pay in cash: Wheeler, 'The price of neutrality', pt 1, 112–13, 119–20.
[59] Medlicott, Economic blockade, ii. 323–36, 598–607: Woodward, British foreign policy, iv, 66–71; A. Milward, War, economy and society 1939–1945, London 1977, 308; Wheeler, 'The price of neutrality', pt 2, 102–4. See also DGFP, D, xiii, no. 489, pp. 808–10.
[60] For a detailed and lucid treatment of British efforts to preserve Spanish non-belligerency during the period under review see Smyth, Diplomacy and strategy of survival, passim. See also Medlicott, Economic blockade, i. 513–15, 529–48; ii. 282–91; Woodward, British foreign policy, iv. 1–6; Sir L. Woodward, British foreign policy in the Second World War, i, London 1970, 433–45; J. A. Cross, Sir Samuel Hoare: a political biography, London 1977, 322–39. For important memoir material see Sir S. Hoare, Ambassador on special mission, London 1946; W. S. Churchill, The Second World War, ii, London 1949; By safe hand.
[61] FO 371/24514 C6538/113/41.
[62] For details of Spanish economic distress during 1940 and 1941 see Smyth, Diplomacy and

interdepartmental discussions in London, Eccles returned to Lisbon and on 23 May presented his government's proposals to Salazar. Under these Britain was prepared to make available at Spanish ports, before the end of June, 100,000 tons of wheat for which payment was to be made through the Anglo-Spanish clearing. Spain would also be helped to buy Portuguese colonial products, subject to a guarantee of non re-export; payment for these should be made through the sterling area account of the Anglo-Spanish clearing which had a large balance in favour of Spain, effectively the underspent portion of the recent £2 million British loan. In return, Salazar was expected to undertake 'the difficult and delicate task' of securing from Spain certain practical assurances on her intention and ability to remain neutral.[63]

These proposals were acceptable to Salazar who was particularly pleased by the one which would allow Spain to purchase Portuguese colonial products; he believed they offered 'a serious basis for a trade that would be of value to both Spain and Portugal'.[64] When Eccles and Selby saw Salazar on 7 June he informed them that the Spaniards were definitely interested and that no time should be lost in proceeding with negotiations. He intimated that he had very gingerly broached the question of assurances, indicating certain features about German activity in Spain which caused Britain anxiety. He had, however, made a request for substantial assurances in Portugal's name and the reception had been favourable.[65]

On 6 July, following discussions with the condé de Tovar and Nicolás Franco, Eccles reached an agreement on a list of Portuguese colonial products which were to be bought through the Anglo-Spanish clearing. This included castor oil seeds, copra, maize, groundnut oil, coffee and sisal. On the 24th Selby, Salazar and Nicolás Franco exchanged notes (the Tripartite Agreement) which provided the necessary credit facilities in the Anglo-Spanish clearing for the Portuguese colonial products. Although the total at this stage was £600,000, further negotiations ensued with various alterations and extensions to the list so that by the end of September a payment of up to £728,000 had been authorised. The assurances were, of course, provided for in the Protocol of 29 July.[66]

While the Tripartite Agreement and the Protocol were a source of much satisfaction to many in British official circles Hugh Dalton, minister of economic warfare, was not convinced of Spanish sincerity. He was disconcerted by Spain's refusal to apply for navicerts, by her disinclination to take the wheat which they were persuaded to offer 'as an act of appeasement' and by the 'anti-British orgies' of the Spanish press. In addition, he was anxious not to build up Spain's war potential in case she followed Italy's example. Dalton's reluctance to proceed with the policy of economic assistance for Spain was not merely dangerous for Anglo-Spanish relations; given Salazar's close association

strategy of survival, 77–82; J. Fontana and J. Nadal, 'Spain 1914–1970' in C. Cipolla (ed.), Fontana economic history of Europe, vi, London 1976, 503–11.
63 FO 371/24490 C6527/379/36; 371/24501 C6938/30/41; DAPE, vii, no. 765, pp. 68–9; By safe hand, 111–13; Telo, Portugal na Segunda Guerra, 162.
64 FO 371/24501 C7009/30/41.
65 FO 371/24515 C7232/113/41.
66 Medlicott, Economic blockade, i. 513–14.

it also threatened Britain's relations with Portugal. He was, however, overruled by Churchill and Halifax and the policy was continued throughout the autumn and winter months of 1940–1 though admittedly in difficult and trying circumstances.[67]

The accession of Ramón Serrano Suñer as foreign minister during October 1940 and Franco's meeting with Hitler at Hendaye the same month naturally aroused fears in British and Portuguese official circles and produced a stiffening in attitude towards Spain. Although information led them, correctly as it turned out, to conclude that Franco had made no major concessions to Hitler, the British authorities recognised that there was still a great danger of the gradual infiltration by Germans into positions of influence in Spain, for example, the police force. Consequently, they shared Salazar's view that it would be wise not to concede too much until they knew rather better where Spain stood. Indeed, Salazar had advised Selby and Eccles, on 26 October, that it would be reasonable and proper to insist, as a condition for continuing economic assistance, on a change of attitude in the Spanish press. In this connection the prime minister had emphasised the failure of the Spanish press to publicise the Tripartite Agreement: as a result the Spanish public was ignorant of the assistance being provided by the British. He had himself vigorously protested to the Spanish government and he was convinced that if Britain continued her policy of economic assistance she had every right to be given the credit for this in Spain, and in the present circumstances to insist on that credit being given.[68]

The need to take a stiffer attitude became patently clear on 3 November when, without warning, the Spaniards annexed the international zone of Tangier, opposite Gibraltar.[69] The United States, which prior to the Tangier crisis had insisted on public assurances of Spanish non-belligerency, was particularly upset and matters were not helped by Serrano Suñer's visit to Berchtesgaden on 18 November. As a result Washington was inclined to drag its heels in the matter of sending relief ships to Spain where famine was imminent. While insisting on conditions such as the removal of obstacles which impeded Anglo-Spanish trade, a fairer attitude in the Spanish press and just treatment of their nationals in Spain, the British, on the other hand, were not inclined to press Franco to make a public statement concerning non-belligerency: they recognised that with German divisions on the Pyrenees frontier Spain could not make such a declaration. Thus on 15 November Salazar advised Selby and Hoare, who was visiting Lisbon, that the only wise policy was for Britain and the United States to continue controlled economic assistance. He warned that

[67] FO 800/323; Halifax to Churchill, 28 Sept. 1940, PREM 4/21/1; Dalton Diaries, xxiii, diary entry 31 Aug. 1940; Dalton Papers, 7/2; By safe hand, 141–2. See also Smyth, Diplomacy and strategy of survival, 60–4, 97.
[68] FO 371/24491 C11741/379/36; 371/24488 C11947/36/36. See also DAPE, vii, no. 1270, 557–61. For details of Franco's meeting with Hitler at Hendaye on 23 October 1940 see DGFP, D, xi, no. 220, pp. 371–6; P. Preston, 'Franco and Hitler: the myth of Hendaye 1940', Contemporary European History i (1992), 1–16.
[69] For a detailed treatment of the Tangier Crisis see Smyth, Diplomacy and strategy of survival, 133–72. See also C. R. Halstead and C. J. Halstead, 'Aborted imperialism: Spain's occupation of Tangier 1940–1945', Iberian Studies vii (1978).

if they stopped Spain would irrevocably collapse into German arms, soon to be followed by Portugal. Even without the combined weight of advice from Salazar, Hoare, Selby and Lord Lothian (Britain's ambassador in Washington who visited Lisbon on 14 November), Halifax would have needed little persuasion to appeal to the United States to soften their attitude with regard to the exportation of foodstuffs and raw materials on credit to Spain. As he told Lord Cranborne, dominions secretary, on 5 December, the policy of controlled economic assistance was dictated by the clearly and frequently expressed opinion of the chiefs of staff that Spain must be kept out of the war and that, if necessary, the blockade must be applied flexibly. In making his appeal on 23 November the foreign secretary emphasised that in view of the desperate food situation the Spanish authorities might finally be driven into co-operation with Germany, with the probable loss of the Iberian Peninsula to Britain's obvious detriment. In addition, United States support would help to stiffen the resistance of the Spanish generals who had recently indicated their willingness to fight if Germany invaded their country.[70] Halifax's appeal was reinforced by a personal telegram from Churchill to President Roosevelt.[71]

Although the United States accepted the British view that a private assurance of Spain's continuing non-belligerency would suffice, the wheat shipment and negotiations for an American loan continued to be delayed. The British, however, agreed to proceed with a loan of £2.5 million, with the provision of a further £2 million should the political situation improve, and the ministry of economic warfare was prepared to grant navicerts for wheat imports up to a million tons for the next twelve months. These offers were conditional upon full publicity in the Spanish press and in broadcasts. On 5 December, following an appeal from the dominions office, Canada agreed to supply wheat to Spain.[72] Unfortunately, the decision of the Spanish authorities on 1 December to incorporate the international zone of Tangier into Spanish Morocco and subsequently to dismiss British nationals employed in administering the zone, coupled with the prolonged stay of Italian submarines, compelled Britain to warn Serrano Suñer, on 14 December, that unless his government showed goodwill in the matter of Tangier it might be found impossible to secure the offer of economic assistance and to implement the arrangements for the delivery of wheat.[73] The British warning coincided with an offer of economic assistance to Spain from Salazar who was convinced that the moment had arrived to make the move and thus forestall the effect of increased German pressure upon Spain resulting from the Italian débâcle in Greece. The British moved quickly to check the Portuguese initiative. Hoare was told that the government did not want the Portuguese to make an independent and concrete offer until the Tangier problem had been overcome and that it would be better if the Portuguese ambassador informed the Spanish authorities that his

[70] FO 371/24508 C11573/40/41; FO 371/24513 C11757/C12249/75/41; Butler Papers, RAB E3/8–127; FO 800/323.

[71] See Woodward, British foreign policy, i. 441–2.

[72] Ibid. 442; Medlicott, Economic blockade, i. 541–2. See also FO 371/24505 C12495/30/41.

[73] Butler Papers, RAB E3/8–131; Woodward, British foreign policy, i. 446; Medlicott, Economic blockade, i. 542.

government was ready 'to associate themselves with and participate in the assistance offered by His Majesty's Government'.[74] At the same time, Noel Charles, the *chargé d'affaires*, was instructed to emphasise to Salazar that Britain was anxious to fulfil her offer of wheat and economic assistance to Spain, that it appreciated the force of his arguments, and to request his assistance either at Madrid or through the Spanish ambassador in Lisbon.[75]

Apart from hinting to the Spanish minister of commerce, Dimitrio Carceller, that Portugal was considering an offer of credit between £500,000 and £1 million, the Portuguese embassy in Madrid avoided any further reference to the subject during the remainder of December 1940. At the same time, Pereira told Eccles on 29 December that Salazar felt it was better to take big economic risks to prevent a collapse in Spain rather than wait for the collapse and see her swallowed up. Pereira was very worried at the delay in providing economic assistance caused by the Tangier negotiations. He gave Eccles the impression that he, and probably his government, did not take the Tangier question very seriously. Following an urgent request from Hoare, Anthony Eden, the new foreign secretary, instructed the Lisbon embassy to explain the details of Britain's case over Tangier to Salazar and to enlist his influence in bringing the Spanish government to reason.[76] When Campbell saw Salazar, on New Year's Day 1941, he emphasised the impossible position in which his government would be placed *vis-à-vis* public opinion if 'they proceeded to mismanage the plans for helping Spain (whose high-handed action had aroused great indignation) without doing what was necessary to safeguard British interests in Tangier'. The Portuguese prime minister indicated his agreement and promised he would try, as he had previously, to induce the Spanish authorities to see reason.[77]

The Tangier negotiations continued throughout January and were completed early in February 1941. Although not satisfied, the British government accepted Spain's assurances with regard to such matters as the maintenance of the existing rights of British nationals and institutions in the zone and full compensation for displaced officials.[78] The British decision was doubtless influenced by the knowledge of increased German pressure on Franco to enter the war on the Axis side.[79] They were also aware that the Germans had approached the Portuguese very recently to ascertain whether the passage of German troops through Spain to Gibraltar ran counter to the Protocol. Salazar had delivered a strong affirmative answer and Pereira was subsequently instructed to see Franco to insist on the full validity of the Protocol and to make it clear that any agreement to allow the passage of German troops through Spain would be a

---

[74] FO 371/24506 C13379/35/41.
[75] FO 371/24517 C13208/113/41.
[76] FO 371/24506 C13955/35/41.
[77] FO 371/26889 C2/2/41.
[78] Woodward, *British foreign policy*, i. 447. See also C. R. Halstead and C. J. Halstead, who claim the Anglo-Spanish entente of February constituted a *de facto* retreat from the assertion of full sovereignty by Spain in Tangier: 'Aborted imperialism', 58.
[79] See Woodward, *British foreign policy*, i. 447–8. For German attempts to persuade Franco to enter the war see DGFP, D, xi, nos 667, 682, 695, 702, 718, 725, pp. 1140–3, 1157–8, 1173–5, 1183–4, 1208–10, 1217–18.

breach of both its letter and spirit. When Pereira made his approach, on 29 January, Franco insisted that his only commitment was to the Protocol which was the basis of his policy. He made no reference to any meeting in the near future with Hitler.[80]

Even before the resolution of the Tangier crisis the ministry of economic warfare had given the go-ahead to the wheat shipments from Canada and Argentina to Spain and had granted the necessary navicerts for an additional 400,000 tons of Argentinian wheat. Following a personal intervention from Churchill on 12 February, and despite Eden's opposition, it was also agreed to grant navicerts for a further 200,000 tons of wheat a month during February and March. Eden, who believed a well-supplied Spain would offer a tempting target to Hitler, reluctantly agreed after discussions in Gibraltar on 17 December with Hoare and the chief of the imperial general staff, General Dill. The foreign secretary accepted that if a contrary, tough line were taken Serrano Suñer would be able to blame Britain for starvation in Spain. This would greatly help him in his efforts to bring Spain into the war on the side of the Axis. Furthermore, Salazar would not appreciate a change of policy.[81]

But despite all attempts to conciliate Spain, the Spanish press launched a venomous attack on Portugal, Britain and the United States during late February and early March 1941. From his conversations with Pereira and Alexander Weddell, United States ambassador at Madrid, it was clear to Hoare that Serrano Suñer was intent on picking a quarrel within the near future. Apart from the press attacks the Spanish foreign minister was doing everything in his power to prevent the projected meeting between Franco and Salazar which had first been broached by the Portuguese dictator.[82] Hoare had told Pereira that in his view it was essential that Salazar meet Franco soon to warn him that Serrano Suñer was determined to push Spain into war and to repudiate the Protocol.[83] The advice of Salazar and Colonel William Donovan, Roosevelt's special adviser on the Axis, was still to continue with the established policy. Shortly afterwards, on 15 March, Hoare and Campbell saw Salazar in Lisbon and complained that the Spanish foreign minister was obstructing the negotiations for a British loan of £2.5 million to Spain. The ambassador wondered whether they ought to make public Serrano Suñer's opposition to the loan and 'pillory him in the eyes of Spain'. Salazar's advice

---

[80] FO 371/26957 C802/802/41; 371/26904 C986/46/41. Although Franco was never to see Hitler again he did see Mussolini on 12 February 1941 at Bordighera on the Italian Riviera: *Ciano's diplomatic papers*, 421–30; P. Preston, *Franco: a biography*, London 1993, 422–3.

[81] Smyth, *Diplomacy and strategy of survival*, 176–8; Medlicott, *Economic blockade*, i. 542–3; FO 371/26904 C1651/46/41. Apart from Eden and Dalton, Lord Cranborne, the dominions secretary, Duff Cooper, the minister of information, and Sir Auckland Geddes and J. N. Buchanan, respectively chairman and financial director of the Rio Tinto company which was the largest British owned company operating in Spain, had reservations about the policy of continuing economic assistance to Spain: FO 800/323; Unpublished diary of Harvey of Tasburgh, diary entries 27 Oct., 13 Nov. 1940, 15 Jan. 1941; Eden Diaries, diary entries, 2, 3, 21 Jan. 1941.

[82] On 29 January Pereira had suggested a visit by Salazar to Spain and Franco had been very receptive to the idea. In the event, Salazar did not visit Spain until March 1942. Nogueira, *Salazar*, iii. 305–6; Preston, *Franco*, 454.

[83] FO 371/26945 C1959/232/41; 371/26939 C2107/222/41. See also *DGFP*, D, xii, nos 66, 89, pp. 119–20, 165; Telo, *Portugal na Segunda Guerra*, 332.

was again cautionary: 'if the Minister for Foreign Affairs continued to object, the only wise course was continued patience'. In addition to the negotiations for a loan proposals were elaborated in London which envisaged a broad approach to Spain involving Britain, Portugal, the United States, and possibly Latin American countries. Hoare, who believed that Salazar was the only man in the peninsula likely to convince Franco against the wishes of Serrano Suñer, advised that the scheme must be made attractive enough to secure the support of the Portuguese leader.[84]

Initially, the prospects for an attractive package deal were promising. The Portuguese offered credits of £500,000 as part of an overall contribution which would make it possible for the Spaniards to purchase Portuguese colonial goods to the value of £1.5 million. The British felt unable to help with the balance because if they permitted the Spanish government to make further sterling payments to the Portuguese this would increase their sterling liability with Portugal which was already £10 million linked to gold. The United States authorities were consulted and initially agreed to assist. Unfortunately, a dispute between Serrano Suñer and Weddell, which ultimately involved Franco and secretary-of-state Cordell Hull, and led to a crisis in Hispano-American relations, removed any further possibility of United States support. Following conversations in Lisbon during June, involving British, Portuguese and Spanish representatives, an agreement was reached which incorporated a list of Spanish first preferences, especially edible oils, to be purchased through the Portuguese credit of £500,000. A tentative list of second preferences was also agreed and these were to be purchased in other ways, provided the United States could be persuaded to reconsider their attitude. The result was very disappointing: in the words of the ministry of economic warfare, 'a puny thing compared with what we hoped to achieve with the Americans in it as well'.[85]

Although some progress had been made in terms of controlled economic assistance to Spain, there was uncertainty as to its effectiveness. Consequently, when Hoare saw Franco on 28 June he asked him directly whether he and his government 'really wished for friendly relations with His Majesty's Government and the United States Government' and whether he wanted 'these economic plans to succeed'. The *Caudillo* was equally frank: he wished the economic plans to succeed. Within a few days, however, the Spanish Blue Division, 18,000 troops under the command of General Muñoz Grandes, was on its way to join the German army on the Russian front and, on 17 July, the fifth anniversary of the military insurrection against the Spanish Republic, Franco declared publicly that the allies had lost the war.[86] Naturally, there was speculation as to

[84] FO 371/26924 C2639/108/41; 371/26904 C2595/46/41; 371/26889 C2403/2/41. For details regarding Serrano Suñer's obstruction of the loan agreement see FO 371/26913 C3753/71/41.
[85] FO 371/26889 C6725/C7566/2/41; Medlicott, *Economic blockade*, i. 524; *By safe hand*, 272. For the dispute between Serrano Suñer and Weddell see C. R. Halstead, 'The dispute between Ramon Serrano Suñer and Alexander Weddell', *Rivista di Studi Politica Internazionali* iii (1974), 445–74. See also Smyth, *Diplomacy and strategy of survival*, 181–9.
[86] FO 371/26906 C7752/46/41. For Franco's speech and the Blue Division's departure for Russia see D. W. Pike, 'Franco and the Axis stigma', *Journal of Contemporary History* xvii (1982), 381–2.

the *Caudillo*'s motives. Salazar instructed Monteiro to communicate his views to Eden:

> It seemed to be a deliberate part of General Franco's policy to create feelings of hostility in Spain against the United States. Dr. Salazar did not believe that this speech had been inspired by the Germans or the Italians. He therefore concluded that either General Franco was preparing for an early rupture of relations with us and with the United States or he believed that the war would shortly be finished and that Spain could join in without much cost to herself. Finally, it might be that General Franco realised that he could not prevent Spain from becoming involved in the war on Germany's side and wished to prevent the United States from entering the war.

The British government had already declared that they were not prepared to continue with their policy of economic assistance while the Spanish authorities adopted so unfriendly an attitude.[87] Salazar accepted this was the minimum they could do in the circumstances. He also felt it would be prudent to stand on the recent declaration and watch Spanish policy: it would either proceed on lines foreshadowed in Franco's speech and become increasingly unfriendly, or would revert to its previous pattern, indicating that the speech was an isolated political act.[88]

Salazar's views exactly coincided with those of the British government.[89] Moreover, owing to the continued hostility of the Falangist press, notably *Arriba*, towards the United States, the foreign office believed there was little they could or should do to smooth the rupture in Hispano-American relations. Strang minuted on 14 August: 'We want relations between the United States and *Portugal* to be good, but it may not be a bad thing, in view of future possibilities, that the United States Government, and United States public opinion should be exasperated with Franco and his Ministers.'[90] Eden, however, recognised that the peninsula was indivisible and that Portugal's benevolent neutrality required Spanish non-belligerency. Accordingly, after consulting Hoare in August and September 1941, he appealed to Washington for an improvement in economic co-operation between the United Kingdom, the United States, Portugal and Spain. In so doing Eden recognised that the first steps had already been taken towards ending the impasse in Hispano-American relations. He regarded this as significant because Britain's own means of action in the economic sphere were nearly exhausted and further developments depended on American co-operation. He also recognised that little progress had been made in drawing the Americans and Portuguese into discussion on subjects such as Portuguese colonial surpluses, United States co-operation in

---

87 See Eden's speech in the house of commons of 24 July 1941: *Hansard parliamentary debates*, HC, 5th ser. ccclxxiii, cols 1074–5. See also CAB 66/17 WP(41)174.
88 FO 371/26812 C8583/149/36; *DAPE*, ix, no. 2116, pp. 101–3.
89 Writing a month after Franco's speech, Churchill concluded that it would not be sound to deduce that 'Franco had given himself over to the Axis' and that by itself it could not be taken as a basis for activating operation 'Pilgrim' ('Puma') for the occupation of the Portuguese and Spanish Atlantic islands: Avon Papers, AP 20/8/669. For operation 'Pilgrim' ('Puma') see ch. ix.
90 FO 371/26925 C8882/108/41. Emphasis in original.

the purchase of goods such as wolfram and olive oil, and the provision of tanker tonnage to secure the minimum requirements of petroleum products for the Portuguese economy.[91] Despite reservations at the Washington embassy Eden insisted, early in December 1941, on an approach being made to the Roosevelt administration for a relaxation of the rationing system to enable the peninsula countries to obtain the minimum quantities of essential imports permitted them by the blockade. American assurances for the policy of pre-emptive purchases in the peninsula were also to be sought.[92]

As far as Britain was concerned the situation became even more urgent with the entry of the United States into the war and reports of increased German activities and increased pressure in the Iberian Peninsula and in Spanish Morocco. On 19 December the embassy in Washington was advised that the chiefs of staff remained of the opinion that it was most important, on strategic grounds, to maintain the neutrality of the peninsula for as long as possible. Neither Portugal nor Spain could be expected to offer organised resistance to a German invasion but the Spanish government might be dissuaded from voluntarily joining the Axis and the Portuguese government might be persuaded to continue to resist overseas. The British therefore hoped that the United States authorities would accept the paramount strategic importance of keeping the Iberian Peninsula out of the war; that with this object in mind they might continue as far as they could to send supplies to Spain; and that they would not be 'too exigent in the negotiations which they have now begun with the Spanish Government'.[93]

Despite their efforts, by the end of 1941 the British were very disappointed at the failure of the Americans to grasp both the importance and the urgency of the problem and the need for action on their part. Further interventions by the Washington embassy notwithstanding, the United States continued to believe that a tough policy towards Spain would pay greater dividends. Consequently, Hispano-American economic negotiations made slow progress during the first part of 1942.[94] While they failed to move the Americans on Spain, the British authorities continued to insist on the maintenance of their generous attitude concerning imports into Portugal and to avoid making difficulties over minor blockade questions. The allied occupation of Timor had damaged Anglo-Portuguese relations and in view of this and of increased Axis pressure in the western Mediterranean, which enhanced the strategic importance of Portugal and her Atlantic islands, it was all the more important 'to endeavour to meet Portuguese needs and susceptibilities and to treat them as far as possible as allies'.[95]

At the level of economic relations therefore, Britain was quite successful during the period 1939-41 in overcoming Portuguese objections to the blockade, objections which the Germans failed to exploit to the full. With regard to the peninsula as a whole the result was somewhat less satisfactory, owing partly

---

[91] FO 371/26926 C10946/108/41.
[92] FO 371/26926 C12977/108/41.
[93] FO 371/26926 C14052/108/41. See also Woodward, British foreign policy, iv. 4–5.
[94] FO 371/26926 C14052/108/41.
[95] Ibid.

to American obduracy. Spanish non-belligerency was, however, maintained, an achievement in which Salazar played a strong supporting role. Although in his memoirs he does not acknowledge the debt he owed to the Portuguese leader Hoare constantly sought his advice and acted upon it. According to Monteiro the Portuguese government sought regularly to impress upon their Spanish colleagues that so long as Britain could maintain her sea and air power, together with the blockade, these conditions would ultimately prove decisive in her favour.[96] In this connection another contemporary, David Eccles, has claimed that there has been a tendency to neglect or undervalue Salazar's role in keeping Spain non-belligerent[97]. However, it is true the Portuguese dictator hardly played the central role in this saga. Franco retained his policy of non-belligerence for reasons other than the wise counsels of his fellow dictator in the peninsula, despite his imperialist ambitions in north Africa and his conviction that since Dunkirk England had lost the war.[98] The sheer exhaustion of the Spanish people, and the army, after the civil war and the lack of military and other resources – particularly foodstuffs for which Franco, in the absence of compensatory supplies from Italy and Germany, was dependent upon Britain and the United States – meant that the Spanish government could not afford a long struggle and would only enter the war when victory seemed certain.[99] Hitler in fact recognised this when he told his military advisers on 8 January 1941 that Franco would only enter the war when Great Britain was ready to surrender.[100] It is worth noting that when Germany appeared on the point of victory against Soviet Russia during July 1941, with the United States still not belligerent, Franco delivered his speech of 17 July. It was as if that moment had come and he was ready for a decisive, if last minute, entry into the war.

As a means of consolidating Britain's position in Portugal, and in accordance with their pre-war views, the Lisbon embassy attached considerable significance to the need to provide help in the organisation of Portugal's land defence. This view was to some degree shared by the authorities in London. During September 1939 the ministry of economic warfare considered that in future customers for arms should be divided into three categories. The first included firm allies, such as France, Egypt and Poland who had broken off relations with Germany; the second prospective allies such as Portugal, Turkey and Iraq who had not yet broken off relations with Germany; the third countries which Britain had

96 FO 371/24491 C11741/379/36; DAPE, vii, no. 1270, pp. 557–61.

97 By safe hand, 419–20.

98 See DAPE, vii, no. 1005, p. 252. Paul Preston argues that Franco consistently tried to use the Portuguese to deceive the British: 'The Caudillo saw Lisbon as a useful conduit to the Foreign Office, to be exploited while the Axis was winning, to mask his own position. In 1943, when the outcome of the war seemed more doubtful, he would use Lisbon to endorse his neutral credentials in the eyes of the Allies. In the summer of 1940, however, he harboured predatory thoughts about Portugal': Franco, 359.

99 For details of Spanish shortages see Smyth, Diplomacy and strategy of survival, 79–81. It was the considered opinion of Hoare and Captain Hillgarth, his naval attaché, that Franco and Serrano Suñer could not sign the Tripartite Pact with Germany, Italy and Japan prior to the fall of Suez because if they did there would be a coup d'état: Eden Diaries, diary entry 26 Apr. 1941.

100 C. B. Burdick, Germany's military strategy and Spain in World War II, New York 1968, 115.

guaranteed but which had not broken off relations with Germany and remained neutral, for example, Greece and Roumania. On fulfilling orders to the first two categories the ministry considered the sole criteria should be Britain's capacity to supply. At the beginning of November 1939 the deputy chiefs of staff, who had concurred with the ministry's categorisation, established a revised list for the supply of arms to foreign countries which was based on their strategical importance. According to this Portugal's naval requirements were considered as being of first importance while her military and air requirements were regarded as having some importance. The foreign office emphasised that if political criteria were applied, Portugal was ranked third equal with Iraq following Egypt and Yugoslavia, the latter still neutral. As an ally Portugal had a special relationship with Great Britain and it was important to retain her goodwill and support. Consequently, it was essential that Portugal's requirements should be met as far as possible and it was particularly important that existing contracts should be fulfilled.[101]

Unfortunately, little was achieved during late 1939 and 1940. At the beginning of the war Portugal's main arms requirements from the United Kingdom consisted of mobile 3.7 inch anti-aircraft guns, submarines and motor torpedo boats, fighter aircraft, and a coastal defence system for the port of Lisbon based on a plan drawn up by Major-General Frederick Barron, inspector of fixed defences at the war office, and accepted by the Portuguese – the fairly detailed specification for this included 9.2 inch guns, 6-pounder twin equipments, 40mm Bofors equipments, static anti-aircraft equipments and anti-aircraft searchlights. It was soon clear that Britain's own deficiencies made early delivery impossible and the foreign office was compelled, during the remainder of 1939, to intervene to salvage even a few concessions from the service departments such as the delivery of fifteen Gladiators and three T class submarines.[102] Severe pressure persuaded the air council to agree to the token delivery of three Spitfires in May 1940 and to supply a further nine in the autumn.[103] The foreign office were less successful with the war office. They could do no more than promise to deliver the coast defence 9.2 inch equipments at the end of 1942 and even that was regarded as optimistic by the ministry of supply in view of Canadian and South African requirements which had precedence. It was not thought possible to supply the 3.7 inch anti-aircraft equipments within the next two or three years.[104]

The Portuguese were therefore determined to retain a large degree of independence. Salazar warned Selby on 6 January 1940 that Portugal needed to accelerate her rearmament and to draw her supplies from available sources. Having expressed his incredulity soon afterwards at Britain's inability to concede the early delivery of such a small order, he made an official complaint

[101] CAB 92/18 AD(39)15 and AD(39)42.

[102] FO 371/23161 C15840/C17167/13834/36; DAPE, vi, No. 187, pp. 159–60

[103] FO 371/23161 C17345/C18717/13834/36; 371/24484 C135/22/36; DAPE, vi, no. 204, pp. 220.

[104] CAB 93/18 AD(39)47; CAB 92/20 AD(S)(39) 1st mtg, allied demands supply subcommittee, 24 Nov. 1939; CAB 92/19 AD(40)8. For details of the offer see ch. iv.

about the delay in the delivery of the Spitfires.[105] This did not, however, deter the Portuguese authorities from announcing their intention to place a firm order for the coastal defence artillery required by the Barron plan and for both static and mobile anti-aircraft equipments.[106]

It was obvious to Halifax that if his government was unable to give the Portuguese at least some satisfaction they could turn to sources of supply which would carry undesirable political connotations. He therefore asked the war office to consider a token early delivery of a few 3.7 inch anti-aircraft guns for training purposes.[107] The war office was less than accommodating: their own requirements and their inability to supply the outstanding orders of allied countries such as Egypt and Iraq made a token delivery to Portugal quite impossible.[108]

With no room for manoeuvre, Halifax sought to calm Portuguese fears by emphasising that Portugal's interests were best served by the concentration of all military resources in the allied war effort; any spare capacity should be devoted to countries in dire need such as Finland.[109] Salazar was unimpressed. On 14 March, he noted his government's view: it did not accept that the Royal Navy alone could assure the security of Portugal. Selby felt Salazar's apprehensions were genuine and he emphasised the extent to which Britain's position in the peninsula would be strengthened if any means could be devised to accelerate Portuguese rearmament.[110] Meanwhile, the decision to defer the whole Portuguese order for anti-aircraft had created consternation within the Lisbon embassy, and had particularly alarmed the military attaché, Lieutenant Colonel Fenton. Although Portugal was in no immediate danger, Fenton believed that the effects of air action against undefended cities in Poland and Finland could hardly reassure the Portuguese government given their total unpreparedness in anti-aircraft defence. Such deficiencies could not be remedied overnight. The military attaché added a further warning:

The consequences of our refusal or inability to deliver at least a token portion of the equipments in question will probably be that the orders will go to Italy with a further resultant increase in the impetus of the strong Italian drive which is going on here and which, let there be no mistake, is directed with full German co-operation, to the undermining of the special British position in this country.

Selby, who understood that Salazar was under enormous pressure from his critics, was very reluctant to tell the Portuguese leader that his order for anti-aircraft guns could not be accommodated. He therefore deferred making a final communication in the matter until Halifax had considered Fenton's analysis.[111]

At the beginning of April the ambassador informed the foreign office that

105 FO 371/24484 C421/22/36; DAPE, vi, no. 319, pp. 261–3.
106 FO 371/24484 C1123/22/36.
107 Ibid; CAB 92/20 AD(S) (40) 2nd mtg, 25 Jan. 1940.
108 FO 371/24484 C2104/C2756/22/36.
109 FO 371/24484 C2378/C3428/22/36; 371/24489 C2886/379/36.
110 FO 371/24489 C3965//C3614/379/36.
111 FO 371/24484 C4068/C4285/22/36.

French circles in Lisbon shared Portuguese fears about a possible *coup* in Spain, especially in view of Axis influences and the large number of Germans in that country. Moreover, the French minister was as convinced as his British colleague that some contribution towards Portuguese arms requirement would consolidate and strengthen the allied cause in the Iberian Peninsula and check any further German advance.[112] Meanwhile, Halifax had written to Chatfield on 28 March as minister for co-ordination of defence to appeal for an early delivery of anti-aircraft guns to Portugal, on the grounds that the *desiderata* of the chiefs of staff would not be met unless Portugal received some supplies and that both the Axis powers were making determined efforts to undermine the British position in Portugal. The end of the Russo-Finnish War had removed one of the strongest arguments against supplying Portugal and it had to be admitted that as long as they remained weak the Portuguese genuinely feared Spanish action against them. Following his appeal, the deputy chiefs of staff unanimously agreed that in spite of the shortage of such equipment the United Kingdom could not afford to turn down the Portuguese request. It was recognised, moreover, that a continued refusal to supply so little might be interpreted by the enemy as a reflection of Britain's own deficiencies. Accordingly, it was agreed that four 3.7 inch anti-aircraft guns should be allotted to Portugal in April and thereafter two per month until the token delivery of sixteen was completed.[113] Salazar indicated his willingness to accept the revised offer when it was put to him on 6 April, provided the sixteen guns were followed by the further twenty his government required and that the additional 48 static 3.7 inch anti-aircraft and 48 Bofors guns, as set out in the Barron report, were also forthcoming.[114] These conditions were accepted by the deputy chiefs of staff.[115]

In taking responsibility for the Bofors guns the British authorities were influenced by the knowledge that a scheme for purchasing them from Hungary was being prepared. The foreign office had learned of the Hungarian connection from a conservative MP, Samuel Hammersly, and from the offices of the head of the civil service, Sir Horace Wilson. Following an interdepartmental meeting at the foreign office on 16 April and a deputy chiefs of staff meeting on 18 April the decision was taken to approach the Portuguese with a proposal which would not only enable them to obtain their requirements but also to provide an incidental service in helping the British government obtain a number of Bofors guns for their own use without endangering Hungary's relations with Germany. The Portuguese authorities were on the point of delivering a favourable reply when Italy entered the war and rendered Hungary's participation out of court.[116] The scheme was revived momentarily during November 1940 when the Hungarians approached Lisbon but Hungary's accession to the Axis during the same month ended any prospects for such a deal.[117]

---

[112] FO 371/24484 C5347/22/36.
[113] CAB 82/2 DCOS(40) 15th mtg, 3 Apr. 1940; CAB 82/5 DCOS(40)50.
[114] FO 371/24490 C5349/379/36; 371/24484 C5369/22/36; DAPE, vi, no. 523, pp. 467–8.
[115] CAB 82/2 DCOS(40) 17th mtg, 18 Apr. 1940; CAB 92/21 AD(S)18; FO 371/24485 C6450/22/36.
[116] FO 371/24484 C5509/C5831/22/36; CAB 82/2 DCOS(40) 17th mtg; FO 371/24485 C5985/22/36; 371/24484 C5758/22/36.
[117] FO 371/24485 C5985/22/36.

By the end of 1940 the only area in Anglo-Portuguese military relations where real progress had been made was in the supply of the 3.7 inch anti-aircraft equipments. No firm dates had been suggested for the Bofors guns. The various dates for delivery during 1941 and 1942 for the two batteries of 9.2 inch guns, two batteries of 6 inch guns and six 6 pounder twin equipments for the Barron plan were unlikely to be adhered to – and the Portuguese had not yet been informed of this fact. At the same time, an offer of four 7.5 inch reconditioned naval guns for Portugal's colonial territories had been indefinitely postponed causing considerable disappointment in Lisbon. The earliest date which could be offered for the delivery of six motor torpedo boats was June 1943 and Portuguese requests for certain equipment for the construction of a destroyer in Portugal had been refused. Finally, despite the revised offer to supply three Spitfires during May 1940 and a further nine in August not one of these aircraft had actually been delivered.[118]

Britain's failure to meet Portugal's arms requirements unquestionably presented the Axis powers with an excellent opportunity to exploit their position to Britain's detriment. Indeed, it was rumoured in November 1940 that the Italians had recently delivered 750 heavy machine guns, 20mm rapid fire guns and 40mm anti-tank guns to Portugal. At the same time, the Germans were seriously considering an agreement with Portugal whereby military equipment would be exchanged for strategic raw materials such as tungsten, tin, sardines in oil and oils. Thus not only would Germany's raw material requirements be met but British purchases of the same raw materials would be disrupted.[119] The situation was to be radically transformed, however, in December 1940, by the decision to hold secret Anglo-Portuguese military conversations in the New Year and by the increasing interest shown in London and Washington in the defence of the Atlantic islands. The strategic dimension of Britain's relations with Portugal had gained significance since the fall of France and the increased possibility of a German invasion of the Iberian Peninsula with or without Spain's approval.

[118] FO 371/24485 C13740/22/36.
[119] *DGFP*, D, xi, no. 390, pp. 690–1.

9

The Atlantic Dimension

For more than half a century Britain's policy-makers had testified to the strategic significance of the Azores and Cape Verde islands and the vital importance of preventing them from falling into enemy hands. During 1940 and 1941 a German threat to Portugal itself and to the islands was, correctly in view of Hitler's operational directives, to be anticipated, and the British authorities were compelled to plan serious and extensive contingency measures.[1] British concern regarding a possible German move against Portugal and the islands was indeed manifest even before the fall of France. Rumours of a pro-German *coup*, which abounded in Portugal during early May, compelled the British government to consider various forms of action. Apart from strengthening British intelligence in Portugal and organising the British communities there, and giving greater priority to Portuguese armaments requirements, the foreign office advised that preparations should be made for seizing strategic points in the Cape Verde islands and the Azores in the event of trouble. Following a meeting of the war cabinet on 15 May the chiefs of staff were instructed to prepare a contingency plan.[2] At the same time, the Portuguese were asked to take early measures to protect the Atlantic islands against a German attack. Selby reported on 1 June that he was satisfied that 'within their possibilities the Portuguese Government are endeavouring to take all necessary precautions. They are responding to our requests with unusual celerity'.[3]

The decision, meanwhile, to proceed with a policy of controlled economic assistance for Portugal (and Spain) raised the problem of German reprisals and of Portuguese national security. On 16 May President Carmona's ADC had informed Selby that if Salazar was given adequate support, Portuguese ports and bases would be placed at the disposal of the British authorities. The question of Portuguese security was remitted to the chiefs of staff who reported that no trained and fully equipped troops were available and that they were unable to provide the Portuguese with artillery and anti-aircraft equipment. Selby was told of the chiefs of staff decision on 27 May but was firmly instructed not to communicate it to the Portuguese government.[4]

---

[1] For details of German operational planning, 1940–2, involving the Atlantic islands see *Brassey's naval annual*, London 1948, 142, 145, 147–8, 152–3, 198–9; *Blitzkrieg to defeat: Hitler's war directives 1939–1945*, ed. H. R. Trevor Roper, New York 1971, 39–43, 81, 121–3; Burdick, *Germany's military strategy*, 17–42, 75, 122–4, 133–49; H. H. Herwig, 'Prelude to *Weltblitzkrieg*: Germany's naval policy towards the United States of America, 1939–1941', *Journal of Modern History* xliii (1971), 657–8.
[2] FO 371/24490 C6527/379/36; CAB 65/7 WM 123(40).
[3] FO 371/24493 C6610/4066/36; *DAPE*, vii, no. 762, pp. 64–5.
[4] CAB 80/11 COS(40)369; CAB 79/4 COS(40) 147th mtg, 24 May 1940; FO 371/24490 C6527/379/36.

In accordance with their brief to examine the strategic implications of Portuguese intervention on the side of Britain's enemies, the chiefs of staff recommended a number of essential measures on 29 May. Given Spanish hostility, the acquisition by Britain's enemies of bases in Portugal itself 'would not be of much additional value to them' since the harbours and aerodromes of Spain 'were sufficient to meet their needs in that area'. As a result no action against the mainland of Portugal was recommended in the event of Portugal changing sides. It was stressed, however, that the Cape Verde islands and the Azores occupied important strategic positions on the Atlantic trade routes between the south Atlantic and the United Kingdom, and that enemy naval and air forces if established on the islands 'would be in a position to seriously threaten Britain's communications'. In view of this, operations 'should be undertaken to deny the facilities of the Cape Verde Islands and the Azores to the enemy'. In addition, the ministry of economic warfare had advised the chiefs of staff that the only economic outlets for much of the trade of Northern and Southern Rhodesia were through Angola and Mozambique respectively, the latter being the most important. Consequently, the main railway in Mozambique and the ports of Beira and Lourenço Marques should be captured and held. The chiefs of staff believed that the government of India would have to take over Goa, where there was a high-powered wireless station, as well as Damão and Diu. They did not envisage operations against Macao or Portuguese Timor, in the latter case so as not to precipitate Japanese aggression.[5]

On 31 May cabinet endorsed the recommendations acknowledging that contingency planning would be necessary in the case of the Atlantic islands, Mozambique and Goa though not Portugal itself. The chiefs of staff were instructed to continue with their detailed operational examination of the possibility of seizing strategic points in the islands while the government of India was assigned responsibility for Goa, Damão and Diu. At the same time, the dominions office with the governments of Southern Rhodesia and South Africa, was to co-ordinate and prepare a plan for the capture of the railway from the frontier of Southern Rhodesia to the coast of Mozambique and the port of Beira.[6]

The preparation of an operations report by the joint planning chiefs during June 1940 was incorporated into planning initiatives involving the Spanish Atlantic islands (Canaries) and Balearic islands. Following their report to the chiefs of staff it was agreed, at a meeting of the latter on 17 June, that as long as Spain and Portugal remained genuinely neutral no action would be taken against their islands. However, if Spain were to enter the war on the side of the Axis, or show signs of so doing, Britain should seize the Azores and Cape Verde islands whether or not Portugal had entered the war against her or had been attacked. It was confirmed that the troops required for the operations would be definitely earmarked and withdrawn from any other role; that navy and army commanders should be nominated immediately and instructed to prepare their detailed landing plans; and that the shipping necessary for the expedition should also be earmarked. The question of priority – whether the Canaries or

5   CAB 66/8 WP(40)180 COS(40)408.
6   CAB 65/7 WM 149(40); FO 371/24495 C11261/7171/36. See also PREM 3/361/4.

the Portuguese islands – was to be examined in the light of the limited forces available. Finally, it was recommended that the joint intelligence committee should consider what 'Fifth Column' activities could be undertaken to assist in the occupation of all or any of the islands.[7] On 21 June Winston Churchill emphasised to the cabinet defence committee that irrespective of any decision on priorities there should be no delay in getting the troops trained and making arrangements for embarkation at short notice.[8]

At this stage it was felt vital that the Portuguese should remain in ignorance, and yet it was recognised that in certain circumstances the government might have to communicate with Salazar. With this in mind Halifax telegraphed Selby on 25 June to request his early advice on how the Portuguese might be approached. The foreign secretary told Selby of the chiefs of staff advice, not only that the Cape Verde islands and the Azores should be occupied immediately if Spain entered the war on the Axis side, but also that precautionary measures might be necessary in advance of actual hostilities if her belligerent intentions became clear. The ambassador was not convinced:

> If, at the present unfavourable junction, we prepare to occupy them before Spain enters the war and without taking the Portuguese Government into our confidence we shall be charged with a breach of the Alliance and of dragging Portugal into the war. Our promise of ultimate salvation will not just now be convincing; we shall demolish our position in the Portuguese mainland; we shall shock Brazil and Latin America profoundly and Portugal, hoping to save her skin will almost certainly throw herself into the arms of Spain and Italy.

Selby was convinced that any communication made after the event would be inadmissable; he believed that Salazar should be taken into their confidence.[9]

The foreign office and the chiefs of staff rejected his advice. The chiefs continued to emphasise that seizure of the islands remained the only option. The alternative of sending an expeditionary force to the Portuguese mainland while shortages of troops and equipment continued and higher priorities existed elsewhere was untenable.[10] Halifax, however, was very concerned that a precipitate occupation of the islands might be counter-productive. He understood that the timing of the operation was of the highest importance and, in view of the advanced preparations, he sought to establish with Churchill that before any force was despatched to the islands the war cabinet, or at least the prime minister, would be consulted. Churchill agreed, minuting on 10 July: 'Nothing must be done without a Cabinet decision.'[11]

Clarification of the circumstances which would activate the operations – code-named 'Accordion' for the seizure of the Azores and 'Sackbut' for the Cape Verde islands – was obviously necessary if the war cabinet was to make a

---

[7] CAB 80/13 COS(40) 465(JP); CAB 79/5 COS(40) 184th mtg.
[8] CAB 69/1 DO(40) 18th mtg.
[9] FO 371/24515 C7429/113/41.
[10] Ibid.
[11] PREM 3/361/1. For details relating to the forces earmarked for the operation see note from General Ismay to Churchill, 12 July 1940, ibid.

considered decision. On 16 July the chiefs of staff specified three possible scenarios: active Spanish or Portuguese hostility; clear Spanish or Portuguese intention to intervene against Britain; failure of economic pressure by control point source or control of shipping to achieve adequate results and consequent British recourse to direct naval action. The chiefs of staff emphasised that unprovoked aggression against the Portuguese islands would provide Japan with a pretext for intervention in Timor and would jeopardise the policy of controlled economic assistance which was showing some prospects of success.[12] The war cabinet, on 22 July, approved in principle the first two conditions for intervention but not the third which was not felt to provide sufficient justification for seizure of the islands.[13]

Churchill was much exercised by the prospect of seizing the islands. On 21 July 1940 he requested an intelligence appraisal on the current state of the Portuguese armed forces. The joint intelligence committee reported within twenty-four hours and emphasised that the coastal defences of the Azores were still under construction while in the Cape Verde islands they were non-existent. The Azores garrison consisted of two light infantry battalions and two coastal batteries. They were not expected to offer much in the way of resistance since their level of training and equipment was felt to be low. There was no air cover: almost all the aircraft of the Portuguese air force were concentrated in and around Lisbon.[14] It was probably the prime minister's awareness of the weak condition of Portuguese defences which prompted him, on 24 July 1940, to suggest an early occupation of the Azores to Halifax:

> All my reflections about the danger of our ships lying under the Spanish howitzers in Gibraltar lead me continually to the Azores. Must we always wait until a disaster has occurred? I do not think it follows that our occupation temporarily, and to forestall the enemy, of the Azores, would *necessarily* precipitate German intervention in Spain and Portugal. It might have the reverse effect. The fact that we had an alternative refuelling base to Gibraltar might tell against German insistence that we should be attacked there, or anyhow reduce German incentive to have us attacked. Moreover once we have an alternative base to Gibraltar, how much do we care whether the Peninsula is overrun or not?[15]

Senior members of the foreign office such as Cadogan and Strang and the chief diplomatic adviser, Vansittart, disagreed stongly, believing that the action Churchill proposed would precipitate German intervention in Spain and Portugal and that in any case the Protocol of 29 July provided clear evidence of improvement in the situation in the peninsula. Halifax therefore advised Churchill to wait 'yet a while before taking action'.[16] In the absence of overt

[12] CAB 66/9 WP 265(40) COS(40)551. See also J. R. M. Butler, *Grand strategy*, II: *September 1939–1941*, London 1957, 239.
[13] CAB 65/14 WM 209(40).
[14] FO 371/24490 C7174/379/36.
[15] PREM 3/361/1.
[16] FO 371/24515 C7429/113/41; PREM 3/361/1. For a brief reference to the debate see E. Barker, *Churchill and Eden at war*, London 1978, 148–9.

Spanish or Portuguese hositility or of any tangible sign that either intended to intervene on the Axis side the forces earmarked for 'Accordion' and 'Sackbut' remained on standby during the late summer of 1940.

While discussions were taking place in London the governments of Southern Rhodesia and South Africa spent June and July considering their joint plans to seize control of the Mozambique railway and the port of Beira; the South Africans were also planning the seizure of the railway from the Transvaal frontier to Lourenço Marques and the port itself. The Dominions authorities were concerned that a delay of even a few hours after operations in the Atlantic had begun might materially prejudice the success of their operations, especially as petrol installations and other British assets in Mozambique were vulnerable. The Southern Rhodesians therefore insisted that they must move before war was declared and as soon as it was clear that Portugal would lose control. It was essential that the authorising telegram from London should arrive in good time.[17] The foreign office were perturbed by Rhodesian assumptions. There was little likelihood of any Portuguese declaration of war against Britain or vice versa. All they had to consider was what preventive action they should take in the event of an attack by Spain on Portugal or if an unfriendly government obtained power in Portugal as a result of an internal *coup*. Salisbury could certainly rely on the foreign office to give as much warning as possible when such preventative action seemed necessary, but 'a great many things would have to happen before such a warning was likely to be issued'.[18]

Jan Smuts, prime minister of South Africa, shared the foreign office's cautious attitude. He doubted the wisdom of taking pre-emptive action against the Atlantic islands and Mozambique as soon as Spain entered, and regardless of Portugal's attitude. He believed such an action would be far more difficult to defend than that which had recently taken place against the French fleet at Oran and Dakar; the British empire's cause rested upon moral grounds which should not be treated lightly. The world's judgement both then and after the war was of the greatest importance.[19] After a meeting of the war cabinet on 22 July 1940 the South African prime minister was informed that His Majesty's Government felt bound to adhere to their original view that Spanish hostility might force them to secure the Cape Verde islands and the Azores, though definite action would not be taken without further consideration by the war cabinet itself and, at that stage, Smuts would be consulted. It was further emphasised that a state of war between Britain and Portugal would not necessarily follow from action against the islands: it was conceivable that the Portuguese would accept the situation under protest. At the same time, the war cabinet agreed with Smuts about timing. They would not encourage his government to take action in Portuguese East Africa until they had given themselves a few days to see whether Portugal acquiesced in their seizure of the islands.[20]

After further consultation between authorities in South Africa and in

---

[17] FO 371/24495 C7171/7171/36.
[18] Ibid.
[19] Ibid.
[20] CAB 65/14 WM 209(40); PREM 3/361/4.

Southern Rhodesia preparations for the seizure of the railways and the ports of Beira and Lourenço Marques were completed in the autumn. The operations were referred to as 'DHQY' and 'DHQZ' respectively. The Southern Rhodesians, however, continued to have reservations about the timing of the operations against the Mozambique railway and Beira, believing that an element of surprise should be retained.[21] The dominions office and the foreign office did not agree. Important political considerations were also involved. If action had to be taken against the Portuguese islands, they would hope to dissuade Portugal by diplomatic means from entering the war against them. Their task would be made all the more difficult if action had also taken place in Mozambique. Any move there should be deferred until the outcome of diplomatic moves had been assessed. Even if Lisbon declared war on Britain action in Mozambique might not be required since there was reason to believe that in the event of a German invasion of Portugal the Portuguese colonies would declare their independence and appeal to Britain for protection. In any case, even if action had to be initiated by the United Kingdom, the alternative of friendly co-operation with Mozambique would remain.[22]

Sir Godfrey Huggins, prime minister of Southern Rhodesia, was far less sanguine. He was not convinced that a British seizure of the islands, in the absence of a German attack on Portugal, would result in friendly co-operation with Mozambique.[23] Smuts was less pessimistic. He continued to appreciate the advantage of deferring action in Mozambique in the hope that Portugal might be persuaded to remain non-belligerent, and he was confident that the military position of South Africa was so strong that Lourenço Marques and Beira could be occupied successfully at any time without undue difficulty. Information in Smuts' possession indicated that the Mozambican authorities might appeal to Pretoria for protection but that any such appeal would almost certainly be accompanied by a request that the *status quo ante* be restored after hostilities had ended. He would find it difficult to give any such assurance. He felt the position of the Portuguese colonies would be analagous to that of the French colonies: their fate would be decided by the issue of war.[24]

Churchill telegraphed Smuts on 17 December 1940. He agreed that any necessary action in the Atlantic islands – now described as operations 'Brisk' (Azores) and 'Shrapnel' (Cape Verde islands) – might be taken without necessarily provoking active Portuguese hostility either in Portugal itself or in her African possessions; and that even if the Portuguese were hostile the Union would be able to deal with Portuguese East Africa. Churchill was equally forthright in rejecting the Southern Rhodesian case for the simultaneous activation of operations 'DHQY' and 'DHQZ' and of 'Shrapnel' and 'Brisk'. He was,

---

21 FO 371/24495 C11261/7171/36; PREM 3/361/4.
22 Ibid.
23 FO 371/24495 C11261/7171/36.
24 PREM 3/361/4. As before the war, so during 1941, both Pretoria and Salisbury cast covetous eyes on Mozambique, particularly Delagoa Bay and the ports of Lourenço Marques and Beira: ibid. Cranborne to Churchill, 28 Feb. 1941. In September 1940 Salazar confessed to Ferreira da Fonseca, the Portuguese minister at Pretoria, that he feared the war would revive South Africa's territorial claims to Portugal's colonies: Telo, *Portugal na Segunda Guerra*, 221. See also Nogueira, *Salazar*, iii. 309.

however, forced to confess that because of 'the need to act quickly and in the greatest secrecy' it would not be possible to consult Smuts when the critical moment arrived. The South African prime minister was none the less assured that no action would be taken without full and careful consideration by the war cabinet.[25] On the same day Huggins was informed of the British prime minister's views and advised that if 'DHQY' and 'DHQZ' were put into operation simultaneously with 'Shrapnel' and 'Brisk' it seemed 'in the highest degree probable' that any chance of maintaining friendly relations with the Portuguese would be lost.[26]

In the course of the discussions in London during the summer of 1940 the possibility of a sudden German move against the Azores had been raised. The chiefs of staff felt this could not be discounted and that a close naval patrol should therefore be instituted despite the greater risk of submarine attack, the additional demand on the navy's attenuated destroyer strength and the opportunity it gave for Axis propaganda in Spain and Portugal. It was essential, however, that the patrol should not enter Portuguese territorial waters. Despite the foreign office view that relations with Portugal were good enough to allow them to give prior information to the Portuguese government, it was agreed that the authorities in Lisbon should not be informed until they asked for information and that the reply would be that the patrol had been established to assist in the British blockade of Germany and of German occupied territories.[27]

A continuous naval patrol close to the Azores seemed to offer a possible solution to the strategic problem. It would deny the islands to Germany while not permitting British use of their facilities. Unfortunately, since the Royal Navy was unable to maintain a continuous patrol, even this limited aim could not be achieved. The only realistic course would be either to occupy the islands at the critical moment or to stand aside and do nothing. The latter was inadvisable, and the former only politically tenable, if Britain was not responsible for precipitating the moment of crisis. During the last months of 1940 the foreign office and the embassies in Lisbon and Madrid were extremely anxious to avoid such an outcome. Towards the end of October Hoare told the foreign office that during his farewell interview with Colonel Juan Beigbeder, the former Spanish foreign minister had emphasised the importance of not allowing any British troops to land on Spanish soil until a Spanish national resistance movement had itself started. He warned that if Britain seized ports in Portugal or landed troops in Spain before the Spanish army had declared its readiness to resist, the Germans would be able to accuse the British of forcing Spain into action in

[25] PREM 3/361/4.
[26] FO 371/24495 C11261/7171/36.
[27] CAB 80/19 COS(40)798; CAB 79/55 COS(40) 11th mtg. (0) part of COS(40) 335th mtg, 4 Oct. 1940; FO 371/24494 C10637/4066/36. British submarines operated close to the Azores with an occasional embarrassing incident such as occurred in December 1940. Halifax's successor as foreign secretary, Anthony Eden, noted this incident in his diary: 'Winston sent for me this morning to meet the Chiefs of Staff. . . . A submarine of ours off the Azores had fired at a suspicious ship and missed, one torpedo landing up on shore! It later transpired that the ship was one of ours and we decided to make a clean breast of the silly business to Salazar': Eden Diaries, diary entry 28 Dec. 1940.

their own interests. On reflection, Hoare concluded that the Portuguese side of the problem should once again be given urgent consideration:

> While I believe that it would be tactically unwise for us to seize bases in Portugal before a Portuguese national movement has started, I think that it is most necessary to consider how best to stimulate a national movement of some kind behind which we could quickly act. . . . The fact of it would give us the justification to enter Portugal as the allies of a Portuguese national movement rather than as invaders who wish to seize bases for their own purposes.[28]

The chiefs of staff were less concerned with the creation of a national movement in Portugal than with forestalling a German move against the Azores. With this in mind Beigbeder's warning sounded ominous. They were anxious to learn whether the seizure of the Azores by British forces would be likely to have the same effect in Spain as the seizure of ports in Portugal itself. The foreign office advised that if Britain seized the Azores in anticipation of German aggression in Spain, the political effect would be Spanish and Portuguese hostility. It would be regarded in both countries as an attack upon the neutrality of the peninsula. It would almost certainly bring Spain into the war, and lead to German occupation of bases for operations in both Spain and Portugal. Apart from creating bitter and lasting resentment among the Portuguese it was likely to arouse American criticism.[29]

The chiefs of staff did not underestimate the political dimension, though strategic considerations alone made it imperative to avoid antagonising Spain and Portugal. Hence their support for a relaxation of the economic blockade during October 1940.[30] Towards the end of November, following a request by Hoare for an assessment of the strategic dangers consequent on Spain joining the Axis powers, the chiefs of staff again emphasised that everything should be done to prevent it. While stressing that Gibraltar must be retained as a base for the rapid prosecution of the campaign against Italy, they also emphasised the dangerous strategic consequences should Portugal follow Spain into the Axis and Lisbon fall under German control:

> The Germans will acquire, in Lisbon, a naval base, which can accommodate all classes of ships, including capital ships, and from which they can directly threaten the Western Patrol. They will thus be in a very favourable position for making a still further breach in the blockade. It will also be open to them to base fast surface craft, including possibly a battle cruiser, at Lisbon with which to raid our communications down the Northern Atlantic to the Middle East. Such raiding forces would be extremely difficult to deal with since they would be operating outside the cover of our main fleet in home waters.[31]

---

28 FO 371/24508 C11460/40/41; PREM 3/405.
29 FO 371/24494 C10637/4066/36.
30 D. Smyth, 'Diplomacy and strategy of survival: British policy and Spanish non-belligerency, 1940–1941', unpubl. PhD diss. Cambridge 1978, 83.
31 CAB 66/13 WP(40)460 COS(40)968.

There was no doubt of the crucial need to avoid antagonising Spain and Portugal, yet a German attack on the Azores and the Cape Verde islands remained a very real possibility. A meeting of the defence committee on 25 November revealed that the chiefs of staff had given 'anxious consideration to the question of whether it would be advisable to carry out operations "Brisk" and "Shrapnel" now, so as to make certain of forestalling the Germans in the Azores and the Cape Verde Islands'. The chiefs agreed on the importance of securing the Azores should Gibraltar become untenable, but they realised that if the operation were carried out immediately a German advance into Spain and Portugal might be precipitated, and Gibraltar lost earlier than might otherwise happen.

The defence committee discussed the matter at some length. Halifax agreed strongly that an occupation of the Azores would cause a very unfavourable reaction in Portugal, would probably activate the Protocol and hence might well precipitate the very crisis they were so anxious to avoid. With Hoare's suggestion in mind it was felt by some members that much would be gained if the Portuguese and Spaniards could be induced to put up even the slightest resistance to a German advance, though it was admitted that a considerable British force would probably have to be sent to the peninsula. If, however, British forces could take and hold Lisbon or Cueta the position would be much better than holding the Azores alone. Sir John Dill, chief of the imperial general staff, demurred: there were not the resources to hold Lisbon, or even Ceuta, and if the Azores were not seized in good time, Britain would be left with nothing. As a counter-argument it was suggested that the Germans might be deterred from entering Spain by the fear of having to hold down yet another hostile population, already in a state of semi-starvation. The fact that Britain had seized the Azores might not therefore be a sufficiently strong reason to precipitate them into an immediate invasion. The first sea lord, Admiral Sir Dudley Pound, added a further consideration. He explained that if the Germans occupied Portugal, Spain and the Canary islands, the navy would have to run their transatlantic convoys across the south Atlantic to Trinidad and thence north to Halifax in Nova Scotia. Enemy occupation of the Canary islands, he stressed, would negate any material advantage in Britain holding the Azores. If, on the other hand, the Spaniards resisted the Germans and gave Britain the use of the Canary islands the navy would be much better placed for controlling European trade than if it held only the Azores. From the discussion it was clear that the arguments in favour of carrying out 'Brisk' and 'Shrapnel' immediately were not overwhelming and that it would be better 'to wait and see whether a suitable moment would not arise before long'. Everything should be ready for when that moment came.[32]

After the meeting the foreign office again sought the advice of their ambassadors in Madrid and Lisbon. Hoare was against occupation of the islands. He believed the effect on the Spanish government in present circumstances would be 'thoroughly bad' and would go a long way towards weakening the steadily growing resistance to a German invasion of Spain or a German march through

[32] CAB 69/1 DO(40) 46th mtg; PREM 3/361/6A.

Spain: Franco's government would clearly regard occupation as an attack on the Iberian Peninsula. He warned that if Britain did occupy the Azores Spain would probably invite the Germans into the Canary islands and he emphasised that, as in 1808, Spanish resistance must start first. Britain should only intervene at the invitation of Spanish resistance forces. An occupation of the Azores would destroy any hope of such an invitation. Seizure of the Azores would be justified, in Hoare's view, only in conditions of over-riding military necessity. In that case it would be essential to take Salazar into British confidence and to enlist the support of the United States. Selby was equally opposed to an occupation of the islands except in the case of dire military necessity. Although the Portuguese might 'swallow' the seizure of the islands and confine themselves to a protest, it was possible that the Spanish government, under pressure from the Germans, would invoke the Protocol. He shared Hoare's view on the need to confide in Salazar but he favoured discussing the matter with the United States government before any approach was made to the Portuguese leader and before any positive action were taken.[33]

The threat of a German descent on Spain without Spanish connivance appeared very real. Italy's disastrous intervention in Greece had been followed by the opening of General Wavell's offensive in North Africa and Churchill was convinced that Hitler would retaliate and that he would do so in Spain. The joint intelligence committee was inclined to agree, though they ruled out the danger of a German attempt to take the Atlantic islands since photographic reconnaissance had revealed that there were no naval forces in the Biscay ports and the chief of the secret service believed Germany would 'do a Norway' on the west coast of the Iberian Peninsula.[34] By mid-December 1940 Churchill was therefore inclined to favour occupation of the Cape Verde islands and the Azores as a precaution. He was opposed, however, by the chiefs of staff who stressed that available forces were insufficient for the operation.[35] Although Churchill still believed a German descent on Spain was more likely than an attack on the Balkans the decision regarding operations 'Brisk' and 'Shrapnel' was deferred though, as his telegram to Smuts of 17 December showed, the matter was kept under review.

Throughout all the months of discussions on the Atlantic islands the British had studiously avoided any communication with the Portuguese authorities. They assumed that Portugal would not risk infringing her neutrality for the sake of co-operation with her ally and that a temporary British occupation with the consent of Lisbon was out of the question. Moreover, while they recognised that because of its strong defences the Grand Canary island would deter a German assault, the British military authorities had not seriously considered helping the Portuguese to fortify the Azores and Cape Verde islands as a deterrent to German action. Indeed, while advising that the Portuguese be encouraged to strengthen their defences on the islands they had offered nothing

---

33 FO 371/24494 C13107/4066/36.
34 F. H. Hinsley, *British intelligence in the Second World War*, i, London 1979, 256–7.
35 CAB79/55 COS(40) 32nd and 33rd mtgs, 14 Dec. 1940; Hinsley, *British intelligence*, i, 257.

in the way of essential equipment. During December 1940, however, a Portuguese initiative forced the government to consider these options seriously.

When Monteiro saw Halifax on 17 December, on personal instructions from Salazar, he raised the question of Anglo-Portuguese military collaboration with regard to the preservation of the integrity and independence of Portugal. The ambassador confirmed that what Salazar intended were staff talks between the British and Portuguese armed forces in London; Portugal's dictator did not wish to be taken by surprise, to see events in Portugal following the pattern of Belgium and Holland.[36] The foreign office and the chiefs of staff agreed that there would be political advantages in staff talks, although the latter seriously doubted whether Salazar would risk infringing his neutrality by granting British forces facilities: these alone would make the staff conversations really worthwhile from a military point of view. The chiefs of staff anticipated that the Portuguese military authorities would press Britain for the supply of arms and ammunition which she simply could not spare. Churchill authorised Halifax to inform Monteiro that His Majesty's Government would welcome Anglo-Portuguese staff talks in London.[37]

The conversations did not start until the beginning of March. Meanwhile, there was a relaxation of operations 'Brisk' and 'Shrapnel' early in the New Year. This resulted from an optimistic assessment, by the chiefs of staff, of the likelihood of Spanish military resistance to a German invasion and from Churchill's own strategic appreciation of the war.[38] At the same time, Monteiro informed Eden that Salazar did not anticipate a German attempt to take the Azores. The Germans did not have superiority at sea and the problem of holding the islands in the face of a hostile population would be too great. The Azores garrison had been strengthened, the Portuguese were prepared to send more troops if it were thought necessary and the German colony on the islands was being carefully watched.[39] These moves strengthened the impression that Portuguese feeling against Germany had hardened and that there was less chance of them resisting a British occupation of the islands. The joint planning staff, therefore argued that operations 'Brisk' and 'Truck' (alternative name to 'Shrapnel') were no longer appropriate and should be cancelled. As an alternative, a battalion of Royal Marines should be held ready to move at short notice from the United Kingdom to the Azores while the commander-in-chief south Atlantic, in conjunction with general officer commanding west Africa, should be instructed to prepare plans for moving at very short notice a detachment from the garrison at Freetown to the Cape Verde islands.

The joint planners also suggested that the Portuguese be persuaded, even before staff conversations began, to accept a small number of technical advisers in the guise of civilians and some defensive material in order to substantially improve the defences of the islands. If the Portuguese did not agree the joint

[36] FO 371/24491 C13546/379/36; DAPE, vii, no. 1376, 677–83.
[37] FO 371/24491 C13546/379/36; CAB 79/8 COS(40) 432nd mtg, 18 Dec. 1940; DAPE, vii, no. 1376, 677–81.
[38] FO 371/26809 C115/115/36; Prime minister's personal minute, 7 Jan. 1941, PREM3/405/8. See also Butler, Grand strategy, ii. 432–3.
[39] FO 371/26793 C237/41/36.

intelligence committee suggested a small number of men be infiltrated into the islands before the outbreak of hostilities. Alternatively, a 'Trojan Horse' expedition might be attempted by a force kept on reserve in ships in the south Atlantic. The chiefs of staff, however, insisted on maintaining the forces as presently constituted for operation 'Brisk' and 'Truck'. The question of infiltrating a small number of technical advisers was remitted to the staff conversations.[40]

Shortly before the arrival of the Portuguese delegation Cadogan emphasised to Churchill the importance which the foreign office attached to their visit. The presence of the mission indicated that the Portuguese might resist aggression by force. It was plainly to Britain's advantage that they should do so and their final attitude would be materially affected by the outcome of the discussions. The prime minister approved the visit but he had doubts about 'the quality and even trustworthiness of the delegation' and insisted that 'they should not be shown anything that matters'. The chiefs of staff shared his doubts: they felt members of the delegation were too junior in rank and that one or two of them had German connections.[41] They were reassured on both points following foreign office intervention with the embassy in Lisbon. In fact, the Portuguese delegation, visiting the United Kingdom ostensibly to study all aspects of the defences of London, was deliberately composed of junior officers as the presence of more senior personnel would have aroused Axis suspicions that the Portuguese were breaking their neutrality. The key member of the delegation was Colonel Barros Rodrigues of the Portuguese general staff. He had the personal confidence of Salazar and he alone was empowered to engage in the staff conversations.[42]

Following preliminary discussions by the joint planning staff and the chiefs of staff[43] it was confirmed that the object of the British delegation, which was headed by the former military attaché in Lisbon, Lieutentant Colonel Fenton, assisted by three junior members of the joint planning staff, Wing Commander Vintras, Commander Evershed and Major Mitford, was to encourage the Portuguese to stiffen their resistance to Axis influence generally and to check German infiltration, particularly into the Atlantic islands. Discussion centred on Portuguese defence plans, British assistance with them and the importance of the Atlantic islands. Subsidiary questions included the supply of war material, infiltration of technical experts into the Azores, British concern regarding the possibility of German submarines using the Bijagós islands off the coast

40 CAB 79/9 JP(41)100 COS(41)23(0); CAB 79/9 COS(41) 65th mtg, 22 Feb. 1941.

41 Cadogan to Churchill, 21 Feb. 1941 and minute by Churchill, 22 Feb. 1941, PREM 3/361/4; CAB79/9 COS(41) 65th mtg.

42 FO 371/26813 C1790/152/36; CAB 80/26 COS(41)123; DAPE, viii, no. 1535, pp. 134–7. The representative of the army and air force among the Portuguese delegation was Lieutenant Colonel Craveiro Lopes, later to be commander-in-chief of the army and president of the Portuguese Republic from 1951 until 1958. Also included in the delegation were artillery major Eduardo Nunes, air captain Carlos Macedo, captain of engineering Joaquim Marques, infantry captain Afonso Cazaes and infantry lieutenant Sá Carneiro: Telo, *Portugal na Segunda Guerra*, 325.

43 For details see CAB 79/9 COS(41) 61st, 65th, 78th mtgs, and JP(41)126. See also CAB 84/28 JP(41)164.

of west Africa as an advanced supply base without Lisbon's knowledge, the importance of preventing Japanese infiltration into Portuguese Timor and specific advice regarding the re-equipment of the Portuguese air force.[44]

Before talks began the chiefs of staff had stressed that the British delegation should avoid giving any impression that Britain might be prepared to provide support on land for the Portuguese.[45] But Rodrigues immediately asked what help Portugal could expect if a German attack came. The British had two alternatives: they could bring the conversations to an end or they could co-operate with Rodrigues in drawing up outline contingency plans but without promising to implement them. The military authorities felt that the second alternative would probably ensure that German infiltration into Portuguese territory was checked, and that in the event of attack British forces would be in a better position to secure the Atlantic islands and achieve the smooth transfer of the Portuguese government. The first was much more problematic as Major-General Sir Hastings Ismay, deputy secretary to the war cabinet and chief of staff to the minister of defence, told Churchill on 8 March:

> The termination of the conversations at this stage would probably lead to a moral deterioration which would render Portugal vulnerable to German infiltration on the Roumanian model. The Portuguese Government might put up a token resistance and might even plan to escape from the country in the event of attack, but our chances of securing the Atlantic Islands would be seriously reduced.

The chiefs of staff had therefore no hesitation, despite the risk of leakage, in recommending the second alternative with the proviso that no promise to send an expeditionary force to Portugal be made. Churchill agreed, emphasising the importance of the proviso.[46]

Within a few days of the prime minister's sanction an outline plan was drawn up which involved all three fighting services. The army was to contribute a force headquarters, one corps of two divisions, one heavy tank brigade, anti-aircraft troops, base and lines of communication units; the navy: naval base staff; and the Royal Air Force: a force headquarters, two fighter squadrons, two medium bomber squadrons and ancillary units. In total the force would consist of approximately 80,000 personnel and 12,000 vehicles and guns requiring twenty-four liners, seventy motor transport and five petrol ships. Approximately one million tons of shipping would be involved. It was calculated that the actual transfer of the force to Portugal would take fifty-four days, that is, fifty-four days would elapse between the day of departure of the first convoy to the arrival of the tenth and last. This did not include the time taken to prepare

---

[44] CAB 99/10 COS(41)181 also AP(41)4. Eight meetings in all took place between 3–12 March 1941. The minutes of these meetings are located in CAB 99/10. Details regarding the re-equipment of the Portuguese air force appear as appendix ix in R. E. Vintras, *The Portuguese Connection*, London 1974, 160–2. This is a rather disappointing memoir of the actual conversations since Vintras devotes far more space to the tour of London's defences. For British concern with regard to the Bijagós Islands see ADM 116/4391.
[45] CAB 79/9 COS(41) 78th mtg, 1 Mar. 1941; CAB 84/28 JP(41)164.
[46] CAB 99/11.

the force after receiving the appeal from Lisbon, which was calculated at ten days.[47] In view of the absence of a prior commitment by the British authorities to send an expeditionary force, the plan was merely academic. Fortunately so because it was clearly flawed, as revealed by a joint intelligence estimation of a timetable for a German attack on Portugal. This assumed that a German attack, launched without Spanish assistance, by four divisions – one armoured, one motorised and two infantry with air support consisting of about 140 aircraft, mainly dive bombers and single engined fighters – would take place on the twentieth day after German forces left the Pyrenean base. If it were optimistically assumed that further forces, totalling fourteen divisions, would also be in process of occupying Spain, the German high command might be compelled to allocate a further period of about ten days for the preparation of advanced bases and the attack against Portugal would not commence until day thirty. In either case the German attack would be launched long before the British expeditionary force was fully established in Portugal.[48]

While reiterating that, in view of their worldwide commitments, no specific promise of armed assistance could be made, the British authorities emphasised strongly that any assistance which could be given would be conditional on the Portuguese Atlantic islands, particularly the Azores, being denied to the Germans. German aircraft and submarines operating from the islands would not only constitute a severe threat to Britain's command of that area, but would also have a serious effect on shipping. Although the Portuguese were aware of possible German intentions and had taken steps recently to improve the defences of the Azores, Rodrigues admitted that his government had not fully realised the importance of the islands. The British offer to supply technical experts was met by an evasive reply from the Portuguese authorities. Finally, discussion on Portugal's armaments requirements made little progress owing to the perennial problem of supply.[49]

Contrary to the expectations of the British delegation, neither Hoare nor the new British ambassador at Lisbon, Sir Ronald Campbell, witnessed a stiffening of Portuguese resolve following the conversations. Indeed, on 21 March Hoare acknowledged this to Churchill himself. Although Portugal was more friendly to Britain than any part of the Continent it seemed to be drifting into 'a state of hopelessness and defeatism'. He was adamant that a good deal more would have to be done to strengthen the Portuguese will to resist; in particular in supplying their armaments requirements.[50] Campbell was convinced that unless the result of the staff conversations was to give the Portuguese very substantial encouragement the resistance offered to a German attack would be merely symbolic at best. His views were reinforced by those of Captain Hilary Owen R.N., the naval attaché, who was particularly worried about the possibility of a simultaneous German sea and air invasion which would ensure an

47 CAB 99/10 AP(41)3.
48 CAB 99/10 AP(41)1.
49 CAB 99/10 COS(41)181 also AP(41)4; Telo, *Portugal na Segunda Guerra*, 327. For details of the latest armaments supply position see CAB 99/10 6th mtg, and annexes i, ii, iii.
50 PREM 3/361/6A.

almost immediate conquest of Portugal and destroy any prospects for future Spanish resistance.[51]

The foreign office, worried that a German setback in the Balkans might result in a drive against the Iberian Peninsula, recommended a suggestion made by Owen – that the position in Portugal should be discussed with the United States Government – to the chiefs of staff. This recommendation was given added urgency by information that German infiltration had begun in the Cape Verde islands with three or four U-boats working from there against Britain's African trade routes. The chiefs of staff opposed Churchill's wish to activate operation 'Brisk' immediately, arguing that so long as there was a chance of Spain resisting German pressure they should refrain from seizing the Cape Verde islands, particularly as such action would probably result in Germany acquiring use of the Canaries. The chiefs agreed with the foreign office that the best deterrent to a German occupation of the Atlantic islands was an increase in American interest which might be achieved by taking them into full confidence. Accordingly, Halifax was instructed, on 28 March, to inform the United States government about their anxieties concerning German fifth column activities in Portugal and increased German activity in the Cape Verde islands and to request that the United States naval squadron, withdrawn early in the war, should return to the Tagus. As a further deterrent the ambassador was asked to recommend an American naval visit to the Atlantic islands.[52]

When R. A. Butler raised the question of German infiltration into the Cape Verde islands with Monteiro on 28 March the ambassador professed his ignorance. At the same time, he assured the parliamentary under-secretary that his government was doing all it could to check German fifth-column activity in Portugal and the islands. On 8 April Monteiro confirmed that the authorities in Portugal had no news whatever of the illegal use of the Cape Verde islands by German submarines.[53] In spite of the increased difficulties should a British occupation prove necessary, the chiefs of staff recommended that the Portuguese be encouraged to reinforce the Atlantic islands and to accept British technical expert advice. Although the Portuguese sent a further three battalions to the Azores and two to the Cape Verdes, they failed to respond on the issue of British technical advisers.[54] As a result, at the beginning of April, the joint planning staff considered the possibility of covert infiltration. However, the success of British pressure in persuading the Portuguese to reinforce the islands and thus reduce the danger of an internal *coup* and of fifth-column activities had increased the risks of infiltration.[55]

Although the Portuguese were actively reinforcing the islands there remained little prospect of viable resistance from within Portugal itself to a

---

[51] FO 371/20834 C2657/900/36; CAB 80/26 COS(41)191, annex i.

[52] Minutes by Churchill, 22, 24 Mar. 1941, chiefs of staff to Churchill, 23 Mar. 1941, PREM 3/361/1; CAB 80/26 COS(41)191; FO 371/26834 C3052/900/36. See also S. Roskill, *Churchill and the admirals*, London 1977, 175.

[53] FO 371/26793 C3057/C351?/41/36; Butler Papers, RAB G12 163, 188.

[54] FO 371/26793 C3586/C3637/C3730/41/36. See also DAPE, viii, nos 1691, 1709, pp. 272–3, 313; Butler Papers, RAB G12 214. For details of Portuguese reinforcements in April and during the second half of 1941 see Telo, *Portugal na Segunda Guerra*, 321, 461–2.

[55] FO 371/26848 C3519/3519/36.

German attack, not least because of Britain's inability to provide rapid and effective assistance. Campbell left the foreign office with no illusions on this score: without a strong British preventative occupation of Portugal there would be no repeat of the Peninsular War. There were only two further options: to encourage the Portuguese to defend their metropolitan territory notwithstanding the probably unfavourable impact on their subsequent resistance overseas; or to inform them candidly that if the blow fell before Britain's position had changed for the better His Majesty's Government would be content to see them accept German occupation of mainland Portugal provided they resisted overseas and accepted British help in defending their islands and colonial possessions.[56] As nothing could be done to help the Portuguese resist a German invasion the chiefs of staff confirmed their support for the second option.[57]

For planning purposes it was vital to know the precise intention of the Portuguese government; in late April and early May 1941 this was anything but clear. On the one hand Monteiro gave Eden the impression that Portugal would resist, while on the other Dr Vieira Machado, minister of colonies, told Campbell that it would be impossible for the Portuguese authorities to escape to the islands or colonies and that consequently they would resign and be replaced, probably by some kind of quisling government.[58] The key lay with Salazar, but to date Campbell had failed to penetrate his reserve. Monteiro, on his return to Lisbon, was equally unsuccessful. In the absence of clarification Campbell advised that an early and clear understanding should be reached between the two governments. Eden and Cadogan, with the recent Greek disaster in mind, agreed that they should be frank with Salazar and tell him that they could not provide effective help in the defence of metropolitan Portugal but that they wished him, in the event, to remove his government to some other part of the Portuguese empire where they would be able to help.[59]

The search for enlightenment with regard to intentions was not confined to the British side. The Portuguese wished to know categorically whether Britain could provide effective support. On 21 May Salazar, having consulted Santos Costa and Sampaio, pre-empted further speculation when he presented his ally with a formidable list of arms requirements, sufficient to equip five full divisions by August of that year. The Portuguese were concerned that Spain would abrogate the Protocol, acquiesce in a German occupation and assist a German invasion of their country. The war material requested was essential for their armed resistance. If the material could be provided, Monteiro assured Eden, the Portuguese would fight, and fight hard but without it they could offer no more than a token resistance. Smaller quantities of material – twenty-four mobile 3.7-inch anti-aircraft guns and thirty-six 40 mm Bofors guns – were also required for the defence of the Cape Verde islands and the Azores.[60]

56 FO 371/26793 C4047/41/36.
57 FO 371/26794 C4794/41/36.
58 FO 371/26984 C4459/4459/41; DAPE, viii, no. 1771, pp. 361–8; FO 371/26793 C4646/41/36.
59 FO 371/26794 C5346/41/36.
60 FO 371/26794 C5460/41/36; DAPE, viii, no. 1832, pp. 425–9; Telo, Portugal na Segunda Guerra, 343–5.

In view of recent events in the Middle East and Balkans the chiefs of staff found it impossible to dispute the Portuguese assumption that Spain would not offer military resistance to Germany, and since Germany had completed her campaign in Greece it was possible that she would be able to spare more forces for the Iberian Peninsula than had been estimated in March. The chiefs reaffirmed that as soon as their country was threatened the Portuguese should transfer the government to the Azores. If the Portuguese authorities agreed to adopt this course really effective assistance could be provided in a number of ways: assistance in the transfer of the Portuguese government to the Azores; early delivery of all the anti-aircraft guns requested by the Portuguese for the defence of the islands and provision of the necessary personnel, either wholly, or in part, to maintain them; the supply of torpedo bombers and the offer of British technicians to assist in carrying out the extension to the aerodrome and its facilities at Terceira Island which they necessitated; and the offer of local naval defence equipment, including boom defence gear and the manpower to install and, if necessary, to operate them. The admiralty was also prepared to make available immediately three 4.7-inch coast defence guns, and the personnel to install and operate them, for the Cape Verde islands. On 29 May the defence committee accepted the recommendations of the chiefs of Staff and they were communicated to the embassy in Lisbon the following day.[61]

Clearly, the decision to offer assistance in the reinforcement of the Atlantic islands was a risk in that Portugal might not co-operate in British plans for their use once they were reinforced, and any miltary operation against them would have been rendered immeasurably more difficult. Moreover, the whole issue of the islands was complicated by the increasing involvement, at Britain's behest, of the United States. President Franklin D. Roosevelt had first raised the subject of the Azores in September 1940. His intervention prompted London to inform him of their contingency plans concerning the Azores and the Cape Verde islands and tentatively to canvass his support.[62] There was, however, no positive American response at that time. Later, Roosevelt was reluctant to provide naval visits to Portugal and the islands following the British request of 28 March 1941. Churchill made a further effort to solicit American support towards the end of April when he appealed to Roosevelt to send 'at the earliest moment' a squadron for a 'friendly visit' to the Azores and Cape Verde islands in order to 'warn Nazi raiders off' and to 'keep the place warm for us as well as giving us valuable information'.[63] The prime minister's appeal, at the beginning of May 1941, coincided with a joint planning recommendation for the preparation of a military operation to capture the Canary islands (subsequently codenamed 'Puma') while simultaneously carrying out the operation against the

---

[61] CAB 65/18 WM 52(41), 22 May 1941; CAB 79/11 COS(41), 26 May 1941 and JP(41)407; CAB 80/28 COS(41)332(Final); CAB 69/2 DO(41) 36th mtg; FO 371/26848 C5883/3519/G; Eden Diaries, diary entry 29 May 1941.
[62] FO 371/24511 C8361/75/41; CAB 65/9 WM 260 (40), 27 Sept. 1940; FO 371/24494 C10637/4066/36.
[63] W. S. Churchill, The Second World War, iii, London 1950, 125. See also J. P. Lash, Roosevelt and Churchill 1939–1941: the partnership that saved the west, London 1977, 308.

Cape Verde islands. The forces and shipping held for the assault on the Azores were to be absorbed into the larger force required for the Canaries. The relegation of the Azores was justified on grounds of the perceived greater strategic importance of the Canaries and the comforting thought that any German occupation of the Azores might only be temporary since British forces ought to be able to recapture them, especially if American help were available. Indeed, American interest in the Azores was growing and was likely to prove a deterrent to any German action against them.[64]

Roosevelt's reaction was not encouraging. He revealed that the Portuguese had protested strongly against his government's offer of a 'friendly visit' to the Azores and Cape Verde islands and this had now been deferred. He was convinced that no expedition should be sent to the Portuguese islands unless Portugal was attacked or definite word of an immediate German attack on the islands was received. Moreover, he insisted that any British occupation of the Azores should be temporary and that the islands should be restored to Portugal in full sovereignty at the end of the war. After consulting Eden the prime minister advised Roosevelt that because of German infiltration his conditions made it almost certain that Britain would be forestalled by the Germans in the islands. At the same time, he assured the president that the islands would be restored to Portuguese sovereignty at the close of the war: 'We are far from wishing to add to our territory, but only to preserve our life and perhaps yours.'[65]

Roosevelt's initial reticence began to fade during the first half of May to a point where he considered sending a confidential emissary to Portugal to ask Salazar whether in the event of a retreat to the Azores he would agree to anti-Axis forces joining in the defence of these islands. When informed of this, Churchill advised that Salazar would not respond positively. If Portugal were occupied, and help in securing the Azores was then welcome, Salazar would prefer it to be exclusively British. In view of Portugal's request for armaments, on 21 May the foreign office concluded that it would be a tactical error to send an American emissary to Lisbon and that, accordingly, American influence should be held in reserve.[66] Roosevelt was not deterred. On 29 May he told Halifax that he was anxious to reach a complete understanding with Churchill regarding the Portuguese islands in the event of a German occupation of Spain and Portugal. He wished to agree a common plan which could function 'on the pressing of a button', and revealed that he was preparing an expeditionary force of 25,000 men and was pressing the military to accelerate their arrangements.[67] He envisaged a situation where Britain would take immediate action perhaps with the help of a token American force. Subsequently the Americans would take over, thus releasing British forces for use elsewhere. Roosevelt attached

---

[64] CAB 84/29 JP(41)313. For full details on the significance of the Canaries and operation 'Puma' see Smyth, Diplomacy and strategy of survival, 221–34.

[65] PREM 3/469. See also Barker, Eden and Churchill, 150; Lash, Roosevelt and Churchill, 308–9.

[66] FO 371/26809 C5297/C5415/115/36.

[67] For details of this planning known as Plan 'Gray', see S. Conn and B. Fairchild, The United States army in World War II: the western hemisphere: the framework of hemisphere defence, Washington, DC 1960, 116–19, 121–5. It was intended that the American force should include a token force from Brazil. See Cordell Hull, The memoirs of Cordell Hull, i, London 1948, 941.

considerable importance to receiving Salazar's assent to intervention; he was considering sending someone like Sumner Welles to see the Portuguese leader.[68]

Ironically, the president's conversion occurred at a most inappropriate time because of the decision to offer to help the Portuguese to reinforce the islands. It was therefore necessary to dampen his new-found enthusiasm. Washington was accordingly informed of the latest developments which aimed at securing what was also the president's objective, namely co-operation in the defence of the Atlantic islands at the invitation of the Portuguese government. The temporary exclusion of the Americans from the islands project was offset by Churchill's request that they relieve the British garrison in Iceland.[69] Roosevelt had recognised that the United States could not play a prominent part with regard to the islands after the uproar created in Portugal by his references, in his fireside chat of 27 May, to the dangers which German control of any of the Atlantic islands posed to the security of the western hemisphere and the need for the United States to extend its naval patrols in the Atlantic. Lisbon had interpreted this as implying that Portuguese sovereignty over the islands might not be respected. Portuguese public opinion had already been alarmed during early May by a speech in which Senator Claude Pepper had publicly invited Roosevelt to occupy the Azores and Cape Verde islands. As Monteiro told Eden on 30 May, things had reached a point where 'a not unimportant section of the Portuguese public was more afraid of the United States than of any other country'.[70] The failure of the Roosevelt administration to provide precise assurances compounded the rift in American-Portuguese relations which continued, despite British attempts to mediate, until mid-July when Roosevelt provided Salazar with a personal assurance concerning the Azores and all Portuguese colonies.[71]

In mid-June the president announced his willingness to leave the business of handling Salazar to the British government. Having previously withheld his final approval to plan 'Gray' owing to changes in the war situation – notably the destruction of the *Bismarck* and the German invasion of Crete which together reduced Germany's naval and air strength and eased the threat to the Azores and Cape Verde islands – and to increased speculation concerning the likelihood of a German invasion of the Soviet Union, Roosevelt suspended the Azores operation. The president's interest in the islands did not diminish

---

[68] PREM 3/469.
[69] FO 371/26794 C4727/41/36; 371/26848 C5883/3519/36. Although he neglects the Portuguese dimension and says little on Iceland, David Reynolds is most informative on Roosevelt's diplomatic manoeuvring during May and June 1941: *The creation of the Anglo-American alliance 1937–1941: a study in competitive co-operation*, London 1981, 199–204.
[70] FO 371/26809 C5052/C6701/115/36; 371/26848 C5883/3519/36. See also J. K. Sweeney, 'The Luso-American connection: the courtship 1940–1941', *Iberian Studies* vi (1977), 4–5. According to João de Bianchi, the Portuguese minister at Washington, Pepper's speech had the prior approval of Roosevelt and his cabinet: Telo, *Portugal na Segunda Guerra*, 368.
[71] *DAPE*, ix, no. 2040, pp. 37–9. For previous correspondence on this issue see ibid. viii, nos 1851, 1855, 1863, 1864, 1871, 1924, 1943, 1952, pp. 451–3, 460–3, 470–4, 488–90, 527–8, 547–8, 560–1. See also *FRUS*, 1941, ii. 836–55. For a brief discussion see A. H. D'Arauzo Stott-Howarth, *A aliança Luso-Britânica e a Segunda Guerra Mundial*, Lisboa 1956, 27–30.

entirely, however, for on 10 July he wrote to President Getulio Vargas of Brazil mentioning use of the Azores as possible German submarine bases and concentration points from which to attack Brazil. If circumstances forced the occupation of the islands Roosevelt hoped the Portuguese would request aid from the United States and Brazil first and that Brazil would be willing to help. He believed that a token Brazilian force would have a positive effect on Portuguese opinion and do much to counter the effects of German propaganda in Portugal. Although the Brazilians would not commit themselves until the operation was more definite and they had solved their own problems of supply they agreed to approach the Portuguese government on behalf of the United States at 'the opportune time'.[72]

Apart from the diplomatic row with the United States, the Portuguese were engaged during June and early July in formulating a response to the British offer of assistance. In his reply of 10 July Salazar agreed that his government would repair to the Azores in the event of an attack upon the mainland, but it was evident that he did not intend to give up the idea of defending the mainland because he hoped the programme for the supply of war material would not be altered or postponed and placed particular emphasis on the completion of the Barron plan for the sea and air defences of Lisbon. Although they readily accepted and appreciated the offer to despatch military equipment to the Azores and Cape Verde islands the Portuguese authorities rejected the offer of technical assistance. Salazar, as Campbell explained later, was not prepared to admit British subjects in any number to the islands for fear of provoking an 'international competition in infiltration' and infringing his policy of neutrality.[73]

With their plans to infiltrate the islands by means of technical assistance thus thwarted, the chiefs of staff were disinclined to implement the offer to supply military equipment unless the Portuguese offered a *quid pro quo* such as an undertaking to grant naval and air facilities in the islands immediately Spain or Portugal was attacked by the Axis powers. The foreign office advised that further staff conversations should be initiated at a fairly high level in order to create the atmosphere in which Britain could secure her requirements without frightening off the Portuguese. Unfortunately, the chiefs of staff would not consider further talks until Lisbon had given an assurance on facilities in the islands; since this was a political matter, it could not be usefully discussed at staff conversations. They also expressed their dissatisfaction with the Portuguese intention to repair to the Azores only in the event of an actual rather than a threatened attack; the Portuguese government would not necessarily do so if German action in the peninsula, including rendering Gibraltar untenable, was restricted to Spain. Consequently, there would be no certainty of Britain securing alternative bases in the Atlantic islands.[74]

---

[72] Conn and Fairchild, *United States army*, 125–5; Sweeney, 'The Luso-American connection', 5; W. L. Langer and S. E. Gleason, *The undeclared war 1940–1941*, New York 1953, 588–9.
[73] *DAPE*, ix, no. 2049, pp. 49–54; FO 371/26848 C8488/3519/36.
[74] CAB 79/12 COS(41) 246th mtg, 15 July 1941; CAB 80/29 COS(41)425; FO 371/26848 C7947/3519/36; CAB 79/13 COS(41) 257th mtg, 23 July 1941.

Although of the same mind, the foreign office did not believe the time was yet ripe for 'a frontal attack upon the Portuguese delusion that a threat to Spain was not necessarily a threat to Portugal'. Equally, they realised it would be most unwise to make the direct approach to Salazar desired by the chiefs of staff. Following discussions between Eden and his senior advisers the war cabinet was warned that the direct approach would involve reneging on their previous undertakings and would lay them open to the charge of having concealed their essential requirements during the discussions which had been proceeding since the previous December. In view of Salazar's character, which demanded frankness in all business discussions, his loyalty to the alliance and the satisfactory progress already achieved, such an approach 'might have the effect of inducing him to reconsider his rather reluctant decision to go to the Islands, and so imperil the prospect of obtaining the use of the Islands at the appropriate time in collaboration with the Portuguese'.[75]

Confirmation that the Portuguese government would be loathe to evacuate to the islands before an actual attack had occurred was provided on 6 August by Monteiro who indicated that any move made without defending the mainland would result in defections among ministers and officials. While recognising the scale of the problem Campbell realised that Salazar must be convinced of the indivisibility of peninsula security. He must be disabused of any illusion that if Spain became belligerent and Portugal remained inviolate Britain would continue to supply arms and other assistance without the reciprocal use of naval and air facilities in the islands. It should be made patently clear to him that with Spain in enemy hands Portugal's neutrality could only be maintained at great cost to his ally. Accordingly, he advised that they should proceed as Eden had proposed with the supply of material and discussion on technical matters at the same time as exchanging views on the point of principle. Salazar would thus be placed under an obligation and there would be a better chance of 'leading him along'.[76]

During the next fortnight, in separate conversations between Eden and Monteiro and Campbell and Salazar, the process of disillusioning the Portuguese authorities continued. A draft official reply to the Portuguese memorandum of 10 July was also prepared which was approved by the chiefs of staff.[77] Progress was threatened, however, by the sudden and unexpected intervention of the prime minister who revealed that during their conversations at Placentia Bay between 9 and 12 August 1941, Roosevelt had indicated his desire to occupy the Azores but only if invited by Salazar. The president had received a personal letter from Salazar which had referred to the provision of war material by the United States should Britain prove unable to supply. Roosevelt had chosen to interpret this as implying a request for armed assistance from the United States in the event of a German move into the Iberian Peninsula. Churchill told the war cabinet on 19 August that in view of the president's interest in the Azores a 'slight' change in British policy ought to be

[75] FO 371/26848 C8258/3519/36; CAB 65/23 WM 77(41), 4 Aug. 1941.
[76] FO 371/26849 C809?/C8763/3519/36.
[77] FO 371/26849 C8870/3519/36; DAPE, ix, no. 2181, pp. 148–53; CAB 79/13 COS(41) 290th mtg, 18 Aug. 1941; CAB 80/59 COS(41)172(0).

considered: the Portuguese should be actively encouraged to apply to the United States for assistance.[78] While it suited Churchill to commit the United States to further intervention in the Atlantic his suggestion would destroy the prospects for Portuguese co-operation with regard to the islands. There was widespread agreement in the foreign office that there was no prospect of Salazar asking America for any assistance other than the provision of military equipment. They were aware from his conversations with Eccles on 19 August that the Portuguese prime minister continued to express his suspicions and fears of American influence.[79] Foreign office assessment of American motives was scarcely less charitable. Roger Makins, supported by Eden, was convinced that 'the obvious anxiety of the United States General Staff to get these islands is a manifestation less of the American desire to assist the Allied war effort than that of American imperialist expansion'.[80] Furthermore, the American illusion that they would receive an invitation from the Portuguese government complicated the carrying out of operation 'Pilgrim' (the substitute codename for 'Puma'). Cadogan emphasised this when he minuted:

> The whole of this depends on the larger decision about operation 'Pilgrim'. If that is decided on, we can try this business, but if the Americans think that in any circumstances they will get an *invitation* from Dr Salazar . . . they are grossly mistaken. The President said that for internal reasons, he must have such an *invitation*. If he doesn't get it, that will presumably mean that he runs out and we are left alone with 'Pilgrim' on our hands and the Azores left in the hands of an antagonised Portugal.

Halifax, on leave in London, concurred. He advised Eden that negotiations with the Portuguese should continue along the present lines and should not be turned 'over to the Americans'. The only dissenting voice was that of Eden's secretary, Oliver Harvey, who stressed the greater danger of American isolationism.[81]

Supported by this weight of opinion Eden informed Churchill on 28 August that his proposal would involve a 'radical' rather than a 'slight' change in the existing policy. The foreign secretary disillusioned Churchill as to the advisability of armed American intervention in the Azores, not least because it would threaten the prospects of Anglo-Portuguese co-operation with regard to the islands. Pending a decision on operation 'Pilgrim', and without prejudice to it, Eden advised the continuation of negotiations with Salazar. Churchill concurred and the United States government was so informed on 3 September.[82]

[78] CAB 65/23 WM 84(41). See also Churchill, *The Second World War*, ii. 338–9; *Chief of staff: the diaries of Lieutenant General Sir Henry Pownall, 1940–1944*, ed. B. Bond, London 1974, 37–8; unpublished diaries of Harvey of Tasburgh, ADD56402, diary entry 12 Aug. 1941.
[79] FO 371/26794 C4727/41/36.
[80] Ibid.
[81] Ibid; unpublished diaries and papers of Harvey of Tasburgh, ADD56402.
[82] FO 371/26794 C4727/41/36; 371/26849 C9735/3519/36. See also *The war diaries of Oliver Harvey*, ed. J. Harvey, London 1978, 38–9.

Following a further interview between Campbell and Salazar on 29 August, in which the ambassador continued the process of undermining Portuguese resistance to their plans, Monteiro was handed, on 6 September, an official British reply to the Portuguese memorandum of 10 July. Britain's position with regard to the islands was made abundantly clear. Disbelief was expressed that it might be possible for Portugal to maintain her neutrality and avoid an occupation once Spain had been drawn into the war. The Axis powers in such circumstances 'would never permit the rearmament of Portuguese forces to be developed to such a state of efficiency that they would be able effectively to defend Portuguese sovereignty on the mainland and to provide an adequate defensive screen behind which allied forces could be landed in Portugal in case of need'. At the same time, Spanish belligerency would compel the abandonment of Gibraltar and this in turn would make it increasingly difficult for British naval forces to maintain sea communications with the Portuguese mainland or to assist when invited in the protection of communications between the various parts of the Portuguese empire since there would be no British naval base between the United Kingdom and the Cape of Good Hope. In addition, the loss of Gibraltar as a naval base would gravely handicap the allied war effort if it were not counter-balanced by the use of some alternative base between the United Kingdom and her African colonies, since 'the defence of Atlantic sea routes against submarines and air attack would in such circumstances become a matter of very great difficulty'. While the Portuguese expressed their confidence in being able to defend the Atlantic islands effectively themselves this depended on the maintenance of British sea power, which in turn depended on the use of facilities in the islands once Gibraltar had become untenable as a naval base. It was hoped that in the event of any threat to Portugal the Portuguese government would not delay in transferring the seat of government to the Azores and would agree 'to afford His Majesty's forces at the earliest possible moment all such facilities as may be necessary to enable them, in the spirit of the Alliance, to collaborate in the defence of the islands and to assist in the protection of communications between the different parts of the Portuguese Atlantic and overseas possessions'.[83]

In the middle of October 1941, after a delay of some six weeks, the Portuguese agreed to discuss, through further staff conversations, the ways and means of withdrawing from Portugal with the aid of their British allies.[84] Two Portuguese staff officers, Colonel Rodrigues and naval captain Sousa Uva, were sent to London. Conversations began on 20 October and ended on 7 November.[85] The British delegation was led by Lieutentant Colonel Myrtle, supported by

---

[83] FO 371/26795 C9731/41/36; 371/26849 C9734/C10096/3519/36; DAPE, ix, nos 2263, 2268, pp. 220–4, 234–42.

[84] According to António Telo there had been increasing contacts since the middle of August 1941 between the Portuguese authorities and two German companies, Krupp and Rheinmetal, with a view to the purchase of artillery. A Portuguese military mission was despatched to Germany headed by Major Costa Padesca and Major Florêncio Cunha. In addition contacts were maintained during this period between junior officers of the Portuguese general staff and their German counterparts: Portugal na Segunda Guerra, 441.

[85] Nine meetings in all took place between 20 October and 7 November 1941. The minutes are located in CAB 99/12.

Wing Commander Vintras and Commander Evershed of the joint planning staff. The Portuguese delegation brought with them a written directive instructing them to work with the British on plans for Anglo-Portuguese collaboration in evacuating the mainland 'from the moment of an attack on Portugal'. The word 'attack' was defined as 'an attack in force'. This was, of course, directly at odds with the British wish to intervene before Portugal was attacked. There was therefore no chance of progress until the Portuguese were persuaded that their ally could not guarantee help if they waited until Portugal was actually attacked. Accordingly, fresh instructions were obtained from Lisbon and as a result a plan for joint action 'from the moment when the Portuguese Government decides to abandon their neutrality', was drawn up. It was made clear that the successful execution of the plan depended on the Portuguese abandoning their neutrality well before they were actually attacked. Although the matter would involve Salazar in a very 'problematic decision' in a moment of stress, the British delegation was confident that his military advisers would do their best to dissuade him from waiting too long. The plan was divided into two phases: first, advance preparations by the Portuguese including the laying in of supplies and the improvement of the defences of the Azores; and second, joint action which would begin the moment the Portuguese government decided it was no longer desirable to maintain their neutrality. The first phase involved British assistance in the form of military equipment for the defence of the Azores and the construction of buildings by the Portuguese to accommodate British personnel on the islands following the departure of the Portuguese government from Portugal. As part of the plan it was agreed that Britain would undertake the training of officers of the Portuguese armed forces and that a Portuguese air force officer should visit London to discuss the development of air facilities in the Azores with the air ministry.[86]

Before the end of the year two further developments in Anglo-Portuguese strategic policy had occurred. The first was a decision by the chiefs of staff to endorse the proposal by General Gifford, the general officer commanding west Africa, that in the event of an invitation by the Portuguese to occupy the Cape Verde islands similar action should be taken in respect of Portuguese Guinea to ensure the security of Bolama and Bissau. The second was the recommendation of the chiefs of staff, made on 25 December, that responsibility for operation 'Pilgrim' should be undertaken by the United States owing to a British shortage of aircraft carriers. All available carriers, then based on Mombasa, were required for operations against the Japanese in the Indian Ocean.[87]

The likelihood of operation 'Pilgrim' being activated was in any case growing more remote. A joint intelligence report at the very end of 1941 concluded that Spain was anxious to remain non-belligerent, to avoid the risk of being at war with the United States and aligned against the Latin American republics as a whole. German attempts to achieve overt co-operation were likely to be resisted unless backed by force and there was no sign of any military movement

---

86 CAB 99/12 AP2(41)1 and COS(41)663.
87 CAB 79/16 COS(41) 417th mtg, 11 Dec. 1941; CAB 80/32 COS(41)729; CAB 79/16 432nd mtg.

towards the Iberian Peninsula.[88] The setbacks suffered by the German armies in Soviet Russia and north Africa during 1942 and the continuation of the policy of controlled economic assistance would suffice to keep Franco's Spain non-belligerent. At the same time, although it was still difficult to pin Salazar down on the question of the timing and circumstances of a Portuguese retreat to the Atlantic islands, further progress was made during 1942 concerning defence preparations on the Azores, particularly on improving air facilities following further conversations in London between the future ill-fated presidential candidate, Staff Major Humberto Delgado, and the British air staff.[89]

From the spring of 1940 until the end of 1941 the British authorities had been involved in discussing contingency plans for the occupation of the Portuguese Atlantic islands and Portuguese East Africa. At one time or another the French, Dominions and United States governments were drawn in. Only the Portuguese were not privy to the decisions concerning the fate of their territories and for some time they continued in the stubborn belief that their neutrality could be preserved under almost any circumstances. Salazar's obduracy with regard to the timing and circumstances of the abandonment of his neutrality was a source of some irritation to the British who failed to convince him that the mere threat of attack ought to be sufficient. The foreign office, in particular, was seriously concerned to prevent any precipitate action which could destroy the alliance and drive Portugal into the Axis camp. Hence their support for the alternative strategy of controlled economic assistance to Portugal and Spain. In the event, and despite Churchill's occasional enthusiasm, the plans laid down so extensively during 1940 and 1941 were never activated; a demonstration of admirable restraint on the part of Britain's policy-makers in view of the perceived German threat to the peninsula. It is surely ironic, therefore, that the British government should abandon restraint in another context – that of the Far East – and precipitate a major crisis in their relations with Portugal. The allied occupation of Portuguese Timor on 17 December 1941 placed, according to Sir Ronald Campbell, the 'greatest strain on Anglo-Portuguese relations since Lord Salisbury's ultimatum of 1890'.[90] The Timor crisis threatened a serious rupture in relations between Britain and Portugal.

[88] FO 371/26946 C14322/300/41.
[89] For details of the air staff conversations during 1942 see CAB 99/14. See also H. Delgado, *The memoirs of General Delgado*, London 1964, 62–7. For Salazar's reluctance with regard to the timing and circumstances of Portugal's *casus belli* see Eden to Campbell, 13 Feb. 1942, Eden Papers, PORT/42/6.
[90] Campbell to Eden, 2 Jan. 1942, PREM 3/361/2.

10

The Far Eastern Context

While it is true that before the mid-1930s Portugal's far eastern possessions –
Macao and the eastern half of the island of Timor – were of little importance in
Anglo-Portuguese relations, they were not entirely neglected. Before the first
world war Portuguese Timor had been included in the Anglo-German colonial
negotiations. Indeed, the Anglo-German Agreement of 1898 had assigned it to
the Germans along with northern Angola and northern Mozambique.[1] However, during negotiations for a revised agreement between 1911 and 1914 the
German government agreed to substitute the Portuguese islands of São Tomé
and Príncipe for Timor.[2]

Macao received attention for different reasons. During the same period it was
a source of considerable embarrassment in Britain's relations with Peking because of its encouragement of gambling and participation in opium smuggling.[3]
Despite their public commitment to preventing the smuggling of opium into
China the Portuguese authorities in Macao proved incapable of taking any
effective measures, a state of affairs which continued throughout the inter-war
years.[4]

In the late 1930s the issue of Japanese activity in Macao and Portuguese
Timor increasingly intruded into Britain's relations with her ally – at just the
time when Axis pressure on Portugal was intensifying. Macao, in the view both
of London and Tokyo, was much less significant. While the Japanese made a
number of attempts to penetrate its economy, through schemes such as that for
for the construction of a waterworks in 1935, for the construction of a deep sea
port in 1939, and for a railway from Macao to Canton, they were more concerned to apply strong pressure on the colony as a way of extracting concessions
in Timor.[5] Japan's motives were fully appreciated in London. Although the
foreign office, with Hong Kong's security in mind, actively discouraged Japanese

[1] In this connection see British documents on the origins of the war, 1898–1914, i, London 1927,
55–6, 63–4, 67, 71–5.
[2] See British documents on the origins of the war, 1898–1914, x, pt 2, London 1938, 429–34,
440–3, 454–7, 469–72, 479–81, 484–5, 497–500, 502–7.
[3] See J. Vincent-Smith, 'Britain and Portugal 1910–1916', unpubl. PhD diss. London 1971,
117–21. This dissertation was subsequently translated into Portuguese and published as As
Relaçoes Políticas Luso-Britânicas 1910–1916, Lisboa 1974.
[4] For example, The opium trade 1910–1941, iv, Wilmington, Del. 1974, pt xxvi, no. 6, pp.
11–43.
[5] For the waterworks scheme see CAB 24/254 CP 67(35); CAB 23/81 CM 16(35), CM
17(35). See also DBFP, 2, xx, nos 267, 279, pp. 463, 490–1. For the deep sea port proposals see
FO 371/23501 F670/F3281/670/10.

schemes for the economic development of Macao through the Lisbon embassy, it was Japan's attempts to penetrate Timor which attracted their sustained interest and also that of the service departments, especially the admiralty. Japanese designs on Portuguese Timor were also a source of increasing anxiety for the governments of Australia and the Netherlands.

Foreign office interest in Portuguese Timor was first aroused early in 1936 when they received reports that an extensive concession for oil boring was available on the island. While recent reports by two major oil companies – the Anglo-Iranian Oil Company and the Anglo-Saxon Petroleum Company – indicated that the prospect of finding oil in Timor in commercially exploitable quantities was not favourable, there was some apprehension that Japanese interests might attempt to obtain the concession as part of the policy of penetration in the Malay archipelago. The admiralty was particularly anxious for the general security of the area and for the defence of the Australian port of Darwin.[6] The foreign office was reminded by Henry Fitzmaurice, the British consul in Batavia, that poor commercial prospects had not prevented the Japanese from previously acquiring a number of dubious mineral concessions in the Netherlands East Indies.[7]

In the event, there were five applications for the sole right of prospecting in Portuguese Timor, four from Japanese companies. The fifth, the Allied Mining Corporation of Manila, was granted the concession. According to intelligence sources, the company, whose president was a Belgian, Dr Serge Wittouck, appeared genuinely interested in exploiting the concession. Although the foreign office were not entirely convinced of its *bona fides* they failed to establish any connection with Japanese interests.[8] At the same time, the granting of the concession to the Allied Mining Corporation caused consternation in Australia, particularly as in September 1936 the Portuguese cancelled the so-called Staughton lease – covering some four thousand acres of Timor in perpetuity – which had recently been taken over by an Australian company, Anglo-Eastern Oil. The Australian government went so far as to request British representations in Lisbon. After interceding with Sampaio during November, Wingfield received assurances that the Portuguese would rescind the cancellation which had been made only as a result of the inactivity of Anglo-Eastern and that the Staughton lease did not clash with the interests of the Allied Mining Corporation.[9]

Before April 1937 Japanese efforts to achieve a foothold in the economy of Portuguese Timor had proved ineffective but then the *Nanyo Kohatsu Kaisha* (South Seas Development Company) made a bid to purchase the *Société Agricole*, which reputedly owned the major share of property on the island. The Japanese authorities also revealed an interest in developing a steamship line from Dili in Timor to Japan via Macao and in making Dili a base for Japanese

6 FO 371/20510 W394/W2799/394/36.
7 FO 371/20271 F2709/1410/10.
8 FO 371/20510 W6834/W13935/394/36; 371/21277 W7966/812/36.
9 FO 371/20510 W11521/W12185/W17259/394/36.

fisheries.[10] Although the foreign office warned the Portuguese to avoid any connection with Japanese interests it was difficult to insist that they should hold back the development of their colony by permanently excluding them. The far eastern department agreed that something should be done to assist in the development of Timor, but because Australia was more closely affected by events in that part of the world it was for Canberra to take the initiative, and sooner rather than later.[11]

The need for urgency was emphasised during September 1937 when it was learned that a joint Portuguese-Japanese company, the Timor Archipelago Development Company (*Timor Gunto Kaihatsu Kaisha*) had been established to develop the lands of the *Société Agricole*,[12] and that the Japanese were making concerted efforts to corner the coffee crop, the principal source of foreign exchange for the administration of Portuguese Timor. A comprehensive foreign office report commissioned late in 1937 underlined the need for action. In commenting on the report Fitzmaurice expressed the view – which was shared by the industrial intelligence committee of the department of overseas trade – that on strategic grounds, the Australians should seriously consider the adoption of a definite policy to establish interests in Timor which could counterbalance those of the Japanese. The report concluded that the importance of Portuguese Timor lay in its strategic importance (which included its possible use as an air base) rather than economic value, current or potential, and hence its future must be a matter of concern to the United Kingdom and Holland as well as to Portugal and Japan.[13]

Early in 1938, the opportunity for an Australian initiative presented itself when it became clear that the Portuguese authorities had not given final approval to the Allied Mining Corporation for the oil concession in Portuguese Timor.[14] It was still therefore possible for an Australian company to step in. In July 1938 the Australian government announced its support for an application by a joint company operation consisting of two Australian companies, Oil Search Limited and Oil Concessions.[15] Despite numerous meetings between representatives of the two companies and Portuguese officials and several representations by Selby with the ministries of foreign affairs and colonies little progress was made until October 1939 when, despite protests from the Belgian legation, Salazar granted Oil Concessions permission to prospect for petroleum and any other mineral oils and hydro-carbonic gases in that part of Portuguese Timor to the east of meridian 125° 50'. The area involved amounted to some 4,000 square miles leaving 1,500 square miles in the hands of the Allied Mining Corporation although the authorities in Lisbon had still not approved that concession.[16]

10 FO 371/21041 F2254/F2721/F5237/615/23.
11 FO 371/21041 F5237/615/23.
12 FO 371/21041 F8060/615/23.
13 FO 371/21041 F10440/615/23; 371/22165 F844/F2978/10/61.
14 FO 371/22165 F202/10/61.
15 FO 371/22165 F7766/10/61.
16 FO 371/23541 F5362/F7042/F11610/179/61; 371/23540 F5520/162/61; 371/24064 W12374/160/61.

The news was not well received in Tokyo, with the result that during March and April 1940 Japanese pressure at Macao was intensified.[17] Portugal insisted that as long as the present holders fulfilled their obligations the concession could not be reassigned, but clearly if it were allowed to lapse, the Portuguese might not be able to withstand further Japanese pressure. Unfortunately, towards the end of April increasing doubts began to be raised about the ability of Oil Concessions to meet the terms of their concession before the 27 November deadline. The Australian high commissioner in London, Stanley Bruce, therefore suggested, at an interdepartmental meeting on 29 April chaired by R. A. Butler, that the big oil companies might be asked to co-operate with Oil Concessions. According to Sir Cecil Kisch, of the mines department, Anglo-Iranian and Royal Dutch Shell were prepared to consider this.[18] The British government rejected the advice of Sir Robert Craigie, the ambassador in Tokyo, who argued that the Japanese should be permitted to co-operate with Australian interests in Timor in exploiting the oil concession.[19]

Negotiations aimed at an agreement whereby the major oil companies would take over the interests of Oil Concessions continued through June and July 1940 but ended in deadlock. Oil Concessions demanded too high a price and the oil companies were not happy with the 'power of veto' held by the Portuguese under the concession.[20] The deadlock had to be broken: Monteiro had warned Strang officially on 7 August that the Portuguese would have to rescind the concession if, as they suspected, Oil Concessions was unable to meet the conditions of its contract in November. In that case the field would be open to other applicants including the Japanese.[21] Following discussions between the treasury, the foreign office, the Australian government and the oil companies, it was agreed that Oil Concessions would receive an initial sum of £12,000, a further £5,000 when a well capable of producing 50 tons of oil per day had been completed, and £16,000 when total production of 500 tons of oil per day was achieved. Of the total of £33,000 the British and Australian Governments were required to contribute £6,000 each; they would receive in return 3 per cent compound interest but relinquished any claim to profit sharing.[22]

In view of Canberra's enthusiastic endorsement of Oil Concessions, Dr Vieira Machado, the Portuguese minister of colonies, was perturbed to learn of the transfer of the company's concession to the major oil companies particularly as Japan was again exerting great pressure at Macao. This was the result of the 'basic national policy' for the establishment of the 'Greater East Asia Co-prosperity Sphere' endorsed by Prince Konoye's government in July 1940. Included in this Japanese *Drang nach Suden* were the vital military resources of the Netherlands East Indies which were to be acquired by diplomatic negotiations if possible but by force if necessary. The most important resource was

---

[17] Telo, *Portugal na Segunda Guerra*, 145.
[18] FO 371/24705 F3051/7/61.
[19] FO 371/24705 F2561/7/61; 371/24700 F3016/2394/10.
[20] FO 371/24706 F3368/F3708/7/61.
[21] FO 371/24706 F3708/7/61.
[22] FO 371/24706 F3841/F3873/F4350/7/61.

unquestionably oil, given Japan's dependence upon imports.[23] Indeed, the consensus at an imperial conference of 19 September 1940 was that there was no other alternative source of oil despite Foreign Minister Matsuoka's belief that considerable supplies might be obtained from the Soviet Union.[24] The takeover of the Timor oil concession by the major oil companies was therefore bound to provoke excitement and speculation in Tokyo where motives in regard to the Portuguese colony were probably not entirely strategic ones.

The British authorities wanted the concession for the western area to be kept in cold storage for at least two years – until all the preliminary work on their eastern concession had been completed. The Portuguese authorities were not so inclined. The Allied Mining Corporation had ceased to have any moral claim to the western area since Wittouck's death in July 1940 and the Portuguese were confronted during the autumn with increased pressure from the Japanese for the western concession. Machado left Selby in no doubt as to his lack of faith in British military assistance should the Japanese be provoked into using force.[25] The minister's response did not deter Halifax from raising the subject of the western concession with Monteiro on 5 November when he emphasised the importance attached to it by both London and Canberra. Machado, however, continued to face Japanese demands and to fear Japanese action in Macao; and he doubted if he could temporise for much longer.[26] That the Portuguese were able to resist was largely because the Japanese were not yet ready to provoke a major crisis in the east Indies at this time. During the imperial conference of 19 September the navy had emphasised the need to use peaceful means in pursuit of oil supplies in the southern seas.[27]

By the end of the year the chiefs of staff had begun to take an active interest in Portuguese Timor, as a result of conversations with the Netherlands military authorities at Singapore.[28] It was hardly surprising that the Dutch should be so anxious about Japanese activities in Timor considering the lack of adequate defences at Koepang in the Dutch half of the island and the apparently lamentable condition of the Portuguese garrison at Dili where, according to Australian intelligence sources, even machine guns were lacking.[29] The Dutch authorities in Batavia were therefore alarmed to learn, shortly before Christmas, that the

[23] For the adoption of the 'basic national policy' see Hosoya Chihiro, 'The Tripartite Pact', in J. W. Morley (ed.), Deterrent diplomacy: Japan, Germany and the USSR 1935–1940, New York 1976, 208–9; I. Nish, Japanese foreign policy 1869–1942: Kasumigaseki to Miyakezaka, London 1977, 236; Akira Iriye, 'Policies towards the United States', in J. W. Morley (ed.), Japan's foreign policy 1868–1941: a research guide, New York 1974, 454. For the significance of the oil resources of the Netherlands East Indies for Japan see Medlicott, Economic blockade, ii. 77–81; and Nagaoka Shinjiro, 'Economic demands on the Dutch East Indies', in J. W. Morley (ed.), The fateful choice: Japan's advance into south east Asia, 1939–1941, New York 1980, 141–6.

[24] Chihiro, 'The Tripartite Pact', 248–9; Japan's decision for war: records of the 1941 policy conferences, ed. Nobutaka Ike, Stanford, Ca. 1967, 7–9.

[25] FO 371/24706 F4350/7/61.

[26] FO 371/24706 F5002/F5221/7/61.

[27] Japan's decision for war, 8; Sumio Hatano and Sadao Asada, 'The Japanese decision to move south (1929–1941)', in Boyce and Robertson, Paths to War, 395.

[28] CAB 79/8 COS(40) 435th mtg; CAB 80/24 COS(40) 1055(JP).

[29] FO 371/24706 F5451/7/61.

Portuguese had given the Japanese permission for six trial flights from Palau to Dili with the object of opening a fortnightly air service.[30] Despite British representations the six trials went ahead and were completed in July 1941.[31] Further consternation was created in government circles towards the end of 1940 by press reports, subsequently confirmed by the Tokyo embassy, that the Japanese ministry of finance had voted 50,000 yen for the establishment of a consulate at Dili.[32] The far eastern department was anxious to counter this move by appointing a British, or preferably Australian consul before the Japanese consulate was established.[33] The foreign office demurred on the grounds that the consular service in the far east was already overstretched and the Australians would do no more than appoint a semi-official representative without consular status.[34]

Through such measures as acquiring the oil concession and persistent representations to the Portuguese government on this and on other issues (such as the establishment of an air service – Quantas Airways – between Darwin and Dili) the British and Australian authorities had succeeded in preventing undue Japanese penetration into Portuguese Timor by peaceful means. At the same time, it was admitted both in Canberra and in London that none of these measures would be effective in preventing an actual Japanese occupation of the island. The question of the defence of Portuguese Timor, hitherto of little importance to Britain, Australia or the Netherlands, assumed greater significance in the autumn of 1941 following the imposition of the economic blockade upon Japan by those countries and by the United States.

By the autumn of 1941 Australian intelligence reports on the lamentable state of the colony's defences had been confirmed by British sources.[35] Military support was now deemed essential. The Australians envisaged discussions between themselves, the British and Dutch authorities. However, the foreign office insisted that the Portuguese be included and that the initial approach be made during the staff conversations with the Portuguese military mission led by Colonel Rodrigues. The Australians agreed in advance to provide the necessary military forces for operations in Portuguese Timor as well as those already earmarked for the defence of Ambon and Koepang in Dutch Timor.[36]

The response of the allied powers to the question of security in Timor can only be regarded as tardy given the importance attached to it as early as

[30] Ibid.

[31] It was hardly surprising that the Portuguese should permit all six trials to proceed in view of Japanese diplomatic pressure which intensified following the signature of the Soviet-Japanese Non-Aggression Pact in April 1941. The Portuguese minister in Tokyo, Esteves Fernandes, advised that the pact had given the 'green light' to Japanese southwards expansion. In May the director general of the Japanese foreign ministry rebuked Fernandes, demanding 'an end to evasion' and threatening 'increased Japanese displeasure': Telo, Portugal na Segunda Guerra, 362.

[32] FO 371/27792 F492/F494/222/61.

[33] FO 371/27792 F494/222/61.

[34] FO 371/27792 F495/F732/222/61.

[35] FO 371/27793 F2795/222/61.

[36] FO 371/27794 F9212/F10787/F10890/222/61.

October 1940 by the first Singapore Conference which had been attended by staff officers from Malaya, India, Australia, New Zealand and Burma. Moreover, in February 1941, during the second Singapore Conference, which included Dutch representatives and United States observers, it was recommended that Japan be engaged by all the powers represented in any one of three contingencies. The first two concerned an attack on American, British or Dutch territory and Thailand. The third contingency was an occupation of Portuguese Timor or the Loyalty Islands or New Caledonia. Nevertheless, the British military authorities avoided making any unequivocal commitment to defend the Netherlands East Indies let alone Portuguese Timor for most of 1941. In this the chiefs of staff, supported by Churchill, were at odds with the foreign office which wanted Britain and the Netherlands East Indies to guarantee mutual support in the event of Japanese aggression. An unequivocal undertaking to this effect was finally communicated to the Netherlands government on 5 December, once Britain had received an assurance of American support.[37] Meanwhile, the Australians had continued to accept Britain's priorities, notably in the middle east, so that although the war cabinet had agreed that Australian troops should reinforce Dutch Timor and Ambon, they had yet to be despatched when the question of Portuguese Timor's security was being considered during October and November 1941.[38]

The urgent need to make progress in discussions with the Portuguese was felt even more keenly in Dutch and Australian circles following Lisbon's acceptance, during October, of a Japanese air service to Portuguese Timor and the appointment of a Japanese consul at Dili.[39] A naval intelligence report produced in Melbourne early in November confirmed the strategic dangers for Australia of a Japanese occupation of Timor: the Australian authorities were only too aware of the vulnerability of Darwin. Nevertheless, despite recognition of the strategic significance of the port by British and Australian naval forces, which made it second only to Singapore in the summer of 1938, it was still being reinforced when Japan entered the war in December 1941.[40]

As part occupants of the island the Dutch were naturally anxious about recent developments in Portuguese Timor and wished to be included in staff conversations about its defence. The central department of the foreign office

[37] P. Lowe, *Great Britain and the origins of the Pacific War: a study of British policy in east Asia 1937–1941*, Oxford 1977, 202, 205; W. N. McIntyre, *The rise and fall of the Singapore naval base*, Cambridge 1979, 174; B. N. Primrose, 'Australian naval policy 1919–1942: a case study in imperial relations', unpubl. PhD diss. Australian National University 1974, 367; J. R. Leutze, *Bargaining for supremacy: Anglo-American naval collaboration 1937–1941*, Chapel Hill, NC 1977, 264–5. For details of the disagreement between the foreign office and the chiefs of staff see P. Lowe, 'Great Britain and the coming of the Pacific War, 1939–1941', *Transactions of the Royal Historical Society*, 5th ser. xxiv (1974), 54–6, and P. Haggie, *Britannia at bay: the defence of the British empire against Japan 1939–1941*, Oxford 1981, 188–9.
[38] Primrose, 'Australian naval policy', 365–6.
[39] The concession of the air service to Japan caused a clamour of protest in London, Washington and Canberra: Nogueira, *Salazar*, iii, 352.
[40] FO 371/27795 F11958/222/61. For details concerning Port Darwin see Roskill, *Naval policy between the wars*, ii. 434; D. A. Thomas, *Japan's war at sea: Pearl Harbour to the Coral Sea*, London 1978, 46–8.

was, however, reluctant to involve them without Portugal's consent; it was vital not to jeopardise the Anglo-Portuguese staff conversations then proceeding on Atlantic defence. When, on 4 November, Eden raised the question of discussions about Timor with Monteiro, he did not mention the Dutch.[41] Moreover, when he saw E. N. van Kleffens, the Netherlands foreign minister, on 6 and 17 November, Eden objected to Dutch participation.[42]

On 13 November, following a preliminary discussion of the Timor question by the British and Portuguese military delegations, Monteiro confirmed that his government would defend their colony against all aggressors, including the Japanese, and that they expected and welcomed British assistance.[43] After consultation with the Portuguese and Australian authorities it was agreed that joint discussions should take place in Singapore.[44] Before issuing the official invitation to the Portuguese Eden was persuaded by the military authorities to admit Dutch military representatives. Consequently, when Monteiro received the invitation on 2 December he warned Cadogan that his government might find it difficult to authorise discussions with the Dutch. In the event, while Salazar predictably rejected the direct participation of Dutch military experts, on the grounds that Portugal and the Netherlands were not allies, he agreed that close contact was necessary and that the Dutch could be kept informed through the British representatives.[45]

Japan's entry into the war on 7 December radically altered the situation. With almost undue haste the Netherlands government proposed to the Portuguese that if Portuguese Timor were attacked Dutch and Australian forces should be called in immediately. In response the Portuguese reminded the Dutch that they had no alliance with Portugal and they did not wish to anticipate the Singapore conversations. Orme Sargent, however, made it quite clear to Monteiro that the British government fully supported the Dutch proposal.[46] Moreover, according to Duff Cooper, who was in Singapore, the governor of the Netherlands East Indies was empowered to take any action necessary to liquidate the Japanese in Portuguese Timor. Military and naval preparations were complete and the Dutch anticipated no difficulty other than that their actions would damage Anglo-Portuguese relations. A joint meeting of officials from the foreign, dominions and war offices, held on 10 December, recognised the extreme urgency and, in view of Portuguese Timor's defenceless condition, the need to take immediate action which, for preference should not be left to the Dutch. After consulting Canberra, Sargent presented Monteiro with an offer of assistance in the event of a Japanese attack: that it would be furnished by Dutch and Australian troops on the understanding that once the emergency

41 FO 371/27794 F10890/222/61; Eden Papers, PORT/41/2; DAPE, x, no. 2511, pp. 11–15.
42 Eden Papers, PORT/41/22; FO 371/27781 F12472/54/61.
43 At this time, although he was prepared to sanction Portuguese participation in military conversations, Salazar remained sceptical about Britain's anxieties, believing that an attack on Timor was unlikely: Telo, Portugal na Segunda Guerra, 479.
44 DAPE, x, no. 2563, pp. 70–6; FO 371/27796 F12289/222/61 and F12505/F12545/222/61.
45 FO 371/27796 F13304/F13306/F13315/222/61; DAPE, x, nos 2654, 2655, 2662, 2678, 2679, pp. 155–6, 165–6, 178–80.
46 FO 371/27797 F13468/F13516/222/61.

was over they would evacuate the colony. The under-secretary expressed the hope that the Portuguese government would accept the offer forthwith and that they would immediately instruct Ferreira de Carvalho, the governor of Portuguese Timor, to ask for such assistance, if the need arose, or to accept it if there was no time for it to be requested via the British government or the local authorities.[47]

Although the Portuguese promptly complied and told Ferreira de Carvalho to proceed with discussions with the governor of Dutch Timor, it was clear that if possible they wished to maintain their neutrality with regard to the Japanese. As with the Atlantic islands, Salazar wished to avoid any action which might imperil his neutrality. This was demonstrated on 11 December when Monteiro demanded that the Australian authorities be warned about flights over Portuguese Timor by their bomber pilots.[48] The risks of ignoring Portuguese susceptibilities were cogently expressed in a foreign office memorandum for the chiefs of staff:

> If we can co-operate successfully with the Portuguese in the matter of Portuguese Timor, it will set an important precedent for co-operation in other parts of the Portuguese Empire. If we ride roughshod over the Portuguese in this matter we may not only prejudice future co-operation, but may cause some immediate political reactions in Lisbon which would be unfavourable to our interests in the Iberian Peninsula.[49]

After the sinking of the *Prince of Wales* and *Repulse* on 10 December[50] these considerations did not weigh with the Dutch and Australian authorities. If danger were seen to be imminent action would be taken; they would not wait for an actual Japanese attack. Consequently, when on 15 December Japanese submarines were identified in the immediate vicinity of Timor a combined force of approximately 350 Dutch and Australian troops was despatched. By the time the foreign office learned of the move it could do little more than try to persuade them not to order a forced occupation if the governor of Timor refused to acquiesce. In the event, this is exactly what happened. Dili was occupied on the morning of 17 December without Carvalho's acquiescence.[51] There followed two months of delicate, and at times strained, negotiations to repair the breach in the Anglo-Portuguese alliance during which sharp differences of opinion arose between the central and far eastern departments of the foreign office.[52]

---

[47] FO 371/27797 F13517/F13576/F13578/F13579/222/61. See also S. W. Kirby, *The war against Japan*, I: *the loss of Singapore*, London 1959, 347.
[48] FO 371/27797 F13619/222/61.
[49] CAB 80/32 COS(41)741.
[50] For British and Australian shocked reactions to the sinking of these capital ships see A. J. Marder, *Old friends, new enemies: the Royal Navy and the Imperial Japanese Navy: strategic illusions 1936–1941*, Oxford 1981, 494–6; C. Thorne, *Allies of a kind: The United States, Britain and the war against Japan 1941–1945*, London 1978, 252.
[51] FO 371/27797 F13607/F13785/222/61.
[52] For brief details of the Timor crisis see Woodward, *British foreign policy*, iv. 42–4; P. Hasluck, *The government and the people*, II, ser. IV: *Civil Australia in the war of 1939–1945*, Canberra 1970, 100–2.

When Campbell warned Sampaio on 16 December of the Dutch and Australian intention to occupy Portuguese Timor his reaction had been almost violent. He insisted that if the occupation went ahead Portugal's neutrality would be fatally compromised and Macao would be seized by the Japanese.[53] Salazar felt betrayed. After a meeting of his council of ministers he sent for Campbell on the evening of 17 December, With 'calm but visibly repressed emotion' the Portuguese leader confirmed that the governor of Timor had been forced to submit to *force majeure*. He then added that before his government considered their position he wanted an explanation of the precise circumstances surrounding the violation of Portuguese territory. Had the local commanders taken the law into their own hands? Had the pace been forced by the Netherlands and Commonwealth governments or had His Majesty's Government been a full and willing party after weighing the implications and the grave consequences for their ally? Simultaneously Monteiro left an official note at the foreign office demanding answers to the same questions.[54] In consultation with Campbell the foreign office drew up a long *note verbale* which was handed to Sampaio on 19 December. While restating the urgent reasons for the occupation the note was intended to be conciliatory. It expressed regret and gave a firm undertaking that the allied troops would be withdrawn from Portuguese Timor as soon as the emergency had passed.[55] Unfortunately, the communication left no doubt as to Britain's complicity in the allied occupation as was inevitable in fairness to the Dutch and Australians. Salazar was distinctly unimpressed as his speech to the National Assembly the same day demonstrated.[56] Because of Salazar's public intervention and a previously published statement by the Netherlands East Indies authorities it seemed advisable, at least to Campbell, that Britain should make a public statement too. Having received the full support of the war cabinet for the line taken so far the foreign office was not convinced but was willing to be guided by the ambassador. It insisted, however, that in view of British public opinion, any statement should not appear apologetic.

Campbell persuaded them that international courtesy demanded a statement; its absence would be interpreted as showing that Britain regarded Portugal as of no account. A public statement was therefore released to the press on the evening of 21 December which regretted the occupation while emphasising the strategic imperatives which made it necessary.[57] That it was going to take more than statements and promises to smooth Portugal's ruffled feathers soon became apparent when Sampaio, adhering to a strictly legal interpretation of events, remarked to Campbell that the show or threat of force had always been bitterly resented by Portugal and the British ultimatum of 1890 had even yet

53 FO 371/27797 F13808/222/61; Nogueira, *Salazar*, iii: 364.
54 FO 371/27797 F13808/F13866/222/61; DAPE, x, no. 2836, pp. 303–5.
55 Ibid. x, no. 2865, pp. 341–5.
56 FO 371/27798 F14004/F14011/222/61; Nogueira, *Salazar*, iii. 366.
57 FO 371/27798 F14007/F14031/F14037/222/61; DAPE, x, no. 2888, pp. 368–71; CAB 65/20 WM 131(41).

not been forgotten. The ambassador ventured the opinion that if no bridge was found Salazar might even break off relations with his ancient ally.[58]

In fact, the Portuguese had no such intention. On 24 December João de Bianchi, the Portuguese minister in Washington, acting on instructions from Salazar, told under-secretary of state Sumner Welles that while his government had felt it necessary to make a show of indignation about Timor it had not 'the slightest intention of throwing itself into the arms of Germany because of this incident'.[59] The Portuguese reply to Campbell's note of 19 December, delivered by Monteiro on 22 December to Sir John Anderson, lord president of the council, indicated a more conciliatory position than hitherto. It informed the British authorities that Portuguese reinforcements were being sent to Timor and expressed the hope that allied forces could then be withdrawn.[60] Unfortunately, matters were greatly complicated by the Portuguese attitude towards the Netherlands government. Their reply to an earlier Dutch note was much stiffer than that delivered to Britain, in fact virtually an ultimatum. It stated, indeed almost threatened that the presence of Netherlands troops in Portuguese Timor was incompatible with the maintenance of correct and friendly relations between the two governments.[61]

Campbell felt that Portugal might be deliberately attempting to drive a wedge between the British and Dutch governments; even that, under strong Axis pressure, she might be manoeuvring towards a break in relations with the Netherlands while maintaining those with Britain. If this was the case it was intolerable. Incensed by the Portuguese action Campbell confronted Sampaio on his own initiative. Having told the secretary-general that he was speaking in a personal capacity Campbell warned that any attempt to differentiate between Britain and the Netherlands would be badly received by British public opinion which admired the valiant support of their Dutch ally in the face of Axis aggression. Moreover, it needed no flight of the imagination to realise what a rupture of relations between Great Britain and Portugal would lead to, namely that with the counterpoise of the alliance removed German submarines would soon be based in Portuguese ports and bombers on Portuguese aerodromes. Campbell believed that would be a tragic ending to an age-old alliance based on a community of interests. Sampaio admitted that it did not do to give free rein to the imagination. Although Campbell's warning had been unofficial the war cabinet agreed that there was no question but that they and the Dutch must stand together. Subsequently, the ambassador's line was 'entirely endorsed' and his action 'warmly approved'.[62]

It was, however, recognised that the Portuguese did not entirely trust the Netherlands or have confidence in their motivation; memories were long and it was not forgotten that Holland had wrested most of Portugal's former far eastern

---

58 FO 371/27798 F14083/222/61.
59 *FRUS*, 1941, ii. 856. Washington was kept fully informed of developments concerning the Timor crisis by the British ambassador, Lord Halifax.
60 FO 371/27798 F14082/222/61; FO 371/27799 F14162/222/61.
61 FO 371/27799 F14163/222/61. See also F14216/222/61.
62 FO 371/27799 F14164/F14166/F14169/222/61; CAB 65/20 WM 134(41).

possessions from her centuries earlier. But a solution to the crisis needed to be found urgently. As Hoare warned: 'from the point of view of the policy of keeping Spain out of the war the sooner the incident could be closed the better'.[63] In order to overcome Portugal's problems with the Dutch a solution was considered during the Christmas period whereby the defence of Portuguese Timor should devolve entirely on Australian troops as a first step towards the ultimate withdrawal of allied troops.[64] Before the proposal could be put to the Portuguese, however, the position was dramatically altered by developments both in Portugal itself and in Portuguese Timor. Sampaio told Campbell on 29 December that Portuguese troops destined for Timor would sail the next day. He suggested, doubtless with Salazar's knowledge, that his government be informed formally that the allied forces would be withdrawn as soon as Portuguese troops had arrived. The Portuguese force consisted of 700 troops (twice the size of the original allied force) and was well-equipped in every respect. The ambassador was surprised by this apparent Portuguese climb-down and could only speculate that Salazar had been thoroughly frightened by the apparent British willingness to contemplate a breach rather than give way on essentials. For Campbell the advantages of the proposal were extremely attractive. The British government had always been ready to support a withdrawal of the allied force as soon as adequate Portuguese forces were in place and provided there was no loss of prestige. It should also suit the Netherlands government which would thus avoid the odium of a virtual ultimatum; Dutch troops would remain with the Australians until the arrival of Portuguese forces rather than withdraw prematurely. From the Portuguese point of view it was a retreat for they would have dislodged neither the Dutch nor the Australian forces in advance of the arrival of their own force. The proposal, of course, spelled the total failure of Axis machinations in Portugal.[65]

Unfortunately, despite its attraction from the diplomatic angle, the Portuguese initiative offered little in the way of military security for Portuguese Timor. The Australians were convinced that Portuguese reinforcements would be insufficient for the task of defending the colony: on 26 December Canberra had insisted that the defence of Portuguese Timor was crucial both to the Netherlands and to the whole British position in the far east and that there should be no retreat. A meeting of the British chiefs of staff on 27 December endorsed this view.[66] The security position was further complicated by news that Governor Carvalho had taken to the hills, literally, with his military forces and entire civil administration, and that there were also Japanese at large in the hills with wireless equipment from a Japanese ship. The allied forces were therefore faced with the possibility of having to take over the civil administration and of coming into conflict with the Portuguese locally,[67] an eventuality which they had sought to avoid since the earliest days of the crisis. On 27

---

63 FO 371/27800 F14293/222/61.
64 CAB 65/20 WM 135(41) and WM 137(41); PREM 3/361/2.
65 FO 371/27800 F14377/222/61.
66 FO 371/27800 F14392/222/61; CAB 79/16 COS(41) 436th mtg.
67 PREM 3/361/2.

December Canberra was left under no illusions as to the consequences of a rupture in Anglo-Portuguese relations:

> There is a serious danger that unless a bridge is found, Dr. Salazar may proceed to the limit of breaking off relations with us. This would not merely mean the end of a long Alliance but might precipitate Axis penetration of the Iberian Peninsula. In this event Gibraltar will become unusable as a base and the vital Portuguese islands in the Atlantic will be denied to us rather than available to our forces. Our air and sea communications through Lisbon to the Middle and Far East and to Australia itself as well as in the Atlantic would then be endangered. Recently highly secret conversations with the Portuguese have gone far to safeguard our position in regard to the Atlantic islands in the event of Axis action in the Iberian Pensinula; the results of these conversations are now in jeopardy.[68]

The dilemma confronting the British authorities in late December 1941 was essentially one of priorities. Should the Atlantic and Iberian, or the south western Pacific dimension prevail? The central department of the foreign office clearly inclined towards the former. Apart from long-standing significant strategic and economic considerations there was an issue of immediate political importance, namely the serious effect a breach between Britain and Portugal would have in Brazil, and, in particular on the Rio Conference.[69] The far eastern department remained distinctly unimpressed, regarding Dutch and Australian anxieties, in particular the latter, as no less important than those of the Portuguese:

> The plain facts are that we and the Netherlands and Australia have got our backs to the wall in the Far East, that Timor is at Australia's front door and that there can be no doubt about the threat to it from Japan except those who wilfully shut their eyes to it. Australia is faced with the possibility of the Netherlands East Indies being overrun and her communications being cut – in fact of being completely isolated. She is not likely to be impressed, therefore, if, when she takes what seems to be an essential defence measure, we squeal about the Iberian Peninsula being overrun and our communications via Lisbon being cut.[70]

The foreign office therefore informed Campbell on 31 December that while they warmly welcomed Portugal's decision to send troops to Timor, allied troops would only be withdrawn if 'adequate Portuguese forces' were provided for its defence. A force of 700 Portuguese troops was unlikely to be adequate especially as there would be no Portuguese reinforcements within call, nor any arrangement for allied assistance. The immediate aim should therefore be to restore the situation as it existed prior to the allied occupation: the staff conversations

---

68 FO 371/27800 F14431/222/61.
69 FO 371/31728 F472/2/61. For details of the Rio Conference see R. A. Humphreys, *Latin America and the Second World War 1939–1942*, London 1981, 165–81.
70 FO 371/31728 F472/2/61.

agreed in November should be resumed before the Portuguese troops arrived or the allied forces withdrew, and should work towards an agreement on the adequate defence of Portuguese Timor in the unprecendented circumstances prevailing in the south west Pacific. It was anticipated that the Portuguese government would agree to invite or accept allied assistance in the event not only of an attack but of the threat of an attack by Japan.[71] Furthermore, the foreign office insisted that the governor of Portuguese Timor should resume contact with the allied commanders with a view to full co-operation pending the arrival of the Portuguese forces.

Campbell viewed these qualifications with horror and telegraphed an immediate reply. Salazar had made a 'big gesture' and if they 'threw it back in his teeth' there was no telling what he might do under 'the stress of righteous indignation'. Campbell emphasised that it was precisely to avoid any quibbling about the relative value of Portuguese, Dutch and Australian troops that Salazar had proposed sending double the number of Portuguese with full equipment, and he advised that it would not be be possible to arrange for secret staff talks until after the allied forces had withdrawn. Moreover, talks could not possibly cover the question of a Portuguese request for assistance in advance of an attack: if Salazar had not agreed to that before, he was even less likely to do so now. In a further telegram Campbell warned that the governor of Portuguese Timor would not co-operate with the allied commanders. Doing so would constitute a breach of neutrality in the eyes of the Axis powers and provoke reprisals.[72]

The defence of Portuguese Timor was raised at the war cabinet on New Year's Day when Sir Earle Page, the special emissary of the Australian government, cast doubt upon the adequacy 'in all contingencies' of 700 Portuguese troops. Eden wondered whether the Australians fully appreciated the practical disadvantages which the British empire would incur if there were a rupture in Anglo-Portuguese relations, while the foreign office remained equally divided, the far eastern department deprecating Campbell's apparently inadequate understanding of Australia's exposed position.[73] To resolve the deadlock the chiefs of staff were invited to pronounce on the strategic priorities. The result was a triumph for the Atlantic dimension for the chiefs of staff agreed on 2 January 1942 that the importance of retaining Australian and Netherlands troops in Portuguese Timor did not justify the risk of a rupture in their relations with Portugal.[74] Naturally, the far eastern department were dismayed, but the strength of their case depended upon the provision of sufficient allied forces to repel a Japanese attack and it was by no means certain that such forces were available. Indeed, at a meeting held the same day at the dominions office at the behest of the war cabinet, involving Cranborne, Strang, Page and Bruce, the latter admitted that if they were unlikely to be able to hold on to Timor it would be foolish to provoke a rupture with Portugal. Consequently, the

---

[71] FO 371/27800 F14402/222/61. Emphasis in original.
[72] FO 371/31727 F8/F11/2/61.
[73] CAB 65/25 WM 1(42); FO 371/31727 F13/2/61.
[74] CAB 79/16 COS(42) 2nd mtg; CAB 80/33 COS(42)4.

Australian chiefs of staff were asked to assess the prospects of holding Timor against a Japanese attack.[75]

Their response was disappointing. While recognising that a Japanese occupation of Portuguese Timor would seriously prejudice the defence of Darwin, they acknowledged that their own forces even when combined with 700 Portuguese would not be able to provide adequate protection. The thousand or so troops would be incapable of withstanding any serious Japanese assault unless, as was most unlikely, very considerable air forces could be brought immediately to their aid. The Australian chiefs of staff concluded their assessment by laying the responsibility for any action firmly at the door of General Sir Archibald Wavell, the supreme commander, south western Pacific.[76] The Australian reply confirmed the wisdom of proceeding with Salazar's proposal. Eden had already informed the war cabinet on 5 January that, on reflection, the allied forces would have to be withdrawn once Portuguese reinforcements had arrived. At the same time it was agreed, at the suggestion of Campbell, who had returned to London for consultations, that Anglo-Portuguese staff conversations should consider what steps should be taken if the Portuguese required assistance in Timor. While it was recognised that Salazar could not possibly agree publicly to the resumption of staff conversations, he might be induced to agree privately that an allied withdrawal, as soon as Portuguese reinforcements arrived, would ensure the immediate institution of staff talks. That allied assistance should be accepted before an actual attack had developed could not, however, form the basis for talks. The only hope was that given a favourable atmosphere, discussions might, if skilfully handled, be widened to cover that issue: in other words the Portuguese military representatives might be persuaded to ask for allied help in good time. The Netherlands government agreed to this approach and on 8 January the Australian authorities were asked to give their approval.[77]

Canberra approved the proposed course of action on 10 January, a change of heart on the part of John Curtin's Labour government, largely as a result of increased optimism concerning the position in northern Australia. The Australian chiefs of staff now felt that, because of American naval and air reinforcements, by the time the Portuguese troops arrived in Timor the position at Darwin might be so improved that they would be able to take more effective action than hitherto in repelling a Japanese attack on Timor.[78]

A consensus having been reached between the allied governments, Campbell returned to Lisbon on 15 January and on the following day presented the agreed proposals to Sampaio. The ambassador emphasised that the ultimate aim of the conversations, which it was proposed should take place at General Wavell's headquarters in Batavia, was to reach an understanding that allied help would be summoned if an attack appeared to be imminent. He advised Sampaio that it was only common prudence to give the Portuguese commander

[75] FO 371/31727 F82/2/61; 371/31728 F474/2/61.
[76] FO 371/31727 F181/2/61.
[77] CAB 65/25 WM 2(42); Unpubl. diaries of Harvey of Tasburgh, diary entry 6 Jan. 1942; FO 371/31278 F474/2/61.
[78] FO 371/31728 F474/2/61.

discretion to summon assistance if he himself was convinced that an attack was about to be launched.[79] On 17 January Salazar agreed to the British proposals and instructed Carvalho that whilst he could not collaborate with the allied commanders he was to put no difficulties in their way in the exercise of their duties pending the withdrawal of their forces. While the Portuguese made no reference to summoning assistance in advance of an attack, Campbell drew the admission from Sampaio that the judgement as to when an attack had already begun was a military matter and the Portuguese commander would not necessarily wait until a landing had been effected.[80]

This was a definite move in the right direction as far as Eden and the foreign office were concerned. But then the whole question was reopened by the intervention of Churchill himself, to whom General Wavell had telegraphed his deep concern (shared by the former minister of colonies and governor general of the Netherlands East Indies, H. J. van Mook, the American representative, General George Brent, and Wavell's senior staff) regarding the inability of the Portuguese reinforcements to resist a Japanese assault on Portuguese Timor. The military authorities were convinced that Japanese intrigue and pressure would be resumed in Timor the moment the allied troops were withdrawn. To forestall any precipitate action on the part of his leader Eden reminded Churchill on 18 January that the chiefs of staff could not justify the retention of allied troops in Portuguese Timor if it meant risking a rupture with Portugal. The foreign secretary added a personal warning:

> I am at all times ready to play the diplomatic hand in accordance with military requirements for the conduct of the war. But at this late stage when we have largely committed ourselves to the Portuguese Government, I am bound to say that it would be dangerous to put our policy into reverse.

Eden also enlightened the Prime Minister as to the actual strength of the allied force in Portuguese Timor: in effect 380 Australian and Dutch troops operating in largely mountainous territory almost as large as Wales, hardly sufficient to hold back the Japanese who could, if they chose, descend in force. Churchill was, however, untroubled by the diplomatic niceties; a willing advocate of subterfuge, he showed a total disregard for Portugal's neutrality:

> We should say to the Portuguese Government that we are guarding Timor until their reinforcements arrive. Nevertheless when they do arrive we should not go. We should leave our troops, the Dutch troops and their troops all on the spot. The Portuguese are obviously not capable of protecting their neutrality, and Timor is a key point. General Wavell should be authorised to take all necessary steps for the military security of Timor regardless of the effects produced on Portuguese pride.[81]

---

[79] FO 371/31278 F474/F532/2/61.
[80] FO 371/31728 F544/2/61.
[81] PREM 3/361/2 and 3/361/3. See also unpubl. diaries of Harvey of Tasburgh, diary entry 20 Jan. 1942.

Although on 19 January the war cabinet endorsed Eden's view that they were committed to withdrawing allied troops from Portuguese Timor, the thought no doubt lingered that when the moment came it would not happen. This despite a public announcement in the Portuguese press on 23 January that the allies had agreed to withdraw when the Portuguese reinforcements arrived.[82] Certainly, Campbell sensed, from the telegrams he had received since his return to Lisbon, that his government were attempting to strengthen their moral ground in case by the time the Portuguese contingent arrived the situation had so changed that allied withdrawal would be undesirable. In a personal letter to Eden, circulated to the war cabinet, he spelled out clearly the consequences of such a decision:

If there is any question of the allied forces not being withdrawn when the Portuguese contingent arrives (thereby obliging it to turn round and sail home again) we must carefully consider the consequences on our wider strategic interests of a definite break with Portugal. If, from the general strategic aspect the local situation is held to be paramount, well and good. But do not let us be deluded into thinking that, having called Dr. Salazar to order once, we could get away with it a second time.[83]

When staff conversations began in Batavia in the first half of February there was every likelihood that allied forces would not leave when the Portuguese reinforcements arrived at the end of the month. The whole issue, however, was rendered superfluous on 19 February when the Japanese invaded Portuguese and Dutch Timor.[84] Because there were allied forces in the Portuguese colony the Japanese were able to make the spurious claim that they were acting in self-defence in attacking it, to protect their operations in Dutch Timor.

The foreign office was incensed by the relatively mild protest of the Portuguese authorities. But it seems that Salazar's hands were tied by the previous action of his ancient ally: allied entry into Portuguese Timor had robbed him of the moral high ground. Certainly, the Portuguese had reason to believe that without the allied presence in their colony the Japanese would not have launched an attack.[85] The British, of course, saw matters differently. For them the Japanese attack was grounded in strategic exigency: the attack upon Darwin, on 19 February, from Admiral Nagumo's Pearl Harbour task force standing off Timor, provided clear proof of this.[86] Significantly, the Japanese were anxious not to alienate the Portuguese government completely because Emperor Hirohito insisted upon viewing Portugal as a possible channel of mediation in Japan's efforts to seek a peace settlement. Hence the Japanese

---

82 CAB 55/25 WM 9(42); FO 371/31729 F823/2/61.

83 CAB 66/21 WP(42)47.

84 See Kirby, *The war against Japan*, i, 428–9.

85 Salazar was most unimpressed by the suggestion of the American minister at Lisbon that a Portuguese severence of relations with Japan would be extremely popular in the United States: Nogueira, *Salazar*, iii, 377.

86 For details of the Japanese attack on Darwin see ibid. 425–6; Thomas, *Japan's war at sea*, ch. iii; D. Bergamini, *Japan's imperial conspiracy*, London 1971, 898.

promise not to intervene in Macao and to respect Portuguese territorial integrity while the occupation continued.[87] Confronted with a Japanese *fait accompli* and recognising the collapse of the whole allied position in the far east Salazar had little option but to accept the Japanese promise.[88] In the event, the Japanese remained in Portuguese Timor until the very end of the war when Portuguese troops participated in its recapture.[89]

[87] Ibid. 899–900; FO 371/31371 F1703/2/61; 371/31732 F1923/2/61.
[88] Japanese promises notwithstanding, they exacted a terrible retribution on the colony's population for help given to the Australian forces, who continued to resist the occupation after February 1942: C. Thorne, *The issue of war: states, societies and the far eastern conflict of 1941–1945*, London 1985, 154.
[89] For details see Woodward, *British foreign policy*, iv. 47–8.

Conclusion

From the British standpoint there was little in the way of positive economic or political affinity with Portugal before and during the period under review. There was little to connect British parliamentary democracy with Portuguese corporatist authoritarianism, which bore some resemblance at least to Italian fascism. Yet successive British governments, whether led by Stanley Baldwin, Neville Chamberlain or Winston Churchill, did not question the alien values of their Portuguese ally. For example, the abuse of human rights by the Salazar regime never figured in foreign office or cabinet discussions, or for that matter in the proceedings of the house of commons, despite the fact that between 1936 and 1939 more than 8,000 political opponents of the regime were incarcerated.[1] Official opinion, shared by the British community in Portugal, tended to admire the achievements of the *Estado Novo*, in particular its success in creating political stability and in adopting policies of financial rectitude not dissimilar to those pursued in the United Kingdom for most of the 1930s.

For his part Salazar never lost sight of the extremes of totalitarianism, not only on the Left but also on the Right. Manuel de Lucena, a critic of his regime, has emphasised the dictator's distrust of Hitler's political creed and his belief, formed early in the second world war, that the allies would be victorious after a long struggle.[2] As a finance minister of long standing, he did not underestimate the financial power of Britain and her association with the United States. Moreover, despite his abhorrence of Stalin's Russia, which he shared with all his associates in Lisbon, Salazar never allowed his emotions to get the better of his judgement in calculating the long-term effects of the failure of 'Operation Barbarossa', although his dismay at the successes of Soviet Russia during 1943–5 probably accounts for his decision to order that flags be flown at half mast throughout Portugal on the death of Hitler in 1945.

The factor which, more than any other, cemented the Anglo-Portuguese alliance was the strategic significance of metropolitan Portugal and her overseas possessions. The consensus in official circles in the United Kingdom between 1890 and 1945 clearly favoured the retention of the alliance whenever its credibility was brought into question. During the period covered by this book two major strategic appreciations by the chiefs of staff, in 1937 and 1940, confirmed that Portugal's possession of the Azores and Cape Verde islands demanded the continuation of the Portuguese connection. In the last resort,

---

[1] See in this context T. Gallagher, 'Salazar's Portugal: the "Black Book" on fascism', *European Studies Review* xiv (1984), 486. For a recent and detailed treatment of the opposition to the Salazar regime see D. L. Raby, *Fascism and resistance in Portugal: communists, liberals and military dissidents in the opposition to Salazar 1941–1974*, Manchester 1988.

[2] Manuel de Lucena, *A evoluçao do sistema corporativo português*, i, Lisbon 1976, cited in Gallagher, *Portugal*, 103.

this implied responsibility for the defence of the whole of the Portuguese empire as well as of Portugal itself. Ironically, the greatest threat to this empire between 1936 and 1941, came not from Nazi Germany or fascist Italy or as a result of Japanese designs on Macao and Portuguese Timor, but from Neville Chamberlain's willingness to use Angola and Mozambique along with the Belgian Congo, as the centrepiece of his scheme for colonial appeasement through an African settlement.[3] In the event, nothing came of the prime minister's scheme or, for that matter, of Churchill's expressed desire during 1940 and 1941 to take precipitate military action with regard to the Azores and Cape Verde islands. The intervention of the two British prime ministers created discomfort for the foreign office and its political masters, Eden and Halifax who, influenced by their officials and the Lisbon embassy, tended to take a sympathetic view of Portugal's problems. This view, which emphasised the value of patient diplomacy, paid dividends on a number of occasions, notably during the civil war in Spain, the crisis over Portuguese Timor and later, in 1943, during negotiations for the lease of bases in the Azores to British forces.[4]

Britain's diplomacy vis-à-vis Portugal was put severely to the test during the Spanish Civil War. The policy of non-intervention was genuinely abhorred in Lisbon where there was unreserved support for the cause of General Franco, and British pressure on the Portuguese to come into line with regard to the Non-Intervention Agreement, membership of the Non-Intervention Committee and participation in the committee's control schemes put an increasing strain on Anglo-Portuguese relations. This was to some degree alleviated by the absence of positive and sustained British criticism when Salazar suspended the observation scheme on the Spanish-Portuguese frontier in June 1937 and by the British government's decision in September 1937 to appoint an agent to the Spanish nationalist administration. However, while the civil war continued, the Portuguese were not entirely mollified and they continued to collaborate, as they had since August 1936, with the Germans and Italians both within the Non-Intervention Committee and through the supply of armaments to Franco's forces. Britain's readinesss to grant de jure recognition to Franco's regime in February 1939 contributed towards healing any residual ill feeling on the Portuguese side. Indeed, after March 1939 Salazar revealed a growing and genuine concern that the western democracies might be permanently alienated from Franco's Spain. His offer to help in reducing the obvious animosity towards Britain, and even more towards France, which still prevailed in nationalist circles, was readily accepted by the British authorities who had seriously considered using the Portuguese dictator as a channel of communication with General Franco during the civil war. Although there was no marked improvement in Anglo-Spanish and Franco-Spanish relations before September 1939 the Portuguese connection was utilised during 1940 and 1941 with the deliberate intention of securing Spanish non-belligerency. While Salazar's contribution was by no means negligible, in particular his role in creating the Protocol

---

[3] It is interesting to note in this context that discussions within the German foreign ministry between 1940 and 1942 tended to exclude Portuguese territory from their lists of colonial desiderata: Hildebrand, Vom Reich zum Weltreich, 645, 674, 722–4.
[4] For the bases deal see Stone, 'The official British attitude', 741–3.

of July 1940, other pressures and influences probably accounted for Franco's decision not to enter the war on the Axis side – not least his desire to see Britain beaten first.

It could be argued with some truth that before 1936 Britain had tended to neglect her Portuguese ally. The Spanish civil war and Portuguese collaboration with Italy and Germany quickly dissipated this tendency. Positive measures were undertaken, with varying degrees of success, in the commercial, cultural and military fields. The most notable success was the despatch to Lisbon in February 1938 of the British military mission which contributed significantly towards countering Axis influence in Portugal. The opposite was true, however, of Britain's failure, largely the responsibility of service departments hampered by the deficiencies of their own rearmament programme, to supply her ally with the land, air and naval armaments she required. On the whole, however, Britain was relatively successful in countering Axis influence before September 1939, a fact highlighted by the Italian government's request, in late August 1939, that Portugal, as the 'ally of England', might use 'her good offices' to persuade the British government to influence the Poles to enter into direct negotiations with Germany on the Danzig problem.[5]

War in Europe provided new opportunities for Axis intervention in Portugal, notably after June 1940 and the fall of France, Italy's entry into the conflagration and Franco's declaration of non-belligerency. As before the war the Axis challenge was vigorously countered with some success in the fields of propaganda and of economic and military relations. The propaganda battle in Portugal, essentially an Anglo-German one, produced no lasting successes for the Axis powers despite a succession of military victories in Europe during 1940 and 1941. On the commercial front, despite the British blockade and the continuation of Portuguese wolfram supplies to the Third Reich, Britain achieved some success, not least Salazar's co-operation in the policy of controlled economic assistance to the Iberian Peninsula. Success was also achieved in military relations even if the priorities of Britain's own war programme prevented the supply of war material on a large scale to Portugal. Given this, it is indicative of the great importance attached to the Azores and Cape Verde islands that the British military authorities were prepared to provide scarce equipment for the defence of these islands. At the same time, the military conversations, held during 1941 in London, served Britain's purposes rather more than Portugal's. Despite contingency plans for the despatch of a British expeditionary force to metropolitan Portugal, Britain had not the slightest intention of intervening in the Iberian Peninsula. Such plans also made it unquestionably more difficult later to persuade the Portuguese government to evacuate Portugal with the minimum of resistance. Although Salazar did finally acquiesce there was no certainty that in the event of a German invasion of the Iberian Peninsula the Portuguese would have repaired in good order to the Azores. As it happened, developments elsewhere in Europe meant that Salazar's regime avoided the opprobrium of evacuation while preparations for the

5   FO 371/22981 C12792/15/18.

defence of the Azores in particular continued, establishing firm foundations for their later use as allied bases of supply.

The general feeling in the foreign office and in the Lisbon embassy during the period 1936–41 was that Salazar's Portugal was basically loyal to the alliance despite differences over non-intervention in the Spanish civil war and contrasting interpretations of benevolent neutrality after September 1939. Certainly, during the early war years, they appreciated the difficulties which Salazar was bound to encounter in his relations with the Axis powers if he became too blatantly pro-allied, not least because of the presence of German troops on the French side of the Pyrenees after June 1940. This view remained unchanged during the remainder of the war and was indeed reinforced by Lisbon's co-operation in various fields such as espionage, and by the Portuguese decision to allow Britain to use the Azores after October 1943.[6] They were therefore hardly likely to contemplate seriously the overthrow of the Estado Novo once the war in Europe had ended. None the less, there were many in the Iberian Peninsula and elsewhere, particularly the American and British left, who anticipated the fall of the Salazar and Franco regimes. It is relevant to note here that critical voices were raised during the war in official circles in Washington concerning the continuation of Portuguese colonialism.[7] In the event, both regimes survived the second world war and went on to play an increasingly respectable role in the defence of a reconstructed and largely democratic western Europe. The Estado Novo's main saving grace, which it shared with Franco's Spain, was of course its impeccable anti-communist credentials: as the cold war developed these were appreciating assets. Doubtless the western democracies had calculated that a restoration of democracy in the Iberian Peninsula might result in a triumph of the left in view of its considerable strength during the previous periods of Portuguese and Spanish parliamentary republicanism.[8] The continuing strategic significance of Portugal and its empire and of Spain demanded that the risks involved in intervening in the internal politics of the two countries be avoided at all costs.[9]

In view of the importance of Portugal and Spain to Britain's foreign and strategic policies both before and after 1941 it is surprising that historians, with the notable exception of Professor Denis Smyth and Sir Llewellyn Woodward, have tended to neglect the Iberian connection. If, as historians constantly acknowledge, Turkey and Greece were considered vital to Britain's strategic

---

[6] For details of Portuguese co-operation with Britain's secret service see Wheeler, 'In the service of order', 6–7.

[7] W. R. Louis, Imperialism at bay 1941–1945: the United States and the decolonisation of the British empire, Oxford 1977, 185.

[8] Gallagher, Portugal, 107–8. For details of the failure of the opposition forces to overthrow the Estado Novo in the aftermath of the second world war see D. L. Raby, 'Controlled, limited and manipulated opposition under a dictatorial regime: Portugal 1945–1949', European History Quarterly xix (1989), 63–84.

[9] For a brief discussion of Portugal's strategical significance after 1945 see D. M. Abshire and M. A. Samuels, Portuguese Africa: a handbook, London 1969, 435–7. For Spain's role in relation to NATO see P. Preston and D. Smyth, Spain, the EEC and NATO, London 1984.

interests in the eastern Mediterranean and the middle east between 1936 and 1941, then Spain's position *vis à vis* both the western Mediterranean and the eastern Atlantic was no less important. And Portugal was of equal if not greater significance for its metropolitan territory and colonial possesions connected with Britain's imperial and strategic interests in many parts of the globe; in the middle and eastern Atlantic, along the west African and east African coast and in the south western Pacific north of Australia. In the final analysis Britain's policy makers proved willing and able to acknowledge this fact. For them the Portuguese connection was anything but obscure.

Bibliography

Unpublished Primary Sources

Public Record Office

CAB2 Committee of Imperial Defence Minutes
CAB4 Committee of Imperial Defence Memoranda Miscellaneous
CAB5 Committee of Imperial Defence Memoranda Colonial Defence
CAB16 Ad Hoc Sub-Committees of Enquiry: Proceedings and Memoranda
CAB21 Cabinet Registered Files
CAB23 Cabinet Minutes
CAB24 Cabinet Memoranda
CAB27 Committees: General Series to 1939 (Cabinet Foreign Policy Committee 1936–9)
CAB53 Chiefs of Staff Committee
CAB54 Deputy Chiefs of Staff Committee
CAB55 Joint Planning Committee
CAB62 International Committee for the Application of the Agreement Regarding Non-Intervention in Spain 1936–9
CAB65 War Cabinet Minutes
CAB66 War Cabinet Memoranda
CAB68 WP(R) series including Ministry of Economic Warfare Papers
CAB69 Defence Committee (Operations)
CAB79 Chiefs of Staff Committee Minutes
CAB80 Chiefs of Staff Committee Memoranda
CAB82 Deputy Chiefs of Staff Committee and Sub-Committees
CAB84 Joint Planning Committees
CAB92 Committees on Supply, Production, Priority and Manpower
CAB99 Commonwealth and International Conferences (Anglo-Portuguese Military Conversations 1941)
PREM1 Prime Minister Files (Chamberlain)
PREM3 Prime Minister Operational Files (Churchill)
PREM4 Prime Minister Confidential Papers (Churchill)
FO371 Political Correspondence Foreign Office
FO372 Treaty Correspondence Foreign Office
FO408 Confidential Print (Germany) Foreign Office
FO425 Confidential Print (Portugal and Spain) Foreign Office
FO800 General and Miscellaneous Collection Foreign Office Ministers and Officials: Various
FO849 International Committee for the Application of the Agreement Regarding Non-Intervention in Spain 1936–9
T161 Supply Files Treasury
ADM116 General Papers Admiralty
AIR40 Directorate of Intelligence and other Intelligence papers Air Ministry

Private Papers
Attlee Papers, Bodleian Library, Oxford
Avon Papers, University of Birmingham
Butler Papers, Trinity College, Cambridge
Cadogan Diaries, Churchill College, Cambridge
Cecil of Chelwood Papers, British Library, London
Chamberlain Papers, University of Birmingham
Chatfield Papers, National Maritime Museum, Greenwich
Dalton Diaries and Papers, British Library of Political and Economic Science, London
Dawson Papers, Bodleian Library, Oxford
Eden Diaries, University of Birmingham
Eden Papers (Official FO954), University of Birmingham
Halifax (Hickleton Papers) (Microfilm), Churchill College, Cambridge
Hankey Papers, Churchill College, Cambridge
Harvey of Tasburgh Diaries and Papers, British Library, London
Hemming Diaries and Papers, Bodleian Library, Oxford
Phipps Papers, Churchill College, Cambridge
Roosevelt Papers, Franklin Delano Roosevelt Library, New York
Simon Papers, Bodleian Library, Oxford
Templewood Papers, University Library, Cambridge
Vansittart Papers, Churchill College, Cambridge
Webster Papers, British Library of Political and Economic Science, London

Published Primary Sources

Official Documents and Publications

Blitzkrieg to defeat: Hitler's war directives, 1939–1945, ed. H. R. Trevor Roper, New York 1971

Brassey's naval annual, London 1948

British Documents on the origins of the war, 1898–1914, i, London 1927; x, pt 2, London 1938

Ciano's diplomatic papers, ed. M. Muggeridge, London 1948

Dez anos de política externa, 1936–1947: a nação portuguesa e a segunda guerra mundial, i, Lisboa 1961; ii, Lisboa 1962; iii, Lisboa 1962; iv, Lisboa 1965; v, Lisboa 1967; vi, Lisboa 1971; vii, Lisboa 1972; viii, Lisboa 1973; ix, Lisboa 1974; x, Lisboa 1974

Documents on British foreign policy, 1919–1939, 2nd ser. xii, London 1972; xv, London 1976; xvi, London 1977; xvii, London 1979; xviii, London 1980; xix, London 1982; xx, London 1984

Documents on British foreign policy 1919–1939, 3rd ser. iii, London 1951; v, London 1952

Documents diplomatiques français, 1932–1939, 2nd ser. iii, Paris 1966; iv, Paris 1967; v, Paris 1968; vi, Paris 1970; vii, Paris 1972; ix, Paris 1974; xii, Paris 1978; xv, Paris 1981

Documents on German foreign policy, 1918–1945, ser. D, i, London 1949; ii, London 1950; iii, London 1951; vii, London 1956; xi, London 1961; xii, London 1962; xiii, London 1964

Foreign relations of the United States, 1936, ii, Washington 1954; 1937, i, Washington 1954; 1938, iv, Washington 1955; 1940, ii, Washington 1957; 1941, i, Washington 1958; 1941, ii, Washington 1959

Foundations of British foreign policy 1792–1902, ed. H. W. Temperley and L. M. Penson, Cambridge 1938

Hansard parliamentary debates, 5th ser. House of Commons, cccxi; cccxvi; cccxviii; cccxix; cccxx; cccxxi; cccxxv; cccxxvi; cccxxvii; cccxxx; cccxxxiv; cccxxxvii; cccxxxviii; cccxli; cccxlii; ccclviii; ccclxxi; ccclxxiii; ccclxxvi
Hansard parliamentary debates, 5th ser. House of Lords, cxix
Japan's decision for war: records of the 1941 policy conferences, ed. Nobutuka Ike, Stanford, Ca. 1967
Parliamentary papers, 1936–7, xxviii, xxix; 1937–8, xxx
The opium trade 1910–1941, iv, Wilmington, Del. 1974

Newspapers and Periodicals
The Times
The Economist
The Listener
The New Statesman and Nation
The Spectator

Contemporary Books and Articles
Atkinson, W. C., 'The polity of Portugal', *Fortnightly Review*, August 1937
——— 'The political structure of the Portuguese "New State" ', *Nineteenth Century and After*, September 1937
——— 'Portugal and her empire', *Fortnightly Review*, July 1939
Ballard, E. A. C., 'Salazar of Portugal', *Contemporary Review*, September 1940
Caldwell, R. G., 'The Anglo-Portuguese alliance today', *Foreign Affairs* xxi (1942)
Deedes, W. F., 'Portugal', *Quarterly Review*, 1939
Derrick, M., *The Portugal of Salazar*, London 1938
——— 'Portugal and Dr Salazar', *The Dublin Review*, October 1937
Fernandes, T. W., *Portugal's financial reconstruction: Professor Oliveira Salazar's record*, Lisbon 1939
Harlech, Lord, 'Salazar: Portugal's prime minister', *The Listener*, June 1940
Hirst, W. A., 'Greater Portugal', *Contemporary Review*, September 1939
Hoijer, O., 'Derrière la façade de la dictature portugaise', *Science Politique*, August 1937
Monteiro, M., *The Portuguese in modern colonialism*, Lisbon 1934
——— 'Portugal in Africa', *Journal of the Royal African Society*, April 1939
Nogales, H. Chaves, 'Franco's Spain', *Fortnightly Review*, October 1937
O'Donnell, T. J., 'Salazar and the new state of Portugal', *Studies*, March 1936
Pick, F. W., *Searchlight on German Africa: the diaries and papers of Dr W Ch Regendanz: a study in colonial ambitions*, London 1939
Prieto, C., *Spanish front*, London 1936
Randle-Elliott, A., 'Spain after civil war', *Foreign Policy Reports* xvi (1940)
RIIA, *Germany's claims to colonies*, London 1939
Schacht, H., 'Germany's colonial demands', *Foreign Affairs* xv (1937)
Secretariado Nacional de Informação, *Portugal: the New State in theory and practice*, Lisbon 1937
Shillan, D., 'Portugal today', *International Affairs* xx (1944)
Taylor, P. B., 'Germany's colonial claims in Africa', *Foreign Policy Reports* xv (1939)
Townsend, M. E., 'The German colonies and the Third Reich', *Political Science Quarterly* lii (1938)
Wakenham, E., 'Portugal today', *Nineteenth Century and After*, September 1938
West, S. G., 'The present situation in Portugal', *International Affairs* xvii (1938)
Woolbert, R. G., 'The future of Portugal's colonies', *Foreign Affairs* xv (1937)

Memoirs, Diaries, Letters, Collected Papers

Avon, Lord, *The Eden memoirs: facing the dictators*, London 1962

By safe hand: letters of Sybil and David Eccles, 1939–1942, ed. D. Eccles, London 1983

Chatfield, Lord, *It might happen again: the autobiography of Admiral of the Fleet Lord Chatfield*, ii, London 1947

Chief of staff: the diaries of Lieutenant General Sir Henry Pownall, II: *1940–1944*, ed. B. Bond, London 1974

Churchill, W. S., *The Second World War*, ii, iii, London 1949–50

Ciano's diary, 1939–1943, ed. M. Muggeridge, London 1947

Dalton, H., *The fateful years: memoirs, 1931–1945*, London 1957

Delgado, H., *The memoirs of General Delgado*, London 1964

The diaries of Sir Alexander Cadogan, 1938–1945, ed. D. Dilks, London 1971

The diplomatic diaries of Oliver Harvey, 1937–1940, ed. J. Harvey, London 1970

Halifax, Lord, *Fulness of days*, London 1957

Hoare, Sir S., *Ambassador on special mission*, London 1946

Hull, Cordell, *The memoirs of Cordell Hull*, i, London 1948

Jones, T., *A diary with letters, 1931–1950*, London 1969

Pereira, P. T., *Memórias postos em que servi e algumas recordações pessoais*, i, ii, Lisboa 1973

Peterson, Sir M., *Both sides of the curtain: an autobiography*, London 1950

Poland and the coming of the Second World War: the diplomatic papers of A. J. Drexel Biddle Jr, United States ambassador to Poland, 1937–1939, ed. P. V. Cannistraro, E. D. Wynot and T. P. Kovaleff, Columbus, Ohio 1976

The private papers of Hore-Belisha, ed. R. J. Minney, London 1960

Salazar, A. O., *Doctrine and action: internal and foreign policy of the new Portugal, 1928–1939*, London 1939

Selby, Sir W. *Diplomatic twilight*, London 1953

Selections from the Smuts papers vi, December 1934 – August 1939, ed. J. van der Poel, Cambridge 1973

Vayo, J. Álvarez del, *Freedom's battle*, London 1940

Vintras, R. E., *The Portuguese connection*, London 1974

The war diaries of Oliver Harvey, ed. J. Harvey, London 1978

Secondary Works

Books

Abendroth, H.-Henning, *Hitler in der spanischen Arena: Die deutsch-spanischen Beziehungen im Spannungsfeld der europäischen Interessenpolitik vom Ausbruch des Bürgerkrieges bis zum Ausbruch des Weltkrieges 1936–1939*, Paderborn 1973

Abshire, D. M. and M. A., *Portuguese Africa: a handbook*, London 1969

Adamthwaite, A., *France and the coming of the Second World War, 1936–1939*, London 1977

Alba, V., *Transition in Spain: from Franco to democracy*, New Brunswick, NJ 1978

Ahlbrandt, W. Kleine, *The policy of simmering: a study of British foreign policy during the Spanish civil war, 1936–1939*, The Hague 1962

Aster, S., *1939 – the making of the Second World War*, London 1973

Barker, E., *Churchill and Eden at war*, London 1978

Bender, G. J., *Angola under the Portuguese: the myth and the reality*, London 1978

Bergamini, D., *Japan's imperial conspiracy*, London 1971

Bond, B. *British military policy between the two world wars*, Oxford 1980

Brazao, R., *The Anglo-Portuguese alliance*, London 1957

Burdick, C. B., *Germany's military strategy and Spain in World War II*, New York 1968

Butler, J. R. M., *Grand strategy*,II: *September 1939–1941*, London 1957

Carlton, D., *Anthony Eden: a biography*, London 1981

Carr, E. H., *Comintern and the Spanish civil war*, London 1984

Cattell, D. T., *Communism and the Spanish civil war*, Berkeley, Ca. 1955

———, *Soviet diplomacy and the Spanish civil war*, Berkeley, Ca. 1957

Clarence-Smith, G., *The third Portuguese empire 1825–1975: a study in economic imperialism*, Manchester 1985

Colodny, R. G., *Spain: the glory and the tragedy*, New York 1970

Conn S. and Fairchild, B., *The United States army in World War II: the western hemisphere: the framework of hemisphere defence*, Washington, DC 1960

Cortada, J. W., *United States-Spanish relations: wolfram and World War II*, Barcelona 1971

Coverdale, J. F., *Italian intervention in the Spanish civil war*, Princeton, NJ 1975

Cross, J. A., *Sir Samuel Hoare: a political biography*, London 1977

Crozier, A. J., *Appeasement and Germany's last bid for colonies*, London 1988

Cruickshank, C., *The fourth arm: psychological warfare, 1938–1945*, London 1977

Delgado, I., *Portugal e a Guerra Civil de Espanha*, Lisboa 1980

Delzell, C. F. (ed.), *Mediterranean fascism, 1919–1945*, New York 1970

Dreifort, J. E., *Yvon Delbos and the Quai d'Orsay: French foreign policy during the Popular Front, 1936–1938*, Lawrence, Ka. 1973

Dülffer, J., *Weimar, Hitler und die Marine: Reichspolitik und Flottenbau 1920 bis 1939*, Düsseldorf 1973

Duroselle, J. B., *La décadence (1932–1939)*, Paris 1979

Edwards, J., *The British government and the Spanish civil war, 1936–1939*, London 1979.

Esch, P. M. van der, *Prelude to war: the international repercussions of the Spanish civil war, 1936–1939*, The Hague 1951

Feiling, K., *Life of Neville Chamberlain*, London 1954

Figueiredo, A. de, *Portugal: fifty years of dictatorship*, New York 1976

Fox, J. P., *Germany and the far eastern crisis 1931–1938: a study in diplomacy and ideology*, Oxford 1982

Fryer P. and P. McGowan Pinheiro, *Oldest ally: a portrait of Salazar's Portugal*, London 1961

Gallagher, T., *Portugal: a twentieth century interpretation*, Manchester 1983

Gibbs, N. H., *Grand strategy, I: Rearmament policy*, London 1976

Graham, L. S., *Portugal: the decline and collapse of an authoritian order*, London 1975

Haggie, P., *Britannia at bay: the defence of the British empire against Japan, 1939–1941*, Oxford 1981

Harper, G. T., *German economic policy in Spain during the civil war*, The Hague 1967

Harvey, C. E., *The Rio Tinto company: an economic history of a leading international mining concern*, Penzance 1981

Haslam, J., *The Soviet Union and the struggle for collective security in Europe, 1933–1939*, London 1984

Hasluck, P., *The government and the people*, II, ser. iv: *Civil Australia in the war of 1939–1945*, Canberra 1970

Henke, J., *England in Hitler's politischen Kalkül, 1935–1939*, Boppard am Rhein 1973

Hildebrand, K., *Vom Reich zum Weltreich: Hitler, NSDAP und koloniale Frage, 1919–1945*, München 1969

——— *The foreign policy of the Third Reich*, London 1973

——— *The Third Reich*, London 1984

Hillgruber, A., *Germany and the two world wars*, Cambridge, Mass. 1981

Hinsley, F. H., *British intelligence in the Second World War*, i, London 1979

Hodgson, Sir R., *Spain resurgent*, London 1953

Holland, R. F., *Britain and the commonwealth alliance, 1918–1939*, London 1981

Homze, E. M., *Arming the Luftwaffe: the Reich air ministry and the German aircraft industry, 1919–1939*, London 1976

Humphreys, R. A., *Latin America and the Second World War 1939–1942*, London 1981

Jacobson, H. A., *Nationalsozialistische Aussenpolitik, 1933–1938*, Frankfurt-am-Main–Berlin 1968

James, R. Rhodes, *Anthony Eden*, London 1986

Kay, H., *Salazar and modern Portugal*, London 1970

Kirby, S. W., *The war against Japan, I: the loss of Singapore*, London 1959

Langer W. L. and S. E. Gleason, *The undeclared war, 1940–1941*, New York 1953

Lash, J. P., *Roosevelt and Churchill, 1939–1941: the partnership that saved the west*, London 1977

Leutze, J. R., *Bargaining for supremacy: Anglo-American naval collaboration, 1937–1941*, Chapel Hill, NC 1977

Little, D., *Malevolent neutrality: the United States, Great Britain and the origins of the Spanish civil war*, Cornell, Ithaca NY 1985

Logan, R. W., *The African mandates in world politics*, Washington, DC 1948

Louis, W. R., *Imperialism at bay, 1941–1945: the United States and the decolonisation of the British empire*, Oxford 1977

Lowe, P., *Great Britain and the origins of the Pacific War: a study of British policy in east Asia, 1937–1941*, Oxford 1977

MacDonald, C. A., *The United States, Britain and appeasement, 1936–1939*, London 1981

McIntyre, W. N., *The rise and fall of the Singapore naval base*, Cambridge 1979

Maisky, I., *Spanish notebooks*, London 1966

Marder, A. J., *Old friends, new enemies. the Royal Navy and the Imperial Japanese Navy: strategic illusions, 1936–1941*, Oxford 1981

Marques, A. H. De Oliveira, *A history of Portugal, II: from empire to corporate state*, New York 1972

Medlicott, W. N., *The economic blockade, i, ii*, London 1952, 1959

——— *Britain and Germany: the search for agreement, 1930–1937*, London 1969

Merkes, M., *Die deutsche Politik gegenüber dem spanischen Bürgerkrieg, 1936–1939*, Bonn 1969

Michalka, W., *Ribbentrop und die deutsche Weltpolitik, 1933–1940: Aussenpolitische Konzeptionen und die Entscheidungsprozesse im Dritten Reich*, München 1980

Middlemas, K., *Diplomacy of illusion: the British government and Germany, 1937–1939*, London 1972

Milward, A., *War, economy and society, 1939–1945*, London 1977

Minter, W., *Imperial network and external dependency: the case of Angola*, Beverley Hills, Ca. 1972

Mitchell, B. R., *European historical statistics 1750–1950*, London 1975

Moradiellos, E., *Neutralidad benévola: el gobierno británico y la insurrección militar española de 1936*, Oviedo 1990

Murray, W., *The change in the European balance of power 1938–1939: the path to ruin*, Princeton, NJ 1984

Newitt, M., *Portugal in Africa: the last hundred years*, London 1981

Newman, S., *March 1939: the British guarantee to Poland*, London 1976

Nish, I., *Japanese foreign policy 1869–1942: Kasumigaseki to Miyakezaka*, London 1977

Nogueira, F., *Salazar, III: As grandes crises (1936–1945)*, Porto 1983

Nolte, E., *Les mouvements fascistes: l'Europe de 1919 à 1939*, Paris 1969

Nowell, C. E., *A history of Portugal*, New York 1953

Oliveira, C., *Salazar e a Guerra Civil de Espanha*, Lisboa 1987

Ovendale, R., *Appeasement and the English speaking world: Britain, the United States, the Dominions and the policy of appeasement 1937–1939*, Cardiff 1975

Parker, R. A. C., *Chamberlain and appeasement: British policy and the coming of the Second World War*, London 1993

Payne, S. G., *A history of Spain and Portugal*, ii, Madison, Wisc. 1973

Peden, G. C., *British rearmament and the treasury 1932–1939*, Edinburgh 1979

Peters, A. R., *Anthony Eden at the foreign office, 1931–1938*, Aldershot 1986

Pike, D. W., *Les français et la guerre d'Espagne, 1936–1939*, Paris 1975

Pratt, L. R., *East of Malta, west of Suez: Britain's mediterranean crisis, 1936–1939*, London 1975

Preston, P., *Franco: a biography*, London 1993

—— and D. Smyth, *Spain, the EEC and NATO*, London 1984

Puzzo, D., *Spain and the great powers, 1936–1941*, New York 1962

Raby, D. L., *Fascism and resistance in Portugal: communists, liberals and military dissidents in the opposition to Salazar 1941–1974*, Manchester 1988

Reynolds, D., *The creation of the Anglo-American alliance, 1937–1941: a study in competitive co-operation*, London 1981

Robinson, R. A. H., *Contemporary Portugal: a history*, London 1979

Rothwell, V., *Anthony Eden: a political biography*, Manchester 1992

Rosas, F., *O Salazarismo e a aliança Luso-Britânica: estudos sobre a política externa do Estado Novo nos anos 30 e 40*, Lisboa 1988

Rose, N., *Vansittart: study of a diplomat*, London 1978

Roskill, S. *Naval policy between the wars*, II: *the period of reluctant rearmament, 1930–1939*, London 1976

—— *Churchill and the admirals*, London 1977

Royal Institute International Affairs, *Survey of international affairs, 1939–1946: the eve of the war, 1939*, London 1958

Schmitz, C. J., *World non-ferrous metal production and prices 1700–1976*, London 1979

Schmokel, W. W., *Dream of empire: German colonialism, 1919–1945*, New Haven, Conn. 1964

Shay Jr, R. P., *British rearmament in the thirties: politics and profits*, Princeton, NJ 1977

Shorrock, W. I., *From ally to enemy: the enigma of fascist Italy in French diplomacy 1920–1940*, Kent State 1988

Smyth, D., *Diplomacy and strategy of survival: British policy and Franco's Spain, 1940–41*, Cambridge 1986

Soares, M., *Portugal's struggle for liberty*, London 1975

Stott-Howarth, A. H. d'Arauzo, *A aliança Luso-Britânica e a Segunda Guerra Mundial*, Lisboa 1956

Taylor, P. M., *The projection of Britain: British overseas publicity and propaganda, 1919–1939*, Cambridge 1981

Telo, A., *Portugal na Segunda Guerra*, Lisboa 1987

Thomas, D. A., *Japan's war at sea: Pearl Harbour to the Coral Sea*, London 1978

Thomas, H., *The Spanish civil war*, 3rd edn, London 1977

Thorne, C., *Allies of a kind: the United States, Britain, and the war against Japan 1941–1945*, London 1978

—— *The issue of war: states, societies and the far eastern conflict of 1941–1945*, London 1985

Toynbee, A. J., *Survey of international affairs 1937*, II: *the international repercussions of the war in Spain (1936–1937)*, London 1938

Vail L. and L. White, *Capitalism and colonialism in Mozambique*, London 1980

Warhurst, P. R., *Anglo-Portuguese relations in south central Africa, 1890–1900*, London 1962

Watt, D. C., *How war came: the immediate origins of the Second World War, 1938–1939*, London 1989

Weinberg, G. L., *The foreign policy of Hitler's Germany*, I: *diplomatic revolution in Europe, 1933–1936*, Chicago 1970
————— *The foreign policy of Hitler's Germany*, II: *starting World War II, 1937–1939*, Chicago 1980
Whealey, R. H., *Hitler and Spain: the nazi role in the Spanish civil war*, Lexington, Kentucky 1989
Wheeler, D. L., *Republican Portugal: a political history, 1910–1926*, Madison, Wisc. 1978
Wiarda, H. J. *Corporatism and development: the Portuguese experience*, Amerst, Mass. 1977
Woodward, Sir L., *British foreign policy in the Second World War*, i, iv, London 1970, 1975
Young, R. J., *In command of France: French foreign policy and military planning, 1933–1940*, Cambridge, Mass. 1978.

Articles, Essays

Abendroth, H.-Henning, 'Die deutsche Intervention im spanischen Bürgerkrieg: ein Diskussionsbeitrag', *Vierteljahrshefte für Zeitgeschichte* xxx (1982)
Adamthwaite, A., 'France and the coming of war', in W. J. Mommsen and L. Kettenacker (eds), *The fascist challenge and the policy of appeasement*, London 1983
Argeron, C. R., 'L'idée d'eurafrique et le débat colonial franco-allemand de l'entre-deux-guerres', *Revue d'Histoire Moderne et Contemporaine* xxii (1975)
Andrew, C. M., 'The French colonialist movement during the Third Republic: the unofficial mind of imperialism', *Transactions of the Royal Historical Society*, 5th ser. xxvi (1976)
Ballhaus, J., 'The colonial aims and preparations of the Hitler regime 1933–1939', in H. Stoecker (ed.), *German imperialism in Africa: from the beginnings until the Second World War*, London 1986
Blinkhorn, M., 'Conservatism, traditionalism and fascism in Spain, 1898–1937', in M. Blinkhorn (ed.), *Fascists and conservatives: the radical right and the establishment in twentieth century Europe*, London 1990
Buckley P. N., E. B. Haslam and W. B. R. Neave-Hill, 'Anglo-French staff conversations, 1938–1939', in Centre Nationale de la Recherche Scientifique, *Les relations franco-britanniques de 1935 à 1939*, Paris 1975
Burdick, C. B., ' "Moro": the resupply of German submarines in Spain, 1939–1942', *Central European History* iii (1972)
Cardozo, M. 'England's fated ally', *Luso-Brazilian Review* vii (1970)
Carlton, D., 'Eden, Blum and the origins of non-intervention', *Journal of Contemporary History* vi (1971)
Chihiro, Hosoya, 'The Tripartite Pact' in J. W. Morley (ed.), *Deterrent diplomacy: Japan, Germany and the USSR 1935–1940*, New York 1976
Cierva, R. de la, 'The nationalist army in the Spanish Civil War', in R. Carr (ed.), *The Republic and the civil war in Spain*, London 1971
Clarence-Smith, G., 'The impact of the Spanish civil war and the Second World War in Portuguese and Spanish Africa', *Journal of African History* xxvi (1985)
Cockett, R. B., 'The foreign office news department and the struggle against appeasement', *Historical Research* lxiii (1990)
Coghlan, F., 'Armaments, economic policy and appeasement: background to British foreign policy 1931–1937', *History* lvii (1972)
Crozier, A., 'Prelude to Munich: British foreign policy and Germany, 1935–1938', *European Studies Review* vi (1976)
————— 'Imperial decline and the colonial question in Anglo-German relations, 1919–1939', *European Studies Review* xi (1981)

Duff, K., 'Portugal', in RIIA, *Survey of international affairs, 1939–1946: the war and the neutrals*, London 1956

Duffy, J., 'Portuguese Africa 1930 to 1960', in L. H. Gann and P. Duignan (eds), *Colonialism in Africa, 1870–1970*, II: *the history and politics of colonialism, 1914–1960*, Cambridge 1970

Dutton, D., 'Eden and Simon at the foreign office, 1931–1935', *Review of International Studies* xx (1994)

Einhorn, M., 'Die ersten Massnahmen des deutschen Imperialismus zur wirtschaftlichen Ausplünderung Spaniens (Juli bis August 1936)', in W. Schieder and C. Dipper (eds), *Der spanische Bürgerkrieg in der Internationalen Politik, 1936–1939*, München 1976

Ellwood, D. W., 'Showing the world what it owed to Britain: foreign policy and cultural propaganda, 1935–1945', in N. Pronay and D. W. Spring (eds), *Propaganda, politics and film, 1918–1945*, London 1982

Fontana J. and Nadal J., 'Spain, 1914–1970', in C. Cipolla (ed.), *Fontana economic history of Europe*, vi, London 1976

Frank Jr, W. C., 'The Spanish civil war and the coming of the Second World War', *International History Review* ix (1987)

——— 'Politico-military deception at sea in the Spanish Civil War, 1936–1939', *Intelligence and National Security* v (1990)

Gallagher, T. 'Controlled repression in Salazar's Portugal', *Journal of Contemporary History* xiv (1979)

——— 'The mystery train: Portugal's military dictatorship, 1926–1932', *European Studies Review* xi (1981)

——— 'Salazar's Portugal: the "Black Book" on fascism', *European History Quarterly* xiv (1984)

——— 'Conservatism, dictatorship and fascism in Portugal, 1914–1945', in Blinkhorn, *Fascists and conservatives*

Girault, R., 'La décision gouvernementale en politique extérieure', in R. Rémond and J. Bourdin (eds), *Edouard Daladier: chef de gouvernement, avril 1938–septembre 1939*, Paris 1977

Le Goyet, P., 'Les relations économiques franco-britanniques à la deuxième geurre mondiale', in *Les relations franco-britanniques*

Halstead, C. R., 'Consistent and total peril from every side: Portugal and its 1940 Protocol with Spain', *Iberian Studies* iii (1974)

——— 'The dispute between Ramon Serrano Suñer and Alexander Weddell', *Rivista di Studi Politica Internazionali* iii (1974)

——— 'Spanish foreign policy, 1936–1978', in J. W. Cortada (ed.), *Spain in the twentieth century world: essays on Spanish diplomacy, 1898–1978*, London 1980

——— and C. J. Halstead, 'Aborted imperialism: Spain's occupation of Tangier, 1940–1945', *Iberian Studies* vii (1978)

Hammond, R. J., 'Economic imperialism: sidelights on a sterotype', *Journal of Economic History* xxi (1961)

——— 'Uneconomic imperialism: Portuguese Africa before 1910', in Gann and Duignan, *Colonialism in Africa, 1870–1960*, I: *the history and politics of colonialism, 1870–1914*, Cambridge 1969

——— 'Some economic aspects of Portuguese Africa in the nineteenth and twentieth centuries', in Gann and Duignan, *Colonialism in Africa, 1870–1960*, IV: *the economics of colonialism*, Cambridge 1975

Hartley, J., 'Recent soviet publications on the Spanish civil war', *European History Quarterly* xviii (1988)

213

Harvey, C. E., 'Politics and pyrites during the Spanish civil war', *Economic History Review*, 2nd ser. xxxi (1978)

Hatano, Sumio and Sadao Asada, 'The Japanese decision to move south (1939–1941)', in R. Boyce and E. M. Robertson (eds), *Paths to war: new essays on the origins of the Second World War*, London 1989

Hauner, M., 'Did Hitler want a world dominion?', *Journal of Contemporary History* xiii (1978)

Herwig, H. H., 'Prelude to *Weltblitzkrieg*: Germany's naval policy towards the United States of America, 1939–1941', *Journal of Modern History* xliii (1971)

Hildebrand, K., 'Deutschland, die Westmächte und das Kolonialproblem ein Beitrag über Hitler's Aussenpolitik vom Ende der Münchener Konferenz bis zum "Griff nach Prag" ', in W. Michalka (ed.), *Nationalsozialistische Aussenpolitik*, Darmstadt 1978

Hillgruber, A., 'England's place in Hitler's plans for world dominion', *Journal of Contemporary History* ix (1974)

Iriye, Akira, 'Policies towards the United States' in J. W. Morley (ed.), *Japan's foreign policy 1868–1941: a research guide*, New York 1974

Kiernan, V. G., 'The old alliance: England and Portugal', *Socialist Register* (1973)

Kuhne, H., 'Zur Kolonialpolitik des faschistischen deutschen Imperialismus (1937–1939)', *Zeitschrift für Geschichtswissenschaft* ix (1961)

Lammers, D., 'From Whitehall after Munich: the foreign office and the future course of British foreign policy', *Historical Journal* xvi (1973)

Louis, W. R., 'Colonial appeasement, 1936–1938', *Revue Belge de Philologie et d'Histoire* xliv (1971)

Lowe, P., 'Great Britain and the coming of the Pacific War, 1939–1941', *Transactions of the Royal Historical Society*, 5th ser. xxiv (1974)

MacDonald, C. A., 'Britain, France and the April crisis of 1939', *European Studies Review* ii (1972)

—— 'Economic appeasement and the German "Moderates", 1936–1939', *Past and Present* lvi (1972)

—— 'Deterrent diplomacy: Roosevelt and the containment of Germany, 1938–1940', in Boyce and Robertson, *Paths to war*

Manne, R., 'Some British light on the Nazi-Soviet pact', *European Studies Review* xi (1981)

—— 'The foreign office and the failure of Anglo-Soviet rapprochement', *Journal of Contemporary History* xvi (1981)

Marques, A. H. de Oliveira, 'The Portuguese 1920's: a general survey', *Iberian Studies* ii (1973)

Martins, H., 'Portugal', in S. J. Woolf (ed.), *European Fascism*, New York 1969

Michaelis, M., 'World power status or world dominion? A survey of the literature on Hitler's "plan of world dominion" (1937–1970)', *Historical Journal* xv (1972)

Michalka, W., 'Conflicts within the German leadership on the objectives and tactics of German foreign policy, 1933–1939', in Mommsen and Kettenacker, *The fascist challenge*

Mills, W. C., 'The Nyon Conference: Neville Chamberlain, Anthony Eden and the appeasement of Italy in 1937', *International History Review* xv (1993)

Monteath, P., 'German historiography and the Spanish civil war: a critical survey', *European History Quarterly* xx (1990)

Moradiellos, E., 'The origins of British non-intervention in the Spanish civil war: Anglo-Spanish relations in early 1936', *European History Quarterly* xxi (1991)

—— 'British political strategy in the face of the military uprising of 1936 in Spain', *Contemporary European History* i (1992)

—— 'Appeasement and non-intervention: British policy during the Spanish civil war', in P. Catterall and J. Morris (eds), *Britain and the threat to stability in Europe 1918–45*, London 1993

Morewood, S., 'Anglo-Italian rivalry in the mediterranean and middle east, 1935–1940', in Boyce and Robertson, *Paths to war*

Nogueira, F., 'Portugal: the ministry for foreign affairs', in Z. Steiner (ed.), *The Times survey of the foreign ministries of the world*, London 1982

Parker, R. A. C., 'British rearmament 1936–1939: treasury, trade unions and skilled labour', *English Historical Review* xcvi (1981)

Payne, S. G., 'Fascism in western Europe', in W. Laquer (ed.), *Fascism: a readers guide – analyses, interpretations, bibliography*, Berkeley, Ca. 1976

Peyrifitte, C., 'Les premiers sondages d'opinion', in Rémond and Bourdin, *Edouard Daladier*

Pike, D. W., 'Franco and the Axis stigma', *Journal of Contemporary History* xvii (1982)

Prestage, E., 'The Anglo-Portuguese alliance', *Transactions of the Royal Historical Society*, 4th ser. xvii (1934)

Preston, P., 'Franco and Hitler: the myth of Hendaye 1940', *Contemporary European History* i (1992)

Raby, D. L., 'Controlled, limited and manipulated opposition under a dictatorial regime: Portugal, 1945–9', *European History Quarterly* xix (1989)

Robertson, E. M., 'Mussolini and Ethiopia: the prehistory of the Rome Agreements of January 1935', in R. M. Hatton and M. S. Anderson (eds), *Studies in diplomatic history*, London 1970

———— 'Hitler's planning for war and the response of the great powers (1938–early 1939)', in H. W. Koch (ed.), *Aspects of the Third Reich*, London 1985

Rüger, A., 'The colonial aims of the Weimar Republic', in Stoecker, *German imperialism in Africa*

Schieder, W., 'Spanischer Bürgerkrieg und Vierjahresplan', in Schieder and Dipper, *Spanische Bürgerkrieg*

Schmitter, P. C., 'The social origins, economic bases and political imperatives, of authoritarian rule in Portugal', in S. V. Larsen, B. Hadtvet and J. P. Myklebust (eds), *Who were the fascists? Social roots of European fascism*, Oslo 1980

Shinjiro, Nagaoka, 'Economic demands on the Dutch East Indies', in J. W. Morley (ed.), *The fateful choice: Japan's advance into south east Asia, 1939–1941*, New York 1980

Smith, A. K., 'Antonio Salazar and the reversal of Portuguese colonial policy', *Journal of African History* xv (1974)

Smyth, D., 'Reflex reaction: Germany and the onset of the Spanish civil war', in P. Preston (ed.), *Revolution and war in Spain, 1931–1939*, London 1984

Stafford, P., 'The Chamberlain – Halifax visit to Rome: a reappraisal', *English Historical Review* xcviii (1983)

———— 'Political autobiography and the art of the possible: R. A. Butler at the foreign office 1938–1939', *Historical Journal* xxviii (1985)

Stone, G. A., 'The official British attitude to the Anglo-Portuguese alliance, 1910–1945', *Journal of Contemporary History* x (1975)

———— 'Britain, non-intervention and the Spanish civil war', *European Studies Review* ix (1979)

———— 'The European great powers and the Spanish civil war', in Boyce and Robertson, *Paths to war*

———— 'Inglaterra, Portugal e a Não Beligerância Espanhola: 1940–1941', *Ler História* xxv (1994)

———— 'Britain, France and Franco's Spain in the aftermath of the Spanish civil war', *Diplomacy and Statecraft* v (1994)

—— 'Britain, France and the Spanish problem, 1936–1939', in R. C. Richardson and G. A. Stone (eds), *Decisions and diplomacy: essays in twentieth century international history*, London 1994

Strandmann, H. P. von, 'Imperialism and revisionism in interwar Germany', in W. J. Mommsen (ed.), *Imperialism and after: continuities and discontinuities*, London 1986

Sweeney, J. K., 'The Portuguese wolfram embargo: a case study in economic warfare', *Military Affairs* xxxviii (1974)

—— 'The Luso-American connection: the courtship, 1940–1941', *Iberian Studies* vi (1977)

Taylor, P. M., 'British official attitudes towards propaganda abroad, 1918–1939', in Pronay and Spring, *Propaganda*

Townsend, M. E., 'Hitler, and the revival of German colonialism', in E. M. Earle (ed.), *Nationalism and internationalism: essays inscribed to Carlton J. Hayes*, New York 1950

Vail, L., 'Mozambique's chartered companies: the rule of the feeble', *Journal of African History* xvii (1976)

—— 'Discussion – the Mozambique company: reply to B. Neil Tomlinson', *Journal of African History* xviii (1977)

Veatch, R., 'The League of Nations and the Spanish civil war, 1936–1939', *European History Quarterly* xx (1990)

Wark, W. K., 'British intelligence on the German air force and aircraft industry, 1933–1939', *Historical Journal* xxv (1982)

Warner, G., 'France and non-intervention in Spain, July – August 1936', *International Affairs* xxxviii (1962)

Watt, D. C., 'German strategic planning and Spain, 1938–1939', *Army Quarterly* (1960)

—— 'Britain, France and the Italian problem, 1937–1939', in *Les relations franco-britanniques*

—— 'British domestic politics and the onset of war', in *Les relations franco-britanniques*

—— 'South African attempts to mediate between Britain and Germany, 1935–1938', in K. Bourne and D. C. Watt (eds), *Studies in international history*, London 1967

Weinberg, G. L., 'German colonial plans and policies, 1938–1942', in *Geschichte Gegenwartsbewusstein: Festschrift für Hans Rothfels zum 70. Geburtstag*, Göttingen 1963

Whealey, R. H., 'How Franco financed his war – reconsidered', *Journal of Contemporary History* xii (1979)

Wheatley, M. R., 'Britain and the Anglo-Franco-Russian negotiations in 1939', in *Les relations Franco-Britanniques*

Wheeler, D. L., 'The military and the Portuguese dictatorship, 1926–1974: "the honor of the army" ', in L. S. Graham and H. M. Makler (eds), *Contemporary Portugal: the revolution and its antecedents*, Austin, Texas 1979

—— 'In the service of order: the Portuguese political police and the British, German and Spanish intelligence, 1932–1945', *Journal of Contemporary History* xviii (1983)

—— 'The price of neutrality: Portugal, the wolfram question, and World War II', pts 1, 2, *Luso-Brazilian Review* xxxiii (1986)

—— 'And who is my neighbor? a World War II hero or conscience for Portugal', *Luso-Brazilian Review* xxvi (1989)

—— 'Review of António Telo's *Portugal na Segunda Guerra*', *Luso-Brazilian Review* xxvii (1990)

Young, R. J., 'The aftermath of Munich: the course of French diplomacy, October 1938 – March 1939', *French Historical Studies* viii (1973).

Index